Investment Portfolio Decision-Making

Edited by

James L. Bicksler
Rutgers University

Paul A. Samuelson
*Massachusetts Institute
of Technology*

Lexington Books
D.C. Heath and Company
Lexington, Massachusetts
Toronto   London

332.67
B473i

Library of Congress Cataloging in Publication Data
Bicksler, James L   comp.
  Investment portfolio decision-making.
    1. Investments—Addresses, essays, lectures. 2. Specula-
tion—Addresses, essays, lectures. 3. Decision-making—
Addresses, essays, lectures. I. Samuelson, Paul Anthony,
1915–   joint comp.   II. Title
HG4527.B45   332.6'7   73–1010
ISBN 0–669–86215–0

Published simultaneously in Canada.

Printed in the United States of America.

International Standard Book Number: 0–669–86215–0

Library of Congress Catalog Card Number: 73–1010

To my parents
John and Katherine Bicksler

Far better it is to dare mighty things, to win glorious triumphs, even though checkered with failure, than to take rank with those poor spirits who neither enjoy much nor suffer much, because they live in the grey twilight that knows not victory nor defeat.

Theodore Roosevelt

Contents

Foreword

"Those who can, do; those who can't, teach." According to this dictum of Shaw, the writings of professors of economics and finance should be of interest only to themselves. Practical men, interested in making a buck, should profitably ignore such academic writings and stick to their studies of corporate earnings, technical conditions of the market, and hot tips down at the midday eating club. Shaw, however, was a notorious joker, not one for the prudent man of investment to rely on. Writings of the last twenty years on the theory of speculative prices are not only of enormous interest for their own sake, but also should be of interest to the practical man who can understand them.

Let me give some illustrations. "Don't put all your eggs in one basket." The wisdom in this old saw gains new dimensions from the models of Harry Markowitz, William Sharpe, and others. Many portfolio men have not realized how strong is the positive correlation among the many securities they hold. They do not have nearly as many effectively different eggs in their baskets as they think.

Or take the question of good performance. The Ford Foundation, in a notable report directed toward non-profit institutions, urged them to be more rational in their investment policies. Who could object to that? Unfortunately, many who read that Report gleaned from it the message, "Be bold!", and this just at a time when the stock market went into its end-of-the-1960s tailspin. Readers who had been familiar with the kinds of analysis represented in this book would not have made this mistake. They would have realized that great performance in a bull market may be simply a reflection of great risk-taking: if two brothers, Cain and Abel, invest in identical securities, but Cain amplifies his leverage and risk by borrowed funds, then in a bull market Cain will spuriously appear to be the great investment genius. Even men innocent of analysis can see this, in the cold dawn of the morning after a bull-market binge. But it takes some analytical sophistication and knowledge of the Sharpe "beta" coefficient to see that certain institutional investors were accomplishing this same enhancement of mean return at the expense of greater risk, not by borrowing a cent, but rather by investing in highly volatile securities. I do not say you have to have read a book like this to sense these subtleties. The best practitioners I have known, many of them never having enjoyed formal schooling in mathematics beyond long division or high school algebra, realized things like this. But that is just the point that needs to be made. Investors who are successful over a long period of time, whether they are self-consciously aware of the fact or not, are essentially following precepts that can only be formulated and defended in terms of quite complicated mathematics.

Here is a final illustration of the need for statistical sophistication. Years ago mutual funds generally could not perform as well as the Dow-Jones or some other index of general stock prices. People in the industry resented this being pointed out, asserting the nonsense that you can't buy the averages. (Nonsense, because if it were true that a portfolio of those thirty stocks could really be expected to do better than the average of the best and most expensive money managers, it would be the duty of money managers simply to invest in the thirty Dow-Jones stocks, thereby bringing down the commission costs to small investors and bringing management fees down to a negligible amount.) In some years of the 1960s, however, mutual funds generally out-performed the Dow Jones or other index numbers of stock prices, and naturally the mutual fund industry called attention to this fact. There is, moreover, an understandable tendency for studies to be made to see which funds have been the most successful in recent years: those that seem to stand out get recommended, and certain of the go-go funds like those of Dreyfus or Fidelity have at times grown mightily at the expense of the rest. What is not sufficiently realized is that, by chance alone, if one picked different samples of fifty securities purely at random from the financial page, some samples would show more past growth than others; but that would not necessarily warrant the slightest credence in the expectation of their superior performance in the future. (It is like a famous study by Alfred Cowles III before World War II of seventeen different forecasting methods; the one that did the best was the "Dow theory," but it was not at all clear that this best performer did any better than the best of seventeen purely-random methods could be expected to do by chance alone.)

Ignoring the crucial question of whether good performance in the past can throw any light at all on good performance in the future. I note the further observation that in any year the fund that seems to show most rapid growth tends generally to be a small rather than a giant fund. People in the industry, who ought to know better, conclude from this fact alone that performance is likely to suffer with growth to giant size. No doubt there are some legitimate reasons to expect this; and to the degree that they are valid, they militate in the direction of starting new funds and stabilizing the size of giant funds. But there is also statistical reason to think that the size effect is spurious. Smaller funds tend to be less diversified; less diversified funds must be expected to show *both* higher and lower *extremes* of performance solely because of their smaller number of stocks held. For it to be legitimate to conclude that mere size hurts performance, we should have to have evidence that across *all* small funds the performance averages out worse than across *all* large funds, and with a deviation that is statistically significant according to the usual probability tests of hypotheses. Such evidence I have never seen marshalled; and casual inspection of what the performance has been of the aggregated portfolios of ten small companies chosen at random, and compared with one giant that is ten times as large, suggests to me that the adverse effects of size are exaggerated. (In any case, a large fund could, in principle, conduct itself like ten independent small funds.) In concluding these practical considerations deduced from the most elementary of sampling considerations, let me mention that contests like that conducted recently by the Chase

Bank among different analysts ought to be appraised for the import of their results by analysts experienced both in stochastic processes and game theory: contestants can rationally go for broke, knowing that the gains to them from purely lucky guesses may outweigh the loss to them of being a big rather than a small loser.

My pitch in this Foreword is not exclusively or even primarily aimed at practical men. Let them take care of themselves. The less of them who become sophisticated the better for us happy few! It is to the economist, the statistician, the philosopher, and to the general reader that I commend the analysis contained herein. Not all of science is beautiful. Only a zoologist could enjoy some parts of that subject; only a mathematician could enjoy vast areas of that terrain. But mathematics as applied to classical thermodynamics is beautiful: if you can't see that, you were born color-blind and are to be pitied. Similarly, in all the branches of pure and applied mathematics, the subject of probability is undoubtedly one of the most fascinating. As my colleague Professor Robert Solow once put it when he was a young man just appointed to the MIT staff: "Either you think that probability is the most exciting subject in the world, or you don't. And if you don't, I feel sorry for you."

Well, here in the mathematics of investment under uncertainty, some of the most interesting applications of probability occur. Elsewhere, in my 1971 Von Neumann Lecture before the Society for Industrial and Applied Mathematics, I have referred to the 1900 work on the economic Brownian motion by an unknown French professor, Louis Bachelier. Five years before the similar work by Albert Einstein, we see growing out of economic observations all that Einstein was able to deduce and more. Here, we see the birth of the theory of stochastic processes. Here we see, if you can picture it, radiation of probabilities according to Fourier's partial differential equations. And finally, as an anticlimax, here we see a way of making money from warrants and options or, better still, a way of understanding how they must be priced so that no easy pickings remain.

One of the troubles of being no longer young is that great experiences are behind you. If I had not already read all the detective works of Dashiell Hammett, I would now look forward to reading them. So I must envy any reader of these essays who reads them for the first time. He has an intellectual treat in store for him!

Paul A. Samuelson
Massachusetts Institute of Technology

Preface

Investment Portfolio Decision-Making contains several, indeed many, recent seminal and exciting essays that have important implications for both (1) normative portfolio decision-making and (2) understanding the empirical structure of the financial markets. It is, one hopes, a well-planned excursion into the rigorous and scholarly literature of investments. While the foundations of investments can be traced back to the 1700s, the real explosion in portfolio and applied capital market theory began in the mid-1960s. The editors are under no illusion that the included articles represent a complete collection of landmark contributions to investments or that one's present views of the empty boxes of investment knowledge will remain invariant over the coming decade. Investments, despite any contrary initial superficial impression, remain still a relatively underdeveloped area of knowledge.

The organization of this volume, like that of any field of knowledge, is to some degree arbitrary and subjective. The present classification scheme, for which I take prime responsibility, seems insightful and intuitively coherent. It is hoped that it will also appear this way to the reader.

It is a pleasure to acknowledge the stimulus of Dr. Giles Mellon, chairman of the Finance Department, Rutgers Graduate School of Business, who has given of his time and creative energies unstintingly over the years. In addition, appreciation is expressed to Professors Kenneth J. Arrow, Amir Barnea, Richard Behnke, Karl Borch, Sidney Nemetz, and Edward O. Thorp for helpful discussion on salient points embedded in this volume. Paul A. Samuelson, of course, merits a special note of thanks for his help, suggestions, and interest. Further, Dean Horace J. DePodwin and Associate Dean David W. Blakeslee of the Rutgers University Graduate School of Business Administration have contributed their patient understanding and encouragement. The good cheer of Conchita G. Gentalia was also a source of great support. Mike McCarroll and Betty Patterson of Lexington Books deserve a round of applause for their cheerful assistance.

James L. Bicksler

Theory of Portfolio Choice and
Capital Market Behavior:
An Introductory Survey

James L. Bicksler

Man continually makes resource allocation choices. Should you vacation in Rio at carnival time, buy a yacht, take out a loan, or/and purchase $50,000 of New York City 1998 6 percent municipal bonds? Questions on variations of this theme are of much interest to individuals having a Horatio Alger dream and who are involved in developing a strategy for gaining riches. Likewise, economists are interested in this genre (the simultaneous portfolio-saving problem) of decision analysis.

The structure of decision-making under uncertainty for the individual has evolved and developed gradually from and into the economics of uncertainty. The basic maximizing rule of normative choice behavior under uncertainty for the individual is that of the expected utility maxim of Bernoulli, Ramsey and Von Neumann-Morgenstern.[1] The expected utility model of the normative theory of choice under uncertainty postulates that an individual behaves as if he (1) assigns utility estimates to each alternative in his opportunity set and (2) chooses that alternative or mix of alternatives that maximizes his expected utility. Alternatively, if one accepts that there is a set of axioms that are a necessary and sufficient prescription for rational behavior under uncertainty, then it follows that the expected utility rule is an optimum selection criterion for ordering an opportunity set of ex ante probability distributions of, for example, claims to wealth.

While this rule is, in and by itself, conceptually eloquent, in order to derive testable hypotheses about capital market phenomena or to prescribe normative investment strategies, more structure must be imposed upon the preference function. This structure may result from either specifying (1) the nature of the probability distributions of one-period returns on all portfolios or (2) the shape of the investor's utility function.

For example, if the individual's utility function can be approximated by a second-degree polynomial, then the individual's preferences can be represented by a quadratic utility function, such as:

$$u(Y) = Y - cY^2.$$

It can be shown that for an individual whose behavior is consistent with a quadratic utility function, choice over any set of probability distributions of, for example, alternative investment portfolios can be made by analyzing the means and standard deviations of the respective return distributions of these portfolios. [2] This means that for this hypothetical individual, use of the efficient set theorem enables one to derive the indifference map consisting of all equally desirable (e.g., constant expected utility) E, S portfolios.

Similarly, the efficient set theorem, which states that the optimal portfolio for a risk averse investor must lie on the E, S indifference map, can be derived from the condition that the probability distributions of one-period portfolio returns are normally distributed.[3] In other words, a preference ordering can be derived by arraying the means and standard deviations of the one-period distributions of portfolio returns provided there is normality of portfolio returns.

Since the seminal contributions of Markowitz and Tobin to the investor portfolio problem of utility maximization under uncertainty postulated that investors' preferences were to be represented over E,S space, the above discussion has particular relevance.[4]

Theory of Choice

Part I on "Theory of Choice" begins with Borch's essay on "A Note on Uncertainty and Indifference Curves." Here, Borch shows that a preference ordering over portfolios in mean-variance space may lead to "incorrect" rankings. Specifically, Borch demonstrates that mean-variance indifference curves do not generally exist as loci of constant expected utility. The assumption of *préfèrence absolue,* which is part of the consistency postulates of von Neumann-Morgenstern, Borch argues, is sufficient to show that arbitrary points on an E,S indifference curve are not equally desirable. These counter-examples are indicative of the inherent paradoxes and contradictions that face a decisionmaker in ordering portfolios in the E,S plane. In sum, mean-variance portfolio analysis does not necessarily lead to expected utility maximization.[5]

Tobin, in his "Comment on Borch and Feldstein," implicitly and explicitly agrees with Borch's point of view regarding the usefulness of E,S portfolio analysis. Tobin does note that the E,S framework has advanced the state of the art. Specifically, normative portfolio choice frameworks now use two-parameters while the previously utilized investment decision rule of one parameter was ensnarled in the conundrum of the St. Petersburgh paradox, in view of the fact that it completely ignored risk.

The scenario whereby individuals in making choices violate the Savage postulates is the focus of the Raiffa note entitled "Risk, Ambiguity, and the Savage Axioms: A Comment." Here, Raiffa argues that while the Savage theorem may not be useful as a descriptive theory of real world behavior, it is the essence of normative decision-making. That is, if the "consistency" conditions are violated, the resulting preference ordering over ex ante probability distributions does not ensure utility maximization. Alternatively stated, individuals who violate the axiom of coherence are subject to a "Dutch book" (e.g., the situation where the individual loses money irrespective of the event outcomes) and that is, of course, irrational.

The essence of a stochastic static decision problem is utility and subjective probability. Its solution is via the Bernoulli rule. When, however, the decision problem shifts from a static context under uncertainty to one incorporating both risk and time preference, the Bernoulli rule is severely challenged, as is pointed out by Mossin in "A Note on Uncertainty and Preferences in a Temporal Context."

Postulate a decision scenario that has both uncertainty and temporal aspects to the random variables of interest. The optimal choice of the decision parameters requires a cardinal utility function in order to derive the preference ordering over the distribution functions. Mossin argues that for opportunities which are both uncertain and temporal there is a violation of the conditions for expected utility maximization. This "violation" results in the preference index for the hedged position on the resolution of distributions to be determined in the future being nonoptimal for any and all, except by chance, of the outcomes that could in fact materialize. Concomitantly, this results in the indifference curves for uncertain temporal prospects in the E,S plane being ellipses. However, expected utility in E,S space cannot have such a representation. Indeed, for this case, the utility function would be quadratic and the investor indifference maps are, in fact, concentric circles. In short, Mossin shows that the ordering of preferences within a joint time-uncertainty decision scenario is a formidable problem.

As previously noted, investment portfolio decision-making under uncertainty or the choice among alternative probability distributions is solved on a formal level by the expected utility maxim. The preference ordering or mapping over outcome spaces implies a cardinal utility function that is unique to a linear transformation. The derivation of this preference structure is on the basis of certain postulates of choice behavior. Thus, a priori a utility function should exhibit certain properties. These might, for example, include nonsatiation, boundness (if the outcome space is not bounded), and risk aversion.

Since the utility function can be thought of as representing an individual's risk-return trade-off, one's initial conjecture would be that the second derivative, $u''(x)$, of the function should represent a measure of risk aversion. This, however, is not the case. The second derivative is not invariant to linear transformations and ergo does not satisfy the invariance principle of the cardinal utility function. Two measures suggested by Arrow-Pratt, however, are useful for providing insights into risk aversion.

Absolute Risk Aversion:

$$R_A(Y) = -\frac{u''(Y)}{u'(Y)}$$

This ratio or function tells how the absolute dollar amount invested in risky assets changes with wealth. Intuitively, if the risk premium required to engage in gambles increases (decreases) with changes in wealth, the investor is said to possess increasing (decreasing) absolute risk aversion. This implies, of course, that if the absolute dollar amount invested in risky assets increases (decreases) with wealth, the utility function of the investor is characterized by decreasing (increasing) absolute risk aversion.[a] It is intuitively appealing to regard the utility functions of investors as having decreasing absolute risk aversion.[b]

Relative Risk Aversion:

$$R_R(Y) = - \frac{Yu''(Y)}{u'(Y)}$$

The relative risk aversion function states that if the proportion of risky assets in one's portfolio increases (decreases) with wealth, then decreasing (increasing) relative risk aversion characterizes the investor's portfolio behavior. This ratio gives insights into the elasticity of the marginal utility of holding risky assets. Indeed, if the wealth elasticity of the demand for cash balances is ≥ 1, it constitutes evidence in behalf of the increasing relative risk aversion hypothesis. Since the studies of Latané, Selden, Friedman, and others are consistent with increasing relative risk aversion, and for additional theoretical reasons, Arrow maintains that the necessary properties of utility functions include not only $u'(Y) > 0, u''(Y) < 0$, decreasing absolute risk aversion, but also increasing relative risk aversion.[6] This hypothesis of Arrow about increasing relative risk aversion is, however, contentious and lacks strong intuitive appeal.[7] For a discussion of the Arrow-Pratt measures of risk aversion see John Pratt's "Risk Aversion in the Small and in the Large," the final essay in this Part.

To conclude, Part I demonstrates, among other things, that there is something intellectually disquieting about the foundations of normative choice under uncertainty. In this regard, one should be reminded of Savage's comment "that the foundations of a subject are usually established long after the subject has been well developed, not before. To suppose otherwise would be a glaring example of 'naive first-things-firstism'."[8]

Dynamic Portfolio Choice Frameworks

Arrow has indicated that the temporal aspect is one of the two most important dimensions of a decision problem.[9] Part II consists of two articles

---

[a]This means that for utility of wealth functions which are characterized by decreasing (increasing) absolute risk aversion, risky assets are noninferior (inferior) goods.

[b]As an aside, the quadratic utility function exhibits increasing absolute risk aversion. For this reason, many economists feel that the quadratic function does not have appealing analytical or economic properties.

representing different rationales and ergo different analytical approaches to the temporal sequential aspect of an investment decision.

The investment literature and portfolio theory a la Markowitz, Tobin, Sharpe, et al., usually postulates decisions to be made within a single period context.[10] Further, the tradition in economics is that the ultimate object of choice is the time dated consumption stream. This view, according to some economists, is more than just a technical detail. It means that this exercise of deriving a preference ordering over the probability distributions of single period terminal wealth relatives is an incomplete description of the individual's normative decision problem. Stated differently, since the theory of choice under uncertainty for the individual postulates that an individual's preference function is specified over intertemporal consumption streams, the discussion of portfolio selection is inseparable from an individual's savings (consumption) behavior under uncertainty. Consequently, a major question becomes how uncertainty affects the optimal savings-investment decision of the individual.

Within this scenario, Phelps' "The Accumulation of Risky Capital: A Sequential Utility Analysis," was the first of a series of seminal contributions to the lifetime consumption-investment strategies literature. In part, it has engendered a string of further developments in the area of optimal lifetime savings-investment choice under uncertainty, including those by Hakansson, Leland, Yaari, Samuelson, Merton, Pye, and others.[11]

The Phelps problem was the determination of the Ramsey optimal consumption-savings path for the individual under uncertainty. Phelps postulated a certain income stream, that the savings of an individual were invested in a portfolio consisting of a single risky asset (this meant the portfolio choice problem was assumed away), the opportunity set did not include a riskless asset, returns were independently distributed, and the utility function for the individual was additive and a member of the isoelastic marginal utility family. The solution of the resulting stochastic functional equation representing the multistage decision process is by stochastic discrete-time programming. Extensions to the portfolio problem have now been made and among the properties of the analytic solution are that: (1) the risky asset ratio of the portfolio is independent of the investor's wealth position and stationary given the invariance over time of the distribution of expected returns and given the individual's choice constraints; (2) the consumption path is contingent, except for the logarithmic utility maximizer, on portfolio choice; (3) the investment opportunity set affects consumption; and, (4) the consumption decision is non-myopic.

This would seemingly suggest that the optimal investment-consumption decision is in several ways significantly different in structure than that of the traditional single-period portfolio problem. First, as indicated in the optimal consumption-investment (static portfolio) literature, utility enters directly (indirectly) via consumption (terminal wealth). Second, the optimization problem is treated within an intertemporal context where the rate of time preference for the individual plays a much more crucial role. Third, the analytical solutions for the simultaneous consumption-investment problem over time for individuals having additive utility functions are much more formidable than for the static portfolio decision problem.

Smith, in "Alternative Procedures for Revising Investment Portfolio," considers empirical aspects of the dynamic portfolio problem for the individual in a world of transactions costs including both search and information costs. The scenario of a Markowitz or Tobin maximizer is, as has been noted, that of a single period investment horizon. This means that the assessment process of means, variances, and covariances of individual securities must begin anew at the end of the stipulated horizon date. The portfolio analysis step deriving the efficient frontier will likely result in a "different" efficient opportunity locus and concomitantly result in a "different" optimal portfolio. Since the decision theoretic context of the Markowitz, Sharpe, and Tobin portfolio theories is that of a single period, no consideration is given to the balancing off of the gains from revision vis-à-vis the costs of implementing the next period's policy. It is, of course, economically relevant to inquire as to what is the preferred revision strategy.

Smith considers four alternative revision strategies. They are (1) the unrevised case—buy and hold, (2) the adjustment case (revise to initial proportions), (3) complete transition (repeat the Markowitz procedure anew), and (4) controlled transition (balancing portfolio revision costs with resulting benefits or advantages gained from revision). Smith argues that a priori the case of controlled transition is the most appealing. The specific portfolio switches à la controlled transition are determined by an iterative procedure that considers the effect in risk-return space of all single security changes under ceteris paribus conditions. The costs of transition include brokerage fees, capital gains, tax opportunity costs, and so forth. This procedure is done on a security by security basis until the newly created "optimal" portfolio is generated. A simulation experiment using a one-period horizon period was performed for each of these four strategies for the period 1946–1955. Interestingly enough, none of the four revision strategies completely dominated the others. However, it seemed that little evidence can be empirically adduced for the adjustment and complete transition strategies being optimal particularly for investor horizons that are relatively short in time. The unrevised case (buy and hold) works well, as obviously it should, when the revision periods are short and, ergo, transactions costs are "relatively" high. Indeed, for investment horizons that are instantaneous and for which transaction costs are positive, the unrevised case would likely asymptotically dominate the other strategies considered.[c]

As the investor revision period is lengthened, the limited revision strategy, according to Smith, begins to become much more desirable than the unrevised

---

[c]A qualification, however, must be noted. Operationally, this condition might result in the portfolios constructed via the unrevised and the controlled transition cases being identical.

strategy on an intertemporal cumulative performance basis. Naturally, as always, in these tests the specification of the expectations generator used for deriving the inputs for the Markowitz-Sharpe diagonal model are crucial.

Smith concludes that "the implications of these findings are that investment managers can profitably take advantage of market information in revising their portfolios, in a manner that is sound, but without sacrificing conservative attitudes towards portfolio turnover."

The Assessment Problem

The essays of Part III focus on a number of germane issues regarding subjective probability. Many psychologists and, for that matter, financial economists are of the opinion that the most important deficiencies in decision-making result from inadequacies in assessing subjective probabilities rather than in processing such information via choice theoretic frameworks. Further, almost all of modern portfolio theory presumes that the probability assessments about risk-return parameters of the securities in the investor's opportunity set are given.

Roberts, in "Risk, Ambiguity, and the Savage Axioms: Comment," argues that the traditional Knightian distinction between risk and uncertainty serves no useful normative purpose. Instead, what is crucial to decision-making is the willingness of the individual to make assessments upon which he will act (e.g., choose an alternative and implement it). The fact that there happens to be a certain "vagueness" about probabilities to be assessed is purely coincidental.

Within this context, Ellsberg has constructed a scenario that induces the asserted behavior of many individuals to violate the Savage postulates. Roberts suggests various possible sources of confusion that might lead to erroneous choices à la the Ellsberg scenario. These include such factors as:

1. The paradox postulates that utility is contingent upon monetary returns while the actual decisionmaker may specify that utility is a function of other arguments.
2. The game is for only one play rather than a series of gambles.
3. The cost of sample information to assess the probabilities of the various alternatives differs across individuals. These possible reasons for computation errors, while interesting from a behavioral viewpoint, have little if any relevance to the normative issue.

One implication of the above is that normative decision rules utilizing assessed subjective probability distributions cannot *operationally* be applied in a cookbook fashion. This means that assessment and quantification of judgment is a task not to be taken lightly. Ergo, the interrrogation techniques utilized, the information parameters generated, the scoring rules employed, decisions regarding the amount of sample information to purchase, and so on, are important issues for inferential and decision-theoretic purposes.

In the Bayesian framework of decision-making and inference, the assessment of subjective probability plays an important role. Formally, the Savage postulates require the decisionmaker to make his assessments consistent with (1) the coherence axiom, and (2) his judgments. Winkler, in "The Quantification of Judgment: Some Methodological Suggestions," discusses the derivation of these probabilities in a careful manner.

The direct interrrogation technique allows the subjective assessments to be derived indirectly from the decisionmaker's expression of betting odds. Unfortunately, under certain conditions, this technique does not offer any incentive for the individual to make assessments consistent with the Savage postulates. The use of penalty functions/scoring rules, however, encourages the individual to express his "true" beliefs and hence to derive probabilities in a "careful" manner. Though much has been learned about the properties of scoring rules, such as the appealing properties of the logarithmic scoring rule, this is still a fertile area for further research.

In addition to a decisionmaker assessing probabilities in a manner consistent with the Savage postulates, it is desirous from a normative standpoint that these probabilities be consistent with reality (e.g., the structure of the world). This is equivalent to saying that ideally we would like the probability assessor to be (1) competent in quantifying judgment à la probability-coherence axioms and (2) an expert in the domain of the forecasting application.[12]

Fama and Laffer's "Information and Capital Markets," considers a host of issues in the economics of information. These queries are, in the main, variations on the themes of costs, benefits, and social welfare implications of information. While information has benefits to the firm via improved decision-making, the genus of the Fama-Laffer essay is the value of information to investors for trading purposes as distinct from its potential value in improving ex ante production decisions. The analysis postulates that both the product and capital markets are perfect, firms issue only equity securities and are market value maximizers, there is no short selling of securities or resale of information by investors of such purchases, and there is homogenous expectations.

Among Fama-Laffer's conclusions are that:

1. Under conditions of monopoly, an independent producer should sell his information instead of engaging in trading activities.
2. The production of such information by an independent producer should be at a level consistent with the maximization of expected profits.
3. The optimum production under monopoly by a firm may be at an output level lower than if the monopolist was an individual. This results from the

consideration by the firm of the effect of such activities on their share-holders.

4. Regardless of the identity of the information producer, under monopoly the information generation process is Pareto suboptimal.

5. Under competitive markets and given that producers can react to the activities of others before the release of such information, equilibrium should be characterized by only one producer and the absence of economic rents.

6. If there is a partial monopoly and the cheapest producer is the firm, the shareholders may or may not benefit (e.g., the expected gains from this activity may be either positive or negative). Again, the optimum output level under partial monopoly will be different for a firm than for an outside individual.

Caveats about the nature of elicited subjective probabilities is the focus of Phillips' "The 'True' Probability Problem."

In the usual formulation of the normative investment decision problem, portfolio analysis begins only after security analysis is completed. Security analysis consists of assessing the required inputs necessary for the portfolio analysis step to generate the efficient frontier. Phillips argues that "a probability is a number between 0 and 1 inclusive" and that "my feelings of uncertainty are feelings, not numbers so they cannot be probabilities." Indeed, Phillips suggests that we interpret subjective feelings in the context of behavioral psychology. Ergo, assessments are verbal response or behavior to an assortment of stimuli. From these premises, Phillips then maintains that "we should discard the idea of a 'true' or 'objective' probability. Instead, we should think of probability judgments as the result of an individual's feelings of uncertainty, translated into a numerical response by internal decision processes. Many factors, both internal and external to the assessor, may influence the feelings of uncertainty, or the decision processes, or both. From this point of view, a probability cannot be wrong; it can, however, be more or less related to stimulus or task characteristics, and it can to varying degrees be affected by memory and cognitive processes, prior experience and information, social and cultural norms, personality, and cognitive styles."

Since the very essence of the meaning of "probability" centers on controversy, it would not be surprising to find substantial debate and even strong disagreement by many on this argument by Phillips.[13] However, perhaps surprising to some, Phillips' views are embedded in much of traditional academic finance as well as consistent with a great deal of the behavioral evidence of the decision processes of businessmen.

Far less likely to be controversial is Phillips' suggestion that assessors can be trained via exposure to "proper" control settings such as, for example, ideas, information, and judgments on "valid" structural relationships about the world.

The Efficient Markets Hypothesis

Much of modern day micro finance theory postulates an efficient capital market. This is particularly true of positive capital market theory. Part IV consists of two essays. The Samuelson essay develops the theoretical underpinnings of the economic rationale of the efficient markets hypothesis. The Black and Scholes contribution considers a scenario in which option prices are in equilibrium and where certain portfolio strategies can result in "superior" risk-adjusted performance. This seemingly is a violation of the efficient market model and might be considered an important empirical paradox of modern financial theory.

The efficient markets literature has produced an amazing anomaly. For one of the few times in economics, significant empirical work has preceded the theory underlying the tested hypothesis. As Fama states, "the impetus for the development of a theory came from the accumulation of evidence in the middle 1950s and early 1960s that the behavior of common stock and other speculative prices could be well approximated by a random walk. Faced with the evidence, and indeed most often contributing to it themselves, economists felt compelled to have some economic rationalization for the data. . . . In short, until the Mandelbrot-Samuelson models appeared, there existed a large body of empirical results in search of rigorous theory.[14]

The empirical work on the efficient markets hypothesis actually dates back to Bachelier's investigation of speculative prices in 1900. In his thesis, Bachelier develops a Wiener Brownian stochastic process with infinitely-divisible independent increments and tests it with data from the Paris Exchange, 1894 through 1898.[15] Outside of scattered research by H. Working and A. Cowles, this thesis about price changes of speculative securities lay essentially dormant until the late 1950s and early 1960s. Then, testing of the random walk model as a description of the movement of speculative prices began in earnest. Studies by Mandelbrot, Cootner, Fama, Alexander, Granger and Morgenstern, and others focused on one aspect or another of the random character or movement of stock prices.[16] A variety of test methodologies were used including cross-spectral analysis, analysis of serial covariances, filters, and the profitability of trading rules. Throughout this period, there were attempts to explain the empirical findings. However, the arguments, while implying a "fair game," did not directly involve the necessary sub-martingale model with which it can be shown that prices fully reflect a given informational parameter.

Samuelson's "Proof that Properly Anticipated Prices Fluctuate Randomly" was the first enunciation of the "fair game" model. Here, Samuelson clearly demonstrates that present prices fully reflect the available information parameter or set and hence expected returns are in equilibrium. Thus if,

$$X_{j,t+1} = P_{j,t+1} - E(\tilde{P}_{j,t+1} \mid \phi_t)$$

then

$$E(\tilde{X}_{j,t+1} \, / \, \emptyset_t) = 0$$

where X is the expected disequilibrium return, the subscripts j and t represent the security and time period respectively, E is the expectations operator, $\emptyset$ is the information parameter or set, P is the price of the security, and the tilde indicates that the parameter is a random variable. Dividends are assumed to be reinvested.

The above implies that the return generating process contingent upon informational parameter ($\emptyset$) will lead to disequilibrium expected returns, $X_{j,t+1}$, of zero. This means that in an efficient market there is no investment trading rule that will generate disequilibrium positive returns. More formally, the fair game model states that the sequence of future price changes in securities will follow a martingale wherein expected disequilibrium returns are zero.

In an important paper entitled "The Pricing of Options and Corporate Liabilities," Black and Scholes show that in a world (1) of no transactions costs, (2) where the borrowing rate equals the lending rate, and (3) where there is a stipulated stochastic return generating process, an optimal instantaneous hedging (long common stock and short warrants) can result in disequilibrium arbitrage profits over the horizon until the warrants expire. The Black and Scholes analysis leading to infinite profits is independent of the assumption of homogenous expectations but is conditional upon the prices of the warrants and the equities being perfectly correlated and hence resulting in perfect hedging. This pricing relationship in turn is derived from the assumption of an instantaneous hedging strategy.

In a companion paper, Black and Scholes present evidence that indeed suggests the prices of options as traded in markets deviate significantly from the prices predicted by the Black and Scholes valuation equation. This combined with the above referred to trading profits presents important challenges to the efficient markets hypothesis.[17]

Since corporate liabilities, except for warrants, can be conceptually viewed as options, this essay also has a number of meaningful implications for corporate financial decision-making. Included among these are comments dealing with the appropriate rate for discounting, default risk in the valuation of corporate bonds, and the effect of corporate debt-equity and dividend policy on the division of market valuation claims to bonds and common. Indeed, in some respects the Black and Scholes article may represent a seminal contribution to modern day corporate finance-valuation theory.

The Time-State Preference
Valuation Framework

Time-state preference theory represents a conceptually elegant theoretical framework for deriving a general equilibrium level of capital asset prices under uncertainty. Part V contains three important articles that develop the time-state framework, or utilize the Arrow-Debreu theory for insights into theoretical, conceptual, or pragmatic issues of capital market behavior.

Arrow, in "The Role of Securities in the Optimal Allocation of Risk Bearing," sets forth the eloquent states of the world model. In this essay, Arrow shows that Pareto optimal allocation of resources under uncertainty for a pure exchange economy, given risk averse utility maximizers, can be achieved via a competitive market structure of commodity claims and a complete array of state securities.

The extension of the Arrow-Debreu theory to portfolio analysis is via integration of the temporal aspect into a time-state preference approach to the valuation of pure securities.[18] Specifically, this partial equilibrium approach then lets risks be subdivided by permitting contingent claims to be time-state dependent. It can be shown that in an Arrow-Debreu world, if investors can both purchase and issue contingent claims, market prices over the fragmented probability distributions can be derived. Further, these prices, given arbitraging, will be in equilibrium.

Radner's essay "Problems in the Theory of Markets Under Uncertainty," focuses on the field of competitive equilibrium under uncertainty. The analysis is of an Arrow-Debreu economy under "standard conditions" and leads to the existence of a Pareto optimal equilibrium of production-consumption relative to some postulated resource endowments and shares.

When economic agents have different information structures, then in an extended Arrow-Debreu world "we get a theory of existence and optimality of competitive equilibrium relative to fixed structures of information for the economic agents." However, when information purchase is independent of the scale of the production process, the solution to this problem results in nonconvex production sets, which is inconsistent with the Arrow-Debreu conditions.

There is a plurality of reasons that would seem to suggest that Arrow-Debreu markets in the "real world" are incomplete. Among these reasons are lack of assessment capabilities by economic agents, moral hazard, unavailability of complex insurance, and speculative markets. Further, the Arrow-Debreu model does not integrate money, a sequence of markets over time, and a stock exchange. However, if the analysis is extended to a sequence of incomplete Arrow-Debreu markets, such can provide a more robust framework inasmuch as uncertainty, a stock exchange, speculative markets, and forecasting are properties that can then be derived. There are a number of different concepts of equilibrium compatible with a sequence of incomplete Arrow-Debreu markets. However, on the query of the optimality of such markets, little can be said until more precise specifications are given to the attainable states of the world and to the restrictions on the time-sequence of allowable contracts.

Also set forth in the Radner article is a menu of "unsolved" problems presently characterizing Arrow-Debreu theory. These include the optimality properties of equilibrium expectations, prices, and strategies, the structure of decision theories under uncertainty for firms, stochastic momentary equilibria for a sequence of markets, the integration of money and credit into the concept of general equilibrium, and so on.

Myers, in "A Time-State-Preference Model of Security Valuation," sets forth, within the Arrow-Debreu framework, a security valuation under uncertainty model.

The present value of contingent returns, given (1) a particular partition of states of nature that is mutually exclusive and exhaustive, (2) perfect markets, and (3) no borrowing or short selling is inferred from the necessary Kuhn-Tucker conditions for the nonlinear programming formulation of the valuation relationships. The derived time-state-preference valuation equation is:

$$P_K \geqslant \sum_{s,t} q(s,t) R_K(s,t)$$

where

$$q(s,t) = \pi(s,t) \frac{u'(s,t)}{u'(0)} .$$

P_K is the ex-dividend market price per share of the kth security at time 0, $q(s,t)$ is the present value of an incremental dollar of portfolio returns to the investor at time t if state (s) occurs, $R_K(s,t)$ represents the vector of returns contingent upon the sequence of states, 1 through $m(t)$ and dates 1 through T, $\pi(s,t)$ is the investor's assessment of subjective probabilities of (s,t) occurring, and $u'(s,t)$ is the marginal utility attributable to (s,t).

The economic meaning of the equation is that it places a lower bound on the security's price that "is at least equal to the expectation of the marginal utility associated with a small increment in his holdings of that security, when the utility of money in future contingencies is measured in terms of the utility of money used for present consumption. If the investor actually holds that security in his portfolio, then its price is exactly equal to the expectation of the marginal utility associated with the security." Myers shows that borrowing does not change the equilibrium conditions for the basic equation of the valuation of time-state securities. However, short selling will. A valuation framework is generalized to this set of market conditions. A number of observations regarding the Arrow-Debreu theory are provided, including the concept of risk equivalent securities, the implication of investor risk aversion for capital market risk-return trade-offs of individual securities, and the effect of "interdependence" on portfolio strategy and capital market relationships (e.g., theory of security valuation).

The Capital Growth Portfolio Criterion

The static normative theory of portfolio choice under uncertainty developed by Markowitz and Tobin is subject to a number of limitations. Part VI considers an alternative portfolio strategy, that of the capital growth model, which has far more appealing conceptual properties than the mean-variance framework.[19]

If the single period context of the investor is changed to a more realistic multiperiod horizon, then the normative strategy for investing in the long run may be a more relevant query.

Postulate that the following properties of the decision outcomes are relevant to the preference ordering of portfolios:

1. A given wealth level should be reached in the shortest time.
2. The expected growth of the portfolio value should be maximized.
3. The strategy should minimize the long-run probability of ruin.

It can be shown that the capital growth criterion that maximizes the expected geometric return of the one-period ex ante distribution of wealth opportunities (the expected logarithm of the one-period wealth relative) fulfills the above three conditions and in the long run, asymptotically dominates alternative portfolio strategies in the above sense. That is, if $u(X)$ is bounded from above and below, then the capital growth model, $E(\log X_T^*)$, will asymptotically dominate the results of any alternative uniform strategy in the sense that:

$$E[u(X_T^*)] > E[u(X_T)], T > T(X_0).$$

Thorp, in "Portfolio Choice and the Kelly Criterion," clearly enunciates these appealing properties of the capital growth model. However, Thorp offers a caveat. Namely, the geometric mean rule is only utility optimal for investors having logarithmic utility. That is, despite the appeal of the rule, it will only maximize utility for investors having logarithmic utility functions.

Unfortunately, it appears at times that certain proponents of the geometric mean rule recommend it as a long-run investing strategy cum utility maximization for all investors regardless of the shape of their utility function. For example, Latané states that "As pointed out to me by Professor L.J. Savage (in correspondence), not only is the maximization of G (the geometric mean) the rule for maximum expected utility in connection with Bernoulli's function but (insofar as approximations are permissible) this same rule is approximately valid for all utility functions."[20]

Samuelson, in "The 'Fallacy' of Maximizing the Geometric Mean in Long Sequences of Investing or Gambling," analyzes under what conditions the growth optimal policy does in fact maximize expected utility. Samuelson conclusively demonstrates that under conditions of bounded utility no uniform strategy, including that of the capital growth model, is optimal. Indeed, Samuelson shows that for the case of bounded utility, limited liability, $u = -e^{-bX}$, and when wealth is above or below a certain stipulated level, the optimal investment portfolio strategy is nonuniform and will be more "desirable" than that of the geometric mean rule and, for that matter, all other uniform and concomitantly suboptimal strategies.

This means that there are rich classes of utility functions for which the capital growth criterion is nonoptimal. Included as examples of such functions would be the power and the exponential, as well as any other utility functions implying either increasing or constant relative risk aversion.

Whether investors should act as if they had a logarithmic utility function is obviously an empirical question. As Thorp points out, those individuals wishing to achieve a stipulated level of wealth in the shortest time or accumulate the largest terminal wealth for a given investment interval will likely find the asymptotic properties of the capital growth model appealing and hence will have logarithmic utility functions. Indeed, Savage argues that "to this day, no other function has been suggested, as a better prototype of Everyman's utility function."[21] In any case, the risk-return preferences of individuals will presumably vary and thus numerous individuals may have power or other utility functions. Hence, despite the capital growth model's property of resulting in almost surely higher terminal wealth than that of alternative strategies, it does not follow that it leads to higher expected utility.[22] This Samuelson terms the "False Corollary" of geometric mean maximizers. An intuitive explanation is the policy's rare outcomes influence expected utility so much that alternative portfolio composition rules dominate the growth optimal model in a utility context.

The Two-Parameter Capital Asset Pricing Model

While there have been several approaches to equilibrium prices of capital assets under uncertainty, the two-parameter capital asset pricing model of Sharpe and Lintner cum modifications appears to be empirically more robust, at least at this point in time, than that of its major competitors.[23, 24] Part VII considers three articles. The first is a clarification essay by Fama of a technical detail regarding the Sharpe and Lintner papers. The Black article details the limitations of the simple version of the Sharpe-Lintner model and sets forth a seminal theoretical extension. Ball's contribution is a practical application of the two-parameter model to detecting the capital market consequences of accounting income reporting changes.

In deriving the two-parameter capital asset pricing model, the Sharpe and Lintner formulations were different in several ways thought to be of economic significance. Their apparent differences included the derivation of different appropriate measures of the risk of an individual asset or security, and different equilibrium risk-return trade-off relationships. Specifically, Sharpe advocated as the appropriate measure of risk the systematic risk of a security, while Lintner advocated a risk measure that integrated both the systematic and residual risk of a security. Further, Lintner's analysis indicated that there was only one equilibrium efficient portfolio (e.g., the market portfolio), while Sharpe concluded that conceivably there could be multiple efficient portfolios (e.g., tangency points).

However, Fama, in "Risk, Return, and Equilibrium: Some Clarifying Comments," showed that properly interpreted there is no necessary conflict between the Sharpe and Lintner analyses. Indeed, Fama demonstrated that if a more general stochastic process generating security returns is postulated, and if a correct specification of the market model is set forth that does not incorporate the restriction of the residual variances of securities being zero, then the risk premium equals:

$$E\left(R_i\right) - R_f = \lambda \left[B_i \sum_{j=1}^{N} X_j \, B_j \, \sigma^2\left(r_m\right) + X_i \, \sigma^2\left(\in_i\right) \right]$$

where E is the expectations operator, R_i equals the return on the individual asset i, R_f is the riskless rate of return, λ is the ratio of the risk premium component of expected market return divided by the variance of the market return, X is the proportion of the asset in the portfolio, B is a parameter specific to asset i, and $\in i$ is the residual term. This is equivalent to Lintner's measure, which can be derived directly from Sharpe's equations.

Empirically, the King and Blume studies indicate that the variance of the residual term is small relative to the variance of the market or common factor. [25] This means that the risk premiums implied by the original Sharpe and Lintner equations will be also approximately equal. Thus, the original Sharpe and Lintner formulations did not lead to any pragmatic viewpoints concerning the structure of security returns that are both important and different.

The equilibrium framework of capital market theory typically postulates a world of (1) homogenous expectations, (2) investors who are risk averse Tobin maximizers, (3) equality of borrowing and lending rates plus the option of the investor to construct whatever long or short portfolios he desires, and (4) the probability distributions on available opportunities measured over instantaneous holding periods are joint normal.

Assumptions (2) and (4) are thought to be descriptive of the real world, while the major relationships of capital market theory can be accommodated to

a world of heterogeneous expectations (see Lintner).[26] Assumption (3) is, to many economists, not a priori appealing.

The recent empirical evidence of Friend-Blume, Miller-Scholes, and Black-Jensen-Scholes casts doubt on the robustness of simple or traditional form of the capital asset pricing model.[27] One bewildering finding is the result that low beta stocks have positive α's while high beta stocks have negative α's. A more robust description of the stochastic process generating security returns is garnered from the two-factor model of Black-Jensen-Scholes. The two-factor model of Black-Jensen-Scholes suggests that during those periods when R_3, the minimum-variance zero-beta portfolio, is positive (negative), low β portfolios do better (worse) than predicted by the traditional form of the capital asset pricing model while high β portfolios do worse (better). Black, in "Capital Market Equilibrium with Restricted Borrowing," suggests that these results along with the empirical findings may be due to assumption (3) being violated. Black then indicates that a modified equilibrium model cum borrowing can be developed which is consistent with the empirical work in this arena.

Specifically, Black shows that in the case where there is no riskless asset and no riskless borrowing or lending, but that all combinations of long and short position in risky assets are permitted, then all efficient portfolios can be regarded as combinations of the market portfolio and the minimum variance zero-beta portfolio. The effect of this on the capital market line is to shift the intercept, and as Black states, "it is possible that restrictions on borrowing and lending would lead to a market equilibrium consistent with the empirical model expressed in equation (3) and developed by Black, Jensen, and Scholes." The expected return on an asset via the Black model can be represented by:

$$E\,(\widetilde{R}_j) = (1 - B_j)\,E\,(\widetilde{R}_3) + B_j\,E\,(\widetilde{R}_m)$$

where $E\,(\widetilde{R}_3)$ is the expected return on the zero-beta minimum variance portfolio. Thus, under conditions of no riskless borrowing or lending, expected returns vary linearly with beta risk.

Under conditions where there is a riskless asset but where investors cannot sell it short, there are now two types of efficient portfolios. One is the less risky efficient portfolio representing a blending of the riskless asset and the market portfolio, where the latter in turn is a combination of a portfolio made up of all risky assets and the minimum-variance zero-beta portfolio. The more risky efficient portfolio represents a portfolio made up of combinations of the minimum-variance zero-beta portfolio and a portfolio comprising all risky assets. Black argues that the case of restricted lending, like the case of restricted borrowing-lending, is consistent with capital market equilibrium. Specifically, capital market equilibrium under this postulated restriction leads to the expected return of a capital market instrument being a linear function of its beta.

Further, the slope of the security market line is now smaller than that of traditional theory and the intercept is now larger. "Thus a model in which borrowing is restricted is consistent with the empirical findings reported by Black, Jensen, and Scholes."

Empirical investigations of market equilibrium involve a host of germane methodological and measurement questions. Ball, in "Risk, Return, and Disequilibrium: An Application to Changes in Accounting Techniques," classifies disequilibrium into four main sources. They are: information about (1) the expected returns on an individual security, (2) the security's expected risk (beta), (3) the expected return on the market portfolio, and (4) the equilibrium risk-return trade-off.

In detecting for the presence of market disequilibrium given a flow of information about a given parameter, a speed of adjustment mechanism must be specified. Further, there are numerous specification problems emanating from the simultaneous impact of the four sources of disequilibrium.

While the market model has distinct advantages over serial-correlation models, it also has a number of potential limitations that impart bias in the estimation of the residuals. Ball thus argues that the cross-sectional model (e.g., the two-factor model of Black) utilizing the grouping technique of Black-Jensen-Scholes and Miller-Scholes can provide major advantages in dealing with the simultaneity problem inasmuch as (1) it can allow for a change in the "riskless" rate (the magnitude of the intercept) over time, and (2) this riskless rate is estimated independently of the mean data of the firm.

The estimation of the betas of the portfolios of securities grouped according to a decile ranking scheme is via a multi-stage procedure that utilizes independent data sources. Thus, the risk-return trade-off relationship is estimated from a sample data source other than that utilized in the grouping procedure. An inspection of the cumulative average error (CAR) of the residuals of the cross-sectional model then indicates the presence or absence of disequilibrium.

In short, the cross-sectional approach allows the risk-return trade-off parameter to change over time and thus makes this methodology appealing vis-à-vis other research designs such as (1) testing for serial correlation in the residuals, (2) a runs test to detect for differences in the rate of return, and (3) analyzing the cumulative average residuals of the expected returns from their sample means for data events grouped before and after income measurement technique changes.

Ball uses the cross-section methodology to investigate the impact of a change in the technique used for measuring accounting income. The empirical finding is that the utilization of alternative accounting schemes for measuring income has no effect on the price of equity shares. Thus, the evidence is consistent with the efficient markets hypothesis inasmuch as accounting processing techniques do not induce market disequilibria.

Ex Post Portfolio Performance

Part VIII considers a number of important queries and problems in performance measurement. The measurement of investment performance may be germane for several reasons. One important reason is the "learning from experience" that may result from the adaptive nature of the portfolio management decision process.

Recent work in portfolio evaluation has focused on two dimensions, risk and return, integrated into a one-parameter measure of performance. In this regard, Sharpe notes that "many measures of past performance have been proposed; most of them ignore risk entirely or treat it inadequately. There are exceptions; at least three measures attempt to account for risk in an acceptable manner. Each is related to the implications of capital market theory."[28] The three measures of performance are Sharpe's reward to variability ratio, Treynor's reward to volatility ratio, and Jensen's differential return. Essentially, what these three measures do is compare returns to a randomly chosen portfolio at a stipulated ceteris paribu risk level.

Smith and Tito, in "Risk-Return Measures of Ex Post Portfolio Performance," compare these three measures along with a fourth measure termed the modified Jensen measure, (differential return a la Jensen divided by a fund's beta or systematic risk). Conceptually, both the Jensen and Treynor measures consider only the fund's systematic risk and posit that the residual risk of the firm is diversified away. The Sharpe measure considers the variance of the portfolio's return, which, in turn, is made of both systematic and residual risk. Smith and Tito point out that the Jensen measure, while useful for indicating whether a fund's performance was better than a buy and hold the market strategy, cannot be utilized for ranking the performance of an array of funds having different risk characteristics.

Empirically, the four alternative measures of ex post performance were highly correlated, at least, for the case of mutual funds. Hence, the choice of which performance criteria to use was not an issue that could be settled ipso facto on grounds of historical evidence.

In measuring the performance of mutual funds vis-à-vis the market, the Sharpe and Treynor measures give quite disparate results. This would appear to mean that the presence of residual risk is important in determining whether funds do or do not outperform the market (e.g., measuring portfolio performance). As to the recommended measure, Smith and Tito advocate the Jensen measure primarily because of (1) its econometric estimation properties and (2) it integrates within it beta or the slope coefficient of the fund's characteristic line.

Fama, in "Components of Investment Performance," suggests finer breakdowns of performance measurement into components suggested by traditional investment analysis.[29] Specifically, measures of the ability (inability) to detect "winners" a la security analysis (e.g., Graham-Dodd-Cottle intrinsic value theory) and to predict future changes in markets levels are propounded.

Further, additional dimensions of performance are set forth including net selectivity (a sub-category of selectivity whereby an appraisal is made of whether the "extra" return generated is sufficient to compensate for the additional risk added to the portfolio), and the incremental return under conditions where the level of the portfolio manager's ex post risk differs from the investor's ex ante target level of portfolio risk.

The multiperiod scenario where there are intraperiod fund flows is of interest inasmuch as it closely approximates the reality of institutional portfolio decision-making. The multiperiod case under a set of rather restrictive assumptions regarding the simultaneity of the dates of evaluation, withdrawal, investment decision transactions, and reinvestment can be generalized from the one-period framework in a quite straightforward manner. Further, Fama shows that the finer breakdowns of performance for the one-period scenario can also be derived for the multiperiod case. In the calculation of intraperiod returns for the multiperiod case, a variation on Fisher's time-weighted rate of return is utilized.

In summary, Fama's analysis suggests a variety of insights into the measurement of ex post performance of various investment portfolio decision-making dimensions. This learning through experience a la performance evaluation should be of much value to portfolio managers in assessing where their talents do or do not reside.

There are two points to make in concluding. First, as Fama and Miller note, "the potential contribution of the theory of finance to the decision-making process, although substantial, is still essentially indirect. The theory can often help expose the inconsistencies in existing procedures; it can help keep the really critical questions from getting lost in the inevitable maze of technical detail; and it can help prevent the too easy unthinking acceptance of either the old clichés or new fads. But the theory of finance has not yet been brought, and perhaps never will be, to the cookbook stage."[30] This point of Fama and Miller needs emphasizing and reemphasizing, particularly to capital market beginners, but more generally to any investor who may have unrealistically high expectations regarding performance.

However, present-day investment knowledge does have relevancy to real-world portfolio decision-making. Indeed, Klein makes an important point in a slightly different vein when he comments "that there is no point trying to construct models that are purely of use in prediction and deny that such models have an existence of their own apart from structural models." Indeed, "the best predictions will be made from best structural models."[31] The same holds true for investments. Only if there is an understanding of the structure of investment interrelationships, both theoretical and empirical, can one formulate "optimal" investment strategies.

Second, there are vast differences between investment knowledge of a decade ago and the present state of this knowledge. What we know today about the empirical state of risk-return relationships and normative portfolio choice is certainly much more impressive than what we knew a decade ago. This means that the empty boxes of investment knowledge today are significantly different in nature than those of the recent past. There is every indication that for the foreseeable future, investments will remain a dynamically changing and exciting field of knowledge offering much indirect wisdom for the practitioner.

Notes

1. D. Bernoulli, "Exposition of a New Theory of the Measurement of Risk," *Econometrica*, 1954, pp. 23–36, sets forth the original intuitive rationale of utility maximization within the scenario of St. Petersburgh paradox. The axiomatic development of the expected utility rule is continued in F.P. Ramsey, "Truth and Probability," *The Foundations of Mathematics and Other Logical Essays* (London: Paul Kegan, 1931), pp. 156–98 and J. von Neumann and O. Morgenstern, *Theory of Games and Economic Behavior*, 2nd edition (Princeton: Princeton University Press, 1947).

2. An alternative choice theoretic approach between probability distributions is via the postulates of stochastic dominance. For an expositon of stochastic dominance, see J. Hadar and W. Russell, "Rules for Ordering Uncertain Prospects," *American Economic Review*, March 1969, pp. 25–34; G. Hanoch and H. Levy, "The Efficiency Analysis of Choices Involving Risk," *Review of Economic Studies*, July 1969, pp. 335–46; and H. Levy and G. Hanoch, "Relative Effectivensss of Efficiency Criteria for Portfolio Selection," *Journal of Financial and Quantitative Analysis*, March 1970, pp. 63–76.

3. In fact, the argument for the two-parameter model can be extended from the normal distribution to the class of symmetric stable distributions of which the normal is a special case. Evidence from the studies of Fama, Roll, and Blume suggest that the characteristic exponent of the stable class of distributions hovers around 1.6. See E. Fama, "The Behavior of Stock Market Prices," *Journal of Business*, January 1965, pp. 34–105; R. Roll, *The Behavior of Interest Rates: The Application of the Efficient Market Model to U.S. Treasury Bills* (New York: Basic Books, Inc., 1970); and, M. Blume, "The Assessment of Portfolio Performance: An Application of Portfolio Theory," unpublished Ph.D. dissertation, University of Chicago, 1968.

4. The pioneering development of the mean-variance or mean-standard deviation portfolio framework is contained in H. Markowitz, *Portfolio Selection: Efficient Diversification of Investments* (New York: John Wiley and Sons, Inc., 1959); and, J. Tobin, "Liquidity Preference as Behavior Towards Risk," *Review of Economic Studies*, February 1958, pp. 65–86. It is particularly from the seminal contribution of Markowitz that modern portfolio theory has evolved.

For a statement of the conditions under which portfolio separation holds in the presence of multiple sets of linear combination of risky opportunity bundles (e.g., mutual funds), when there is or is not a riskless asset, see D. Cass and J.E. Stiglitz, "The Structure of Preferences and Returns and Separability in Portfolio Allocation: A Contribution to the Pure Theory of Mutual Funds," *Journal of Economic Theory,* June 1970, pp. 122–60.

For theorems regarding mutual funds or separation theorems for intertemporal portfolio decisions, see R.C. Merton, "An Intertemporal Capital Asset Pricing Model," *Econometrica,* forthcoming.

5. A recent manuscript by Borch, entitled "Uncertainty and Indifference Curves: A Correction," *Review of Economic Studies,* 1973, p. 141, attempts to clarify, by an illustrative example, this basic inconsistency or flaw in mean-variance analysis.

Hakansson, however, takes issue with Borch. His argument is that "When the range of each attainable wealth distribution X is bounded, however, as it clearly is in any real-world situation and in any reasonable model thereof (see Lemma 1), this proposition is false." Further, "Borch's proposition is true of course if one demands that indifference curves must exist in the whole (E,S)-space. But in any decision problem, indifference curves are only needed to choose among attainable (E,S)-points—which can be specified independently of, and therefore in advance of, the preference ordering." See Nils H. Hakansson, "Mean Variance Analysis in a Finite World," *Journal of Financial and Quantitative Analysis,* September 1972, p. 1877.

6. See R. Selden, "Monetary Velocity in the United States," *Studies in the Quantity Theory of Money,* M. Friedman (ed.), (Chicago: University of Chicago Press, 1956), pp. 179, 257; M. Friedman, "The Demand for Money: Some Theoretical and Empirical Results," *Journal of Political Economy,* Vol. 67, 1959, pp. 327–51; H. Latané, "Income Velocity and Interest Rates: A Pragmatic Approach," *Review of Economics and Statistics,* 1960, pp. 445–49; A. Meltzer, "The Demand for Money: The Evidence from Time Series," *Journal of Political Economy,* Vol. 71, 1963, pp. 219–46, esp. p. 225.

7. Stiglitz, for example, argues that both theoretical and empirical reasons exist that suggest relative risk aversion is decreasing. See J. Stiglitz, "Review of Arrow's 'Aspects of the Theory of Risk Bearing'," *Econometrica,* 1969, p. 742. Recent empirical work by Professor Irwin Friend, using survey data from the Federal Reserve Board study of Financial Characteristics of Consumers and Changes in Family Finances and Federal personal income tax returns, indicates that investors have either constant or increasing relative risk aversion if wealth is measured all inclusive including human capital. See Irwin Friend, "Rates of Return on Bonds and Stocks, the Market Price of Risk and the Cost of Capital," preliminary draft, August 1973, pp. 27ff.

8. Savage, *op. cit.,* p. 1.

9. K. Arrow, "Statistical and Political Economy," *Econometrica,* October 1957, p. 523.

10. An exception to this is the article by Fama, which shows that under certain conditions (investor risk aversion and perfect capital markets) an investor's

behavior in a multiperiod world is indistinguishable from choice in a two-parameter world in which a risk averse investor has a single period horizon. See E. Fama, "Multiperiod Consumption−Investment Decisions," *American Economic Review,* March 1970.

11. N. Hakansson, "Optimal Investment and Consumption Strategies Under Risk for a Class of Utility Functions," *Econometrica,* September 1970; H. Leland, "Dynamic Portfolio Theory, Ph.D. dissertation, Harvard University, May 1968; M. Yaari, "Uncertain Lifetime, Life Insurance, and the Theory of the Consumer," *Review of Economic Studies,* April 1965; P. Samuelson, "Lifetime Portfolio Selection by Dynamic Stochastic Programming," *Review of Economics and Statistics,* August 1969; R. Merton, "Lifetime Portfolio Selection Under Uncertainty: The Continuous-Time Case," *Review of Economics and Statistics,* August 1969; and, G. Pye, "Lifetime Portfolio Selection with Age Dependent Risk Aversion," Working Paper, IP–167, University of California at Berkeley, Institute of Business and Economic Research, May 1971.

12. For an elaboration on this point see A. Tversky and D. Kahneman, "Judgment Under Uncertainty: Heuristics and Biases," Invited paper for the Fourth Conference on Subjective Probability, Utility, and Decision Making, Rome, September 1973.

13. For an excellent discussion of alternative interpretations of probability, see W. Salmon, *The Foundations of Scientific Inference* (Pittsburgh, Pa.: University of Pittsburgh Press, 1966).

14. For an excellent summary of much of the empiricism of the efficient markets model through 1969, see E. Fama, "Efficient Capital Markets: A Review of Theory and Empirical Work," *Journal of Finance,* May 1970, pp. 383–417.

15. L. Bachelier, *Théorie de la Speculation* (Paris: Gauthier-Villars, 1900).

16. Many of these papers are reprinted in P. Cootner's *The Random Character of Stock Market Prices* (Cambridge: M.I.T. Press, 1967).

17. Black and Scholes show, using ex post data to estimate ex ante variances, that portfolios formed by purchasing options on high variance securities and selling options on low variance securities result, given the absence of transactions costs, in substantial positive excess returns. See F. Black and M. Scholes, "The Valuation of Option Contracts and a Test of Market Efficiency," *Journal of Finance,* May 1972.

18. Arrow's original formulation was in an atemporal context. Debreu extended the model to the temporal domain. See G. Debreu, *Theory of Value* (New York: John Wiley and Sons, 1959).

19. Note Samuelson's comment that "These remarks critical of the criterion of maximum expected average compound growth do not deny that this criterion, arbitrary as it is, still avoids some of the even greater arbitrariness of conventional mean-variance analysis." See P. Samuelson, "The 'Fallacy' of Maximizing the Geometric Mean in Long Sequences of Investing or Gambling," *Proceedings of the National Academy of Sciences,* October 1971, p. 2496.

For an enumeration of the appealing economic properties of the growth optimal model see N. Hakansson, "Multi-Period Mean-Variance Analysis: Toward a General Theory of Portfolio Choice," *Journal of Finance,* pp. 857–84.

20. H. Latané, "Criteria for Choice Among Risky Ventures," *Journal of Political Economy,* 1959, p. 151.

21. Savage, *op. cit.,* p. 94.

22. The literature on the log-normal approximation in portfolio decision-making has recently been burgeoning. Counterarguments include M. Goldman, "A Negative Report on the 'Near Optimality' of Max-Expected-Log Policy as Applied to Bounded Utilities for Long-Lived Programs," M.I.T., November 1973, (mimeo.); R. Merton and P. Samuelson, "Fallacy of the Log-Normal Approximation to Optimal Portfolio Decision-Making over Many Periods," *Journal of Financial Economics,* March 1973; and P. Samuelson and R. Merton, "Generalized Mean-Variance Tradeoffs for Best Perturbation Corrections to Approximate Portfolio Decisions," *Journal of Finance,* forthcoming.

23. Witness Fama's statement that "the important basis for the conclusion that the two-parameter model is useful is that it does well, relative to any other capital market model of which I am aware, in describing return data." See E. Fama, "Risk, Return, and Portfolio Analysis: Reply," *Journal of Political Economy,"* May–June 1973, pp. 753–55.

24. Two recent pioneering empirical tests of the capital growth model's robustness in explaining the equilibrium level of asset prices are: E. Fama and J. MacBeth, "Long-Term Growth in a Short-Term Market," *Journal of Finance,* forthcoming; and R. Roll,"Evidence on the Growth-Optimal Model," *Journal of Finance,* June 1973.

25. B. King, "Market and Industry Factors in Stock Price Behavior," *Journal of Business,* Supplement, January 1966, pp. 139–90; and M. Blume, "The Assessment of Portfolio Performance," Ph.D. dissertation, University of Chicago, 1967.

26. J. Lintner, "The Aggregation of Investors' Diverse Judgment and Preferences in Purely Competitive Securities Markets," *Journal of Financial and Quantitative Analysis,* December 1965, pp. 347–400.

27. I. Friend and M. Blume, "Measurement of Portfolio Performance Under Uncertainty," *American Economic Review,* September 1970. M.H. Miller and M. Scholes, "Rates of Return in Relation to Risk: A Re-examination of Some Recent Findings," *Studies in the Theory of Capital Markets,* M.C. Jensen (ed.), (New York: Praeger Publishers, 1972), pp. 47–78; F. Black, M. Jensen, and M. Scholes, "The Capital Asset Pricing Model: Some Empirical Tests," *Studies in the Theory of Capital Markets,* M.C. Jensen (ed.), (New York: Praeger Publishers, 1972), pp. 79–121.

28. W. Sharpe, *Portfolio Theory and Capital Markets* (New York: McGraw-Hill Publishing Company, 1970), p. 52.

29. M.C. Jensen, "Optimal Utilization of Market Forecasts and the Evaluation of Investment Performance," in *Mathematical Methods in Investment and Finance,* G. Szego and K. Shell (eds.) (New York: American Elsevier

Publishing Company, 1972), contains numerous ideas on the same theme of Fama's article.

30. E. Fama and M.H. Miller, *The Theory of Finance* (New York: Holt, Rinehart, and Winston, 1972), p. viii.

31. L.R. Klein, *An Essay on the Theory of Economic Prediction* (Chicago: Markham Publishing Company, 1971), p. 99.

**Part I
Theory of Choice**

1

A Note of Uncertainty and Indifference Curves

Karl Borch
*Norwegian School of Economics
and Business Administration
Bergen, Norway*

1. A decision problem under uncertainty consists essentially in establishing a preference ordering over a set of stochastic variables. We do not lose much if we interpret these stochastic variables as monetary gains, with the distribution functions $F_1(x), F_2(x) \ldots F_i(x) \ldots$. The problem is then to establish a preference ordering over a set of such functions.

If the ordering is consistent in the sense of von Neumann and Morgenstern [7], it can be represented by a utility function $u(x)$ so that

$$\int_{-\infty}^{+\infty} u(x)dF_i(x) > \int_{-\infty}^{+\infty} u(x)dF_j(x).$$

if, and only if $F_i(x)$ is ranked above $F_j(x)$ in the preference ordering.

2. If the initial set is a family of distributions $F(x, a_1 \ldots a_n)$, which are completely determined by n parameters, the problem is evidently to establish a preference ordering over a set of fectors $\{a_1 \ldots a_n\}$. It is then natural to represent this preference ordering by a utility function $U(a_1 \ldots a_n)$ of the kind used in classical economic theory. One should then be able to analyze the problem with the familiar tools of economic analysis.

This is a natural and very attractive idea, which has a long history. The idea is the foundation of the subject which actuaries call "the theory of risk" [4], and which has its origin in the work of Tetens [8], who studied orderings depending on the mean and the mean deviation of distribution functions.

There will—apart from degenerate cases—be a one-to-one correspondence between the n parameters $a_1 \ldots a_n$, and the n first moments of the distribution $m_1 \ldots m_n$, provided that these exist. We do, therefore, not lose much generality if we assume that the preference ordering can be represented by a utility function of the form $U(m_1 \ldots m_n)$.

3. Let us now try to combine this old model with the theory of von Neumann and Morgenstern. If a preference ordering over a family of distributions

Reprinted by permission of the publisher and author from *Review of Economic Studies*, January 1969, p. 1–4.

$F(x, m_1 \ldots m_n)$ is consistent in the sense of von Neumann and Morgenstern, there exists a utility function $u(x)$ so that

$$U(m_1 \ldots m_n) = \int_{-\infty}^{+\infty} u(x) \, dF(x, m_1 \ldots m_n).$$

This relation can only be satisfied if $u(x)$ is a polynomial of degree n, i.e., if

$$u(x) = x + c_2 x^2 + \ldots + c_n x^n,$$

and if $U(m_1 \ldots m_n)$ is linear, i.e. if

$$U(m_1 \ldots m_n) = m_1 + c_2 m_2 + \ldots + c_n m_n,$$

where $c_2 \ldots c_n$ are constants. The result is really trivial. If $u(x)$ is not a polynomial of degree n, the preference ordering will depend on properties of the distributions which cannot be described by the first n moments.

4. The function $u(x)$ can be interpreted as the *utility of money*. Economic common sense requires that $u'(x) > 0$, and there are usually good reasons for assuming that $u''(x) < 0$, i.e. that marginal utility of money is decreasing. These two assumptions imply that $u(x)$ cannot be a polynomial. This again means that the old approach to the economics of uncertainty must violate:

    (i) either the consistency conditions of von Neumann and Morgenstern,

    (ii) or the usual assumptions about the utility of money.

One might have expected that this fairly simple conclusion should have discouraged economists from continuing to explore the old approach. It appears, however, that exactly the opposite has happened. The expected utility theorem of von Neumann and Morgenstern seems to have revived the interest in the old model—particularly in its simplest form, i.e., for $n = 2$. A number of authors: Allais [1], Markowitz [5], [6], Tobin [9] and others have used this model as the corner stone of general theories. Most of them seem, however, to be aware of the possibility of such violations as mentioned above. Allais is probably most outspoken on this point, since he [2] explicitly rejects the consistency conditions of von Neumann and Morgenstern. The others seem to believe that these conditions can be ignored, at least as a first approximation. For instance if $u(x)$ is a polynomial, the conditions $u'(x) > 0$ and $u''(x) < 0$ may be satisfied in certain intervals. If we confine our attention to distribution functions concentrated on these intervals, we can of course establish a consistent preference ordering depending only on moments. If we apply this ordering to other distributions, we will inevitably run into contradictions of the kind indicated in the following paragraphs. We can avoid these contradictions and obtain a consistent preference ordering over the set of all distributions by assuming that $u(x)$ is made up of "pieces" of polynomials, so that the two conditions above are satisfied. Such orderings will however not depend exclusively on the moments of the distribution functions.

5. For $n = 2$ we have

$$u(x) = x + cx^2$$

and

$$U(m_1, m_2) = m_1 + cm_2 = E + cE^2 + cS^2,$$

where

$E = m_1$ = the expected gain,

$S^2 = m_2 - m_1^2$ = the square of the standard deviation of the gain.

In the terms of classical economic theory this means that the indifference curves in an ES-plane are concentric circles with the centre on the S-axis. Markowitz and Tobin do not seem to accept this implication. Bierwag and Grove [3] are aware of it, and to their credit, seem to feel a bit unhappy about this observation.

Most authors who have worked with the model, ignore this implication—and the expected utility theorem from which it follows. Instead they assume that a reasonable preference ordering over a set of probability distributions can be represented by a family of indifference curves in the ES-plane. This seems to be a very innocent assumption, and it may be worth while showing that it contains a contradiction, without using the conditions in para 4.

6. Let us write (x, p, y) for the following distribution:

Gain x with probability $1 - p$

or gain y with probability p.

If $y_1 > y_2$, we assume that (x, p, y_1) is preferred to (x, p, y_2). Allais [2] calls this assumption *préférence absolue*. It is a part of the consistency conditions of von Neumann and Morgenstern, and the only part which Allais accepts.

Let us now assume that it is claimed that the two points (E_1, S_1) and (E_2, S_2) lie on the same indifference curve in the ES-plane. We can then take

$$x = \frac{S_1 E_2 - S_2 E_1}{S_1 - S_2},$$

$$p = \frac{(E_1 - E_2)^2}{(E_1 - E_2)^2 + (S_1 - S_2)^2} \, ,$$

$$y_1 = E_1 + S_1 \frac{S_1 - S_2}{E_1 - E_2} \, ,$$

$$y_2 = E_2 + S_2 \frac{S_1 - S_2}{E_1 - E_2} \, .$$

It is easy to verify that the mean and standard deviation of (x, p, y_i) are E_i and S_i. Hence the points (E_i, S_i) and (E_2, S_2) can lie on the same indifference curve only if $y_1 = y_2$, i.e. if

$$E_1 + S_1 \frac{S_1 - S_2}{E_1 - E_2} = E_2 + S_2 \frac{S_1 - S_2}{E_1 - E_2}$$

or

$$(E_1 - E_2)^2 + (S_1 - S_2)^2 = 0$$

or

$$E_1 = E_2 \text{ and } S_1 = S_2.$$

This means that it is impossible to draw indifference curves in the *ES*-plane. If a person claims that he can do this, we can pick two arbitrary points on one of his indifference curves, and construct two distributions which are represented by these two points, and which cannot be equally desirable under the assumption of *préférence absolue*.

7. The counter example we have given should at least indicate that theories based on indifference curves in an *ES*-plane must be used with some caution. It is, however, clear that a portfolio theory depending on such curves, does not make sense if it is possible to offer the decision maker any two-point distribution of the type considered above. This ought to have led the enthusiasts of portfolio theory to specify the validity of their models—a question they seem reluctant to answer.

The usual starting point of a portfolio model is a finite set of stochastic variables $x_1, x_2 \ldots x_n$, representing the securities available in the market. A portfolio is then represented by a stochastic variable

$$x = \sum_{i=1}^{n} t_i x_i,$$

where

$$\sum_{i=1}^{n} t_i = 1.$$

A reasonable preference ordering over the set of such portfolios can usually be represented by a family of indifference curves in the ES-plane. To demonstrate the inherent contradiction, we must use two-point distributions which do not belong to the set.

The situation is not quite so simple if the initial set consists of all stochastic variables which have distributions belonging to a particular two-parameter family of functions $F(x, a_1, a_2)$. A portfolio will then have a distribution which does not belong to the family. If, for instance, we start with a set of Poisson variables

$$\Pr(x = b + cn) = \frac{a^n e^{-a}}{n!} \quad (n = 0, 1, 2, \ldots)$$

any infinitely divisible distribution can be obtained as a portfolio. The two-point distribution is not infinitely divisible, but it seems odd to deny this distribution a place in a preference ordering over a large family of distributions. The only possibility of "staying within the family" is to take the initial set as the set of all normal distributions. This assumption is made explicitly by Allais [1], but not by the other revivers of the classical model.

References

1. Allais, M. "L'Extension des Théories de l'Equilibre Economique Général et du Rendement Social au Cas du Risque", *Econometrica* (1953), pp. 269–290.
2. Allais M. "Le Comportement de l'Homme Rationnel devant le Risque: Critique des Postulates et Axiomes de l'Ecole Americaine", *Econometrica* (1953), pp. 503–546.
3. Bierwag, G.O. and Grove, M.A. "Indifference Curves in Asset Analysis", *The Economic Journal* (1966), pp. 337–343.
4. Borch, K. "The Theory of Risk", *Journal of the Royal Statistical Society,* Series B (1967), pp. 432–467.

5. Markowitz, H. "Portfolio Selection", *The Journal of Finance* (1952), pp. 77–91.

6. Markowitz, H. *Portfolio Selection – Efficient Diversification of Investments* (John Wiley & Sons, 1959).

7. Neumann, J. von and Morgenstern, O. *Theory of Games and Economic Behavior,* 2nd Edition (Princeton University Press 1947).

8. Tetens, J.N. *Einleitung zur Berechnung der Leibrenten und Anwartschaften* (Leipzig, 1789).

9. Tobin, J. "Liquidity Preference as Behavior Towards Risk", *The Review of Economic Studies,* 25 (1958), 65–86.

2

Comment on Borch and Feldstein

James Tobin
Yale University

Both Mr. Borch and Mr. Feldstein remind us that it is very difficult to derive propositions that are simultaneously *interesting* and *general.* In particular the Neumann-Morgenstern hypothesis of utility maximization will not, unaided, tell us much about portfolio choices. To get propositions with significantly more content than the prescription that the investor should maximize expected utility, it is necessary to place restrictions on his utility function or his subjective probability estimates or both. These propositions, naturally, will not hold if these restrictions are removed.

I do not believe that any of us who have found mean-variance analysis illuminating have been under any illusions on this basic point. We have known, and we have said, that "$E - \sigma$"indifference curves, as loci of constant expected utility, do not in general exist. I am not surprised that Mr. Borch can demonstrate their non-existence by contriving probability distributions that the $E - \sigma$ criteria will rank incorrectly, given that the utility function meets everywhere his canons of good behaviour. We all know, to give another example, that no amount of risk aversion will cause an investor to prefer a portfolio with a certain return of zero to one with a wide dispersion of possible non-negative returns.

We are considering an investor deciding how much, if any, of each of n assets to hold in his portfolio for a definite period of time: the portfolio is $(x_1, x_2, \ldots, x_n)$ where $\Sigma x_i = 1$. The portfolio return R will be $\Sigma x_i r_i$ where the r_i are random variables.

Strictly speaking, the portfolio choices of an expected-utility-maximizing investor can be analyzed in terms of the two parameters, mean and variance, of his subjective probability distributions of the returns from alternative possible portfolios only if one or both of the two following assumptions is met:

(a)   the investor's utility function is quadratic;
(b)   he regards the r_i as normally distributed.

In the absence of (a), the second assumption is required. Without it, the alternative possible portfolios $(x_1, x_2, \ldots, x_n)$ cannot be described and ranked in

Reprinted by permission of the publisher and author from *Review of Economic Studies,* January 1969, p. 13–14.

terms of mean and variance, even if the individual assets (pure portfolios with one $x_i = 1$ and all the rest equal to zero) can be so described and ranked.

As Mr. Feldstein points out, I tried erroneously to stretch the admittedly restricted generality of the approach. I should have recognized that the family of 2-parameter distributions with the requisite property has only one member, the normal. In the "proof" which Mr. Feldstein criticizes I used the property of replication under mixing mentioned in the preceding paragraph without realizing or stating that the normal is the only 2-parameter distribution for which it holds. It is this same point—not, as Mr. Feldstein seems to assert in his third section, a different one—that is involved in the necessity to assume either quadratic utility or normal probability distributions in applying mean-variance analyses to choices involving more than one risky asset.

As for the convexity of the $E - \sigma$ indifference curves, my assertion was simply this: If they exist and are derived from expected utility maximization, then they must be convex. This is true, whether (a) or (b) is the simplifying assumption made. Mr. Feldstein's indifference curve, with a concave range, is not a relevant example to counter this assertion. His logarithmic utility and log-normal probability distribution might be used to rank a designated list of basic portfolios all of which have by assumption log-normally distributed returns. But they could *not* be used to rank any portfolios that are linear blends of those basic portfolios, because the returns on the blends will not be log-normal. Now the fact that the market makes linear blends available to the investor is of the very essence of the portfolio choice problem. An analytical apparatus that does not handle this essential fact is as useless as a model of consumer choice that does not allow the consumer to move within his budget constraint to any market basket of goods he wants.

I do not believe it is an exaggeration to say that, until relatively recently, the basic model of portfolio choice used in economic theory was a one-parameter model. Investors were assumed to rank portfolios by reference to one parameter only—the expected return, possibly corrected by an arbitrary "risk premium", constant and unexplained. This approach was rationalized, if at all, by assuming either subjective certainty or constant marginal utility. It is now more than a decade ago that I participated in the modest endeavour of doubling the number of parameters of investors' probability estimates involved in economists' analyses of asset choice. This extension from one moment to two was never advertised as the complete job or the final word, and I think that its critics in 1968 owe us more than demonstrations that it rests on restrictive assumptions. They need to show us how a more general and less vulnerable approach will yield the kind of comparative-static results that economists are interested in. This need is satisfied neither by the elegant but nearly empty existence theorems of state preference theory nor by normative prescriptions to the individual that he should consult his utility and his subjective probabilities and then maximize.

3 Risk, Ambiguity, and the Savage Axioms: Comment

Howard Raiffa
Harvard University

Ellsberg writes:

I propose to indicate a class of choice-situations in which many otherwise reasonable people neither wish nor tend to conform to the Savage postulates, nor to the other axiom sets that have been devised. But the implications of such a finding, if true, are not wholly destructive. First, both the predictive and normative use of the Savage or equivalent postulates might be improved by avoiding attempts to apply them in certain, specifiable circumstances where they do not seem acceptable. Second, we might hope that it is precisely in such circumstances that certain proposals for alternative decision rules and nonprobabilistic descriptions of uncertainty (e.g., by Knight, Shackle, Hurwicz, and Hodges and Lehmann) might prove fruitful. I believe, in fact, that this is the case.[1]

Let me introduce myself as one who accepts Savage's postulates or equivalent rules for a much wider domain of problems than does either Ellsberg or Fellner. In particular, I find that I would want to behave in a manner consistent with Savage's normative prescriptions of behavior in the examples cited by the above authors. At the outset I will agree with them that it is not hard to elicit from most people (and I include myself in this category) a set of mutually inconsistent responses to questions or to observe in their actions inconsistent behavior. But I wish to reaffirm, what these authors also emphasize, that Savage's theory is not a descriptive or predictive theory of behavior. It is a theory which purports to advise any one of its believers how he *should* behave in complicated situations, *provided* he can make choices in a coherent manner in relatively simple, uncomplicated situations.

The fact that most people can be shown to be inconsistent in their manifest choice behavior cuts two ways: First, it emphasizes the difficulties encountered in putting into practice a model which demands in each application that the

Reprinted by permission of the publisher and author from *The Quarterly Journal of Economics,* November 1961, p. 690–694.

1. Daniel Ellsberg, "Risk, Ambiguity, and the Savage Axioms," *The Quarterly Journal of Economics,* LXXV (Nov. 1961), p. 646.

decision-maker assign a set of preferences to a host of simple problems which are internally consistent. Second, it clearly demonstrates how important it is to have a theory which can be used to aid in the making of decisions under uncertainty. If most people behaved in a manner roughly consistent with Savage's theory then the theory would gain stature as a descriptive theory but would lose a good deal of its normative importance. We do not have to teach people what comes naturally. But as it is, we need to do a lot of teaching; and to help point out this need, I particularly like the examples cited in Ellsberg's and Fellner's papers.

Several years ago, Ellsberg tested some of his observations on me. As an experimental subject I was hopelessly contaminated because I had already thought hard about the discussion in Jimmy Savage's book on the Allais Paradox. My immediate impulse was to break apart some of the options he asked me to consider into simpler components and then to force internal consistency on myself by means of the Savage model. But as Ellsberg pointed out, this was not playing *his* game and he asked me for a reply to his questions without any pencil pushing. I complied and I was found wanting. I was inconsistent. But I was uncomfortably inconsistent, because some of the options he posed seemed too complicated to me and I wanted to reduce them by means of the Sure-thing Principle. Of course, if I had done this, I would have forced consistency on myself. Naturally, when he pointed out that I was inconsistent I insisted that if I were playing the game for real I would pay a premium to be allowed to change my choices so that I would not violate the Sure-thing Principle. Each of us went away from that meeting with different messages: he with the notion of the limitations of the Savage theory; I with renewed respect for the importance of the Savage theory.

I started to experiment on my own with adaptations of Ellsberg's counter-intuitive examples. My subjects were students at the Harvard Business School and a few seasoned business executives—"men of experience." Immediately I observed what I shall call the "two-shift-effect." I found that when relative frequencies or so-called objective probabilities were given in numerical form as data of a decision problem, then these were often used in computing various indices (e.g., expected or actuarial values) which served as a guide to action. But if certain uncertainties in the problem were in cloudy or fuzzy form, then very often there was a shifting of gears and no effort at all was made to think deliberately and reflectively about the problem. Systematic decomposition of the problem was shunned and an over-all "seat of the pants" judgment was made which usually graphically reflected the temperament of the decision-maker. (I refer here to the pessimism-optimism polarity.) In reporting this, I am just confirming the experience of Ellsberg and Fellner (and also of Shackle, Knight, etc.). However, I draw a different message from this exprience. There is a need to teach people how to cope with uncertainty in a purposive and reflective manner, and to break down the taboo that probabilities should only be assigned if one has clearcut relative frequency data at hand. As *one* step toward making this view more palatable I have regularly used in my classes the following adaptation of one of Ellsberg's thought-provoking problems.

I believe the following questionnaire (two questions plus the brief pre-amble) should be clear enough. You might enjoy trying this yourself now. In the classroom I usually emphasize the fact that "You," the subject, *have complete freedom* of calling "red" or "black" in both of the questions below.

Exhibit: An Experiment Involving
Objective and Subjective Probabilities

Please answer the following questions as fairly as you can, indicating how *you personally* would act if faced with the choices described. *This is not a quiz;* there is no single "right" answer to either question.

Question 1

Suppose you have been offered the following proposition: You will be given an urn containing exactly 50 red balls and 50 black balls; there are no balls of other colors in the urn. You will name a color (red or black), and then without looking, draw a single ball from the urn. Suppose, further, that the pay-offs are as follows:

   (a) If the color *you* name differs from *your* drawing you get nothing.

   (b) If the color *you* name agrees with *your* drawing your gain is $100.

Keeping in mind your financial position as of today, and remembering that the game is to be played just once, up to how much would you be willing to pay in order to participate in this game? $_____

Question 2

Suppose now, that you have been offered the same proposition as above, except that in this case the urn contains an *unknown* number of red balls and an unknown number of black balls; that is, the urn may contain all black balls, all red balls, or a mixture of the two, but there are no balls of other colors in the urn. The procedure and the pay-offs are exactly the same as in Question 1.

Keeping in mind your financial position as of today, and remembering that the game is to be played just once, up to how much would you be willing to pay in order to participate in this game? $_____

The answers for the first question clustered somewhere around $30. Several subjects go down as low as $10 and a few go as high as $45. Of course, although the actuarial or expected value of the game is $50 there is nothing "incorrect" about any of these answers. A *majority* of the subjects offered considerably more for question 1 than for question 2. For example, an answer of $35 for question 1 and $5 for question 2 would be a typical pair. On the other hand, a minority gave like amounts: $40 and $40 or $10 and $10, etc. According to the Savage Axioms the second option should be worth at least as much as the first. It's fun to listen to a group of subjects argue in class whether or not the second option is worse than the first. There is not only division of opinion but opinions do not change easily. But then someone—all too often that someone is I—comes up with the following argument: Suppose you withdraw a ball from the urn with unknown composition but do not look at its color. Now toss a fair (unbiased) coin and call "red" if heads, "black" if tails. The "objective" probability of getting a match is now .5 and therefore it is just as desirable to participate in the second game as in the first. I have found out that after the student convinces himself it does not matter whether the ball is drawn first or whether the coin is tossed first, that he is most willing to increase his price for the second game up to the price he was willing to pay in the first game. Incidentally, I tried this same experiment on a graduate class in statistics in which all the students had prior courses in mathematical statistics and the pattern of answers, as well as the ensuing free-for-all discussion, was very much like the experiences I had with business school students who had had no previous courses in statistics.

As a second example let us use the very ingenious example given by Ellsberg where a subject chooses a ball from an urn containing 30 red balls and 60 (black and yellow) balls, the latter in unknown proportion. Recall that the four acts he considers lead to the array:

		Red	Black	Yellow
			State	
	I	100	0	0
Act	II	0	100	0
	III	100	0	100
	IV	0	100	100

I concur with Ellsberg that most subjects choose act I over II and IV over III, thus violating the Savage Axioms. Also I admit that many of these subjects are reluctant to change their choices when it is pointed out to them that their behavior is inconsistent with the Sure-thing Principle. Many are also not very impressed with the argument that *no* partition of the sixty (black, yellow) balls would lead to the pattern I over II and IV over III. Well, I would like to undermine further their confidence in their initial choices! I find the following argument is quite persuasive. Suppose you register I > II and IV > III. I now offer you the paired comparison between the following two options. In option A a fair (unbiased) coin is tossed and act I is taken if heads appears, whereas act IV is taken if tails appears; with option B, heads leads to act II and tails to act III. In table form we get:

	Heads	Tails
Option A	Act I	Act IV
Option B	Act II	Act III

Now by strict dominance option A is better than B *for you* since you prefer I to II and IV to III. So far there is no trouble but let's take a closer look at options A and B. The final outcomes of either option depend on the toss of the coin and the selection of a ball. Now let's do the accounting by analyzing the implications of the options conditional on the color of the withdrawn ball. Our analysis takes the form:

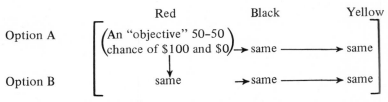

	Red	Black	Yellow
Option A	An "objective" 50–50 chance of $100 and $0 → same	same →	same
Option B	same	→ same →	same

But this reasoning should lead everyone to assert that options A and B are *objectively identical!* Something must give! I cannot see how anyone could refute the logic leading to the conclusion that given your initial choices, you should prefer option A to option B. This bit of logic is certainly not the weak link in the argument. But then again these options look awfully alike to me! Therefore, on thinking it over, wouldn't you like to change your mind about your initial preferences?

4

A Note on Uncertainty and Preferences in a Temporal Context

Jan Mossin
*Norwegian School of Economics and Business Administration
Bergen, Norway*

When someone asks you which of a set of uncertain prospects you prefer you should answer: "That depends upon when the outcomes will become known." The importance of this qualification was clearly pointed out by Markowitz [3, Chs. 10–11]. The reason why the temporal aspect is important is not only that it will affect your choice, but, more fundamentally, because it has to do with the question of whether or not it is possible to represent such choices by means of a utility function. Markowitz gives an example which illustrates that this may not be so.

If there are situations where choices among probability distributions cannot be represented by a utility function, then the rule for making those choices violates te consistency conditions of von Neumann and Morgenstern. This note examines the problem in the context of a simple two-period consumption model, with the purpose of finding out just what it is that is violated, and to see why such a violation is not unreasonable.

Consider an individual faced with the problem of allocating his wealth y between present consumption c_1 and future consumption c_2. To make things simple it will be assumed that the interest rate on savings (positive or negative) is zero with certainty. Thus, $c_2 = y - c_1$. Total wealth could be conceived of as consisting of present income y_1 and future income y_2 with y_1 known with certainty and y_2 being a random variable. It is, however, only their sum that matters; the important point is that the precise value of y will not become known before the end of the initial period, i.e., after c_1 has been chosen. Dreze and Modigliani [2] refer to the probability distribution for y, $F(y)$, in such a case as a *temporal* uncertain prospect.

The determination of an optimal value of c_1 requires the existence of a cardinal utility function $u(c_1, c_2)$ representing preferences among consumption profiles (or among gambles involving consumption profiles). This function is assumed to be determined on the basis of the ordinary consistency conditions of von Neumann and Morgenstern. Thus, when the optimal c_1 is chosen, expected utility will be

---

Reprinted by permission of the publisher and author from *American Economic Review,* March 1969, p. 172–74.

43

$$U(F) = \max_{c_1} \int u(c_1, y - c_1) dF(y).$$

This expression defines indirectly the utility (or preference index) U associated with the probability distribution $F(y)$ and thus establishes a preference ordering over all such probability distributions. That is,

$$\max_{c_1} \int u(c_1, y - c_1) dF_1(y) \geqslant \max_{c_1} \int u(c_1, y - c_1) dF_2(y)$$

if an only if $F_1(y)$ is preferred or indifferent to $F_2(y)$.

The question now is: can the preference ordering $U(F)$ be represented by means of a utility function $v(y)$ for wealth? That is, is it possible to write

$$\max_{c_1} \int u(c_1, y - c_1) dF(y) = \int v(y) dF(y)?$$

Clearly, if choices among distributions $F(y)$ satisfy the von Neumann-Morgenstern conditions, it always would. However, as will be demonstrated, the answer is that such a representation does not generally exist. This result must mean that the von Neumann-Morgenstern conditions are violated, even though the individual acts in a perfectly rational and consistent manner.[1]

To see what is involved, consider an example with the utility function

$$u(c_1, c_2) = 72 - (8 - c_1)^2 - (8 - c_2)^2 \ (c_1 \leqslant 8, c_2 \leqslant 8).$$

Substituting $c_2 = y - c_1$, this becomes

$$u(c_1, y - c_1) = 72 - (8 - c_1)^2 - (8 + c_1)^2 + 2(8 + c_1)y - y^2$$

so that expected utility is

$$\int u(c_1, y - c_1) dF(y) = 72 - (8 - c_1)^2 - (8 + c_1)^2 + 2(8 + c_1)E - E^2 - S^2,$$

where E and S are the expectation and standard deviation of y, respectively. The optimal value of c_1 is here given by $c_1 = E/2$, which, upon substitution, gives

$$U(F) = \max \int u(c_1, y - c_1) dF(y) = 72 - \tfrac{1}{2}(16 - E)^2 - S^2.$$

---

1. The concept of the indirect (derived, tangential utility functional was pioneered by Roy [6]. It has been applied to sequential decision problems under uncertainty by, among others, Radner [5] and Mossin [4], as well as in [2]. However, in none of these papers is the representation problem explicit. A general discussion of representation of preferences over distributions is forthcoming in a book by Karl Vind, University of Copenhagen.

Thus, preferences among probability distributions are specified in terms of their means and standard deviations according to the formula above. This could be used to plot indifference curves for such prospects in the E,S-plane; these would be ellipses with center at $(16,0)$ and eccentricity $1/2$. Clearly, for an arbitrary $F(y)$, no function $v(y)$ such that $\int v(y)dF(y) = 72 - \frac{1}{2}(16 - E)^2 - S^2$ exists. The only utility function giving expected utility in terms of E and S only (for arbitrary distributions) is the quadratic. In that case, however, the indifference curves are concentric circles with center on the E-axis (see Borch [1]).

The explanation of the result in the preceding paragraph is not far to seek. Consider a specific distribution $F_1(y)$ such that $y = 6$ or $y = 10$ with equal probability. This has mean $E_1 = 8$ and standard deviation $S_1 = 2$. Under this prospect maximum expected utility would be $U(F_1) = 36$. This probability distribution carries the same expected utility as the *certain* outcome $y = 16 - 6\sqrt{2} = 7.51$, or, to put it differently, the individual is indifferent between $F_1(y)$ and the degenerate distribution of $F_2(y)$ which gives $y = 7.51$ with certainty.

Since $F_1(y)$ and $F_2(y)$ are ranked indifferently the individual may consider letting the choice be decided by help of a coin toss. This device may seem simple enough, but in a temporal context it must be used with care: it makes a great deal of difference whether the coin is tossed now or a year from now. If the coin is tossed *now* everything is fine: he will know which of the two distributions will apply; in either case he will, by choosing the appropriate c_1, obtain a utility level of 36, hence he should not mind letting chance decide which one will apply.

If the coin is to be tossed *after* c_1 has been chosen, however, he faces the temporal prospect $F(y) = \frac{1}{2}F_1(y) + \frac{1}{2}F_2(y)$ which has as outcomes

$\qquad$ 6 with probability $\frac{1}{4}$

$\qquad$ $16 - 6\sqrt{2}$ with probability $\frac{1}{2}$

$\qquad$ 10 with probability $\frac{1}{4}$

For this prospect, $E = 12 - 3\sqrt{2}$ and $S^2 = 36 - 24\sqrt{2}$ so that maximum expected utility is $U(F) = 19 + 12\sqrt{2} \approx 35.97$. Thus, the probability distribution F ranks below F_1 and F_2, i.e., $U(\frac{1}{2}F_1 + \frac{1}{2}F_2) < U(F_1)$ even though $U(F_1) = U(F_2)$. This represents an obvious violation of the independence condition (or "compounding of probabilities" condition) for an expected utility representation of $U(F)$. Such a representation requires that $U(\alpha F_1 + (1 - \alpha)F_2) = \alpha U(F_1) + (1 - \alpha) U(F_2)$ for any two distributions.

It is not difficult to see why this condition is not satisfied. In determining his optimal c_1 under the mixed prospect F the individual will take into account the need for hedging against the uncertain outcome of the coin toss. But a decision made on this basis is quite obviously optimal against *neither* of the original distributions F_1 and F_2. Relative to F_1 he will, in retrospect, have consumed too little; relative to F_2 too much.

The situation is illustrated in somewhat generalized form in Figure 1, where $g_i(c_1)$ is written for $\int u(c_1, y - c_1)dF_i(y)$. $g_1(c_1)$ and $g_2(c_1)$ attain the same maximum value; this value is higher than the maximum attained by the function $g = \frac{1}{2}g_1 + \frac{1}{2}g_2$.

The general idea is that having to wait until the end of the period for the outcome to become known is bad enough in itself; not even knowing the exact distribution according to which the outcome will be determined is still worse. The following analogy should be familiar: I may be indifferent between teaching Course A and Course B next fall, but, in view of the preparations that must be made in the meantime, I would certainly not want the decision to be postponed until classes begin.

The example given above demonstrates the importance of the temporal aspect in risk-taking situations. As emphasized by Markowitz, the representation of preferences among probability distributions by means of a utility function is meant to apply to cases of *timeless* prospects, i.e., to situations where the outcome is determined at once, without any intervening decisions involving commitment of the outcome. For such prospects, the derivation of an indirect utility function for wealth from the solution of the allocation problem causes no difficulty (see [2]). For temporal prospects, however, representation of preferences in terms of a utility function for wealth may be inappropriate—and for reasons that are obvious once you think of it. On further reflection it is also apparent that in the real world *temporal* prospects, not timeless ones, are the rule rather than the exception. Even in a controlled experimental setting they seem difficult to avoid; in a gamble with payoffs depending upon the outcome of, say the next presidential election, subjects may easily be led to take the possibility of intermediate decisions into account. This should serve as a reminder of the constant need for caution in applying a utility function for wealth to the analysis of risk-taking behavior.

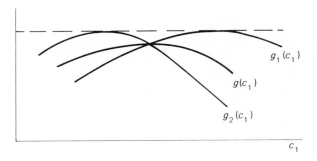

Figure 1

References

1. K. Borch, "A Note on Uncertainty and Indifference Curves," *Rev. Econ. Stud.* (forthcoming, 1969).
2. J. Dreze and F. Modigliani, "Epargne et consommation en avenir aléatoire," *Cahiers du Seminaire d'Econometrie,* 1966, *9,* 7-33.
3. H. Markowitz, *Portfolio Selection.* New York 1959.
4. J. Mossin, "Optimal Multiperiod Portfolio Policies," *Jour. Bus.,* April 1968, *41,* 215-29.
5. R. Radner, "Equilibre des marchés à terme et au comptant en cas d'incertitude," *Cahiers du Seminaire d'Econometrie,* 1966, 9, 35-52.
6. R. Roy, "La distribution du révénu entre les divers biens," *Econometrica,* July 1947, *15,* 205-25.

5

Risk Aversion in the Small and in the Large[1]

John W. Pratt
Harvard University

1. Summary and Introduction

Let $u(x)$ be a utility function for money. The function $r(x) = -u''(x)/u'(x)$ will be interpreted in various ways as a measure of local risk aversion (risk aversion in the small); neither $u''(x)$ nor the curvature of the graph of u is an appropriate measure. No simple measure of risk aversion in the large will be introduced. Global risks will, however, be considered, and it will be shown that one decision maker has greater local risk aversion $r(x)$ than another at all x if and only if he is globally more risk-averse in the sense that, for every risk, his cash equivalent (the amount for which he would exchange the risk) is smaller than for the other decision maker. Equivalently, his risk premium (expected monetary value minus cash equivalent) is always larger, and he would be willing to pay more for insurance in any situation. From this it will be shown that a decision maker's local risk aversion $r(x)$ is a decreasing function of x if and only if, for every risk, his cash equivalent is larger the larger his assets, and his risk premium and what he would be willing to pay for insurance are smaller. This condition, which many decision makers would subscribe to, involves the third derivative of u, as $r' \leqslant 0$ is equivalent to $u'''u' \geqslant u''^2$. It is not satisfied by quadratic utilities in any region. All this means that some natural ways of thinking casually about utility functions may be misleading. Except for one family, convenient utility functions for which $r(x)$ is decreasing are not so very easy to find. Help in this regard is given by some theorems showing that certain combinations of utility functions, in particular linear combinations with positive weights, have decreasing $r(x)$ if all the functions in the combination have decreasing $r(x)$.

The related function $r^*(x) = xr(x)$ will be interpreted as a local measure of aversion to risks measured as a proportion of assets, and monotonicity of $r^*(x)$ will be proved to be equivalent to monotonicity of every risk's cash equivalent measured as a proportion of assets, and similarly for the risk premium and insurance.

Reprinted by permission of the publisher and author from *Econometrica* Vol. 32, 1–2 (April 1964), pp. 122–136.

1. This research was supported by the National Science Foundation (grant NSF–G24035). Reproduction in whole or in part is permitted for any purpose of the United States Government.

These results have both descriptive and normative implications. Utility functions for which $r(x)$ is decreasing are logical candidates to use when trying to describe the behavior of people who, one feels, might generally pay less for insurance against a given risk the greater their assets. And consideration of the yield and riskiness per investment dollar of investors' portfolios may suggest, at least in some contexts, description by utility functions for which $r^*(x)$ is first decreasing and then increasing.

Normatively, it seems likely that many decision makers would feel they ought to pay less for insurance against a given risk the greater their assets. Such a decision maker will want to choose a utility function for which $r(x)$ is decreasing, adding this condition to the others he must already consider (consistency and probably concavity) in forging a satisfactory utility from more or less malleable preliminary preferences. He may wish to add a further condition on $r^*(x)$.

We do not assume or assert that utility may not change with time. Strictly speaking, we are concerned with utility at a specified time (when a decision must be made) for money at a (possibly later) specified time. Of course, our results pertain also to behavior at different times if utility does not change with time. For instance, a decision maker whose utility for total assets is unchanging and whose assets are increasing would be willing to pay less and less for insurance against a given risk as time progresses if his $r(x)$ is a decreasing function of x. Notice that his actual expenditure for insurance might nevertheless increase if his risks are increasing along with his assets.

The risk premium, cash equivalent, and insurance premium are defined and related to one another in Section 2. The local risk aversion function $r(x)$ is introduced and interpreted in Sections 3 and 4. In Section 5, inequalities concerning global risks are obtained from inequalities between local risk aversion functions. Section 6 deals with constant risk aversion, and Section 7 demonstrates the equivalence of local and global definitions of decreasing (and increasing) risk aversion. Section 8 shows that certain operations preserve the property of decreasing risk aversion. Some examples are given in Section 9. Aversion to proportional risk is discussed in Sections 10 to 12. Section 13 concerns some related work of Kenneth J. Arrow.[2]

Throughout this paper, the utility $u(x)$ is regarded as a function of total assets rather than of changes which may result from a certain decision, so that $x = 0$ is equivalent to ruin, or perhaps to loss of all readily disposable assets. (This is essential only in connection with proportional risk aversion.) The symbol $\sim$ indicates that two functions are equivalent as utilities, that is, $u_1(x) \sim u_2(x)$

---

2. The importance of the function $r(x)$ was discovered independently by Kenneth J. Arrow and by Robert Schlaifer, in different contexts. The work presented here was, unfortunately, essentially completed before I learned of Arrow's related work. It is, however, a pleasure to acknowledge Schlaifer's stimulation and participation throughout, as well as that of John Bishop at certain points.

means there exist constants a and b (with $b > 0$) such that $u_1(x) = a + bu_2(x)$ for all x. The utility functions discussed may, but need not, be bounded. It is assumed, however, that they are sufficiently regular to justify the proofs; generally it is enough that they be twice continuously differentiable with positive first derivative, which is already required for $r(x)$ to be defined and continuous. A variable with a tilde over it, such as $\tilde{z}$, is a random variable. The risks $\tilde{z}$ considered may, but need not, have "objective" probability distributions. In formal statements, $\tilde{z}$ refers only to risks which are not degenerate, that is, not constant with probability one, and interval refers only to an interval with more than one point. Also, increasing and decreasing mean nondecreasing and nonincreasing respectively; if we mean strictly increasing or decreasing we will say so.

2. The Risk Premium

Consider a decision maker with assets x and utility function u. We shall be interested in the *risk premium* π such that he would be indifferent between receiving a risk $\tilde{z}$ and receiving the non-random amount $E(\tilde{z}) - \pi$, that is, π less than the actuarial value $E(\tilde{z})$. If u is concave, then $\pi \geqslant 0$, but we don't require this. The risk premium depends on x and on the distribution of $\tilde{z}$, and will be denoted $\pi(x,\tilde{z})$. (It is not, as this notation might suggest, a function $\pi(x,z)$ evaluated at a randomly selected value of z, which would be random.) By the properties of utility,

$$u(x + E(\tilde{z}) - \pi(x,\tilde{z}) = E\{u(x + \tilde{z})\}. \tag{1}$$

We shall consider only situations where $E\ u(x + \tilde{z})$ exists and is finite. Then $\pi(x,\tilde{z})$ exists and is uniquely defined by (1), since $u(x + E(\tilde{z}) - \pi)$ is a strictly decreasing, continuous function of π ranging over all possible values of u. It follows immediately from (1) that, for any constant μ,

$$\pi(x,\tilde{z}) = \pi(x + \mu, \tilde{z} - \mu). \tag{2}$$

By choosing $\mu = E(\tilde{z})$ (assuming it exists and is finite), we may thus reduce consideration to a risk $\tilde{z} - \mu$ which is actuarially neutral, that is, $E(\tilde{z} - \mu) = 0$.

Since the decision maker is indifferent between receiving the risk $\tilde{z}$ and receiving for sure the amount $\pi_a(x,\tilde{z}) = E(\tilde{z}) - \pi(x,\tilde{z})$, this amount is sometimes called the cash equivalent or value of $\tilde{z}$. It is also the asking price for $\tilde{z}$, the smallest amount for which the decision maker would willingly sell $\tilde{z}$ if he had it. It is given by

$$u(x + \pi_a(x,\tilde{z})) = E\{u(x + \tilde{z})\}. \tag{3a}$$

It is to be distinguished from the bid price $\pi_b(x,\widetilde{z})$, the largest amount the decision maker would willingly pay to obtain $\widetilde{z}$, which is given by

$$u(x) = E\{u(x + \widetilde{z} - \pi_b(x,\widetilde{z}))\}. \tag{3b}$$

For an unfavorable risk $\widetilde{z}$, it is natural to consider the insurance premium $\pi_I(x,\widetilde{z})$ such that the decision maker is indifferent between facing the risk $\widetilde{z}$ and paying the non-random amount $\pi_I(x,\widetilde{z})$. Since paying π_I is equivalent to receiving $-\pi_I$, we have

$$\pi_I(x,\widetilde{z}) = -\pi_a(x,\widetilde{z}) = \pi(x,\widetilde{z}) - E(\widetilde{z}). \tag{3c}$$

If $\widetilde{z}$ is actuarially neutral, the risk premium and insurance premium coincide.

The results of this paper will be stated in terms of the risk premium π, but could equally easily and meaningfully be stated in terms of the cash equivalent or insurance premium.

3. Local Risk Aversion

To measure a decision maker's local aversion to risk, it is natural to consider his risk premium for a small, actuarially neutral risk $\widetilde{z}$. We therefore consider $\pi(x,\widetilde{z})$ for a risk $\widetilde{z}$ with $E(\widetilde{z}) = 0$ and small variance σ_z^2; that is, we consider the behavior of $\pi(x,\widetilde{z})$ as $\sigma_z^2 \to 0$. We assume the third absolute central moment of $\widetilde{z}$ is of smaller order than σ_z^2. (Ordinarily it is of order σ_z^3.) Expanding u around x on both sides of (1), we obtain under suitable regularity conditions[3]

$$u(x - \pi) = u(x) - \pi u'(x) + O(\pi^2), \tag{4a}$$

$$E\{u(x + \widetilde{z})\} = E\{u(x) + \widetilde{z}u'(x) + \tfrac{1}{2}\widetilde{z}^2 u''(x) + O(\widetilde{z}^3)\}$$

$$= u(x) + \tfrac{1}{2}\sigma_z^2 u''(x) + O(\sigma_z^2). \tag{4b}$$

Setting these expressions equal, as required by (1), then gives

$$\pi(x,\widetilde{z}) = \tfrac{1}{2}\sigma_z^2 r(x) + O(\sigma_z^2), \tag{5}$$

where

$$r(x) = -\frac{u''(x)}{u'(x)} = -\frac{x}{dx}\log u'(x). \tag{6}$$

---

3. In expansions, $O(\ )$ means "terms of order at most" and $o(\ )$ means "terms of smaller order than."

Thus the decision maker's risk premium for a small, actuarially neutral risk $\tilde{z}$ is approximately $r(x)$ times half the variance of $\tilde{z}$; that is, $r(x)$ is twice the risk premium per unit of variance for infinitesimal risks. A sufficient regularity condition for (5) is that u have a third derivative which is continuous and bounded over the range of all $\tilde{z}$ under discussion. The theorems to follow will not actually depend on (5), however.

If $\tilde{z}$ is not actuarially neutral, we have by (2), with $\mu = E(\tilde{z})$, and (5):

$$\pi(x,\tilde{z}) = \tfrac{1}{2}\sigma_z^2 r(x + E(\tilde{z})) + O(\sigma_z^2). \tag{7}$$

Thus the risk premium for a risk $\tilde{z}$ with arbitrary mean $E(\tilde{z})$ but small variance is approximately $r(x + E(\tilde{z}))$ times half the variance of $\tilde{z}$. It follows also that the risk premium will just equal and hence offset the actuarial value $E(\tilde{z})$ of a small risk $(\tilde{z})$, that is, the decision maker will be indifferent between having $\tilde{z}$ and not having it, when the actuarial value is approximately $r(x)$ times half the variance of $\tilde{z}$. Thus $r(x)$ may also be interpreted as twice the actuarial value the decision maker requires per unit of variance for infinitesimal risks.

Notice that it is the variance, not the standard deviation, that enters these formulas. To first order any (differentiable) utility is linear in small gambles. In this sense, these are second order formulas.

Still another interpretation of $r(x)$ arises in the special case $\tilde{z} = \pm h$, that is, where the risk is to gain or lose a fixed amount $h > 0$. Such a risk is actuarially neutral if $+h$ and $-h$ are equally probable, so $P(\tilde{z} = h) - P(\tilde{z} = -h)$ measures the *probability premium* of $\tilde{z}$. Let $p(x,h)$ be the probability premium such that the decision maker is indifferent between the status quo and a risk $\tilde{z} = \pm h$ with

$$P(\tilde{z} = h) - P(\tilde{z} = -h) = p(x,h). \tag{8}$$

Then $P(\tilde{z} = h) = \tfrac{1}{2}[1 + p(x,h)]$, $P(\tilde{z} = -h) = \tfrac{1}{2}[1 - p(x,h)]$, and $p(x,h)$ is defined by

$$u(x) = E\{u(x + \tilde{z})\} = \tfrac{1}{2}[1 + p(x,h)]u(x + h) + \tfrac{1}{2}[1 - p(x,h)]u(x - h). \tag{9}$$

When u is expanded around x as before, (9) becomes

$$u(x) = u(x) + hp(x,h)\, u'(x) + \tfrac{1}{2}h^2 u''(x) + O(h^3). \tag{10}$$

Solving for $p(x,h)$, we find

$$p(x,h) = \tfrac{1}{2}hr(x) + O(h^2). \tag{11}$$

Thus for small h the decision maker is indifferent between the status quo and a

risk of $\pm h$ with a probability premium of $r(x)$ times $\frac{1}{2}h$; that is, $r(x)$ is twice
the probability premium he requires per unit risked for small risks.

In these ways we may interpret $r(x)$ as a measure of the *local risk aversion*
or *local propensity to insure* at the point x under the utility function u; $-r(x)$
would measure locally liking for risk or propensity to gamble. Notice that we
have not introduced any measure of risk aversion in the large. Aversion to
ordinary (as opposed to infinitesimal) risks might be considered measured by
$\pi(x,\tilde{z})$, but π is a much more complicated function than r. Despite the absence
of any simple measure of risk aversion in the large, we shall see that comparisons
of aversion to risk can be made simply in the large as well as in the small.

By (6), integrating $-r(x)$ gives $\log u'(x) + c$; exponentiating and integrating
again then gives $e^c u(x) + d$. The constants of integration are immaterial because
$e^c u(x) + d \sim u(x)$. (Note $e^c > 0$.) Thus we may write

$$u \sim \int e^{-\int r}, \tag{12}$$

and we observe that the local risk aversion function r associated with any utility
function u contains all essential information about u while eliminating everything
arbitrary about u. However, decisions about ordinary (as opposed to "small")
risks are determined by r only through u as given by (12), so it is not convenient
entirely to eliminate u from consideration in favor of r.

4. Concavity

The aversion to risk implied by a utility function u seems to be a form of
concavity, and one might set out to measure concavity as representing aversion
to risk. It is clear from the foregoing that for this purpose $r(x) = -u''(x)/u'(x)$
can be considered a measure of the concavity of u at the point x. A case might
perhaps be made for using instead some one-to-one function of $r(x)$, but it
should be noted that $u''(x)$ or $-u''(x)$ is not in itself a meaningful measure of
concavity in utility theory, nor is the curvature (reciprocal of the signed radius
of the tangent circle) $u''(x)(1 + [u'(x)]^2)^{-3/2}$. Multiplying u by a positive
constant, for example, does not alter behavior but does alter u'' and the curvature.

A more striking and instructive example is provided by the function
$u(x) = -e^{-x}$. As x increases, this function approaches the asymptote $u = 0$ and
looks graphically less and less concave and more and more like a horizontal
straight line, in accordance with the fact that $u'(x) = e^{-x}$ and $u''(x) = -e^{-x}$ both
approach 0. As a utility function, however, it does not change at all with the
level of assets x, that is, the behavior implied by $u(x)$ is the same for all x,
since $u(k + x) = -e^{-k-x} \sim u(x)$. In particular, the risk premium $\pi(x,\tilde{z})$ for any risk
$\tilde{z}$ and the probability premium $p(x,h)$ for any h remain absolutely constant as

x varies. Thus, regardless of the appearance of its graph, $u(x) = -e^{-x}$ is just as far from implying linear behavior at $x = \infty$ as at $x = 0$ or $x = -\infty$. All this is duly reflected in $r(x)$, which is constant: $r(x) = -u''(x)/u'(x) = 1$ for all x.

One feature of $u''(x)$ does have a meaning, namely its sign, which equals that of $-r(x)$. A negative (positive) sign at x implies unwillingness (willingness) to accept small, actuarially neutral risks with assets x. Furthermore, a negative (positive) sign for all x implies strict concavity (convexity) and hence unwilling-ness (willingness) to accept any actuarially neutral risk with any assets. The absolute magnitude of $u''(x)$ does not in itself have any meaning in utility theory, however.

5. Comparative Risk Aversion

Let u_1 and u_2 be utility functions with local risk aversion functions r_1 and r_2, respectively. If, at a point x, $r_1(x) > r_2(x)$, then u_1 is locally more risk-averse than u_2 at the point x; that is, the corresponding risk premiums satisfy $\pi(x,\tilde{z}) > \pi_2(x,\tilde{z})$ for sufficiently small risks $\tilde{z}$, and the corresponding probabil-ity premiums satisfy $p_1(x,h) > p_2(x,h)$ for sufficiently small $h > 0$. The main point of the theorem we are about to prove is that the corresponding global properties also hold. For instance, if $r_1(x) > r_2(x)$ for all x, that is, u_1 has greater local risk aversion than u_2 everywhere, then $\pi_1(x,\tilde{z}) > \pi_2(x,\tilde{z})$ for every risk $\tilde{z}$, so that u_1 is also globally more risk-averse in a natural sense.

It is to be understood in this section that the probability distribution of $\tilde{z}$, which determines $\pi_1(x,\tilde{z})$ and $\pi_2(x,\tilde{z})$, is the same in each. We are comparing the risk premiums for the same probability distribution of risk but for two different utilities. This does not mean that when Theorem 1 is applied to two decision makers, they must have the same personal probability distributions, but only that the notation is imprecise. The theorem could be stated in terms of $\pi_1(x,\tilde{z}_1)$ and $\pi_2(x,\tilde{z}_2)$ where the distribution assigned to $\tilde{z}_1$ by the first decision maker is the same as that assigned to $\tilde{z}_2$ by the second decision maker. This would be less misleading, but also less convenient and less suggestive, especially for later use. More precise notation would be, for instance, $\pi_1(x,F)$ and $\pi_2(x,F)$, where F is a cumulative distribution function.

Theorem 1: Let $r_i(x)$, $\pi_i(x,\tilde{z})$, and $p_i(x)$ be the local risk aversion, risk premium and probability premium corresponding to the utility function u_i, $i = 1$, 2. Then the following conditions are equivalent, in either the strong form (indi-cated in brackets), or the weak form (with the bracketed material omitted).

(a) *$r_1(x) \geqslant r_2(x)$ for all x [and $>$ for at least one x in every interval].*

(b) *$\pi_1(x,\tilde{z}) \geqslant [>] \pi_2(x,\tilde{z})$ for all x and $\tilde{z}$.*

(c) $p_1(x,h) \geqslant [>] \, p_2(x,h)$ for all x and all $h > 0$.

(d) $u_1(u_2^{-1}(t))$ is a [strictly] concave function of t.

(e) $\dfrac{u_1(y) - u_1(x)}{u_2(w) - u_1(v)} \leqslant [<] \dfrac{u_2(y) - u_2(x)}{u_2(w) - u_2(v)}$ for all v, w, x, y with $v < w \leqslant x < y$.

The same equivalences hold if attention is restricted throughout to an interval, that is, if the requirement is added that x, $x + \widetilde{z}$, $x + h$, $x - h$, $u_2^{-1}(t)$, v, w, *and* y, *all lie in a specified interval.*

Proof: We shall prove things in order indicating somewhat how one might discover that (a) implies (b) and (c).

To show that (b) follows from (d), solve (1) to obtain

$$\pi_i(x, \widetilde{z}) = x + E(\widetilde{z}) - u_i^{-1}(E\{u_i(x + \widetilde{z})\}). \tag{13}$$

Then

$$\pi_1(x, \widetilde{z}) - \pi_2(x, \widetilde{z}) = u_2^{-1}(E\{u_2(x + \widetilde{z})\}) - u_1^{-1}(E\{u_1(x + \widetilde{z})\})$$

$$= u_2^{-1}(E\{\widetilde{t}\}) - u_1^{-1}(E\{u_1(u_2^{-1}(\widetilde{t}))\}), \tag{14}$$

where $\widetilde{t} = u_2(x + \widetilde{z})$. If $u_1(u_2^{-1}(t))$ is [strictly] concave, then (by Jensen's inequality)

$$E\{u_1(u_2^{-1}(\widetilde{t}))\} \leqslant [<] \, u_1(u_2^{-1}(E\{\widetilde{t}\})). \tag{15}$$

Substituting (15) in (14), we obtain (b).

To show that (a) implies (d), note that

$$\frac{d}{dt} u_1(u_2^{-1}(t)) = \frac{u_1'(u_2^{-1}(t))}{u_2'(u_2^{-1}(t))}, \tag{16}$$

which is [strictly] decreasing if (and only if) $\log u_1'(x)/u_2'(x)$ is. The latter follows from (a) and

$$\frac{d}{dx} \log \frac{u_1'(x)}{u_2'(x)} = r_2(x) - r_1(x). \tag{17}$$

That (c) is implied by (e) follows immediately upon writing (9) in the form

$$\frac{1 - p_i(x,h)}{1 + p_i(x,h)} = \frac{u_i(x + h) - u_i(x)}{u_i(x) - u_i(x - h)}. \tag{18}$$

To show that (a) implies (e), integrate (a) from w to x, obtaining

$$-\log\frac{u_1'(x)}{u_1'(w)} \geq [>] - \log\frac{u_2'(x)}{u_2'(w)} \text{ for } w < x, \tag{19}$$

which is equivalent to

$$\frac{u_1'(x)}{u_1'(w)} \leq [<] \frac{u_2'(x)}{u_2'(w)} \text{ for } w < x. \tag{20}$$

This implies

$$\frac{u_1(y) - u_1(x)}{u_1'(w)} \leq [<] \frac{u_2(y) - u_2(x)}{u_2'(w)} \text{ for } w \leq x < y, \tag{21}$$

as may be seen by applying the Mean Value Theorem of differential calculus to the difference of the two sides of (21) regarded as a function of y. Condition (e) follows from (21) upon application of the Mean Value Theorem to the difference of the reciprocals of the two sides of (e) regarded as a function of w.

We have now proved that (a) implies (d) implies (b), and (a) implies (e) implies (c). The equivalence of (a) - (e) will follow if we can prove that (b) implies (a), and (c) implies (a), or equivalently that not (a) implies not (b) and not (c). But this follows from what has already been proved, for if the weak [strong] form of (a) does not hold, then the strong [weak] form of (a) holds on some interval with u_1 and u_2 interchanged. Then the strong [weak] forms of (b) and (c) also hold on this interval with u_1 and u_2 interchanged, so the weak [strong] forms of (b) and (c) do not hold. This completes the proof.

We observe that (e) is equivalent to (20), (21), and

$$\frac{u_1(w) - u_1(v)}{u_1'(x)} \geq [>] \frac{u_2(w) - u_2(v)}{u_2'(x)} \text{ for } v < w \leq x. \tag{22}$$

6. Constant Risk Aversion

If the local risk aversion function is constant, say $r(x) = c$, then by (12):

$$u(x) \sim x \qquad \text{if} \quad r(x) = 0; \tag{23}$$

$$u(x) \sim -e^{-cx} \qquad \text{if} \quad r(x) = c > 0; \tag{24}$$

$$u(x) \sim e^{-cx} \qquad \text{if} \quad r(x) = c < 0. \tag{25}$$

These utilities are, respectively, linear, strictly concave, and strictly convex.

If the risk aversion is constant locally, then it is also constant globally, that is, a change in assets makes no change in preference among risks. In fact, for any k, $u(k + x) \sim u(x)$ in each of the cases above, as is easily verified. Therefore it makes sense to speak of "constant risk aversion" without the qualification "local" or "global."

Similar remarks apply to constant risk aversion on an interval, except that global consideration must be restricted to assets x and risks $\tilde{z}$ such that $x + \tilde{z}$ is certain to stay within the interval.

7. Increasing and Decreasing Risk Aversion

Consider a decision maker who (i) attaches a positive risk premium to any risk, but (ii) attaches a smaller risk premium to any given risk the greater his assets x. Formally this means

(i) $\pi(x,\tilde{z}) > 0$ for all x and $\tilde{z}$;
(ii) $\pi(x,\tilde{z})$ is a strictly decreasing function of x for all $\tilde{z}$.

Restricting $\tilde{z}$ to be actuarially neutral would not affect (i) or (ii), by (2) with $\mu = E(\tilde{z})$.

We shall call a utility function (or a decision maker possessing it) *risk-averse* if the weak form of (i) holds, that is, if $\pi(x,\tilde{z}) \geqslant 0$ for all x and $\tilde{z}$; it is well known that this is equivalent to concavity of u, and hence to $u'' \leqslant 0$ and to $r \geqslant 0$. A utility function is *strictly risk-averse* if (i) holds as stated; this is equivalent to strict concavity of u and hence to the existence in every interval of at least one point where $u'' < 0, r > 0$.

We turn now to (ii). Notice that it amounts to a definition of strictly decreasing risk aversion in a global (as opposed to local) sense. One would hope that decreasing global risk aversion would be equivalent to decreasing local risk aversion $r(x)$. The following theorem asserts that this is indeed so. Therefore it makes sense to speak of "decreasing risk aversion" without the qualification "local" or "global." What is nontrivial is that $r(x)$ decreasing implies $\pi(x,\tilde{z})$ decreasing, inasmuch as $r(x)$ pertains directly only to infinitesimal gambles. Similar considerations apply to the probability premium $p(x,h)$.

Theorem 2: *The following conditions are equivalent.*

(a') *The local risk aversion function* $r(x)$ *is* [*strictly*] *decreasing.*

(b') *The risk premium* $\pi(x,\tilde{z})$ *is a* [*strictly*] *decreasing function of x for all* $\tilde{z}$.

(c') *The probability premium* $p(x,h)$ *is a* [*strictly*] *decreasing function of x for all* $h > 0$.

The same equivalences hold if "increasing" is substituted for "decreasing" throughout and/or attention is restricted throughout to an interval, that is, the requirement is added that x, x + $\tilde{z}$, x + h, and x - h all lie in a specified interval.

Proof: This theorem follows upon application of Theorem 1 to $u_1(x) = u(x)$ and $u_2(x) = u(x + k)$ for arbitrary x and k.

It is easily verified that (a') and hence also (b') and (c') are equivalent to

(d') $u'(u^{-1}(t))$ is a [strictly] convex function of t.

This corresponds to (d) of Theorem 1. Corresponding to (e) of Theorem 1 and (20)–(22) is

(e') $u'(x)u'''(x) \geqslant (u''(x))^2$ [and $>$ for at least one x in every interval].

The equivalence of this to (a')–(c') follows from the fact that the sign of $r'(x)$ is the same as that of $(u''(x))^2 - u'(x)u'''(x)$. Theorem 2 can be and originally was proved by the way of (d') and (e'), essentially as Theorem 1 is proved in the present paper.

8. Operations which Preserve Decreasing Risk Aversion

We have just seen that a utility function evinces decreasing risk aversion in a global sense if an only if its local risk aversion function $r(x)$ is decreasing. Such a utility function seems of interest mainly if it is also risk-averse (concave, $r \geqslant 0$). Accordingly, we shall now formally define a utility function to be [*strictly*] *decreasingly risk-averse* if its local risk aversion function r is [strictly] decreasing and nonnegative. Then by Theorem 2, conditions (i) and (ii) of Section 7 are equivalent to the utility's being strictly decreasingly risk-averse.

In this section we shall show that certain operations yield decreasingly risk-averse utility functions if applied to such functions. This facilitates proving that functions are decreasingly risk-averse and finding functions which have this property and also have reasonably simple formulas. In the proofs, $r(x)$, $r_1(x)$, etc., are the local risk aversion functions belonging to $u(x)$, $u_1(x)$, etc.

Theorem 3: Suppose a > 0: $u_1(x) = u(ax + b)$ *is* [*strictly*] *decreasingly risk-averse for* $x_0 \leqslant x \leqslant x_1$ *if and only if* $u(x)$ *is* [*strictly*] *decreasingly risk-averse for* $ax_0 + b \leqslant x \leqslant ax_1 + b$.

Proof: This follows directly from the easily verified formula:

$$r_1(x) = ar(ax + b).$$ (26)

Theorem 4: If $u_1(x)$ is decreasingly risk-averse for $x_0 \leqslant x \leqslant x_1$, and $u_2(x)$ is decreasingly risk-averse for $u_1(x_0) \leqslant x \leqslant u_1(x_1)$, then $u(x) = u_2(u_1(x))$ is decreasingly risk-averse for $x_0 \leqslant x \leqslant x_1$, and strictly so unless one of u_1 and u_2 is linear from some x on and the other has constant risk aversion in some interval.

Proof: We have $\log u'(x) = \log u_2'(u_1(x)) + \log u_1'(x)$, and therefore

$$r(x) = r_2(u_1(x))u_1'(x) + r_1(x).$$ (27)

The functions $r_2(u_1(x))$, $u_1'(x)$, and $r_1(x)$ are $\geqslant 0$ and decreasing, and therefore so is $r(x)$. Furthermore, $u_1'(x)$ is strictly decreasing as long as $r_1(x) > 0$, so $r(x)$ is strictly decreasing as long as $r_1(x)$ and $r_2(u_1(x))$ are both > 0. If one of them is 0 for some x, then it is 0 for all larger x, but if the other is strictly decreasing, then so is r.

Theorem 5: If $u_1, \ldots, u_n$ are decreasingly risk-averse on an interval $[x_0, x_1]$, and $c_1, \ldots, c_n$ are positive constants, then $u = \Sigma_1^n c_i u_i$ is decreasingly risk-averse on $[x_0, x_1]$, and strictly so except on subintervals (if any) where all u_i have equal and constant risk aversion.

Proof: The general statement follows from the case $u = u_1 + u_2$. For this case

$$r = -\frac{u_1'' + u_2''}{u_1' + u_2'} = \frac{u_1'}{u_1' + u_2'}r_1 + \frac{u_2'}{u_1' + u_2'}r_2;$$ (28)

$$r' = \frac{u_1'}{u_1' + u_2'}r_1' + \frac{u_2'}{u_1' + u_2'}r_2' + \frac{u_1''u_2' - u_1'u_2''}{(u_1' + u_2')^2}(r_1 - r_2)$$

$$= \frac{u_1'r_1' + u_2'r_2'}{u_1' + u_2'} - \frac{u_1'u_2'}{(u_1' + u_2')^2}(r_1 - r_2)^2.$$ (29)

We have $u_1' > 0, u_2' > 0, r_1' \leqslant 0$, and $r_2' \leqslant 0$. Therefore $r' \leqslant 0$, and $r' < 0$ unless $r_1 = r_2$ and $r_1' = r_2' = 0$. The conclusion follows.

9. Examples

9.1. *Example* 1. The utility $u(x) = -(b - x)^c$ for $x \leqslant b$ and $c > 1$ is strictly increasing and strictly concave, but it also has strictly *increasing* risk aversion:

$r(x) = (c - 1)/(b - x)$. Notice that the most general concave quadratic utility $u(x) = \alpha + \beta x - \gamma x^2$, $\beta > 0$, $\gamma > 0$, is equivalent as a utility to $-(b - x)^c$ with $c = 2$ and $b = \frac{1}{2}\beta/\gamma$. Therefore a quadratic utility cannot be decreasingly risk-averse on any interval whatever. This severely limits the usefulness of quadratic utility, however nice it would be to have expected utility depend only on the mean and variance of the probability distribution. Arguing "in the small" is no help: decreasing risk aversion is a local property as well as a global one.

9.2. Example 2. If

$$u'(x) = (x^a + b)^{-c} \text{ with } a > 0, c > 0, \tag{30}$$

then $u(x)$ is strictly decreasingly risk-averse in the region

$$x > [\max\{0, -b, b(a - 1)\}]^{1/a}. \tag{31}$$

To prove this, note

$$r(x) = -\frac{d}{dx} \log u'(x) = \frac{ac}{x + bx^{1-a}}, \tag{32}$$

which is $\geqslant 0$ and strictly decreasing in the region where the denominator $x + bx^{1-a}$ is $\geqslant 0$ and strictly increasing, which is the region (30). (The condition $x \geqslant 0$ is included to insure that x^a is defined; for $a \geqslant 1$ it follows from the other conditions.)

By Theorem 3, one can obtain a utility function that is strictly decreasingly risk-averse for $x > 0$ by substituting $x + d$ for x above, where d is at least the right-hand side of (31). Multiplying x by a positive factor, as in Theorem 3, is equivalent to multiplying b by a positive factor.

Given below are all the strictly decreasingly risk-averse utility functions $u(x)$ on $x > 0$ which can be obtained by applying Theorem 3 to (30) with the indicated choices of the parameters a and c:

$a = 1, 0 < c < 1$: $\quad u(x) \sim (x + d)^q$ $\qquad$ with $d \geqslant 0, 0 < q < 1$; $\quad$ (33)

$a = 1, c = 1$: $\qquad u(x) \sim \log(x + d)$ $\qquad$ with $d \geqslant 0$; $\qquad$ (34)

$a = 1, c > 1$: $\qquad u(x) \sim -(x + d)^{-q}$ $\qquad$ with $d \geqslant 0, q > 0$; $\quad$ (35)

$a = 2, c = .5$: $\qquad u(x) \sim \log(x + d + [(x + d)^2 + b])$ with $d \geqslant |b|^{\frac{1}{2}}$; $\quad$ (36)

$a = 2, c = 1$: $\qquad u(x) \sim \arctan(\alpha x + \beta)$ or
$\qquad\qquad\qquad \log(1 - (\alpha x + \beta)^{-1})$ $\qquad$ with $\alpha > 0, \beta \geqslant 1$; $\quad$ (37)

$a = 2, c = 1.5$: $u(x) \sim [1 + (\alpha x + \beta)^{-2}]^{-\frac{1}{2}}$ or
$-[1 - (\alpha x + \beta)^{-2}]^{-\frac{1}{2}}$ with $\alpha > 0, \beta \geqslant 1$.   (38)

9.3 *Example* 3. Applying Theorems 4 and 5 to the utilities of Example 2 and Section 6 gives a very wide class of utilities which are strictly decreasingly risk-averse for $x > 0$, such as

$$u(x) \sim -c_1 e^{-cx} - c_2 e^{-dx} \quad \text{with } c_1 > 0, c_2 > 0, c > 0, d > 0. \quad (39)$$

$$u(x) \sim \log(d_1 + \log(x + d_2)) \text{ with } d_1 \geqslant 0, d_2 \geqslant 0, d_1 + \log d_2 \geqslant 0. \, (40)$$

10. Proportional Risk Aversion

So far we have been concerned with risks that remained fixed while assets varied. Let us now view everything as a proportion of assets. Specifically, let $\pi^*(x, \tilde{z})$ be the *proportional risk premium* corresponding to a proportional risk $\tilde{z}$; that is, a decision maker with assets x and utility function u would be indifferent between receiving a risk $x\tilde{z}$ and receiving the non-random amount $E(x\tilde{z}) - x\pi^*(x, \tilde{z})$. Then $x\pi^*(x, \tilde{z})$ equals the risk premium $\pi(x, x\tilde{z})$, so

$$\pi^*(x, \tilde{z}) = \frac{1}{x} \pi(x, x\tilde{z}). \tag{41}$$

For a small, actuarially neutral, proportional risk $\tilde{z}$ we have, by (5),

$$\pi^*(x, \tilde{z}) = \frac{1}{2}\sigma_z^2 r^*(x) + o(\sigma_z^2), \tag{42}$$

where

$$r^*(x) = xr(x). \tag{43}$$

If $\tilde{z}$ is not actuarially neutral, we have, by (7),

$$\pi^*(x, \tilde{z}) = \frac{1}{2}\sigma_z^2 r^*(x + xE(\tilde{z})) + o(\sigma_z^2). \tag{44}$$

We will call r^* the *local proportional risk aversion* at the point x under the utility function u. Its interpretation by (42) and (44) is like that of r by (5) and (7).

Similarly, we may define the *proportional probability premium* $p^*(x,h)$, corresponding to a risk of gaining or losing a proportional amount h, namely

$$p^*(x,h) = p(x,xh). \tag{45}$$

Then another interpretation of $r^*(x)$ is provided by

$$p^*(x,h) = \tfrac{1}{2}hr^*(x) + O(h^2),\tag{46}$$

which follows from (45) and (11).

11. Constant Proportional Risk Aversion

If the local proportional risk aversion function is constant, say $r^*(x) = c$, then $r(x) = c/x$, so the utility is strictly decreasingly risk-averse for $c > 0$ and has negative, strictly increasing risk aversion for $c < 0$. By (12), the possibilities are:

$$u(x) \sim x^{1-c} \qquad \text{if } r^*(x) = c < 1,\tag{47}$$

$$u(x) \sim \log x \qquad \text{if } r^*(x) = 1,\tag{48}$$

$$u(x) \sim -x^{-(c-1)} \qquad \text{if } r^*(x) = c > 1.\tag{49}$$

If the proportional risk aversion is constant locally, then it is constant globally, that is, a change in assets makes no change in preferences among proportional risks. This follows immediately from the fact that $u(kx) \sim u(x)$ in each of the cases above. Therefore it makes sense to speak of "constant proportional risk aversion" without the qualification "local" or "global." Similar remarks apply to constant proportional risk aversion on an interval.

12. Increasing and Decreasing Proportional Risk Aversion

We will call a utility function [strictly] increasingly or decreasingly proportionally risk-averse if it has a [strictly] increasing or decreasing local proportional risk aversion function. Again the corresponding local and global properties are equivalent, as the next theorem states.

Theorem 6: The following conditions are equivalent.
(a″) The local proportional risk aversion function $r^*(x)$ is [strictly] decreasing.
(b″) The proportional risk premium $\pi^*(x,\tilde{z})$ is a [strictly] decreasing function of x for all $\tilde{z}$.
(c″) The proportional probability premium $p^*(x,h)$ is a [strictly] decreasing function of x for all $h > 0$.
The same equivalences hold if "increasing" is substituted for "decreasing"

throughout and/or attention is restricted throughout to an interval, that is, if the requirement is added that x, $x + x\widetilde{z}$, $x + xh$, and $x - xh$ all lie in a specified interval.

Proof: This theorem follows upon application of Theorem 1 to $u_1(x) = u(x)$ and $u_2(x) = u(kx)$ for arbitrary x and k.

A decreasingly risk-averse utility function may be increasingly or decreasingly proportionally risk-averse or neither. For instance, $u(x) \sim -\exp[-q^{-1}(x + b)^q]$, with $b \geqslant 0$, $q < 1$, $q \neq 0$, is strictly decreasingly risk-averse for $x > 0$ while its local proportional risk aversion function $r^*(x) = x(x + b)^{-1}[(x + b)^q + 1 - q]$ is strictly increasing if $0 < q < 1$, strictly decreasing if $q < 0$ and $b = 0$, and neither if $q < 0$ and $b > 0$.

13. Related Work of Arrow

Arrow[4] has discussed the optimum amount to invest when part of the assets x are to be held as cash and the rest invested in a specified, actuarially favorable risk. If $\widetilde{i}$ is the return per unit invested, then investing the amount a will result in assets $x + a\widetilde{i}$. Suppose $a(x, \widetilde{i})$ is the optimum amount to invest, that is $a(x, \widetilde{i})$ maximizes $E\{u(x + a\widetilde{i})\}$. Arrow proves that if $r(x)$ is [strictly] decreasing, increasing, or constant for all x, then $a(x, \widetilde{i})$ is [strictly] increasing, decreasing, or constant, respectively, except that $a(x, \widetilde{i}) = x$ for all x below a certain value (depending on $\widetilde{i}$). He also proves a theorem about the asset elasticity of the demand for cash which is equivalent to the statement that if $r^*(x)$ is [strictly] decreasing, increasing, or constant for all x, then the optimum proportional investment $a^*(x, \widetilde{i}) = a(x, \widetilde{i})/x$ is [strictly] increasing, decreasing, or constant, respectively, except that $a^*(x, \widetilde{i}) = 1$ for all x below a certain value. In the present framework it is natural to deduce these results from the following theorem, whose proof bears essentially the same relation to Arrow's proofs as the proof of Theorem 1 to direct proofs of Theorems 2 and 6. For convenience we assume that $a_1(x, \widetilde{i})$ and $a_2(x, \widetilde{i})$ are unique.

Theorem 7: Condition (a) *of Theorem 1 is equivalent to*
(f) $a_1(x, \widetilde{i}) \leqslant a_2(x, \widetilde{i})$ *for all x and $\widetilde{i}$ [and $<$ if $0 < a_1(x, \widetilde{i}) < x$].*
The same equivalence holds if attention is restricted throughout to an interval,

---

4. Kenneth J. Arrow, "Liquidity Preference," Lecture VI in "Lecture Notes for Economics 285, The Economics of Uncertainty," pp. 33–53, undated, Stanford University.
        Addendum (1969). In retrospect, I wish footnote 2 had made clear that Robert Schlaifer's contribution included formulating originally the concept of decreasing risk aversion in terms of the probability premium and proving that it implies $r(x)$ is decreasing, i.e., that (c') implies (a') in Theorem 2. J.W.P.

that is, if the requirement is added that x and x + $\tilde{\imath}x$ lie in a specified interval.

Proof: To show that (a) implies (f), note that $a_j(x, \tilde{\imath})$ maximizes

$$v_j(a) = \frac{1}{u_j'(x)} E\{u_j(x + a\tilde{\imath})\}, \qquad j = 1,2. \tag{50}$$

Therefore (f) follows from

$$\frac{d}{da}\{v_1(a) - v_2(a)\} = E\left\{\tilde{\imath}\left(\frac{u_1'(x + a\tilde{\imath})}{u_1'(x)} - \frac{u_2'(x + a\tilde{\imath})}{u_2'(x)}\right)\right\} \leqslant [<]0, \tag{51}$$

which follows from (a) by (20).

If, conversely, the weak [strong] form of (a) does not hold, then its strong [weak] form holds on some interval with u_1 and u_2 interchanged, in which case the weak [strong] form of (f) cannot hold, so (f) implies (a). (The fact must be used that the strong form of (f) is actually stronger than the weak form, even when x and $x + \tilde{\imath}x$ are restricted to a specified interval. This is easily shown.)

Assuming u is bounded, Arrow proves that (i) it is impossible that $r^*(x) \leqslant 1$ for all $x > x_0$, and he implies that (ii) $r^*(0) \leqslant 1$. It follows, as he points out, that if u is bounded and r^* is monotonic, then r^* is increasing. (i) and (ii) can be deduced naturally from the following theorem, which is an immediate consequence of Theorem 1 (a) and (e).

Theorem 8: If $r_1(x) \geqslant r_2(x)$ for all $x > x_0$ and $u_1(\infty) = \infty$, then $u_2(\infty) = \infty$. If $r_1(x) \geqslant r_2(x)$ for all $x < \epsilon, \epsilon > 0$, and $u_2(0) = -\infty$, then $u_1(0) = -\infty$.

This gives (i) when $r_1(x) = 1/x$, $r_2(x) = r(x)$, $u_1(x) = \log x$, $u_2(x) = u(x)$. It gives (ii) when $r_1(x) = r(x)$, $r_2(x) = c/x$, $c > 1$, $u_1(x) = u(x)$, $u_2(x) = -x^{1-c}$.

This section is not intended to summarize Arrow's work,[4] but only to indicate its relation to the present paper. The main points of overlap are that Arrow introduces essentially the functions r and r^* (actually their negatives) and uses them in significant ways, in particular those mentioned already, and that he introduces essentially $p^*(x,h)$, proves an equation like (46) in order to interpret decreasing r^*, and mentions the possibility of a similar analysis for r.

Part II
Dynamic Portfolio Choice Frameworks

The Accumulation of Risky Capital:
A Sequential Utility Analysis

Edmund S. Phelps
Columbia University

This paper investigates the optimal lifetime consumption strategy of an individual whose wealth holding possibilities expose him to the risk of loss. The vehicle of analysis is a stochastic, discrete-time dynamic programming model that postulates an expected lifetime utility function to be maximized. All wealth consists of a single asset, called capital.

The problem described belongs mainly to the theory of personal saving. Models of saving behavior thus far have been entirely deterministic [4, 7, 8, 11, 12, 13),[2] whereas, in fact, the saver is typically faced with the prospect of capital gain or loss. So it seems appropriate to determine whether the results of the conventional theory carry over or have to be qualified upon admitting capital risk into the theory.[3] The question also arises as to the effect of capital risk itself upon the level of consumption. This neglected factor may play a role in the explanation of certain inter-group differences in saving behavior.

These questions are easier to raise than to answer, and this paper is frankly an exploratory effort. No generality or definiteness is claimed for the results obtained. A brief outline of the paper and sketch of some of these results follow.

In the first two sections, a utility function and a stochastic capital growth process are postulated and discussed. Subsequently, the "structure" of the optimal consumption policy, that is, the way in which consumption depends upon the individual's age and capital, is established. One's expectations, based on existing "deterministic" theory, are confirmed: Optimal consumption is an increasing function of both age and capital. Little else appears deducible without further restrictions upon the utility function.

Thereafter attention is confined to certain monomial utility functions. These special cases cannot yield general theorems but they do have the function

---

Reprinted by permission of the publisher and author from *Econometrica*, Vol. 30, 4 (October 1962), pp. 729–743.

1. For helpful discussions on this subject I am grateful to T.N. Srinivasan and S.G. Winter.

2. An exception is a Cowles Foundation Discussion Paper by Martin Beckmann [2]. That paper (which deals with wage rather than capital uncertainty) uses a technique similar to the one here.

3. The model below resembles Ramsey's more than contemporary models [7, 11] so that it is largely his results that are modified.

of providing counter-examples to conjectures and of serving to suggest other hypotheses for empirical test.

For example, it is shown that the classical phenomenon of "hump saving" [8, 12] need not occur, quite apart from reasons of time preference, if capital is risky. Instead a low-capital "trap" region is possible in which it is optimal to maintain or decumulate capital, no matter how distant the planning horizon.

These utility functions all make consumption linear homogeneous in capital and permanent nonwealth income, and linear in each of these variables. But the straight-line classroom consumption function is not really upheld: Consumption cannot be expressed as a function of aggregate expected income because expected income (treated as certain) and expected capital income have different variances, whence different impacts upon the level of consumption. The marginal propensity to consume out of risky income is smaller than out of sure income. This result may help to explain why households which depend primarily upon (risky) capital income (e.g., farmers, wealthy heirs) are comparatively thrifty.

Finally, we consider the effect upon the consumption level of variations in the riskiness and in the expected rate of return of capital (given capital and nonwage income). Not surprisingly, the direction of effect of both are unpredictable without knowledge of the type of utility function; the familiar conflict between substitution and income effects applies as much to risk as to the rate of return. Two closely related utility functions give opposite results. But it is interesting that risk always "opposes" return. Where increase of the rate of return raises (reduces) the propensity to consume, an increase in risk reduces (raises) it; and where return has no effect, neither does risk.

1. The Behavior of Capital

Capital is treated as homogeneous in the sense that each unit of the asset experiences the same rate of return.[4]

The individual's consumption opportunities occur at discrete, equally spaced points in time. These points divide the lifetime of the consumer into N periods. The state of the system at the beginning of each period, $n = 1, 2, \ldots, N$, is described by the variable x_n, the amount of capital then on hand. At this time the individual chooses to consume some amount c_n of this capital.

The unconsumed capital is left to grow at a rate which is not then known. In addition to the capital growth, the individual receives an amount, y, of nonwealth income at the end of the period. This income is the same each period. Consequently the amount of capital available for consumption in the next period is given by the difference equation

---

4. Alternatively, capital might have been envisioned more like identical female rabbits. In any short time period, some units of the asset would multiply while others not. This might be termed subjective or *ex ante* homogeneity.

$$x_{n+1} = \beta_n(x_n - c_n) + y, \qquad x_1 = k, \tag{1.1}$$

where $\beta_n - 1$ is the rate of return earned on capital in the nth period.

We shall assume that the random variables β_n are independent and drawn from the same probability distribution. There are m possible rates of return, $0 \leqslant \beta_i$, $i = 1, 2, \ldots, m$. The probability of the ith rate of return will be denoted by p_i (the same from period to period). In addition we shall assume that $\bar{\beta} = \Sigma_1^m \, p_i\beta_i > 1$ so that the consumer expects capital to be productive. However, $\Sigma_1^m \, p_i(\beta_i - \bar{\beta})^2 > 0$, and so the realized return may differ from the expected one.

2. The Utility Function

This model postulates a consumer who obeys the axioms of the von Neumann-Morgenstern utility theory. His consumption strategy (or policy) can therefore be viewed as maximizing the expected value of utility, which is determined up to an increasing linear transformation.

Second, we suppose that the lifetime utility associated with any consumption history is a continuously differentiable function of the amount consumed at the beginning of each period.

The lifetime utility function is assumed to be of the independent and additive form

$$U = \sum_{i=1}^{N} \alpha^{n-1}u(c_n), \qquad 0 < \alpha \leqslant 1. \tag{2.1}$$

The implications of this functional form are several. Preferences for the consumption "chances" or distributions of any period are invariant to the consumption levels befalling the individual in other periods (separability). Preferences among consumption subhistories in the future are independent of the age of the individual (stationarity). Preference for a consumption strategy is independent of or unaffected by any serial correlation in the random consumption sequence associated with that strategy (independence).[5]

The same axioms which yield the von Neumann-Morgenstern utility indicators also imply that $U(c_1, \ldots, c_N)$ is bounded from above and below.[6] Con-

---

5. However the necessary and sufficient conditions for independence of utilities when choice takes place under uncertainty have yet to be investigated. The independence of utilities when choice takes place in an environment of certainty has been axiomatized by Debreu [6]. The meaning of additivity with a variable utility discount factor and an infinite number of periods has also been investigated by Koopmans [9].

6. A proof of boundedness may be found in [1] and [5]. The proof uses the "continuity axiom" and a generalization of the St. Petersburg game, the idea for which Arrow [1] credits to K. Menger.

sequently $u(c_n^{\cdot})$ is also a bounded function. Let $\bar{u}$ and $\underline{u}$ denote the upper and lower bounds of $u(c_n)$, respectively.

Finally, we postulate that the individual strictly prefers more consumption to less (monotonicity) and that he is strictly averse to risk (concavity). The latter means that for every pair of consumption histories $(c_1, \ldots, c_N)$ and $(c_1^o, \ldots, c_N^o)$ to which he is not indifferent, he will strictly prefer the certainty of the com-promise history $Oc + (1 - O)c^o$ to the mixed prospect offering him the history c with probability $\bar{O}$ and the history c^o with probability $1 - O, 0 < O < 1$. It follows trivially that $u(c_n)$ is a strictly increasing and strictly concave function.

3. Derivation of the Functional Equations

We seek the consumption strategy (or, equivalently, policy)—denoted by the sequence of functions $\{c_n(x)\}$ for $x \geqslant 0, n = 1, 2, \ldots, N$—which maximizes expected lifetime utility:

$$J_N(c) = \exp_\beta U \tag{3.1}$$

subject to the relation (1.1). Notice that the optimal $c_n, n = 1, \ldots, N$, will be a stochastic rather than a predetermined function of n.

To treat this variational problem we turn to the technique of dynamic programming [3]. Observing that the maximum expected value of lifetime utility depends only upon the number of stages in the process and the initial capital, k, we define the function

$$w_N(k) = \max J_N(c) \tag{3.2}$$

where the maximum is taken over all admissible policies. The function defined may be interpreted as the utility-of-wealth function of the optimizing consumer having N periods of life remaining.

Next one reduces the problem with N decision variables to a sequence of N problems, each involving only one policy variable, the decision which must be taken at the current moment. This approach leads to the following functional equations:[7]

---

7. The argument starts with the observation that with the elapse of each period the individual is confronted with another multistage decision problem which differs only in having one less stage and, in general, a different initial capital. By the "principle of opti-mality"[3], if the individual's consumption strategy is optimal for the original N-stage process then that part of the strategy relating to the last N-1 stages must also constitute a complete optimal strategy with respect to the new N-1 stage process. This principle, equa-tion (1.1), the additive utility function (3.1) and the definition (3.2) combine to yield the sequence of equations in the unknown utility of wealth functions in (3.3) and (3.4).

$$w_N(x) = \max_{0 \leqslant c \leqslant x} \left[u(c) + \alpha \sum_{i=1}^{m} p_i w_{N-1}(\beta_i(x-c) + y) \right], \qquad N \geqslant 2,$$

$$\tag{3.3}$$

and

$$w_1(x) = \max_{0 \leqslant c \leqslant x} u(c) \tag{3.4}$$

which defines the utility of wealth in the single stage process. Without a subscript, the symbol c shall always denote the value of consumption in the first period of the (not necessarily original) multistage process. Similarly x shall denote capital at the start of whatever process is being considered.

4. Properties of the Optimal Consumption Policy

A number of standard results follow from this model: First, the optimal consumption strategy is unique; the optimum value of c_n is a unique function of x_n for every n.

The proof consists of showing that the utility of wealth function is strictly concave if the utility of consumption function is strictly concave; therefore the maximand in each period is a strictly concave function of current consumption, whence the maximizing consumption level is unique.[8]

Second, consumption is an increasing function of capital and age. The latter result depends upon the further assumption made now that $\alpha\beta > 1$. It will become clear in the next section that this inequality is also a necessary condition for positive accumulation of capital.

The proof is rather involved and is omitted here. It can be shown that if $\alpha\bar{\beta} > u'(0)/u'(y)$ then, with $N \geqslant 2$ periods remaining, consumption is the following function of capital:

$$c = \begin{cases} 0, & 0 \leqslant x \leqslant \bar{x}_N, \\ c_N(x), & x \geqslant \bar{x}_N, \end{cases} \tag{4.1}$$

where $c_N(x) = 0$ at $x = \bar{x}_N$, $c_N'(x) > 0$, and $c_N(x) < x$. The function $c_N(x)$ repre-

---

8. Readers who are unfamiliar with this type of proof may wish to consult [3]. Proofs of the result above and of the other results stated but not proved in this section can be found in an earlier version of this paper (same title) by the author, published as Cowles Foundation Discussion Paper No. 109, which is available on request to the Cowles Foundation.

sents the interior portion of the solution where consumption is not constrained by the nonnegativity requirement.

It can be further shown that the marginal utility of wealth declines with age and capital and that the "consumption function" in (4.1) shifts leftward and upward as age increases:

$$w_1'(x) < w_2'(x) < \ldots < w_N'(x) < \ldots,$$

$$c_2(x) > \ldots > c_N(x) > \ldots,$$

$$0 < \bar{x}_2 < \ldots < \bar{x}_N < \ldots. \tag{4.2}$$

Of course, when $N = 1$, $c = x$.

In the other case, where $\alpha\bar{\beta} \leq u'(0)/u'(y)$, the constraint that consumption cannot exceed capital becomes binding for $N = 2$ and possibly for larger N—when capital is sufficiently small. If there is a value of $x \geq 0$ for which $c_N(x) = x$ then, denoting this value by $\hat{x}_N$, we obtain

$$c = \begin{cases} x, & 0 \leq x \leq \hat{x}_N, \\ c_N(x), & x \geq \hat{x}_N. \end{cases}$$

Again, as age increases, N decreases, the marginal utility of wealth function decreases and the consumption function shifts upward. Consequently the intersection where $c = x$ shifts rightward:

$$\hat{x}_2 > \ldots > \hat{x}_N \geq 0.$$

A typical possibility is graphed in Figure 1. This consumption function is of the second type. As N becomes small, the consumption schedule shifts upward. When $N = 2$, the function intersects the $c = x$ line. When $N = 1$, $c = x$ at all x.

The $I(x)$ function is defined in the next section.

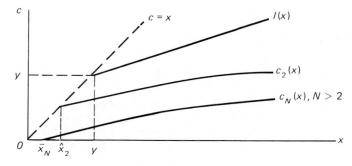

Figure 1

5. Conditions for Expected Accumulation

The preceding theorems confirm our expectations about the qualitative behavior of optimal consumption. They do not go far enough to permit inferences about the behavior of capital as a function of age and initial capital. One might ask if the model generates "hump saving" [8, 12], so important in the theory of aggregate capital formation. The "hump saver" saves when he is young and dissaves as he grows older. Therefore we ask: Can one find a value of N sufficiently large to induce the individual to save—more precisely, to cause the expected value of his subsequent capital to exceed the value of his present capital?[9]

Let us define "expected income," $I(x)$, to be the amount of consumption such that the expected value of capital in the next period equals present capital. Now $\exp x_{n+1} = y + \bar{\beta}(x_n - c_n)$. Expected stationarity, $\exp x_{n+1} = x_n$, implies $c_n = (y/\bar{\beta}) + [(\bar{\beta} - 1)/\bar{\beta}]x_n = I(x)$. Expected income is displayed as a function of capital in Figure 1. Our question is then whether, in the limit, as N approaches infinity, $c_N(x) < I(x)$ for all $x \geq y$.

The answer is clear cut when capital is riskless. Then $\beta_i = \beta$ for all i and we obtain the following recurrence relation in the limiting utility of wealth function:

$$w(x) = \max_c \left\{ u(c) + \alpha w(\beta(x - c) + y) \right\}. \tag{5.1}$$

The maximum is an interior one for $x \geq y$ so that $c(x)$ defined by

$$u'(c) - \alpha\beta w'(\beta(x - c) + y) = 0 \tag{5.2}$$

determines c as a function of x.

Differentiating totally with respect to x gives

$$w'(x) = \alpha\beta w'(\beta(x - c) + y) + c'(x)[u'(c) - \alpha\beta w'(\beta(x - c) + y)]$$

$$= \alpha\beta w'(\beta(x - c) + y) \qquad [\text{by } (5.2)]. \tag{5.3}$$

Since $w'(x)$ is monotone decreasing, (5.3) implies that $x_{n+1} > x_n$ if and only if $\alpha\beta > 1$. Therefore, denoting the limiting consumption function by $c(x)$, $c(x) < I(x)$ for all $x \geq y$.

This simple result fails to extend to risky capital. When $\beta_i \neq \bar{\beta}$ for some i, (5.3) becomes

$$w'(x) = \alpha \sum_i p_i \beta_i w'(\beta_i(x - c) + y). \tag{5.4}$$

---

9. Of course, an affirmative answer would not be very interesting if the necessary value of N exceeds human life expectancy!

From (5.4) no general conclusions concerning the conditions for expected capital growth can be drawn. Of course capital cannot be expected to grow very long unless $\bar{\beta} > 1$. But $\alpha\bar{\beta} > 1$ is insufficient to guarantee "expected" capital growth.[10]

It is clear that the critical value which $\alpha\bar{\beta}$ must exceed if capital growth is to be expected will depend upon the distribution of β_i and the shape of the marginal utility function $w'(x)$. The only practical procedure here is to investigate the implications for capital growth of particular classes of utility functions.

6. Implications of Selected Monomial Utility Functions

In this section we investigate the implications of certain types of monomial utility functions for the consumption function and for the expected path of capital.

We consider first the utility function[11]

$$u(c_n) = \lambda c_n^{-\gamma} \qquad \bar{u}, \gamma > 0, \lambda > 1. \tag{6.1}$$

Solving successively for the sequence of unknown functions $\{w_n(x)\}$, $N = 1, 2, \ldots$, yields

$$w_N(x) = \bar{u}(1 + \alpha + \ldots + \alpha^{N-1}) - \lambda(\alpha b^{-\gamma})^{N-1} [1 + (\alpha b^{-\gamma})^{\frac{-1}{\gamma+1}} +$$

$$\ldots + (\alpha b^{-\gamma})^{\frac{-(N-1)}{\gamma+1}}]^{\gamma+1} [x + (b^{-1} + \ldots + b^{-(N-1)})y]^{-\gamma} \tag{6.2}$$

and

$$c_N(x) = \frac{(\alpha b^{-\gamma})^{\frac{-(N-1)}{\gamma+1}}}{1 + (\alpha b^{-\gamma})^{\frac{-1}{\gamma+1}} + \ldots + (\alpha b^{-\gamma})^{\frac{-(N-1)}{\gamma+1}}} [x + (1 + b + \ldots + b^{N-2})y] \tag{6.3}$$

---

10. Several plausible cases are the following. First, there may be no capital level at which the expected returns to saving repays the risks. Or it may be that the individual can "afford" the risks of net expected saving only when capital exceeds a critical value at which $c(x)$ intersects $I(x)$ from above. In the opposite case, additional wealth is worth the risks only as long as capital falls short of the level where $c(x)$ intersects $I(x)$ from below.

11. The function (6.1) fails to have the boundedness property assumed up to this point and thus it contradicts the "continuity axiom" mentioned in Section 2. Whatever the merits of that axiom, the function has received sufficient study in the context of deterministic models [4, 12, 13] to deserve our attention here.

where

$$b = (\Sigma p_i \beta_i^{-\gamma})^{\frac{-1}{\gamma}}.$$

If the reader applies (6.3) to $c_{N+1}(x)$ and uses (6.2) he will obtain an expression for $w_{N+1}(x)$ having the same form as (6.2). Note also that if $\alpha = \beta_i = 1$ for all i, formula (6.3) calls for consuming a fraction $1/N$ of the individual's net worth, $x + (N - 1)y$.

Provided that $\alpha b^{-\gamma}$ (for which $\alpha < 1, \beta > 1, \gamma > 0$ is sufficient in the certainty case), the expressions in (6.2) and (6.3) converge as N approaches infinity, giving the solutions to the "infinite state" process:

$$w(x) = \frac{\bar{u}}{1 - \alpha} - \lambda \left[\frac{(\alpha b^{-\gamma})^{\frac{-1}{\gamma+1}}}{(\alpha b^{-\gamma})^{\frac{-1}{\gamma+1}} - 1} \right]^{\gamma+1} \left(x + \frac{y}{b - 1} \right)^{-\gamma} \tag{6.4}$$

and

$$c(x) = (1 - (\alpha b^{-\gamma})^{\frac{1}{\gamma+1}} \left(x + \frac{y}{b - 1} \right). \tag{6.5}$$

This limiting consumption function is useful as an approximation to $c_N(x)$ for large N.

(i) Properties of the consumption function.

A number of properties of the consumption functions (6.3) and (6.5) can be observed immediately. First, the consumption function is linear homogeneous in capital and nonwealth income. Of two households, both having identical utility functions like (6.1), if one household enjoys twice the capital and non-wealth income of the other, it will aslo consume twice as much.

Second, consumption is linear in capital and nonweatlth income. The co-efficient of wealth, $\partial c/\partial x$, may be called the marginal propensity to consume (MPC) out of wealth.

The convergence condition $\alpha b^{-\gamma} < 1$ insures that $\partial c/\partial x > 0$. And $\partial c/\partial x < 1$ for all finite $\alpha, b > 0$.

The coefficient $\partial c/\partial y$ may be called the MPC out of "permanent," sure, (nonwealth) income. Clearly $\partial c/\partial y > 0$ if and only $b > 1$ (given the convergence condition). What can be said concerning this condition?

When capital is risky (that is, when $\beta_i \neq \bar{\beta}$ for some i), then $b < \bar{\beta}$.[12] There-for the postulate $\bar{\beta} > 1$ does not imply $b > 1$. We see thus that Keynes' "psychological law" stating that MPC > 0 applies only if capital has a positive net expected productivity and only if capital is sufficiently productive at that. However, we do observe positive MPC and if we were to fit this model to data we should presumably find that $b > 1$. At any rate, we shall assume $b > 1$ unless we indicate the contrary.

Is the MPC also less than one, as Keynes had it? Of course, with $b > 1$, the MPC out of an income stream beginning sufficiently far in the future is bound to be less than one. Usually one considers the effect on (immediate) consumption of immediate income. To do that in the present model—where the paycheck is received at the end of the period—suppose capital increases by the same amount as y, as if last period's paycheck were increased too. Is this MPC out of 'imme-diate," nonwealth income smaller than one?

This MPC is

$$\left[1 - (\alpha b^{-\gamma})^{\frac{1}{\gamma+1}} \right] \frac{b}{b-1}$$

and is smaller than one if and only if $\alpha b > 1$.

This is an interesting condition. This same condition, we show now, is neces-sary and sufficient for positive capital accumulation at all possible values of income and capital.

Note first that $c(x) < I(x)$ for all $x \geq y$—causing the expected growth of capital—if and only if $c(y) < y$ and $c'(x) \leq I'(x)$. Now $c(y)/y$ equals the MPC just analyzed so that $\alpha b > 1$ means $c(y) < y$. The condition that $c'(x) < I'(x)$ is

$$1 - (\alpha b^{-\gamma})^{\frac{1}{\gamma+1}} < \frac{\bar{\beta}-1}{\bar{\beta}}$$

for which $\alpha b > 1$ is sufficient (although unnecessary).[13]

The significance of this exercise lies in the possibility that $1 < b \leq 1/\alpha$, in which case capital will be expected to grow only if it exceeds a certain threshold. Suppose $\alpha b = 1$. Then all nonwealth income is consumed and there is "net expected saving"—that is, $c(x) < I(x)$—only if $x > y$, i.e., only if the individual starts the period with some capital over and above his just-received wage of the previous period. Otherwise there will be no "hump saving" (in this case), even though $\bar{\beta} > 1/\alpha$.

---

12. To see this, draw a diagram showing $\bar{\beta}_i^{-\gamma}$ as a function of β_i. Since $\beta^{-\gamma}$ is a convex function of β, $\Sigma p_i \beta_i^{-\gamma} > \bar{\beta}^{-\gamma}$ whence $b = (\Sigma p_i \beta_i^{-\gamma})^{-1/\gamma} < \bar{\beta}$.
13. Note that all these conditions reduce to $b > 1$ if $\alpha = 1$.

A comparison of the MPC's leads to an interesting finding: The greater non-wealth income, y, as a proportion of total expected income, $I(x)$, the larger is the ratio of consumption to expected income. This is because the MPC out of (sure, immediate) nonwealth income, $c'(x)b/(b - 1)$, is greater than the consumption effect of that increase in current capital which is required to raise expected income by one dollar. Writing

$$x = \frac{\bar{\beta}}{\bar{\beta} - 1} \left[I(x) - \frac{y}{\bar{\beta}} \right],$$

we see that the latter consumption effect is $c'(x)\bar{\beta}/(\bar{\beta} - 1)$. Recalling that $b < \bar{\beta}$, we find that "sure" income has the stronger effect. This implies that, among households who have like utility functions and who face the same capital growth process, those whose expected income depends relatively heavily on risky capital will be observed to be relatively thrifty. This may help to explain why wealthy heirs, farmers, and certain other groups save a comparatively large proportion of their incomes. Further, the result suggests that capital income and labor income ought not to be aggregated in econometric analyses of consumption.

(ii) *Variations of risk and return.*

The last question taken up here relates to the effect upon consumption of variations in the riskiness and expected return from capital. Since the consumption function is linear homogeneous we can write

$$c = \frac{\partial c}{\partial x} x + \frac{\partial c}{\partial y} y,$$

whence these variations influence consumption through the marginal propensities, which are a function of b (and independent of x and y).

Let us consider first the effect of variations in risk and return on the value of b.

An increase in the expected return on capital is defined here as a uniform shift in the probility distribution of β_i which leaves all its moments the same except the mean, $\bar{\beta}$. Such a shift *increases* $\bar{\beta}$ and b.

What effect has risk on the value of b? When capital is risky, $b < \bar{\beta}$. Thus the presence of risk (as distinct from marginal increases therein) *decreases* b.

Hence, capital's (net) productivity and its riskiness affect consumption in the opposite direction.

A second kind of risk effect results from a change in the degree of risk, somehow measured.

A probability distribution which offers a simple measure of risk is the uniform or rectangular distribution. This is a two-parameter distribution with mean $\bar{\beta}$ and range $2h$. The variance is $h^2/3$ so that h is the measure of risk.

We show now that increases in h reduce b so that the "structural" and "marginal" effect of risk on b are in the same direction. Noting that $db/dh < 0$ means $db^{-\gamma}/dh > 0$, we examine $b^{-\gamma}$.

By definition of b,

$$b^{-\gamma} = \int_{\bar{\beta}-h}^{\bar{\beta}+h} \beta^{-\gamma}\left(\frac{1}{2h}\right)d\beta.$$

Evaluating the integral we find

$$b^{-\gamma} = \frac{1}{(1-\gamma)2h}\,[(\bar{\beta}+h)^{1-\gamma} - (\bar{\beta}-h)^{1-\gamma}].$$

Differentiating with respect to h yields

$$\frac{db^{-\gamma}}{dh} = \frac{1}{2(1-\gamma)h^2}\,[(\bar{\beta}-h)^{-\gamma}(\bar{\beta}-\gamma h) - (\bar{\beta}+h)^{-\gamma}(\bar{\beta}+\gamma h)].$$

Assuming $\gamma > 1$, $db^{-\gamma}/dh > 0$ if and only if

$$\frac{\bar{\beta}-\gamma h}{\bar{\beta}+\gamma h} < \left(\frac{\bar{\beta}-h}{\bar{\beta}+h}\right)^{\gamma}.$$

β equal zero is excluded, for otherwise b is not defined. Consequently $h < \bar{\beta}$ and the right hand side of the inequality must be positive. But so may be the left hand side (if $\gamma < \bar{\beta}/h$). The following shows the inequality is satisfied for all $\gamma > 1$.

Dividing both sides of the inequality by $\bar{\beta}$, and defining $z = h/\bar{\beta}$, we obtain

$$\frac{1-\gamma z}{1+\gamma z} < \left(\frac{1-z}{1+z}\right)^{\gamma}$$

which, taking the logarithm on both sides, we find to be satisfied if and only if

$$\log(1-\gamma z) - \log(1+\gamma z) < y\,[\log(1-z) - \log(1+z)].$$

Expansion of the logarithmic functions into Taylor's series yields

$$\left(-\gamma z - \frac{(\gamma z)^2}{2} - \frac{(\gamma z)^3}{3} - \ldots\right) - \left(\gamma z - \frac{(\gamma z)^2}{2} + \frac{(\gamma x)^3}{3} - \ldots\right)$$

$$< \gamma\left[\left(-z - \frac{z^2}{2} - \frac{z^3}{3} - \ldots\right) - \left(z - \frac{z^2}{2} + \frac{z^3}{3} - \ldots\right)\right]$$

whence

$$\left(\gamma z + \frac{(\gamma z)^3}{3} + \frac{(\gamma z)^5}{5} + \ldots\right) > \left(\gamma z + \frac{\gamma z^3}{3} + \frac{\gamma z^5}{5} + \ldots\right).$$

This inequality can be seen to hold for all $\gamma > 1$. Therefore a marginal increase in risk reduces the value of b. Recalling that an increase in the expected return increases b, we note that changes in risk and return have opposite effects on consumption.

We consider now the effect of a change in b upon consumption. Does the substitution effect dominate here—so that a rise in b encourages saving and reduces consumption? Or does the income effect dominate?

Turning first to $\partial c/\partial x$, we see from (6.5) that an increase in b raises $\partial c/\partial x$.

Turning next to $\partial c/\partial y$, we note from (6.5) that $\partial c/\partial y = 1/(b-1) \cdot \partial c/\partial x$. It would appear that a rise in b might reduce $\partial c/\partial y$, because of the downward recapitalization (using $1/(b-1)$) of the y stream, if b were sufficiently small ($b > 1$). It can be shown that $d(\partial c/\partial y)/db \geq 0$ if and only if $(\alpha b^{-\gamma})^{-1/(\gamma+1)} \leq (1 + b\gamma)/(1 + \gamma)$. If $\alpha = 1$ this is satisfied for all $b > 1$; otherwise it is satisfied only for values of b above some value $\hat{b} > 1$.

Thus, if there is no utility discount, the income effect dominates here; then a rise in the expected return on capital weakens the incentive to save and an increase in risk compels more saving in order to reduce the insecurity of the future. But if the future is discounted, the individual feels "poorer"; then a rise in the expected return may encourage saving up to a point, after which the income effect dominates; this point comes sooner the smaller is y. In either case, risk and return variations have opposing qualitative effects upon consumption.

(iii) *Other utility functions.*

To see that the implications of the utility function (6.1) for the effects of variations in risk and return are not general, one has only to modify the utility function thus:

$$u(c_N) = \lambda c^{\gamma}, \qquad \lambda > 0, 0 < \gamma < 1. \tag{6.6}$$

All the equations (6.2) – (6.5) continue to hold with the difference that λ and γ are then replaced by $-\lambda$ and $-\gamma$, respectively. Hence the limiting consumption function is

$$c(x) = \left[1 - (\alpha b^{\gamma})^{\frac{1}{1-\gamma}}\right] \left(x + \frac{y}{b-1}\right) \tag{6.7}$$

where $b^{\gamma} = \Sigma p_i \beta_i^{\gamma}$.

An increase in $\bar{\beta}$, other moments of the distribution unchanged, will increase b.

Once again the effect of risk is easy to ascertain. Since β^{γ} is a concave function of β, $\Sigma p_i \beta_i^{\gamma} < \bar{\beta}^{\gamma}$ whence $b = (\Sigma p_i \beta_i^{\gamma}) < \bar{\beta}$.

Turning finally to the effect of a marginal increase in risk upon b, we find that the "natural" result $db^{\gamma}/dh < 0$ (meaning that global and marginal risk effects have like signs) depends upon the condition $(\bar{\beta} - \gamma h)/(\bar{\beta} + \gamma h) > [(\bar{\beta} - h) /(\bar{\beta} + h)]^{\gamma}$, which is satisfied for all $\gamma < 1$.

Once again, risk and return work in opposite directions.

Consider now the effect of an increase in b upon consumption. Unlike the previous example, $\partial c/\partial x$ decreases with increasing b, as can be seen from (6.7); the substitution effect dominates the income effect. And, as (6.7) clearly shows, $\partial c/\partial y$ is also a decreasing function of b for all values of $b > 1$; the downward recapitalization of future income merely reinforces the substitution effect against the weaker income effect.

Thus an increase in expected return encourages saving while an increase of the riskiness of capital discourages saving. The implications of the utility function (6.6) are essentially opposite to those of the utility function (6.1).

To what can this contrast of results be attributed? The utility function is determined only up to a linear transformation, meaning that we can set $\bar{u} = 0$ in (6.1) without effect. Doing this reveals that both (6.1) and (6.6) are constant-elasticity utility functions with elasticity parameter γ. The income effect dominates (unless b is small and y large) in the elastic case and the substitution effect dominates in the inelastic case.

Finally we examine a utility function that can produce some odd results, the logarithmic function in (6.8):

$$u(c_N) = \log c_N. \tag{6.8}$$

It appears to be impossible to solve for $c_N(x)$ explicitly in terms of x and y except in the case $y = 0$. Then we easily find

$$w_N(x) = (1 + \alpha + \ldots + \alpha^{N-1}) \log x + v(\theta, \alpha, N) \tag{6.9}$$

where $v(\theta, \alpha, N)$ depends only upon the parameters, denoted by θ, of the probability distribution of β_i, α and N, and not upon x.

Also

$$c_N(x) = \frac{x}{1 + \alpha + \ldots + \alpha^{N-1}}.$$ (6.10)

When the utility function is logarithmic, the optimum consumption rate is independent both of the expected return and riskiness of capital. Consumption is linear homogeneous in capital. As N is increased, the consumption function flattens asymptotically until, in the limit,

$$c(x) = (1 - \alpha)x.$$ (6.11)

A limiting function exists only if $\alpha < 1$.[14]

References

1. Arrow, K.J.: *Bernoulli Utility Indicators for Distributions Over Arbitrary Spaces,* Technical Report No. 57 of the Department of Economics, Stanford University, July, 1958.
2. Beckmann, M.J.: "A Dynamic Programming Model of the Consumption Function," Cowles Foundation Discussion Paper No. 69, March 1959.
3. Bellman, R.: *Dynamic Programming,* Princeton: Princeton University Press, 1957.
4. Champernowne, D.G.: Review of "A Theory of the Consumption Function" by Milton Friedman, *Journal of the Royal Statistical Society,* Series A, Vol. 121, Part I, 1958.
5. Chernoff,. H., and L. Moses: *Elementary Decision Theory,* New York: John Wiley and Sons, 1959.
6. Debreu, G.: "Topological Methods in Cardinal Utility Theory," *Mathematical Methods in the Social Sciences,* Stanford: Stanford University Press, 1960.
7. Friedman, M.: *A Theory of the Consumption Function,* Princeton: Princeton University Press, 1957.
8. Graaff, J. De V.: "Mr. Harrod on Hump Saving," *Economica,* February, 1950, pp. 81–90.
9. Koopmans, T.C.: "Stationary Ordinal Utility and Impatience," *Econometrica,* April, 1960, pp. 287–309.

---

14. For certain utility functions the existence of a limiting solution does not require $\alpha < 1$. Ramsey [12] argued that boundedness was sufficient but a condition on the elasticity or rate of approach to the upper bound is also necessary, at least in models not containing risk. Samuelson and Solow [14] assume that the upper utility bound is attained at a finite consumption rate, which is not a necessary condition.

10. Markowitz, H.M.: *Portfolio Selection,* New York: John Wiley and Sons, 1959.
11. Modigliani, F., and R. Brumberg: "Utility Analysis and the Consumption Function: An Interpretation of Cross-Section Data," in K. Kurihara, ed., *Post-Keynesian Economics,* New Brunswick, New Jersey: Rutgers University Press, 1954.
12. Ramsey, F.P.: "A Mathematical Theory of Saving," *Economic Journal,* December, 1928, pp. 543–559.
13. Robertson, D.H.: *Lectures on Economic Principles,* Vol. II, Ch. 5, pp. 69–87.
14. Samuelson, P.A., and R.M. Solow: "A Complete Capital Model Involving Heterogeneous Capital Goods," *Quarterly Journal of Economics,* November, 1956, pp. 537–562.

7

Alternative Procedures for Revising Investment Portfolios*

Keith V. Smith
University of California, Los Angeles

I. Introduction

Investment management is a decision-making process which ranges from an individual managing his own small portfolio of securities to institutional investors who manage portfolios valued in millions of dollars. The importance of investment management is readily observed in the increased activity of the securities markets, the close scrutiny given by regulatory agencies to various institutional investors and professional investment managers, the growing market value of pension funds, trust funds, and investment companies, and finally, the increasing number of related research studies which are reported in the financial literature.

Beginning where security analysis leaves off, portfolio selection is a decision-making process which ideally results in the purchase of specified quantities of certain securities, which, taken collectively, best satisfy the stated objectives of the investor. Although portfolio objectives may vary considerably among investors, they may be conveniently categorized as expectations for income, expectations for capital appreciation, and the risk level associated with such expectations. Clearly, the outstanding theoretical approach to the portfolio selection problem is the efficient-set concept developed by Markowitz [8]. His methodology is based on expected portfolio return (income plus appreciation) and the standard deviation of this return which is used as a measure of portfolio risk. It assumes that investors desire return and are risk averters. A central feature of the efficient-set solution to portfolio selection is that it specifies the investment level for each security at a single point in time.

Portfolio revision, on the other hand, is the continuing process of evaluating

Reprinted by permission of the publisher and author from *Journal of Finance and Quantitative Analysis*, December 1968, p. 371–403.

*Part of the research for this paper was conducted while attending the Workshop in Research in Business Finance at the Graduate School of Business Administration, Harvard University, June–July 1967. The author benefited from discussions with J. Lintner, R.R. Glauber, and other attendees of this workshop. Research assistance was also provided by the Division of Research, U.C.L.A. A preliminary version of the paper was presented at the Thirty-First National Meeting of the Operations Research Society of America, New York City, June 2, 1967.

and changing the investment holdings of a given portfolio so as to continue to satisfy investor objectives. Unfortunately, however, most of the important research to date has centered on portfolio selection decisions and on the problems of measuring portfolio performance.[1] This paper is concerned with extending the efficient-set concept of portfolio selection to the larger problem of revising portfolios over time. In particular, the purpose of this paper is to (1) present a revision framework which extends the Markowitz concept to an intertemporal basis, (2) suggest alternative procedures for revision portfolios within such a framework, and (3) test these alternatives by simulating portfolio selection and revision over the postwar period using a population of common stocks.

Section II introduces a theoretical framework for considering the problem of portfolio revision, while Section III presents four alternative procedures for revising investment portfolios within such a framework. This is followed in Section IV by a description of a portfolio simulation experiment which was designed to test empirically the four revision alternatives. Section V discusses the results of the portfolio simulation and explores the cost-effectiveness of one of the revision alternatives. The important question of how frequently a portfolio should be revised is considered in Section VI. The final section of the paper summarizes findings, explores the implications of the reported research, and suggests certain areas for continuing effort.

II. Portfolio Revision

For each security j in a population of m possible investments, the Markowitz formulation of portfolio selection requires an expected value of portfolio return, r_j, the variance of this return s_j^2, and its covariance, s_{ij}, with all other security returns. These input values are based on expectations for the next period. Solution of the selection problem is accomplished by an efficient set of portfolios in return-variance (risk) space, such as the curve, *abcd* in Figure 1. A portfolio is efficient if (1) it has the highest possible expected return for a given level of risk, and (2) the lowest possible variance (risk) for a given expected return.[2] Each portfolio along the efficient frontier can be described by a vector $X = [x_j]$, where x_j is the proportion of the entire portfolio value invested in

---

1. For a brief discussion of the inter-relationships between security analysis, portfolio selection, portfolio revision, and performance measurement, see Smith [12].

2. In this paper, the formulation of an efficient portfolio is made with respect to a point in time one period later than when portfolio selection is made. That is, the expectational horizon is a single period, although revision procedures are examined over an investment horizon of several periods. For a discussion of a multi-period expectational horizon, see Pogue [9].

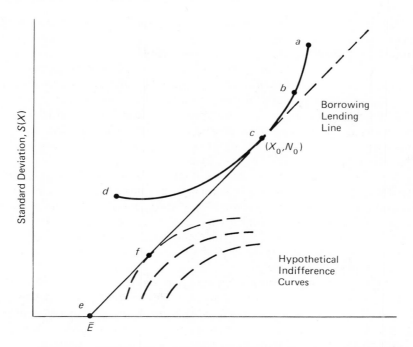

Figure 1. Efficient Set at the Beginning of an Investment Period

security j.[3] The characteristics of a given portfolio, X, are expected return

$$E(X) = \sum_{j=1}^{m} x_j r_j \tag{1}$$

and standard deviation

$$S(X) = \left[\sum_{i=1}^{m} \sum_{j=1}^{m} x_i x_j s_{ij} \right]^{1/2} \tag{2}$$

___

3. Solution of the portfolio selection problem, which is formulated into a quadratic programming context, consists of a series of corner portfolios. A corner portfolio is a point along the efficient set where a single security enters or leaves the portfolio. The set begins, for example, with point a in Figure 1, which is a portfolio consisting of one security which has the highest expected return. Subsequent corner portfolios typically have additional members as diversification reduces portfolio variance. Point d represents the "last" corner portfolio which has the lowest attainable variance.

If an investor's portfolio is to consist only of risky securities, he must select a particular portfolio along the efficient frontier based on his preferences for return and risk. Tobin [15], Lintner [7], and Sharpe [11] have all shown that, if a riskless asset (such as a savings account) is included as a member of the investor's portfolio, the efficient frontier becomes *abce* in Figure 1 where point *e* represents the riskless asset with return $\bar{E}$ and point *c* is the point of tangency with a straight line segment from *e*. An investor will then select the particular portfolio along *abce* which best satisfies his return-risk preferences. This occurs at the tangency of the modified efficient set and his highest attainable indifference curve—such as at point *f* in Figure 1.[4]

If the investor is also able to borrow at rate $\bar{E}$, the straight line segment is extended and the portfolio at *c* is the optimal portfolio of risky securities selected in conjunction with borrowing and lending opportunities. Since it is impossible to specify indifference curves in general, and because the focus of this paper is only on portfolios of risky securities (common stocks), it is convenient simply to consider the portfolio at *c*, and assume that the investor will borrow or lend accordingly.

At the beginning of an investment period, it is assumed that an investment of size M_0' is made in the unique portfolio at *c*. This portfolio is described by the vector $X_0 = [x_{0j}]$, and also the vector $N_0 = [n_{0j}]$, where n_{0j} is the number of shares of security *j* that are held. This holding of security *j* corresponds to its participation level x_{0j} by the expression

$$n_{0j} = \frac{x_{0j} M_0'}{P_{0j}}, \tag{3}$$

where P_{0j} is the market price of security *j* at the time of purchase.[5] The characteristics of this initially selected portfolio (X_0, N_0) are return $E(X_0)$ and standard deviation $S(X_0)$.

At the end of the investment period, it is possible for the investor to revise his expectations for the *m* securities under consideration, and to compute a new or revised efficient frontier, such as *ghijk* in Figure 2. Moreover, when the investor's existing holdings are combined with revised expectations, his portfolio can also be located in the return-risk space, using equations (1) and (2). The existing portfolio is denoted by the vector $X_1 = [x_{1j}]$ where

---

4. In this context, the highest indifference curve means the curve which is furthest to the right in Figure 1. Tobin [15] has shown that if investors are risk-averters and diversifiers, and select portfolios based solely on $E(X)$ and $S(X)$, their indifference curves are concave from below, as indicated in Figure 1.

5. The resulting fraction was truncated so that only an incremental group of shares was purchased. This, plus the inclusion of brokerage fees necessary to purchase (X_0, N_0) resulted in an exact investment, M_0, which was approximately equal to M_0'.

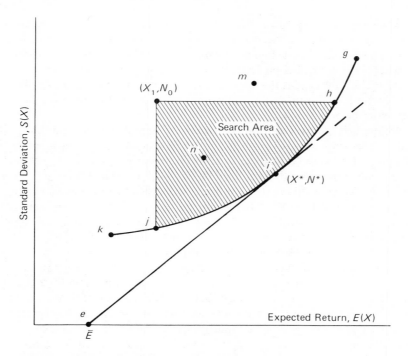

Figure 2. Efficient Set, Existing Portfolio, and Search Area at the End of the Investment Period

$$x_{1j} = \frac{n_{0j}p_{1j}}{\displaystyle\sum_{k=1}^{m} n_{0k}p_{1k}} \qquad (4)$$

and p_{1j} is the current price of security j. In general, $x_{1j} \neq x_{0j}$ since changing prices have effectively changed the participation level of each non-zero security. Although X_1 is different from X_0, the actual share holdings are still described by N_0.

Depending on the overall economic climate for risky securities, and the particular expectations for individual issues, the revised efficient set *ghijk* may have shifted either way from the former efficient frontier. Furthermore, the existing portfolio (X_1, N_0) will typically be inefficient when re-evaluated at the end of the first investment horizon. And, provided that the investor prefers to hold an efficient portfolio based on his revised expectations, he will thus want to change his holdings to reflect the inefficiency of (X_1, N_0).

When a riskless asset (point e in Figure 2) is included, the unique (tangency) portfolio at i is identified. This particular portfolio is the efficient combination of risky assets, which, when combined with borrowing or lending opportunities, best satisfies the return-risk preferences of the investor. The portfolio at i is denoted by (X^*, N^*) and is the target portfolio which the investor would like to hold—provided, of course, that he is willing to revise his expectations for all securities in the population.

Within such a framework, the portfolio revision problem can clearly be stated. The investor currently owns the portfolio denoted by (X_1, N_0), but he would prefer to change his holdings to reflect his revised expectations. Although any portfolio in the shaded area defined by (X_1, N_0), point h, and point j, would be preferable to his existing portfolio, the investor would ideally like to hold the portfolio at (X^*, N^*).[6] In the absence of transaction costs and capital gains taxes, the investor would simply make such a change. In a more realistic world, however, the investor must consider the advantage of holding (X^*, N^*) versus the total costs of obtaining such a portfolio.

If revision costs are excessive, the investor may consider changing to an intermediate portfolio, such as point n, which is inefficient but clearly preferable to his existing holdings. If it is assumed that certain portfolios, such as those at point m, are undesirable because the investor's risk position would be degraded, the shaded area of Figure 2 can be thought of as a search area for possible portfolio changes.[7] Such changes are not optimal in the Markowitz efficient sense, but they do offer the investor an improvement in portfolio position, which, under certain realistic conditions, may be in his best interest.

III. Four Alternative Procedures for Revision

The situation summarized in Figure 2 is a suggested framework for portfolio revision which extends the Markowitz efficient-set concept to an intertemporal basis. This section is a presentation of four distinct procedures, or

---

6. In an earlier paper [13], this author presented an alternative framework, in which the investor accepts the risk inherent in the existing portfolio (X_1, N_0), and attempts to make a transition, or change, to the portfolio at point h in Figure 2. This was justified because (1) the focus was only on horizons of two periods, and (2) it facilitated the comparison of the expected returns and costs involved. If such a procedure were followed over an extended investment horizon, there would tend to be an upward drift in portfolio risk over time. By continually focusing on the tangent portfolio (X^*, N^*), however, such a degradation is eliminated.

7. Unfortunately, Figure 2 does not fully illustrate all possibilities. For example, if either $S(X_1) < S(X^*)$ or $E(X_1) > E(X^*)$, the search area would not include the target portfolio. For this reason, the assumption of a well-defined search area was not adhered to in this study. Because of the investor's lending and borrowing opportunities, however, it is reasonable to always consider a movement from the existing to the target portfolio. This is explained further in the next section.

strategies, for revising investment portfolios within such a framework. The alternatives differ in their degree of conservatism concerning portfolio turnover, as well as the manner in which changing expectations are handled.

A. Unrevised Case

The first revision alternative is simply to do nothing. That is, the investor holds the unrevised portfolio (X_1, N_0), over the next investment period, or over an extended horizon of w periods. It is assumed that after-tax dividends are not reinvested in particular securities, but are simply made available to the investor. Although the total market value of the unrevised portfolio after w periods is given by

$$M'_w(UNR) = \sum_{k=1}^{m} n_{0k} P_{wk}, \tag{5}$$

it would be necessary to pay brokerage fees and capital gains taxes in order to obtain the actual cash value, $M_w(UNR)$, accruing to the investor.

The entire investment can be summarized by the initial cash outlay, M_0, a series of after-tax dividend payments over time, D_t, and the final cash value, $M_w(UNR)$. Annual yield to the investor for the unrevised case, $Y(UNR)$, is the rate-of-return which makes the present value of such a cash flow stream equal to zero. It is a cash-to-cash value, in the spirit of the empirical work of Fisher and Lorie [3], since the cash costs of both purchasing and selling the portfolio are included.

Although the primary focus of this paper is on revision alternatives, the unrevised case serves as a useful benchmark for comparison. In addition, it is a conservative strategy, in that costs of revision are minimized, as well as portfolio turnover.

B. Adjustment Case

The second revision alternative is also somewhat conservative in avoiding portfolio turnover, but it does involve an adjustment at the end of each period. It recognizes that the Markowitz selection methodology is based on return expectations for the next period only, but insists that initial expectations be maintained over the entire investment horizon. Moreover, it has already been shown that price fluctuations cause an existing portfolio to be inefficient when evaluated at the end of the next period. The adjustment strategy is simply to make the necessary changes in security holdings that will restore the original participation levels, X_0, at the beginning of each new investment period.

After the first period, for example, the required adjustment would be to change from (X_1, N_0) to (X_0, N_1). The revised share holdings are summarized by the vector $N_1 = [n_{ij}]$ where

$$n_{ij} = \frac{x_{0j} \sum_{k=1}^{m} n_{0k}(p_{1k} + d_{1k})}{p_{1j}} \qquad (6)$$

and d_{1k} is the after-tax per share dividend for security k assumed paid at the end of the first period. That is, the current market value of the portfolio is redistributed among the same securities according to initial participation levels.

Cash flow in the investor, at this point in time, C_1, is the composite effect of (1) after-tax cash dividends paid for that period, (2) all brokerage fees necessary to adjust the investor's holdings, and (3) capital gains taxes applicable when shares of any security are sold. This cash flow, which can be positive or negative depending on the particular situation, is treated as a residual rather than an active member of the portfolio. It would be expected to be quite small relative to the market value of the entire portfolio at the time of adjustment.

At the end of w periods, the total market value of the adjusted portfolio is

$$M_w'(ADJ) = \sum_{k=1}^{m} n_{w-1,k} p_{wk}, \qquad (7)$$

where $n_{w-1,k}$ represents the share holdings of security k after the last adjustment. Again, it would be necessary to pay brokerage fees and capital gains taxes in order to obtain the cash value, $M_w(ADJ)$. The investor's annual yield, $Y(ADJ)$, is computed as before, from the investment stream consisting of the initial investment, M_0, and the cash flow series, C_t, during the horizon, and the terminal value, $M_w(ADJ)$.

The adjustment strategy is based on the premise that expectations are stable over time, and that they will not be influenced by what happens in the securities markets during subsequent periods. The need to periodically adjust a portfolio back to its initial proportions was first suggested by Latané [6] in developing his balance model. It has also been discussed in a recent paper by Renshaw [10].

On *a priori* grounds, one might well argue that expectations should be expected to change over time, and, in fact, the underlying hypothesis of the revision framework (Figure 2) is that "new" efficient sets can be computed periodically. The adjustment alternative to portfolio revision also means that only those securities in the initial portfolio selected can ever appear in the investor's holdings. That is, revision, in the adjustment case, is limited to changes in holding levels within the initial set of securities. There is no entering or exiting of securities from the portfolio. Once committed, a given level of a particular security must be maintained.

C. Complete Transition

The third and fourth alternatives for portfolio revision are based on the opposite belief that expectations do change when investors are exposed to market performance and additional information about securities. However, they differ only in the procedure for reflecting such expectations.

The complete transition alternative was alluded to in the previous section. At the beginning of each period, a complete change is made from the existing (and re-evaluated) portfolio (X_1, N_0) to the appropriate target portfolio (X^*, N^*). The actual share holdings in the target portfolio are given by $N^* = [n_j^*]$ where

$$ n_j^* = \frac{x_j^* \left[\sum_{k=1}^{m} n_{0k}(p_{1k} + d_{1k}) \right]}{p_{1j}} \qquad (8) $$

This differs from Equation (6) in that new participation levels for the target portfolio, x_j^*, replace the levels, x_{0j}, which are maintained over the entire investment horizon in the adjustment case. It also infers that securities may leave or enter the portfolio as expectations change over time.

The cash flow associated with a complete transition includes the effects of after-tax dividends, brokerage fees, and capital gains tax. Again, the cash flow may be positive or negative, but its absolute size would still be expected to be small, relative to the overall portfolio investment. The annual yield to an investor, when complete transitions are made at the end of w periods, is designated as $Y(TAR)$. It is the internal rate-of-return corresponding to the cash flows and terminal value for the complete transition alternative.

Complete transitions are at an opposite extreme from the unrevised case, in that revised expectations are fully reflected in the revision strategy. Moreover, transitions are made without any ex ante consideration of the relevant costs involved.[8] So, depending upon the extent to which expectations change, the

---

8. In the earlier paper [13], transition costs were explained and a complete transition was not considered feasible unless the gain in expected return exceeded the transition costs

turnover in security holdings can be quite high as securities enter or leave
the portfolio. But, as previously mentioned, in the absence of transition costs,
complete transitions would represent the optimal revision strategy and the
Markowitz concept of efficient portfolios would be continually reflected
throughout the investment horizon.

D. Controlled Transition

The fourth alternative strategy is motivated by a desire to avoid the
excessive turnover of a complete transition, but still reflect changing expectations
and the efficient-set concept. The basic idea is to consider changes in the
investment level of individual securities in an iterative fashion. The search region
for such iterations is the indicated area in Figure 2. It is possible that a few
chosen changes will achieve the majority of the gain in expected return in
moving from (X_1, N_0) to (X^*, N^*), but at a considerable savings in total transition cost.

A major difficulty, in an ex ante sense, of making a transition of any sort is
comparing changes in risk position with possible improvements in expected
portfolio return. That is, there is a problem in trying to reduce return and risk to
a common denominator. For the purpose of a controlled transition, however,
this problem is handled by remembering that the investor is assumed to have
borrowing and lending opportunities. Furthermore, by combining a risk-free
asset with a risky portfolio in the appropriate proportions, an investor can
induce any desired level of risk. This levering possibility is the cornerstone of
the controlled transition concept.

Consider the situation depicted in Figure 3. The existing and target
portfolios are (X_1, N_0) and (X^*, N^*), respectively, and the risk-free asset has a
return of $\bar{E}$. Since (X^*, N^*) is the desired portfolio, its risk characteristic,
$S(X^*)$, is taken as a reference level (in risk-return space) for possible security
changes.

The straight line from $\bar{E}$ to (X_1, N_0) represents all possible combinations
of the existing portfolio and the risk-free asset. This line crosses the risk reference
at an expected return of $E_c(X_1)$, which may be thought of as the risk-equivalent
return associated with the portfolio $(X_1 N_0)$. Moreover, *any* portfolio in the
return-risk space may be evaluated in terms of its unique risk-equivalent return,
which is determined in a similar manner. Such a procedure effectively reduces
the separate dimensions of risk and return to a single scale—the reference (risk)
level associated with the target portfolio.

---

involved. In this study, the tradeoff between expected gain and expected cost provided
the impetus for developing the controlled transition procedure. For all cases, however,
actual (as opposed to expected) transition costs were included in the ex post measurement
of portfolio performance.

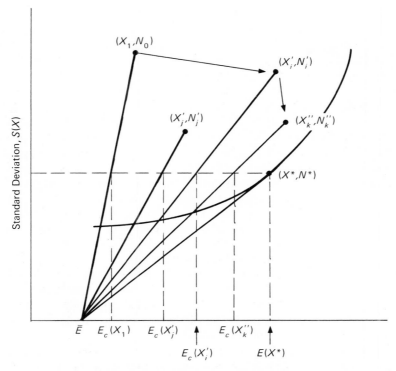

Figure 3. Risk Equivalent Analysis of Typical Iterations For a Controlled Transition

The controlled transition begins by considering all possible changes of a single security. By such a change for security j is meant the change in share holdings from the existing portfolio, n_{0j}, to that indicated for the target portfolio, n_j^*. This could involve buying or selling of security j, depending on the particular situation. The portfolio resulting from changing n_{0j} to n_j^* is denoted by the vectors (X_j', N_j').[9] Note that only one element in the share vector changes, while all values in the participation-level vector necessarily are affected. Finally, the risk-equivalent return associated with a single transition to (X_j', N_j') is denoted by $E_c(X_j')$.

The suggested procedure is to compute the risk-equivalent return for each single-security change, and then to determine the change which has the largest value. For example, in Figure 3, a change of holdings for security i is seen to

9. It is well to clarify the notation which is used. Subscripts on the vectors in the representation (X_j', N_j') indicate the single security whose holding was changed. The primes indicate that this is the first iteration of the controlled transition. Conversely, (X_k'', N_k'') means that on the second iteration, the holdings of security k are altered.

be preferable to a change in security j because $E_c(X_i') > E_c(X_j')$. For convenience, assume that $E_c(X_i') = MAX_j[E_c(X_j')]$. The gain in expected return from this change, on an equivalent-risk level, is simply $E_c(X_i')$ minus $E_c(X_1)$. The expected costs associated with the change consist of (1) the brokerage fees necessary to effect the change in the security i, and (2) the tax opportunity cost if shares are sold and taxable capital gains result.[10] If expected gain exceeds expected cost, the single-security change is feasible, the transition is made, and a successful iteration is recorded.[11] It should be noted that the risk-equivalent return concept is only used to establish a common denominator among various portfolios. It is not intended to infer the extent to which an investor might use a risk-free asset to adjust his risk position.

Once a successful iteration is made, the procedure enters the next phase, which is simply a continuation using the "pseudo-existing" portfolio (X_i', N_i') and the same target (X^*, N^*). A search is made of possible single-security changes, and the one with the largest risk-equivalent return is determined. Suppose $E_c(X_k'') = MAX_j[E_c(X_j'')]$. The gain in return, as measured from the previous iteration, is $E_c(X_k'')$ minus $E_c(X_i')$ and is compared with cost of change from (X_i', N_i') to (X_k'', N_k''). The iterative procedure continues as long as feasible changes can be found. It is easy to show that such an iterative process converges to the target portfolio (X^*, N^*). That is, if any portfolio has a risk-equivalent return greater than $E(X^*)$, it must necessarily lie outside the efficient frontier, but this contradicts the basic idea of the Markowitz concept.

The upper bound on the controlled iterative process, therefore, is a complete transition to the target (X^*, N^*), which is the alternative previously discussed. The final iteration of the controlled procedure is then held for the next investment period, after which it is re-evaluated in light of revised expectations and the procedure is applied once more. The realized yield after w periods is designated by $Y(CON)$, and it is consistent with the internal rate used for the previous revision alternatives. The only difference is that the cash flows may be larger than in the previous cases, particularly if only a few iterations are made. For example, if the only iteration is to sell a certain number of shares of a certain security, the cash flow would be an inflow to the investor. Conversely, the purchase of additional shares would necessitate an additional investment outlay. Over several iterations, however, such flows would tend to balance out.

In particular, the controlled transition alternative is an iterative search for single-security changes which satisfy the expected return—expected cost criterion. Although the procedure typically results in investors holding inefficient port-

---

10. For an explicit treatment of tax opportunity costs associated with taking a capital gain, see Smith [13].

11. An alternative procedure would be to select the single-security change which gives the largest net improvement of expected return less transition cost. Because expected return typically exceeds transition cost by a large amount, the two methods give almost identical sequences of iterations.

folios, focus remains on the aggregate portfolio rather than on individual securities. The controlled transition strategy is intended as a compromise between the theoretical content of the Markowitz selection model and the real-world consideration of transition costs and portfolio turnover.

Although his model essentially deals with portfolio selection at a certain point in time, Markowitz was well aware of the illiquidities that would be encountered over time.[12] The need to consider the costs of making periodic changes in a portfolio has also been pointed out by Fanning [2] in his survey discussion of investment management. Finally, the concept of a controlled transition is a particular example of a recent statement by Heller [4] that "the economic practitioner has to operate deep in the heart of realism, and has to deal with movement toward rather than to the ideal."

IV. Simulation Experiment

The previous section has explained four alternative procedures for revising investment portfolios. The procedures range from no change, to change based on stable expectations, to change based on revised expectations. As such, they represent a spectrum of revision strategies rather than an exhaustive set of possible procedures.

In order to subject the four alternatives to an empirical test, portfolio selection and revision were simulated over the 1946–1965 period. The population of securities which was used consisted of the common stocks of 132 firms. All of these firms, whose shares are traded on the New York Stock Exchange, are large and well-known. Basic data for the simulation consisted of adjusted year-end prices and annual cash dividends for the 132 common stocks.[13]

The methodology used for portfolio selection was the diagonal reformulation, by Sharpe [11], of the Markowitz efficient-set model. By relating security yield to an index of market activity in a linear formulation, the diagonal model infers each covariance term s_{ij} from the mutual relationship of securities i and j with the given index. In addition to being computationally advantageous, Smith [14] has shown that if a stock price index is used, the Sharpe model can be expected to capture the true (historical) covariance relationships that are involved in diversification. Finally, Cohen and Pogue [1] have indicated that the single-index model is preferable to the more complicated multi-index model, particularly when the universe consists of a single type of security, such as common stocks.

Inputs for the Markowitz-Sharpe selection model were generated using

12. See Markowitz [8], pp. 274–303.
13. Data was provided by the Standard and Poor's Compustat Service. The population is a subset of 150 common stocks used in the earlier study [13]. The total number was necessarily reduced so that complete data for the 20-year horizon would be available.

Standard and Poor's industrial stock price index, which consists of 425 issues. Five years of prior data were used in each case, although recent data were weighted more heavily using multiple observations. Input data were weighted in this manner so that the revision process would be sensitive to recent market information. Furthermore, the expected returns, used in preparing inputs for each security, were calculated on an after-tax basis. Dividends were taxed at a rate of 59 percent (the 1962 marginal tax rate for an investor with taxable income of $50,000 and filing a joint rate) and capital gains at 25 percent. The input values generated in this manner for each of the 132 securities were then used to generate efficient sets.

An efficient set of portfolios was generated at the end of 1951, and similarly for each of the next 12 years. A risk-free asset was also included so that the tangent portfolio (point c in Figure 1) could be located. The risk-free asset was assigned an expected, after-tax return of 2.05 percent, which corresponded to a 5 percent dividend return, such as for a savings and loan account, taxed at 59 percent. Using participation levels from the efficient set analysis, X_0, a total portfolio investment of $200,000 was distributed among the indicated participants. Using the appropriate prices, the incremental number of shares for each security was calculated. The exact investment at the beginning of the two-period horizon, M_0, reflected the simulated purchase of such a portfolio, and included an exact brokerage fee function.

Each portfolio thus selected was held until the end of 1965. An investment period was taken to be one year, so that each initial portfolio was subjected annually to each of the four revision procedures.[14] For each of the 52 situations (4 revision alternatives times 13 starting points), dividends were totaled and taxed at the 59 percent rate at the end of each year. When adjustments or revisions were made, depending on the particular alternative being examined, capital gains taxes (25 percent rate) were paid on all terminated positions. The net effect of dividends, taxes, and the buying or selling of different shares resulted in a unique cash flow for each year. The internal rate-of-return for each investment pattern was then calculated by solving the appropriate polynomial equation.[15]

In addition to a research design covering extended horizons from various starting points to the end of 1965, portfolio operations were also simulated over abbreviated horizons of two years. For example, an initial portfolio was purchased at the end of 1951. One year later, at the end of 1952, a revision alternative was applied, and the resulting portfolio was held for a second year before holdings were terminated. The same was done for each of the four

---

14. Application of the four revision alternatives at more frequent intervals is discussed in Section VI.

15. The method of solution which was used is an approximating procedure which computes the internal rate-of-return in less than ten iterations. Such a method was discussed and used by Herzog [5] and also by Fisher and Lorie [3].

alternatives. Although primary emphasis was on results over extended horizons, the results for abbreviated horizons served to illustrate the highly situational nature of certain revision alternatives, as well as to indicate the cyclical movement of the securities markets during the 1951-1965 period.

V. Discussion of Results

Consider first the portfolio yields which resulted when the four revision alternatives were applied over extended horizons. These results appear as Table 7-1. A cursory comparison of these values suggests that no single procedure or strategy dominated the others. Highest yields for a given horizon were achieved five times for controlled, four times for adjusted, and two times each for unrevised and complete. Although the controlled strategy worked best in more cases, it gave these results during the earlier (and hence longer) horizons.

Sub-comparisons are also of interest. There was very little difference (seven versus six horizons of higher yields) between the unrevised and adjusted cases which suggests that there was little added payoff in continually adjusting back to the initial participation levels. Conversely, controlled transitions gave higher yields than their complete transition counterparts in eight of thirteen horizons. Finally, either a complete or controlled transition gave higher yields than the unrevised strategy in nine of thirteen horizons, which tentatively suggests that there is an advantage to reflecting expectational changes in an investment strategy over time.

Table 7-1

Cash-to Cash Portfolio Yields from Alternative Revision Procedures over Extended Horizons (Percents)

Investment Horizon	Unrevised Case Y(UNR)	Adjustment Case Y(ADJ)	Complete Transition Y(TAR)	Controlled Transition Y(CON)
1952–1965	12.22	10.80	11.48	12.51
1953–1965	11.47	10.90	11.57	12.86
1954–1965	13.16	12.58	12.19	12.91
1955–1965	10.02	10.08	10.46	12.15
1956–1965	8.91	8.82	9.82	11.81
1957–1965	10.49	11.32	10.95	12.50
1958–1965	11.11	11.65	10.69	11.33
1959–1965	7.08	8.26	7.15	7.12
1960–1965	6.14	6.98	5.67	5.57
1961–1965	3.57	3.28	8.15	7.78
1962–1965	1.59	1.42	6.43	5.97
1963–1965	15.65	16.62	13.74	13.50
1964–1965	19.19	18.15	16.46	17.40

It should be noted, however, that these results are influenced by the cumulative effects inherent in the research design. That is, a bad result in a certain year could seriously affect the yields for all horizons which include that year. For that reason, and also to examine cyclical effects, the results over abbreviated horizons were also investigated. These results appear as Table 7-2. The last rows of Tables 7-1 and 7-2 are identical, of course, since they represent the same two-year horizon, 1964-1965. With the exception of the unrevised case where no action was taken, abbreviated horizons represent a single application of the adjustment or revision procedure. In a rough sense, the extended horizon results are a composite of those for the abbreviated horizons. Results are not multiplicative, however, because of different starting conditions and, because for the former, portfolios were not sold until the end of the extended horizon.

In comparing portfolio yields presented in Tables 7-1 and 7-2, one quickly notes the higher variation in yields over abbreviated horizons. Values range from over 40 percent, in one instance, to negative yields for certain of the horizons, including 1962, which featured a sharp market break. Conversely, these cyclical effects tended to even out over the longer, extended horizons.

Largest yields over abbreviated horizons were achieved primarily by the unrevised and controlled strategies with no particular pattern over time. Only twice did the adjustment case give better results than an unrevised strategy,

Table 7-2
Cash-to-Cash Portfolio Yields from Alternative Revision Procedures over Abbreviated Horizons (Percents)

Investment Horizon	Unrevised Case Y(UNR)	Adjustment Case Y(ADJ)	Complete Transition Y(TAR)	Controlled Transition Y(CON)
1952-1953	6.49	6.27	5.64	6.13
1953-1954	14.73	14.62	18.87	18.90
1954-1955	29.18	28.82	27.09	27.18
1955-1956	8.87	8.52	7.75	8.01
1956-1957	2.47	1.93	5.52	5.65
1957-1958	25.86	24.37	27.00	28.82
1958-1959	40.05	38.47	28.19	28.19[a]
1959-1960	7.67	4.50	4.46	7.67[b]
1960-1961	-2.47	-2.96	3.82	3.87
1961-1962	-1.47	-1.42	0.28	0.56
1962-1963	0.55	0.25	-2.90	-3.05
1963-1964	14.18	14.20	13.86	13.12
1964-1965	19.19	18.15	16.46	17.40

[a]Controlled yield was same as complete yield because target portfolio was reached in successive iterations.
[b]Controlled yield was same as unrevised yield because no successful iterations were made.

and a controlled strategy outperformed the complete transition method except in the last three horizons. These results suggest that over shorter horizons, investors should either buy and hold, or buy and revise in a limited manner. That is, the higher portfolio turnover, which is characteristic of the adjusted and complete alternatives, is more useful over longer investment horizons.

Certain results in Table 7-2 also serve to illustrate the highly situational nature of controlled transition strategy. For the 1958-1959 horizon, the controlled alternative continued until a complete transition was reached—as noted by similar yields for the two revision alternatives. At the other extreme, not a single iteration was feasible for the 1959-1960 horizon, and thus the controlled yield was the same as that for the unrevised case. That is, at the end of 1959, it was not possible to find a single-security change which gave a dollar improvement in expected return (on a risk-equivalent basis) that exceeded the expected dollar cost of such a change. These two extremes occurred only once, however, and typically the controlled transitions ended with an intermediate portfolio that offered some improvement in return for only a fraction of the total cost necessary to reach the target portfolio.

Further details on the complete and controlled transition alternatives are presented in Table 7-3. For each abbreviated horizon, it is seen that complete transition was feasible in the sense that increased expected return, in moving

Table 7-3

Cost-Effectiveness of Controlled versus Complete Transitions over Abbreviated Horizons

Investment Horizon	Complete Transitions		Controlled Transitions		
	Increased Expected Return	Expected Transition Cost	Number of Iterations	Expected Return Achieved	Transition Cost Incurred
1952-1953	$12,700	$2,095	34	73.6%	58.3%
1953-1954	19,799	1,973	59	99.0	84.0
1954-1955	23,049	6,414	4	11.5	4.2
1955-1956	7,885	2,509	10	96.3	84.9
1956-1957	24,323	1,403	34	99.8	96.1
1957-1958	20,654	1,550	12	65.9	21.6
1958-1959	17,847	6,617	18	100.0	100.0[a]
1959-1960	4,505	2,171	0	0.0	0.0[b]
1960-1961	35,060	718	17	99.9	93.1
1961-1962	28,897	1,449	12	99.6	90.8
1962-1963	12,055	114	20	95.8	—[c]
1963-1964	4,867	1,528	5	82.3	57.4
1964-1965	4,496	1,246	10	85.9	50.4

[a]Controlled same as complete.

[b]Controlled same as unrevised.

[c]Not applicable. Transition cost for controlled transition was negative because of capital gains tax offset.

from the existing portfolio to the appropriate target, exceeded the expected cost of transition.[16] And, in most cases, return was several times greater than cost. This is explained, in large part, by the length of the period under consideration. Obviously, expectations can change radically during a 12-month period, as witnessed by the relatively wide range of return and cost expectations.[17] If a revision alternative, such as the complete transition, was applied at more frequent intervals, return would not be expected to dominate cost in every case.

Complete transitions are also useful to explore the cost-effectiveness of the controlled transition procedure, since they represent the upper limit on the single-chance iterations that can be made. The highly situational nature of controlled transitions are again noted in the number of successful iterations for each application.[18] This high variability is attributed to cyclical market trends together with changing expectational patterns. The latter are inherent in the historical extrapolation method for preparing inputs for the portfolio selection model.

The final two columns of Table 7-3 indicate how effectively the controlled procedure was able to move the existing portfolio toward its corresponding target portfolio. Consider, for example, the 1952-1953 horizon. At the end of 1952, after 34 iterations, the final portfolio achieved 73.6 percent of the total gain in the expected return that a complete transition would have realized, but at only 58.3 percent of the total expected cost of a complete transition. Again, high variability was observed for the iterative procedure ranging between the two extremes, 1957-1958 and 1958-1959, which have already been discussed. For many of the horizons, however, it was possible to almost reach the target at a significant savings in transition costs. This analysis, of course, is ex ante since it is the expectations for benefits and costs which are compared, and should not be confused with the ex post results of Table 7-2.

VI. Frequency of Revision

Complete transitions, and controlled transitions to a lesser but perhaps more realistic degree, capture the essence of the Markowitz efficient-set concept

16. It should be clear that these are ex ante estimates prior to actually making the transition. Furthermore, expected transition cost is not a cash flow but rather an opportunity cost measure which includes the foregone expected return when capital gains are taken, as well as all brokerage fees incurred in the transition.

17. Extremely low cost values for the 1960-1961 and 1962-1963 horizons occurred because of the offsetting effect of high capital losses during 1960 and 1962, respectively.

18. The upper limit on possible iterations is the number of securities in the union of two sets—the set of participants in the existing portfolio, and the set of participants in the target portfolio. Typically, the tangent portfolio along the efficient frontier had less than 20 participants. The lone exception to this was the year-end 1952 tangent portfolio which had a higher level of diversification. This explains the high number of iterations for the 1953-1954 investment horizon.

on an intertemporal basis. The foregoing empirical results suggest that, over many horizons, investors could well have profited from a periodic updating of their portfolios reflecting their changing expectations for various securities. The failure of any single revision alternative to dominate over all horizons is attributed to cyclical movements of the security market, the highly situational nature of particular securities within particular portfolios, and an overall uncertainty associated with the investment process.

Furthermore, the ex post portfolio yields of Tables 7-1 and 7-2 suggest that the complete and controlled transition procedures worked better during the strong upward market of the late 1950's and less well during the early 1960's, when substantial downturns were experienced. Whereas these revision alternatives both reflect current market information, the frequency of revision itself becomes an important variable. If the market turned downward during an investment period of one year, it could well be several months before the revision routine would have an opportunity to reflect this information and eliminate certain issues whose expectations had changed substantially.

It seemed of interest, therefore, to see if the suggested procedures for revising investment portfolios could produce better yields if applied at more frequent intervals. To this end, the research design was extended to include investment periods of three months and six months, as well as twelve months for yearly revision. A smaller population of fifty securities was used to compare the four revision alternatives—applied annually, semi-annually, and quarterly.[19] This additional simulation was conducted for the extended horizon 1952-1965, and the two-period, abbreviated horizon 1952-1953. As such, it was intended as a representative, rather than an exhaustive, testing of the revision alternatives at selected frequencies.

At first blush, the approach seemed to be one of simply applying the four revision alternatives at the three different frequencies and comparing ex post yields. In so doing, however, one would, in effect, be considering not only the revision alternatives, but the methods used for generating inputs for the Markowitz/Sharpe diagonal model. In the previous simulation, five years of historical price and dividend data (five observations) were extrapolated, using an appropriate weighting scheme, to generate inputs for the portfolio selection model. When one applies revision alternatives on a quarterly basis, however, a comparable five years of historical data would involve twenty observations.

It became necessary, therefore, to disentangle the input preparation process from the revision alternatives. This was accomplished by first applying

19. Data for this phase of the research was provided by the Center for Research in Security Prices (sponsored by Merrill, Lynch, Pierce, Fenner and Smith, Inc.), Graduate School of Business, University of Chicago. The particular tape which was used includes adjusted monthly closing prices of common stocks listed and traded on the New York Stock Exchange. The population of fifty common stocks was a non-random sample. It consisted of the first fifty stocks from the tape that had been listed continuously from 1946 to the present.

the revision procedures with the input process effectively held constant. That is, on each occasion when inputs were prepared for all securities in the population, only five observations were used, one each for the preceding five years. Although the process was identical to that previously used for an investment period of one year, it deliberately ignored certain data when the investment period was either six months or three months. This is referred to as the "partial" information procedure.

Then this restriction was relaxed, and all available information was used in each application of the complete and controlled transition alternatives. In the "full" information procedure for semi-annual revision, a total of ten observations on security price were used to generate data inputs—namely, two observations from each of the previous five years. Unlike the previous design, however, dividends were assumed to be zero for all securities, and thus only price appreciation effects were reflected in the ensuing experiment. Correspondingly, twenty observations were used for quarterly revisions. In all other respects, the research design was identical to the previous work, and yields again were the internal rate-of-return for particular cash flow patterns.

Ex post portfolio yields are presented in Table 7–4 for both extended and abbreviated horizons. The first column of results is for the unrevised case, and the values are seen to be independent of the frequency of revision. This occurred because dividends were not considered, and because no further changes were made once the initial portfolio was selected. Expectations also were not changed in the adjustment case, and there was no realized advantage in a periodic adjustment back to the initial participation levels determined by the portfolio selection model. In fact, a degradation in ex post yield was experienced when

Table 7–4

Cash-to-Cash Portfolio Yields from Alternative Revision Procedures at Selected Frequencies Over Representative Investment Horizons

Frequency	Unrevised Case	Adjusted Case	Complete Transition		Controlled Transition	
			Partial	Full	Partial	Full
Extended Horizon 1952–1965						
Annually	8.92	7.89	8.74	8.74	8.63	8.63
Semi-Annually	8.92	7.40	8.50	9.22	5.78	9.13
Quarterly	8.92	7.34	8.35	10.38	7.37	12.04
Abbreviated Horizon 1952–1953						
Annually	0.85	0.33	1.19	1.19	1.70	1.70
Semi-Annually	0.85	0.28	2.18	2.18	1.24	1.94
Quarterly	0.85	0.13	1.59	2.51	1.23	2.14

the adjustment was made at more frequent intervals. This was doubtless due to higher transition costs associated with more frequent adjustments.

Conversely, ex post yields for complete and controlled transitions were highly dependent on the type of input process used. In the case of "partial" information where certain available data was ignored, the return to investors did not improve when the method was applied more frequently. But for the "full" information design, where all available information was used, yields improved significantly when the revision procedure was used more often. For example, in the case of using complete transitions over the extended horizon, annual yields improved from a small disadvantage to a sizable advantage, relative to the unrevised case.

Comparable yield patterns were also observed for the controlled transition alternative over both the abbreviated and extended horizons. These preliminary results affirmed the hypothesis that frequency of revision is, itself, an important aspect of the investment management process, and that investors should avail themselves of available market information.

As before, the abbreviated horizon can be used to examine the cost-effectiveness of the iterative feature of controlled transitions. Consider the full information case over the 1952–1953 horizon. The number of individual applications of the revision procedure over this two-year period was $2T - 1$ where T equaled the number of investment periods per year. Thus, complete or controlled transitions were applied 1, 3, and 7 times, respectively, for annual $(T = 1)$, semi-annual $(T = 2)$, and quarterly $(T = 4)$ revision. Results of the cost-effectiveness analysis are presented as Table 7–5.

Table 7–5
Cost-Effectiveness of Controlled versus Complete Transitions for Selected Frequencies Over Abbreviated Horizon 1952–1953

	Complete Transitions		Controlled Transitions		
Frequency	Increased Expected Return	Expected Transition Cost	Number of Iterations	Expected Return Achieved	Transition Cost Incurred
Annually	$15,031	$1,504	28	94.0%	85.9%
Semi-Annually	$ 1,287 2,137 2,878	$ 686 783 972	6 10 12	85.0% 89.5 89.5	32.1% 66.3 58.0
Quarterly	$ 418 484 1,129 446 213 910 683	$ 680 592 636 528 531 1,005 658	3 2 8 4 1 3 3	65.7% 60.4 81.0 79.9 31.5 54.6 70.3	21.5% 37.8 59.9 35.6 7.9 16.6 28.0

A first consideration is the feasibility of complete transitions. For both annual and semi-annual revision, increase in expected dollar returns exceeded expected transition cost, and each complete transition was feasible. When applied quarterly, however, only two of seven complete transitions were feasible. This is attributed to the fact that expectations do not change as much over three-month periods, and hence the difference, $E(X^*) - E_c(X_1)$, was typically quite smaller than comparable amounts in the annual case.

The degree of expectational change for different frequencies was also reflected in the number of successful iterations which were made in the iterative process of controlled transitions. As seen in Table 7–5, there was a positive relationship between number of iterations and length of investment period. Hence, a longer interval between revisions results in greater changes in expectations, a larger search area between (X_0, N_1) and (X^*, N^*), and a larger sequence of single-security changes which improve the risk-equivalent return of the portfolio.

Finally, the last two columns of Table 7–5 compare the benefits and costs of revision at different frequencies. A comparison of these results with those from Table 7–3 suggests that cost-effectiveness also improves with lengthening of the investment period. But this is merely consistent with the observation that both size of search area and number of iterations increase with investment period length. Certainly, improved yields, from more frequent use of the controlled procedure, offsets such a degradation in cost-effectiveness.

VII. Implications

This study was concerned with the development and empirical test of alternative procedures for revising investment portfolios over time. The revision alternatives differ mainly in their treatment of changing expectations for all securities under consideration. The unrevised case ignores such change; the adjusted case insists on maintaining initial expectations; while the complete and controlled transitions reflect changing expectations. Although the latter two alternatives are both based on the efficient-set concept of Markowitz, they differ in their consideration of transition costs and portfolio turnover.

In addition to providing the investor with portfolios having preferable ex ante characteristics, complete and controlled transitions resulted in higher ex post yields than did the alternative strategies over many of the horizons investigated. Although complete transitions periodically return the investor's portfolio to the efficient frontier, the controlled transition was able to achieve near-efficiency with a substantially lower portfolio turnover. Finally, a preliminary investigation of investment timing indicated that yields could be significantly improved if complete or controlled transitions were applied at more frequent intervals. The implication of these findings is that investment managers can profitably take advantage of market information in revising their portfolios, in a manner that is theoretically sound, but without sacrificing conservative attitudes toward portfolio turnover.

The controlled transition procedure is essentially a search for single-security changes which iteratively improve the return-risk position of the investor's portfolio. It should be noted that this is only one of many possible search procedures within the framework of Figure 2. For example, one could investigate simultaneous changes in two, or three, or even more securities. Higher levels are equivalent to a combinatorial search, however, and necessitate inclusion of search costs along with transition costs.

Beyond the usual qualifications attributable to research design, two important limitations should also be mentioned. The first is that the Markowitz/ Sharpe model, which was used, does not include an upper-bound constraint on the participation level of any given security. Although the average number of participants in an efficient portfolio was about 20 for the horizons covered, occasionally an individual common stock comprised as much as 15–20 percent of the total portfolio investment. This may well be objectionable in view of certain legal constraints which prohibit investment levels beyond 5 percent, for example. The implication of adding a constraint set, which prohibits high participation levels, is to induce greater diversification within the portfolio, but in adopting such a conservative strategy, the full power of the Markowitz concept is reduced. It was felt that upper-bound constraints, as well as other restraints peculiar to particular institutional investors, could always be added as further refinement to the methodology.

The second limitation has to do with the revision framework and the length of the planning horizon. Probably the strongest argument which can be levied against the revision methods developed in this study is that they are in no sense optimal. That is, they involve the successive application of a single-period static model over a multi-period horizon. A truly optimal model for dynamic portfolio revision would necessarily involve the forming of expectations for all securities over all periods of the planning horizon. And, although portfolio changes could still be made periodically, based on current information, such changes would always be optimal with respect to the remainder of the horizon.

A multi-period model for portfolio revision was not attempted, however, because of the nature of the input generating process. It can be noted that the entire process, described in this paper, is based on an historical record of price and dividend data—plus a few arbitrarily chosen parameters such as tax and brokerage fee rates. Paralleling any attempt to refine the procedures suggested in this paper, or to extend them to a multi-period basis, it is important to again consider the neglected problem of how to generate the necessary expectational data for each security in the population. At best, this study revealed the benefits of using all available information in the input process. If portfolio revision can improve an unrevised portfolio, such as has been shown, then improved inputs, utilizing the subjective but experienced feelings of security analysts, should add even greater potential to the suggested alternatives for revising investment portfolios.

References

1. Cohen, K.J., and J.A. Pogue, "An Empirical Evaluation of Alternative Portfolio Selection Models," *Journal of Business*, 40 (April 1967), pp. 166–193.
2. Fanning, J.E., "How to Improve Investment Decisions," *Harvard Business Review*, 44 (January–February 1966), pp. 156–168.
3. Fisher, L., and J.H. Lorie, "Rates of Return on Investments in Common Stocks," *Journal of Business*, 37 (January 1964), pp. 1–21.
4. Heller, W.W., *New Dimensions of Political Economy* (Cambridge, Mass.: Harvard University Press, 1966).
5. Herzog, J.P., "Investor Experience in Corporate Securities: A New Technique for Measurement," *Journal of Finance*, 19 (March 1964), pp. 46–62.
6. Latané, H.W., "Investment Criteria: A Three Asset Portfolio Balance Model," *Review of Economics and Statistics*, 45 (November 1963), pp. 427–430.
7. Lintner, J., "The Valuation of Risk Assets and the Selection of Risky Investments in Stock Portfolios and Capital Budgets," *Review of Economics and Statistics*, 47 (February 1965), pp. 13–37.
8. Markowitz, H.M., *Portfolio Selection: Efficient Diversification of Investments* (New York: John Wiley & Sons, Inc., 1959).
9. Pogue, J.A., "An Adaptive Model for Investment Management," Paper presented at the Thirty-First National Meeting of the Operations Research Society of America, New York City, June 1, 1967.
10. Renshaw, E.A., "Portfolio Balance Models in Perspective: Some Generalizations That Can Be Derived from the Two Asset Case," *Journal of Financial and Quantitative Analysis*, 2 (June 1967), pp. 123–149.
11. Sharpe, W.F., "A Simplified Model for Portfolio Analysis," *Management Science*, 9 (January 1963), pp. 277–293.
12. Smith, K.V., "Needed: A Dynamic Approach to Investment Management," *Financial Analysts Journal*, 23 (May–June 1967), pp. 115–117.
13. ——, "A Transition Model for Portfolio Revision," *Journal of Finance*, 22 (September 1967), pp. 425–439.
14. ——, "Stock Price and Economic Indices for Generating Efficient Portfolios," *Journal of Business* (forthcoming).
15. Tobin, J., "Liquidity Preference as Behavior Towards Risk," *Review of Economic Studies*, 25 (February 1958), pp. 65–86.

Part III
The Assessment Problem

8

Risk, Ambiguity, and the Savage Axioms: Comment*

Harry V. Roberts
University of Chicago

I. Are There Uncertainties That Are Not Risks?

Daniel Ellsberg has recently revived interest in the distinction between "measurable uncertainties," or "risks," and "unmeasurable uncertainties," or "uncertainties."[1] Ellsberg argues that vagueness about probabilities can lead people to violate the axioms of consistent behavior, the "Savage axioms," upon which modern Bayesian decision theory and inference is based. He contends that some of these violations are conscious and deliberate, not careless mistakes that would be retracted after careful reflection. From this Ellsberg concludes that Bayesian theory is applicable to decision-making under risk but not to decision-making under uncertainty. For dealing with uncertainty a more elaborate theory is needed, and Ellsberg proposes such a theory.

The problem of uncertainty that concerns Ellsberg is real and important, but his diagnosis and therapy seem to me to be a step in the wrong direction. People who are reluctant to use Bayesian theory are likely to be even more reluctant to use Ellsberg's modification of it. The modification demands additional formal assessments of things that are hard to assess, and difficulties of formal assessments are really at the heart of almost all objections to the Bayesian approach, at least by skeptical statisticians.[2] I shall not, however, press my

Reprinted by permission of the publisher and author from *The Quarterly Journal of Economics*, May 1963, pp. 327–36.

*Valuable comments on earlier drafts of this paper have been given by Gordon Antelman, Selwyn Becker, Ward Edwards, Bruno de Finetti, Giora Hanach, William Kruskal, John Pratt, L.J. Savage, Robert Schlaifer, Lester Telser, and members of the Econometrics Workshop, University of Chicago.

1. Daniel Ellsberg, "Risk, Ambiguity, and the Savage Axioms," *The Quarterly Journal of Economics*, LXXV (Nov. 1961), 643–69. See also William Fellner, "Distortion of Subjective Probabilities as a Reaction to Uncertainty," this *Journal*, LXXV (Nov. 1961), 670–89.

2. The other objection commonly advanced by skeptical statisticians is that Bayesian methods, applied to some particular problem, might involve prohibitive computation or prohibitive analytical difficulty. This objection seems less fundamental than the one mentioned in the text. If the only difficulties were computational or analytical, the Bayesian framework would still seem useful in suggesting approximate solutions or in evaluating rules-of-thumb.

objections to Ellsberg's therapy. Rather, I shall argue that his diagnosis is wrong, and that the "risk-uncertainty" dichotomy is not really a fruitful one from a normative point of view.

II. Vagueness

People often feel that their judgments about probabilities are too vague, ambiguous, volatile, uneasy, or shaky to be taken seriously as a basis for a formal analysis. While these adjectives perhaps have different shades of meaning, let us fix on "vague" as a basis for further discussion. Savage himself has long recognized the problem occasioned by "vagueness." In Savage's terminology, a person is vague about the probability assigned to a single trial if he cannot obtain from himself a clear answer as to what probability to assign to it. He is vague about a probability distribution if introspection fails to reveal clearly what the distribution is. Savage comments, "Some people see the vagueness phenomenon as an objection; I see it as a truth, sometimes unpleasant but not curable by a new theory."[3]

Vagueness in probability judgments is a matter of degree; we are always more or less vague. The important question is whether or not we are so vague about a probability as to be unwilling to make an assessment of it. If we are willing to make an assessment, we mean that we are willing to incorporate the assessment into a formal decision-theoretic analysis. We can always write down a number, but we may or may not feel that the number is worth basing anything on. This is tantamount to saying that we may wish to make a formal analysis or that we may wish to fall back on an informal one.[4] It is the distinction between formal and informal analysis, rather than between risk and uncertainty, that seems really helpful.

Vagueness should not be confused with the difficulty or unpleasantness of making assessments. Decisions, however arrived at, can be tough and unpleasant. We may have afterthoughts and misgivings when we make them. But some decisions are unavoidable and must be made somehow. If we do not face up to them, we avoid unpleasantness at the expense of a retreat from our problems. Probability assessments, as one ingredient in decisions, can also be unpleasant. They may sometimes be bypassed or partially bypassed, but the decision to do so should not be based on unpleasantness, except insofar as unpleasantness can be considered a cost to be taken into account in making the decision.

The problem of vagueness is most serious in complicated probability

---

3. L.J. Savage, "Bayesian Statistics," to appear in *Decision and Information Processes* (New York: Macmillan, forthcoming).

4. Of course, even an abortive attempt at formal analysis may be helpful in a subsequent informal analysis by clarifying the issues that need to be mulled over, or by focusing suspicion on any snap decision that might casually emerge from informal analysis alone.

assessments, such as an assessment of a multivariate prior distribution in an analysis of variance problem. The essential issues, however, can be illustrated by the probabilities associated with a Bernoulli process. We therefore present the following terminology. Denote the probability of success on a single Bernoulli trial by p. If we think of p as a random variable that has a distribution of its own, we write $\tilde{p}$ (p – tilde). If we somehow assess the distribution of $\tilde{p}$, the assessment of p is the expected value of this distribution, $E(\tilde{p})$.[5] We could be vague about the distribution of $\tilde{p}$ yet not about $E(\tilde{p})$. If we were vague about $E(\tilde{p})$, we would necessarily be vague about the distribution of $\tilde{p}$.

It is tempting to say that vagueness has something to do with the dispersion of the distribution of $\tilde{p}$. While we may find it more difficult or unpleasant to make a judgment about a dispersed distribution, we are not vague if we do make a judgment. A dispersed distribution of $\tilde{p}$ will, however, be more sensitive to revision in the face of sample data from the Bernoulli process.

III. Ellsberg's Paradox

Ellsberg's first example contains all the ingredients needed for further discussion, so we quote his description in full.

> Consider the following experiment. Let us suppose that you confront two urns containing red and black balls, from one of which a ball will be drawn at random. To "bet on Red$_I$" will mean that you choose to draw from Urn I; and that you will receive a prize a (say $100) if you draw a red ball ("if Red$_I$ occurs") and a smaller amount b (say, $0) if you draw a black ("if not-Red$_I$ occurs").
>
> You have the following information. Urn I contains 100 red and black balls, but in a ratio entirely unknown to you; there may be from 0 to 100 red balls. In Urn II, you confirm that there are exactly 50 red and 50 black balls. An observer—who, let us say, is ignorant of the state of your information about the urns—sets out to measure your subjective probabilities by interrogating you as to your preferences in the following pairs of gambles:
>
> 1. "Which do you prefer to bet on, Red$_I$ or Black$_I$: or are you indifferent?" That is, drawing a ball from Urn I, on which "event" do you prefer the $100 stake, red or black: or do you care?

---

5. Since there seems to be some confusion on this point, a proof may be in order. We use the discrete case to show the method:

$$P \text{ (success on one trial} \mid \text{distribution of } \tilde{p}) = \sum_{p} P(\tilde{p} = p) \, P(\text{success} \mid p)$$
$$= \sum_{p} P(\tilde{p} = p) \cdot p$$
$$= E(\tilde{p})$$

2. "Which would you prefer to be on, Red_{II} or $Black_{II}$?"
3. "Which do you prefer to bet on, Red_I or Red_{II}?"
4. "Which do you prefer to bet on, $Black_I$ or $Black_{II}$?"[6]

Ellsberg reports that many people are indifferent in questions 1 and 2, yet express a preference for Red_{II} in question 3 and $Black_{II}$ in question 4. (Presumably this pattern of responses reflects a preference for dealing with a "known" distribution.) He goes on to demonstrate that this set of answers cannot be reconciled with the Savage axioms, *given Ellsberg's interpretation of the problem that he has formulated*. A person must either modify his answers or violate the axioms. Ellsberg argues essentially that the intuitive conviction underlying the set of answers may be stronger than the intuitive conviction of the axioms in which case the axioms should yield. To me the intuitive conviction of the axioms is strong and direct. But my experience in trying to apply them has convinced me of two things: (1) it is easy to make mistakes, or at least to misinterpret the problem to be solved; (2) I have thus far succeeded in tracing all my violations of the axioms to mistakes or misinterpretations. My recommendation to a person giving the answers reported by Ellsberg is this: "Put yourself temporarily within the Bayesian framework and see what a careful Bayesian analysis can contribute to your understanding of your answers."

An analogy may be helpful. Optical illusions are well known to distort perception, and the study of such illusions has been an important and fruitful area of psychology. We all know that there are circumstances in which we cannot trust our own eyes. If I watch a magician, the plain evidence in front of me tends to undermine my confidence in certain natural laws. Yet I firmly believe that, whether or not I can find it, there *is* a natural explanation. It does not occur to me to discard or modify well-known laws of nature.

The analogy is unfair in that it seems to suggest that we should put the same trust in the Savage axioms as we would, say, in the law of conservation of mass and energy.[7] But the analogy is useful in suggesting that apparent violations of the Savage axioms might be fruitfully studied in the same spirit that we might study the moon illusion, the fact that the moon looks larger very near the horizon than when it is higher in the sky, a phenomenon that has invited explanation for centuries.[8]

---

6. *Op. cit.*, pp. 650–51.

7. Ellsberg points out the danger that the Savage axioms may somehow "abstract away from vital considerations." *Op. cit.*, p. 669. Luce and Raiffa remind us, ". . . before committing ourselves on the acceptability of a set of axioms . . . , we are well advised to investigate some of the consequences with an idea of ferreting out the hidden jokers." R. Duncan Luce and Howard Raiffa, *Games and Decisions* (New York: Wiley, 1957), p. 124. My own confidence in the Savage axioms stems mainly from their fruitfulness in statistical problems, although their direct intuitive appeal is also important to me.

8. Lloyd Kaufman and Irvin Rock, "The Moon Illusion," *Scientific American*, Vol. 207 (No. 1, 1962), pp. 120–30.

We begin by noting that each of the four answers mentioned by Ellsberg could be interpreted as a probability assessment, and that the probability assessments are *not* vague. The trouble is that the set of answers displays inconsistent probability assessments. Thus:

1. $P(Red_I) = P(Black_I) = .5$
2. $P(Red_{II}) = P(Black_{II}) = .5$
3. $P(Red_{II}) > P(Red_I)$
4. $P(Black_{II}) > P(Black_I)$.

On any one question, the subject *has* obtained from himself a clear answer about the probability to be assigned to an individual trial. He is presumably prepared to act upon it in making a decision.

Two important lessons can be drawn from this. (1) Suppose that a decision *must* be made about an individual trial, and that the decision turns only on how a probability would be assessed *if* he tried to assess it. Then to say that the subject is vague is to say that his power of decision is paralyzed. He can afford the luxury of vagueness only if the decision can somehow be deferred or avoided. (2) By noticing his inconsistent probability assessments, he can study the inconsistencies carefully to see which assessments he holds to and which ones should yield. This process lies wholly within, and indeed typifies, the Bayesian approach, for which internal consistency is the major part of "rationality."

In assessing the probability p of "success" on an individual trial one approach is to assess the distribution of $\tilde{p}$ and compute $E(\tilde{p})$ from this distribution. A second approach is to assess $E(\tilde{p})$ directly. There is an option here, and there is no *logical* principle to say which approach should be used. (Indeed the subject might try it *both* ways, and, if he discovers inconsistencies, reflect further to learn better his own mind.) Let $p_I = P(Red_I)$, $q_1 = 1 - p_1$, $p_{II} = P(Red_{II})$, and $q_{II} = 1 - p_{II}$. Presumably everyone agrees, without any problem of vagueness, that $E(\tilde{p}_{II}) = .5$ *and* that for all practical purposes the distribution of $\tilde{p}_{II}$ concentrates mass unity at $p_{II} = .5$. The answer given by the subject to question 1 suggests that, for him, $E(\tilde{p}_I) = .5$. The distribution of $\tilde{p}_I$ is presumably *not* concentrated at .5 but rather spread out in some way that leads to an expectation of .5. The subject could quite properly have claimed vagueness about all other details of this distribution, since it was not necessary to remove vagueness about the distribution in order to assess its expected value.

In answering questions 3 and 4, the subject, who, recall, is now trying to reapproach the problem in the spirit of the Savage axioms, finds that he has assessed

$$E(\tilde{p}_{II}) > E(\tilde{p}_I)$$

and

$$E(\widetilde{q}_{\,II}) > E(\widetilde{q}_{\,I})$$

It is hard to see that questions 3 and 4 have given him any insight about the urns that he did not have when he answered 1 and 2. Yet his intuitive feelings about his answers to 3 and 4 are still strong and he is tempted, with Ellsberg, to feel that the Savage axioms will have to yield. But before giving up on the axioms a more careful examination of the answers to 3 and 4 is wise.

In preparation for this, let me state my own understanding of certain points about Ellsberg's problem that are not made explicit by his wording. I assume that Ellsberg meant that the problem should be analyzed as a single, unique choice; that the utility of the outcomes of the games depended solely on money; that the money outcomes depended only on the outcomes of an individual trial; and that there are no concealed possibilities, such as the possibility of buying sample information. With this in mind let us consider the various ways of resolving the preference for II over I in spite of indifference as to color within I or II separately.

(1) Ellsberg's analysis of his paradox is based on the assumption that the utilities of outcomes are a function only of the monetary consequences. But this is not necessarily the assumption that the subject was making. As just one illustration,[9] the subject might feel that his choice of Red_I could lead to unpleasant second guesses by someone who observed the experiment: he could be criticized, however unfairly, for not taking an apparently "safe" course of action (Red_{II}) if he lost by taking an "unsafe" one (Red_I). An analysis of utility, formal or informal, might reveal the reason for the subject's willingness to pay more for Red_{II} than Red_I, and similarly for $Black_{II}$ over $Black_I$. At the same time he could resolve his confusion about probabilities by deciding that he really feels $P(Red_I) = P(Red_{II}) = P(Black_I) = P(Black_{II}) = .5$, without taint of vagueness.

(2) The subject may have assumed erroneously that the monetary outcomes are a function of p rather than of the outcome of a single trial. For example, he may subconsciously have been thinking that the payoff was proportional to the number of red balls in the chosen urn. If each red ball was worth \$1, the choice Red_{II} is worth \$50 *for sure* in this game. The choice Red_I has, by the answer to question 1, an expected *monetary* value of \$50. But even without a careful assessment of the distribution of $\widetilde{p}_I$, it will be clear that expected *utility* will be less (assuming a conditional utility curve representing "risk aversion") than the utility of \$50 certain. For this game, therefore, the choice Red_{II} would be indicated by a utility argument and no inconsistent probability assessments need be involved. It does not to me seem fantastic that the subject should get mixed up about which game he is playing. I have done the experiment in

---

9. For another in the same vein, the subject may fear that Urn I might contribute to an ulcer, regardless of what a rational analysis of other aspects of the problem may suggest.

statistics classes and encountered the following kind of argument. "If I pick Red_I, I would be completely out of luck if there were no red balls in the urn." Students seem less ready to see the fact that one is equally out of luck if he picks Red_{II} and a black ball is drawn.

Closely related logically to the previous paragraph, but more subtle—the subject may not want to analyze the problem as a single unique choice. He may have it in mind that he will play the game again. One simple example is easily analyzed and instructive. Suppose that the subject must decide now on his choice of red or black for 100 independent repetitions either from Urn I or Urn II. By independent, I mean in the sense of drawing *with* replacement repeated samples of size 1. It is now quite possible that he is indifferent between Red and Black for either urn separately, but prefers Urn II to Urn I. This is because: (a) Monetary return is a function of 100 trials rather than one trial. (b) Given a uniform prior[10] for $\widetilde{p}_I$, the distribution of monetary return has the same expected value for each urn but approximately three times the standard deviation for Urn I. (c) In the presence of risk aversion, larger dispersion of the distribution of monetary return implies smaller expected utility.

(3) The subject may now notice that the "cost of uncertainty," in the technical sense, is higher for Urn I and Urn II. That is, if he had the option of paying for sample information before making a choice, he would pay nothing at all for sample information from Urn II, while he might well pay something for sample information from Urn I. If we assume that the subject is not vague about the distribution of $\widetilde{p}_I$ and is willing to assess it for rough calculation as a continuous uniform distribution[11] from 0 to 1, and that he is guided by expected monetary value, it turns out that he should be willing to pay up to $16.67 for a sample of *one* ball before making his choice. For, if the sample turns out red, Bayes' theorem will cause him to revise his expectation for $\widetilde{p}_I$ from .5000 to .6667. If it turns out black, he will revise from .5000 to .3333. In either case, the expected income for the choice that looks best after the sample (red if red, black if black) is increased from $50 to $66.67. The question of how much he would be willing to pay for sample information is logically irrelevant since none of Ellsberg's questions admit this option, but it is easy to be confused.[12]

(4) The subject may decide that the choice of Red_{II} over Red_I would be held only if all other considerations were evenly balanced, but that upon reflection he would be willing to pay nothing at all for the privilege to choose Red_{II}.

---

10. Introduced only for concreteness. Any nondegenerate prior leads to the same qualitative conclusion.

11. See preceding footnote.

12. In commenting on this paragraph, Robert Schlaifer described a theoretical problem for which he and Arthur Schleifer, Jr., initially made a false conjecture about the solution because they were confused by the existence of a cost of uncertainty that was not relevant to the problem they were investigating.

His original preference was really a second order preference, so to speak, and should not lead him to abandon the axioms.

(5) The subject may have had a much harder time in answering question 1 than question 2. The probability assessment of question 2 was trivial, whereas the assessment of $E(\widetilde{p}_1)$ in question 1 was difficult. Granted that he cannot afford the luxury of vagueness under the circumstances, the subject would certainly not have an easy mind about what he had done. He might feel that if he had to make the assessment repeatedly, he would be wildly volatile in his choices according to his latest feelings about the whims of the experimenter who had filled up Urn I. It is easy to carry over this feeling into questions 3 and 4, and want to have no further part of Urn 1.

(6) The subject may realize he is vague, in Savage's sense, about the *distribution* of $\widetilde{p}_1$, and that he failed to realize that this distribution is irrelevant to either question 3 or 4.

I cannot claim dogmatically that all subjects are confused by one or more of the six points just suggested. Presumably psychological experiments could be designed to shed further light on the question. From the point of view of psychology, errors of perception are interesting and knowledge about the causes of these errors is valuable. My interest, however, is mainly normative. I contend that it is irresponsible and unwise for a subject to persist in his four original answers unless he has first carefully examined these six points and if he has not looked for other possible explanations in the same vein. (My list is intended to be suggestive rather than exhaustive.)[13] Almost everyone seems to accept the Savage axioms in the absence of vagueness about probability assessments. Violation of the axioms because of vagueness should not be contemplated lightheartedly if the decisions or inferences involved are taken seriously.

IV. Discussion and Conclusion

It is hard to see any important role for vagueness in Ellsberg's paradox, at least for a person who makes definite choices for all four questions. Yet vague-

---

13. Ward Edwards, after reading an earlier draft of this paper, did some informal experimentation. He comments: "I found the opinion that a seventh source of error, different from the six you list, was controlling. That is, a simple preference for more information . . . over less. Such a preference is a natural consequence of the experimental fact that information cannot hurt and almost always helps in decision-making." Gordon Antelman suggested in the same vein: "Subject may be pretty sure he doesn't know how to analyze the game and yet be fairly certain that Urn II *is at least* as good as Urn I."

A different line of reasoning, based on mixed strategies, also tends to reinforce the appeal of the Savage axioms in examples closely related to, though not identical with, Ellsberg's. Raiffa points out that the subject can assure himself an objective probability of .5 for Urn I by tossing a fair coin to decide which color to pick. See Howard Raiffa, "Risk, Ambiguity, and the Savage Axioms: Comment," this *Journal*, LXXV (Nov. 1961), 690–94.

ness and the threat of it are often important problems in application of Bayesian decision theory. Irresponsible handling of vagueness renders the whole apparatus hazardous, just as would any form of self-deception in any scheme of decision-making. It would be helpful to look more closely at the process of arriving at assessments of probabilities to see just how vagueness may enter in and what can be done about it. But this would lead to a rather technical chapter in Bayesian statistics, one that can be written convincingly in the present state of the art only for relatively simple problems. While I shall not here undertake even a summary of this chapter, it is worth pointing out my conviction that people skeptical of the Bayesian approach are likely to be convinced only by seeing concrete Bayesian methods that can cope with serious problems. A Bayesian can only wish that skeptics would not make firm judgments until they have given the approach a fair chance.

Ellsberg's paradox serves as a useful example for showing that one's first intuitive judgments may be analyzed and illuminated by the very approach that they seem at first to threaten. I do not contend that all subjects would hold to the Savage axioms as a result of such analysis, but I believe, partly on the basis of informal experimentation, that many of them would.

In any event the remedy for vagueness is an honest attempt to recognize genuine vagueness, to deal with it directly if possible, or to bypass it skillfully by less formal and complete analyses. My personal opinion is that the problem of vagueness will be most successfully met in situations in which at least part of the information comes from sample data, that is, numbers generated by such processes as the Bernoulli, Poisson, or normal. When sample data are absent or when vagueness threatens our attempts to assess the sampling process, the role of formal analysis may have great conceptual value, for example, in disentangling the *probabilities* of events from the *utilities* of the consequences of events. The formal approach may hint at good informal ones, as when we graph data in ways that cast light on such assumptions as independence or normality. But the literal application of formal methods is likely to be much more restricted. Even so, the normative value of Bayesian decision theory can be great. If we cannot always eliminate vagueness about the answers, we never need be vague about the right questions to ask.

The Quantification of Judgment: Some Methodological Suggestions*

Robert L. Winkler
Indiana University

1. Personal Probability

In the personalistic theory of probability, probability measures the confidence that a particular individual has in the truth of a particular proposition. This can be expressed intuitively in terms of betting odds or translated, if desired, from odds to probability. The personalistic view differs from other approaches by not attempting to specify what assessments are "correct." All self-consistent, or coherent, assessments are admissible as long as the individual feels that they correspond with his judgments.

It can be shown [4, 14] that personal probabilities assessed in accordance with certain plausible behavioral postulates of coherence must conform mathematically to a probability measure. In essence, the postulates of coherence (the term "consistency" is often used in place of "coherence") are such that it is impossible to set up a series of bets against a person obeying the postulates in such a manner that the person is sure to lose regardless of the outcome of the event(s) being wagered upon.

In denying the existence of "correct" probability assessments, we are denying a normative interest in the expertise of assessors with regard to events for which the assessments are made. In other words, we are not interested (in a normative sense) in how well probability assessments correspond to something in reality. Instead, we are interested in how well the assessments correspond to the assessor's judgments. For example, suppose I assess the probability of rain tomorrow to be 0.10 and you assess the same probability to be 0.95. If in fact it does rain tomorrow, you would appear to be the "better" assessor. But according to the personalistic theory of probability, the two assessments are equally "good" provided that they correspond to our respective judgments. If our respective judgments are such that we both feel that the probability of rain is in the neighborhood of 0.10, then according to the theory I am the "better" assessor (whether or not it rains) because my assessment corresponds

Reprinted by permission of the publisher from *Journal of the American Statistical Association*, Vol. 62, 320 (December 1967), pp. 1105-1120.

*The author is grateful to Bruno de Finetti, Ward Edwards, a referee and the Editor for helpful comments on an earlier draft of this paper.

with my judgments whereas your assessment fails to correspond with your judgments. It must be emphasized that although the theory is not concerned with the expertise of the assessor, presumably we would be concerned about this in applications of the theory. If a third person were to consider the assessments which you and I have made regarding rain tomorrow in making a decision as to whether or not to plan a picnic, he would probably be quite interested in our respective expertise in weather forecasting. This question is discussed further in Section 6 of this paper [see also 3, 11].

Our interest in personal probability assessments, then, focuses on two requirements: (1) The assessments should obey certain postulates of coherence; and (2) the assessments should correspond with the assessor's judgments. Given a set of assessed probabilities, it is a fairly simple mathematical exercise to verify (or disprove) requirement (1). On the other hand, it is not possible to verify (or disprove) requirement (2). A probability assessment is the result of the interaction (or intuitive processing) of numerous beliefs or judgments which exist only in the assessor's mind. Also, any one set of assessed probabilities is defined only at a given point in time and is subject to revision as the assessor obtains new information. For example, I might wish to change my assessment of the probability of rain tomorrow if just after making the assessment I see an ominous-looking dark cloud. Good states that: "The difficulties become clear when it is realized that we estimate probabilities every minute of the day, at least implicitly, and that how we do this is unknown."[7, p. ix] "Nevertheless, for the purposes of making decisions, we do manage to make approximate estimates of probabilities. How this is done is an interesting problem in psychology and neurophysiology."[7, p. 4].

Although we cannot verify (or disprove) requirement (2), we can attempt to develop methods to help the assessor assess probabilities which are in accordance with his judgments. One approach to the assessment of probabilities is direct interrogation, which consists of questions regarding probabilities, betting odds, contemplation of future samples, hypothetical lotteries, graphing probability distributions, and so on [19]. This approach has been criticized [14, pp. 27–30] on the grounds that the assessor has no incentive to make his assessments correspond with his judgments. For example, if you are asked for your assessment of the probability of rain tomorrow, you may state the first number that comes to mind. If there is a payoff involved which depends on your assessment and on whether or not it actually rains, it is to your advantage to choose the response which maximizes your payoff. This paper is concerned with methods involving payoffs (bets and penalty functions) which, when used alone or in conjunction with direct interrogation, should encourage careful assessments. Following de Finetti [5, p. 117]: "We want to build and propose for practical use such methods as will automatically favour the genuine expression of anybody's beliefs."

2. Assumptions and Notation

Assume that a person, the Assessor, is faced with the task of assessing his probabilities through the use of direct interrogation methods. The particular methods being used are not of concern. The Assessor possesses the following ideal properties:

1. He never violates the postulates of coherence. Following Savage [15, p. 11]: "This person is idealized; unlike you and me, he never makes mistakes, never gives thirteen pence for a shilling, or makes such a combination of bets that he is sure to lose no matter what happens."
2. He fully understands both the methods used to obtain his probability assessments and the methods used to encourage careful assessments. That is, he understands the alternatives open to him and the implications of each alternative.
3. He has a utility function which is linear with respect to money in the relevant range (that is, the range of monetary amounts used in conjunction with the assessment procedure). Furthermore, he chooses his responses in such a way as to maximize his expected utility.[1]

Assume further that the judgments of the Assessor with regard to the problem being considered may be fully represented by a probability distribution, $f(x)$, of a random variable X. Consider an n-fold partition $X_1, X_2, \ldots, X_n$ on the real line. Then $f(x)$ can be summarized by $p_1, p_2, \ldots, p_n$, where $p_1 = P(x \in X_i)$, $i = 1, 2, \ldots, n$.

The actual assessed probability distribution or set of responses will be denoted by $r(x)$ or by $r_1, r_2, \ldots, r_n$ if an n-fold partition is considered. The only restriction on the responses is that they must not violate the postulates of coherence. We are interested in investigating methods which should lead the Assessor to make $r(x)$ identical to $f(x)$ or to set $r_i = p_i$ for $i = 1, 2, \ldots, n$.

3. Actual Bets

The first method to be discussed involves offering the Assessor a series of bets. These are actual bets, not hypothetical bets, in the sense that in each case the winner of the bet is determined and the amount of money involved actually changes hands. Good states [7, p. 49] that: "Probability judgments can be sharpened by laying bets at suitable odds. If people always felt obliged to back

---

1. A systematic development of the theory of utility as well as a historical discussion is found in [14]. For a more elementary discussion, see [1].

their opinions when challenged, we would be spared a few of the 'certain' predictions that are so frequently made."

In each case presented, the Assessor must choose between two bets (he is not allowed to abstain from betting). In the first case, the Assessor must choose between a bet with fixed probabilities q and $1 - q$ of winning and losing and a bet dependent on whether or not some event E occurs.

Bet 1a: Win $\$A$ if the event E occurs.
            Lose $\$B$ if E does not occur.
Bet 1b: Win $\$A$ with probability q.
            Lose $\$B$ with probability $1 - q$.

The expected values of Bets 1a and 1b to the Assessor are, respectively, $Ap + Bp - B$ and $Aq + Bq - B$, where p is his probability that E will occur. Therefore we may draw the following inferences from his decision: if Bet 1a is chosen, $Ap + Bp - B \geqslant Aq + Bq - B$, so $p \geqslant q$; similarly, if Bet 1b is chosen, $p \leqslant q$. Thus, we see that the result of this bet is inequality involving p. It is interesting to note that the Assessor's choice of a bet is independent of our choice of A and B.[2]

Suppose that there is an event E' with a well-established probability q of occurring with which the Assessor is intuitively familiar (an example might be the occurrence of a six on one toss of a fair die). Then Bet 1b could be made conditional on whether or not E' occurs. Here q is not explicitly stated, but it is implied by the choice of E'. For most values of q, it seems that a suitable E' could be found, although this would depend on the Assessor's experience with various classes of events.

The second case differs from the above situations in that the assessor must choose between two sides of the same bet.

Bet 2a: Win $\$A$ if E occurs.
            Lose $\$B$ if E doesn't occur.
Bet 2b: Win $\$B$ if E doesn't occur.
            Lose $\$A$ if E occurs.

The expected values of Bets 2a and 2b are, respectively, $Ap - B(1 - p)$ and $B(1 - p) - Ap$. If Bet 2a is chosen, $Ap - B(1 - p) \geqslant B(1 - p) - Ap$, which reduces

---

2. This raises an interesting question concerning the game theoretic aspects of the betting situation. We contemplate probing the Assessor by a number of bets to be proposed from time to time. Thus, the Assessor should be concerned about the bets to be offered in the future; and he might consider passing up an attractive bet in order to be freer to make still more attractive bets in the future. His choice of a bet is independent of our choice of A and B only if he can be convinced that the bets to be offered in the future do not depend on his present behavior.

to $p \geqslant B/(A + B)$. If Bet 2b is chosen, the inequality is reversed. Once again the result is an inequality involving p, and in this case the Assessor's choice of a bet is dependent on our choice of A and B.

The bets presented elicit information about the probability attached by the Assessor to an event E. By letting E consist of any combination of intervals on the real line, we can elicit information about $f(x)$. In particular, we might consider intervals of the form $(-\infty, x)$ in order to obtain probability inequalities for fractiles of $f(x)$.

Now that some betting situations have been presented, a new question must be posed: how can the actual bets be used to advantage in encouraging careful probability assessment? One suggestion might be to use them in place of, rather than in addition to, direct interrogation. Indeed, this follows the spirit of Savage's (and de Finetti's) formulation of the theory of personalistic probability [14, pp. 27–30; 4, p. 101].

The better situations presented here, however, result only in inequalities involving the assessed probabilities. Certainly we could use the betting situation to determine a probability to any desired degree of precision, but this might require a large number of bets. Ten carefully selected bets will determine any probability to the third decimal place. Fewer might be needed if we have some initial idea regarding the Assessor's probability, especially if it is expected to be close to either zero or one. Also, there is often an element of vagueness involved in the assessment of probabilities, so that a few bets might determine a probability as precisely as possible. Nevertheless, the total number of bets might still be large if, in the course of attempting to assess $f(x)$, several probabilities were considered.

One way to avoid the problem of a large number of bets would be to assess the probabilities through the use of direct interrogation and then to use the betting situation as a check on the assessed probabilities. The direct interrogation should get us "in the ballpark" by suggesting which bets might be most illuminating. For example, if the Assessor assesses $p_i = 0.35$, we might wish to use Bets 1a – 1b with $q = 0.37$ or $q = 0.33$. If we really wished to push our Assessor to the limit (after all, we have endowed him with such ideal qualities that it would be a shame not to take advantage of them), we could set q equal to 0.3499 or 0.3501. At any rate, it is clear that the assessed probabilities give us some idea of which bets to present to the Assessor. A drawback of this procedure, however, is the possibility of gamesmanship on the part of the Assessor. If he is aware of the procedure, he could intentionally falsify his responses to direct interrogation in order to receive an attractive choice of bets.

One final note regarding bets is concerned with their use in connection with different methods of direct interrogation. It has been demonstrated that different questioning methods may produce different responses [19]. If we consider k different methods, we may get responses $r_{1j}, r_{2j}, \ldots, r_{nj}$ [or $r_j(x)$] for the jth method, $j = 1, 2, \ldots, k$. By a proper selection of bets to be presented to the Assessor, it may be possible to determine which set of responses best approximates the $p_1, p_2, \ldots, p_n$ [or $f(x)$] by determining which set of responses (if any) is consistent with all of the bets.

A simple example should illustrate this proposition. Consider a dichotomous sample space with events X_1 and X_2. Two methods are used, with respective responses $r_{11}, r_{21} = 1 - r_{11}$ and $r_{12}, r_{22} = 1 - r_{12}$. Suppose we use Bets $1a$ - $1b$ with $q = (r_{11} + r_{12})/2$. But the Assessor's choice of a bet determines which side of q the probability p_1 is on and thus determines which response, r_{11} or r_{12}, is a better approximation to p_1.

4. Penalty Functions

The use of penalty functions, or scoring methods, is discussed in some detail by de Finetti [3, 5] Toda [17], and others [16, 18]. The penalty functions, or scoring methods, involve the computation of a score according to a scoring rule which is designed to lead the Assessor to reveal his true beliefs. "The scoring rule is constructed according to the basic idea that the resulting device should oblige each participant to express his true feelings, because any departure from his own personal probability results in a diminution of his own average score as he sees it." [3, p. 359].

The scoring rules must be tied in with the use of some reward (or punishment), the amount of which should be directly proportional to the score. The score could be considered a reward in itself, or monetary rewards proportional to the score could be introduced. These methods, then, can be thought of as scoring rules in the sense that the Assessor should attempt to maximize his expected score. On the other hand, the methods can be thought of as penalty functions in the sense that the Assessor is penalized (through a lower expected score and the related lower expected reward) for deviating from his true beliefs. While we shall call the actual rules for computing the Assessor's score scoring rules, we shall label this entire class of methods penalty functions.

The general scoring rule proposed by de Finetti [5, p. 91] is $S_1 = 2r_h$ $- \Sigma_{j=1}^{n} r_j^2$, where the actual value of X lies in X_h. He also suggests two variants, $S_1' = (S_1 + 1)/2$ and $S_1'' = (S_1 - 1)/2$, which serve only to change the scale: for r_j satisfying the postulates of coherence, the ranges of S_1, S_1', and S_1'' are, respectively, $[-1, 1]$, $[0, 1]$, and $[-1, 0]$. In general, $aS_1 + b(a > 0)$ will have range $[-a + b, a + b]$. The scoring rule $aS_1 + b(a > 0)$ leads the Assessor to express his true judgments, since he must set $r_i = p_i$ $(i = 1, 2, \ldots, n)$ in order to maximize $E(aS_1 + b)$.

In the special case where $n = 2$ (a dichotomous situation), S_1' is equivalent to $S_2 = 1 - (1 - r_h)^2$ and to the "Brier score," which is used in the verification of probabilistic forecasts in meteorology [13] .[3] The computation of the score is easier with S_2 than with S_1'. Toda suggests $S_2' = S_2 - 1$ for dichotomous situations and calls it the quadratic loss game [17, p. 16] .

Two other scoring rules discussed by Toda are the spherical gain game (S_3) and the logarithmic loss game (S_4):

$$S_3 = r_h \Big/ \left(\sum_{j=1}^{n} r_j^2 \right)^{\frac{1}{2}}$$

$$S_4 = \log r_h.$$

It can be shown that S_3 and S_4 (and their positive linear transformations) oblige the Assessor to express his true judgments. The logarithmic loss game is discussed by Good [6] and by van Naerssen [18] , and the spherical gain game is discussed by Roby [12] .

With respect to the penalty functions, a note of caution is warranted. There are many scoring rules which seem reasonable but turn out not to be upon further investigation. The scoring rule $S = r_h$ seems intuitively reasonable at first glance. The score is equal to the probability assigned to the interval containing the actual value. It turns out, however, that the Assessor can maximize his expected score by setting one of the r_i equal to one (the r_i corresponding to the highest p_i) and the other r_i equal to zero. Consider a dichotomous situation with $p_1 = .6$ and $p_2 = .4$. By setting $r_i = p_i, i = 1, 2$, the Assessor has an expected score of $(.6)^2 + (.4)^2 = .52$. If $r_1 = 1$ and $r_2 = 0$, the Assessor's expected score is $1(.6) + 0(.4) = .60$. This points out the fact that it is not sufficient for a method

---

3. If $n > 2, S_1 + (n - 1)$ is equivalent to a sum of S_2 scores. An n-fold partition can be regarded as a set of n interrelated dichotomies, or two-fold partitions, where each dichotomy consists of one element of the n-fold partition versus the remaining $n - 1$ elements. Then there are n S_2 scores corresponding to the n dichotomies:

$$S_{2i} = 1 - (1 - r_i)^2 \qquad \text{if } X \in X_i$$

$$= 1 - r_i^2 \qquad \text{if } X \notin X_i, i = 1, 2, \cdots, n.$$

Now, if $X \in X_h$,

$$\sum_i S_{2i} = 1 - (1 - r_h)^2 + \Sigma(1 - r_i^2)$$

$$= 2r_h - \sum_i r_i^2 + n - 1$$

$$= S_1 + (n - 1).$$

to seem intuitively reasonable; it must be shown that the method will actually oblige the Assessor to reveal his true judgments. McCarthy [9] states that a scoring rule S is admissible (i.e., keeps the Assessor honest) if and only if it is of the form $S = \partial s(r_1, r_2, \ldots, r_n)/\partial r_h$, where s is a convex function of the r_i which is homogeneous of the first degree. From this it is easy to show that any linear combination (with positive coefficients) of admissible scoring rules is an admissible scoring rule.

The penalty functions are functions of the r_i, $i = 1, \ldots, n$, and thus they are dependent upon the choice of an n-fold partition. In some situations, the nature of X may make the choice of a partition obvious. In other situations, we must balance off the desire to obtain as much information as possible about the Assessor's distribution (implying a fine partition) against the desire to simplify the calculations (implying a coarse partition).

In some cases, the Assessor's entire distribution, $f(x)$, may be of interest. The penalty functions can be used in these cases even though the assessment consists of $r(x)$ rather than a set of r_i. If the partition is not predetermined (or, equivalently, if the Assessor has no knowledge regarding the partition), the Assessor must make $r(x)$ identical to $f(x)$ in order to maximize his expected score. This is the only $r(x)$ that assures him that $r_i = p_i$, $i = 1, \ldots, n$, and hence that his expected score is maximized, regardless of the choice of a partition.

Here the choice of a partition is not as important as it is when it determines the probabilities to be assessed. To eliminate the possibility of gamesmanship, however, the Assessor should have no knowledge regarding the partition. One way to guarantee this would be to randomly select $n - 1$ real numbers from some distribution $g(y)$ which is independent of X. These $n - 1$ values, when ordered, divide the real line into n disjoint and exhaustive intervals (assuming no single value occurs more than once). In this manner, the choice of a partition is simple once n and $g(y)$ have been chosen.

If more control is desired over the width and general location of the intervals, a set of n intervals could be completely determined except for their specific location. This could be done by tentatively choosing a partition and a real number T and then allowing the $n - 1$ dividing points to be shifted t units to the right, where t is randomly selected from a uniform distribution on $[0, T]$. In practice we may feel confident that the Assessor has no knowledge of the partition, but the randomization procedures are still valuable in case our confidence is not warranted.

If the Assessor's entire probability distribution is not wanted, penalty functions can also be used for finding other parameters of the distribution. For example, if the assessor is asked to predict the actual value of X subject to a penalty proportional to the square of his error, it will be to his interest to give the mean of his distribution. If the penalty is proportional to the absolute error, he should reveal the median of his distribution, and so on. Two other techniques deserving mention are the range betting and partition betting methods proposed by Toda [17]. Here the Assessor's responses are in the form of intervals [not in the form of r_i or $r(x)$] , and the score is dependent on whether or not the actual value falls in a particular interval.

5. Implications for the Personalistic Theory

The distinction we have drawn between direct interrogation and the methods discussed in this paper should be clearer now. Direct interrogation provides a way for the Assessor's beliefs and judgments to be expressed in probabilities or in some form (such as betting-odds) which can be translated into probabilities. In other words, it serves as a vehicle for the Assessor to quantify his judgments. The methods discussed here, on the other hand, serve to lead the Assessor to make his assessments agree with his true judgments by making it advantageous for him to do so.

As we have noted, direct interrogation has been criticized on the grounds that there is no way of knowing if the resulting assessments are actually in accordance with the Assessor's beliefs and judgments. This criticism has played an important role, both explicitly and implicitly, in the development of the personalistic theory. An example is the discussion by Savage, cited in Section 1, in which he rejects the verbal approach [14, pp. 27-8] :

> Attempts to define the relative probability of a pair of events in terms of the answers people give to direct interrogation has justifiably met with antipathy from most statistical theorists. . . . What could such interrogation have to do with the behavior of a person in the face of uncertainty, except of course, for his verbal behavior under uncertainty? . . . It would, in short, be preferable, at least in principle, to interrogate the person, not literally through his verbal answer to verbal questions, but rather in a figurative sense somewhat reminiscent of that in which a scientific experiment is sometimes spoken of as an interrogation of nature. Several schemes of behavioral, as opposed to direct, interrogation have been proposed.

If the Assessor is presented with no actual bets and no penalty functions, what incentive does he have to make his assessments correspond with his judgments? In some cases he may have incentive to intentionally falsify his judgments because he perceives (whether correctly or incorrectly) a reward (or punishment) scheme which encourages him to do so. For example, in a particular situation he may feel that overestimation is a more serious error than underestimation, so he intentionally assesses a lower value than his true beliefs would justify. This may be because his past experiences have indicated that overestimation is usually penalized ("It failed to come up to your expectations, eh?") while underestimation is not ("How about that—it did even better than you expected!").

The above criticism might lead some to insist that subjective probabilities can be given an operational meaning only in terms of actual choices, or decisions, made by the Assessor. This places a heavy burden on the betting situations (or similar notions involving a decision, or choice of acts, by the Assessor), which are fairly inefficient (in the sense of resulting only in inequalities and being quite time-consuming).[4] It seems that the primary usefulness of the bets should be to encourage careful assessment.

The criticism can be removed without discarding direct interrogation. This can be accomplished simply by using it in conjunction with bets and/or penalty functions. For example, the results of using direct questions about probabilities could be thought of as a reliable quantification of the Assessor's judgments if some bets and/or a penalty function were used to encourage careful assessment. The penalty functions are extremely valuable in this sense, for they are not time-consuming in the sense that the bets are. That is, they do not increase the time required for assessments to be made, except in the sense that the Assessor may be more careful and hence may take more time. Once the Assessor understands the penalty functions, their task is performed automatically. The element of time is involved in computing the score, especially when n is large, but computations can easily be done on a computer if necessary. The two classes of methods (direct interrogation and bets or penalty functions) complement each other well, with one providing the vehicle for the quantification of judgment and the second providing the incentive for a quantification consistent with the Assessor's judgments.

6. Implementation of the Methods

Up to this point we have been interested in the general development of the methods and their use under ideal conditions (that is, with the hypothesized Assessor). We now address ourselves to this question: are the methods practicable?

A. Reasonableness of the Assumptions

Several rather strong assumptions were made about the ideal Assessor. Could we reasonably expect them to hold for actual assessors? First, it was assumed that the postulates of coherence would never be violated. Of course, the theory of personalistic probability and the underlying principles of coherence constitute a normative theory and do not claim to describe actual behavior. We would no more expect people to never violate the postulates of coherence than we

---

4. When bets are used merely as an introspective way of arriving at one's own personal probabilities, they are valuable and not particularly time consuming.

would expect them to never violate the rules of logic or arithmetic [4, p. 111] .
Presumably, the degree to which an assessor obeys the rules of coherence would
depend on such variables as the familiarity of the assessor with the terminology
of probability and statistics and his general competence in quantitative reasoning. Some descriptive studies have indicated that naive subjects do not obey the
rules of coherence unless the problem is quite simple or the subjects have under-
gone fairly extensive training [see, for example, 2 and 8] . Naive subjects are
not alone, though. Even an assessor sophisticated in probability and statistics
and familiar with the coherence axioms is apt to violate the axioms if he is not
careful. After all mathematicians have a reputation for their inability to balance
checkbooks; yet we would not question their knowledge of the laws of addition
and subtraction.

But how serious are these incoherences which may arise from time to time?
If a person is aware of making an arithmetic error, he will no doubt review
his calculations and correct the error. Similarly, if an assessor is aware of a
violation of the postulates of coherence (let us call such a violation an inconsistency), he should review his assessments and remove the inconsistency. A
subtle difference between the arithmetic error and the inconsistency must be
pointed out. One person can correct another person's arithmetic error since
there is a "correct" answer which can be determined and which different people
will agree on. A probability assessment, however, is "private" to an assessor in
the sense that it represents the judgments of the assessor and of no one else. The
removal of and inconsistency involves a reconsideration of the judgments upon
which the inconsistent assessments were based, and only the original assessor
can make such a reconsideration. For example, a set of assessments may be
inconsistent because the sum of the probabilities is 1.2 rather than 1.0. To a
person other than the assessor, it might seem convenient to remove the inconsistency by "normalizing" the probabilities, or dividing each probability by 1.2
so they will sum to 1.0. The original assessor, on the other hand, if faced with
the inconsistency, might reassess his probabilities in some different manner
(for instance, by subtracting 0.2 from one probability in the set, provided that
this will not result in a negative number). If he decides to "normalize," this
is an allowable choice; but the choice is his and no one else's.

The seriousness of inconsistencies, then, is greatly reduced by the possibility
of their removal. The problem which remains concerns the recognition of
inconsistencies, since they can only be removed if they are identified. Indeed,
one function of the theory of personal probability is to enable assessors to
detect and remove inconsistencies in their assessed probabilities. With some
training and experience at assessing, the assessor should be able to recognize his
inconsistencies. In a recent study by the author [19] , the rate of occurrence
of inconsistencies was reduced with training and experience. De Finetti [5, p. 88]
states: "Although it is known that people often do not exhibit logical or probabilistic coherence, this only makes it more important to use probability theory

to show them how to avoid unnecessary losses due to such inconsistency." In essence, what we are suggesting here is that assessors can be taught, to a certain degree, to identify and reconcile inconsistencies. Because of this, the fact that people do violate the postulates of coherence should not create a serious problem.

A second assumption concerned the assessor's understanding of the methods. The naive assessor is not likely to understand the methods at first because of difficulties with the concepts and terminology. This problem should be eliminated by sufficient training, as is suggested by the results presented in [19]. It would be worthwhile to develop improved instructional procedures for the various techniques of direct interrogation. With respect to the bets and penalty functions, the assessor should be informed of their purpose. He should be convinced that these methods will penalize him for assessments which are not consistent with his judgments. If a penalty function is used, he should be informed about (and should understand) the scoring rule. The question of learning through experience will be discussed later in this section.

The assumption of a utility function which is linear in the relevant range depends not only on the assessor but also on the choice of the "relevant range." The monetary amounts used as rewards (or punishments) should be neither too small nor too large. If they are too small, they will not be important enough to the assessor to warrant his taking the time to make careful assessments. That is, the difficulty of taking the time to make careful assessments outweighs the utility of the expected gain due to careful assessments. If the amounts are too large, utilities will no longer be linear with respect to money and we enter the realm of risk-avoiding and risk-taking behavior. It must be emphasized that the terms "small" and "large" are relative terms and depend on the particular assessor. What is a "small" amount to one person may seem quite "large" to another. This raises the question of the measurement of utility functions, which is an important problem and is beyond the scope of this paper. Certainly work in this area would be helpful in investigating the assumption of linear utility functions.

Even if the assessor's utility function is linear with respect to money, there may be factors other than money involved, as de Finetti points out [5, p. 119]:

> The main factor of distortion lies in the unavoidable presence of other data possibly acting as aims besides the score: first of all the rank attained by a subject among his group, or the desire to achieve an extraordinary performance. In such cases, a subject may be willing to take a chance by a hazardous response or forecast so that, if by good luck he guessed correctly, it would give him a larger probability to be alone at the first place. . . . As for material rewards, it is easy (although unusual) to eliminate any additional advantage for the first place besides the reward rigorously proportional to the total score; as for moral

reward, it is difficult to obviate this danger completely, especially at the end of a long series.

The presence of a penalty function, or scoring rule, might lead some people to behave as gamblers and completely defeat the purpose of the rule. For instance, suppose a person of this type is assessing probabilities for a dichotomous situation and the scoring rule S_1 is being used. A specific example might be the assessment of probabilities for the two events "rain tomorrow" and "no rain tomorrow." If an assessor thinks that "rain" is more likely than "no rain" (note that nothing is said about *how much* more likely "rain" is), he might assess a probability of 1.0 to "rain," thereby hoping to attain a perfect score of +1.0 (which he will attain if it does rain). In doing so, he runs the risk of attaining the worst possible score, −1.0, if it does not rain. In contrast to this risk-taking behavior, a risk-avoider might tend to follow a minimax strategy by assessing a probability of 0.5 for each of the two alternatives. His score is "guaranteed"—it will be 0.50 whether it rains or not. If he assessed his probabilities in any other way other than 0.50 and 0.50, he would be admitting the possibility of a lower score. In general, a risk-taker might assess a distribution which is highly concentrated about a single point, thereby hoping to "catch" the actual value and obtain a very high score. A risk-avoider, on the other hand, might assess a uniform distribution to assure himself of a certain minimum score while forfeiting his chances for a very high score. These examples are extreme cases, but any intentional distortion (even if only slight) of one's assessments toward one of these extremes is a form of risk-taking or risk-avoiding. Risk-taking and risk-avoiding may affect the betting situations as well as the penalty functions.

Despite these problems involving utility, the methods may still be feasible, especially if an assessor is to make quite a few assessments. The assessor who wishes to maximize his expected score (or expected gains in the betting situation) over a number of trials will soon learn that risk-taking or risk-avoiding doesn't work in the long run. If an assessor continues to act as a risk-taker or a risk-avoider, he is really operating with a different penalty function than the one intended.

One very important assumption which has remained implicit throughout the discussion is the restriction of the random variable X to that class of random variables for which an actual value can be determined. Without such an actual value, there would be no way of determining the winner of any bets or computing a score. For example, suppose a manufacturer has developed a new product and wishes to assess a probability distribution for the proportion of consumers in a given city who possess a certain characteristic which is considered relevant for a marketing decision regarding the new product. The only way to determine an "actual value" here would be to interview every consumer in the city, but this would be impractical. Perhaps we could get around such problems by offering the assessor indirect bets, such as bets regarding sample outcomes, and by developing scoring rules based on sample outcomes rather than actual values. This would require further investigation.

B. "Good" vs. "Bad" Assessors and Learning from Experience

The concept of a "good" or a "bad" assessor can be thought of in two different contexts. First, we have a criterion of "goodness" with respect to the personalistic theory of probability. In this context, a "good" assessor is one who obeys the postulates of coherence and makes assessments which correspond to his judgments [i.e., makes $r(x)$ identical to $f(x)$]. The ideal Assessor postulated in Section 2 is the extreme example of a "good" assessor in this sense. We would expect another criterion of "goodness" to be considered in applications of the theory. In this context, a "good" assessor is one who is extremely knowledgeable in the area under consideration. Essentially, the first context concerns expertise in the general area of probability assessment; the second context concerns expertise in some area of application. The first requires probabilities to correspond with judgment; the second requires them to correspond with something in reality.

Ideally, we would like both criteria to be satisfied. That is, we would like the assessor to be competent in both probability assessment and the area of application. Unfortunately, this is not usually the case. Consider once again the weather forecasting example. A satistician who is familiar with the theory of personal probability may be able to make coherent assessments in accordance with his judgments; but he may know very little about meteorology. A meteorologist, on the other hand, may be an expert in his field; but he may not understand the concept of probability. This statistican satisfies the first criterion but not the second; the meteorologist satisfies the second but not the first. Who is the "better" assessor?

In a normative sense (regarding coherence), the statistician is clearly the "better" assessor. A person who must base a decision on the assessed probability of rain tomorrow, however, may be more interested in how much the assessor knows about meteorology. In this case he might claim that the meteorologist is the "better" assessor.

If the problem at hand is important enough to warrant serious consideration, it is not necessary to make a choice between the two criteria of "goodness." With some instruction and practice, the meteorologist could be trained in the use of the assessment methods (this should be infinitely easier than giving the statistician instruction in meteorology). With this training, perhaps the meteorologist could satisfy both criteria of "goodness."

Hopefully, then, people can be trained to be "good" assessors. Also, we would expect them to learn from experience; that is, with more experience they should become "better" assessors. It has already been noted that as the assessor gains experience, fewer inconsistencies would be expected. Experience should increase his understanding of the methods, which in turn should reduce the number of inconsistencies. Also, experience should help the assessor to understand the correspondence between judgments and probabilities. Naive assessors tend to overuse certain round numbers, such as 0, 0.25, 0.50, 0.75, and 1.0. They often label events as being impossible rather than assess small probabilities for them (e.g., by truncating the distribution rather than including extreme tail areas with very small probabilities). Experience should serve to lessen these tendencies [5, p. 120].

Experience should make the assessor a "better" assessor in the second sense as well as in the first sense. By considering feedback concerning the relationship between his assessments and the actual values, he can check for tendencies such as bias—the tendency to consistently underestimate or consistently overestimate. This feedback could be in the form of direct comparison of the assessments with the actual values, evaluation of the scores determined by some penalty function, or consideration of the sums of money won and lost through the betting situations or the penalty functions. Thus, the methods considered in this paper serve not only to encourage careful assessment, but also to encourage the assessor to evaluate his assessments in light of the actual values determined later. This sort of evaluation should make him a "better" assessor.

One final way of learning from experience is through interpersonal comparisons. For example, the assessor could compare his assessments with the assessments of another person who consistently obtained higher scores and won more money from the bets. The assessor might try to determine what additional factors could have been considered by the other person to enable him to obtain the higher scores. An assessor whose scores are consistently lower than those of others might wish to reevaluate the mental processes involved in his assessments. This suggests another use for the methods presented here: namely, as means of evaluation of different assessors in the long run. If a number of persons make assessments for the same variables over a period of time, we could see which assessor earned the highest total score. This information might be of interest for future applications. It should be pointed out that the scores reflect the disparity of the assessed values and the actual values, so the scores are evaluations of the "goodness" of the assessors in the second sense rather than in the normative sense.[5] Also, interpersonal comparisons of scores are only valid if the different

---

5. This is not to say that the scores are *objective* measures of "goodness" in the second sense or that such "goodness" can be measured objectively. The "goodness" of an assessor should be thought of as a subjective judgment of another person concerning the assessor. To the extent that the other person feels that the scores are related to factors such as skill or expertise rather than to chance, he should feel that the relative scores provide a rough evaluation of "goodness."

assessors have made assessments of the same nature. This is because the score is dependent upon such things as the variable(s) considered, the choice of a partition, and so on.

C. Considerations Regarding the Choice of Methods

The choice of methods in any specific situation is dependent on such considerations as: the choice of a model for the situation (choice of a partition, probabilities to be assessed, etc.); the familiarity of the assessor with the methods; and time and monetary considerations with respect to the administration of the methods (personnel, computing, etc.). The first consideration, choice of model, limits the number of admissible methods. Factors such as time and money are also important; the betting situation requires more time than the penalty functions, for example.

An example should serve to illustrate the choices available in the selection of a model. Suppose an investment firm decides to have its security analysts assess probabilities for the prices of certain stocks at some point in the future (e.g., one year from the date of assessment). What probabilities should be assessed? Actual stock prices are generally measured in dollars and fractional dollars (usually eighths of dollars), implying a discrete sample space. It would, however, be unreasonable (and impractical) to ask the assessor to assess a probability of each possible price. For a volatile stock, this could necessitate hundreds of assessments. The numerous possibilities could be grouped into intervals and assessments made for each interval, where the width of the intervals would depend upon the range of expected prices. For a stock selling in the $5–$20 range, intervals of width $1 might be chosen. On the other hand, for a stock selling in the $50–$100 range, intervals of width $5 might be used. Another alternative would be to approximate the discrete distribution by a continuous distribution. This might be reasonable because of the large number of sample points (possible prices). Also, this may well be the most useful model in the sense of providing the most information, since probabilities for any intervals (and hence for any n-fold partition) can be determined from a continuous distribution, but the reverse procedure is not possible.

Once the model is chosen, an equally important problem is the determination of the specific procedures to be used. Within the betting situation, how many bets are to be used? Which set of bets is to be used? With Bets $1a$ – $1b$, what values of q are to be used and what event E' is to be chosen? With all the bets, how are A and B to be selected? Some of these questions cannot be answered without reference to a specific situation, while others admit partial answers at this time (some of these problems are briefly discussed elsewhere in this paper). The number of bets is dependent upon the time and money available. We have suggested that the betting situation is time-consuming (and expensive if the assessor wins often), so presumably we would want only a minimum number of bets—just enough to discourage careless assessments. The selection of q could be made after some assessments are actually made—see Section 3. The event E' should be one for which historical frequencies are readily available and for which the assessor had a good intuitive feel. The amounts wagered, A and B, should be large enough to be worthwhile to the subject, but not so large as to bring non-linear utilities into play. These answers are admittedly not completely satisfactory, but perhaps they can serve as a starting point.

Within the penalty functions there are also some questions. Which penalty function should be used? How should we determine the monetary rewards (or punishments) to be used? In considering a scoring rule such as $aS_1 + b$, what values of a and b should be used? How should he choose a partition? Again, some of these items admit only partial answers and some are discussed elsewhere in the paper. The problem of the monetary values to be used here is the same problem as the determination of A and B in the betting situation, and the choice of a partition is discussed briefly in Section 4. The choice of a and b determines the range of the scoring rule. A convenient range might be from zero to one hundred, since this is a range commonly used in other types of evaluations (e.g., in the measurement of academic achievement). If we set $a = b = 50$, then $aS_1 + b$ will have this range.

As for the different penalty functions, more empirical work is needed to compare them. Phillips and Edwards investigated assessments made under a number of payoff functions, including the quadratic and logarithmic functions. They found [10, p. 352] that "logarithmic payoffs are more effective than no payoffs, quadratic payoffs, or linear payoffs in producing estimates more nearly like probabilities calculated from Bayes' theorem." One attractive feature of the logarithmic scoring rule, as opposed to the quadratic and spherical scoring rules, is the fact that the score depends only upon the probability assigned to the "actual event" and not upon the probabilities assigned to the other events. Shuford, Albert, and Massengill [16] point out that the logarithmic scoring rule is unbounded on the left and suggest truncating it (say, at log .01) to prevent a score of $-\infty$ (an infinite penalty).

It may even be possible to combine the betting situation and the penalty functions. One suggestion (due to Ward Edwards) is as follows. In a dichotomous situation, it has been determined that the assessor thinks that event A is more probable than event B. He is then asked to choose one of fifty-one bets:

Bet	If Event A occurs, win	If Event B occurs, win
1	100.00	0
2	99.99	1.99
3	99.96	3.96
.	.	.
.	.	.
.	.	.
50	75.99	73.99
51	75.00	75.00

This is simply another way of presenting a quadratic scoring rule. The payoff is quadratic, and the choice of bets determines $P(A)$ to two decimal places [If Bet 1 is chosen, $P(A) = 1.00$; If Bet 2, $P(A) = 0.99$; and so on to Bet 51, where $P(A) = 0.50$].

The questions posed in this section indicate directions for further research. A number of methods have been discussed here, and certainly other methods could be developed. In addition to further theoretical developments, more empirical work would be most welcome. Many of the questions posed here can be answered only by empirical investigations, and the results of such empirical investigations may lead in turn to the development of more refined methods.

References

1. Chernoff, Herman, and Moses, Lincoln E., *Elementary Decision Theory*. New York: John Wiley, 1959.

2. Edwards, Ward, and Phillips, Lawrence D., "Man as Transducer for Probabilities in Bayesian Command and Control Systems," in Maynard W. Shelley and Glenn L. Bryan, eds., *Human Judgments and Optimality*. New York: John Wiley, 1964, 360–401.

3. de Finetti, Bruno, "Does It Make Sense to Speak of 'Good Probability Appraisers'?," in Irving John Good, gen. ed., *The Scientist Speculates—An Anthology of Partly-Baked Ideas*. New York: Basic Books, 1962, 357–63.

4. de Finetti, Bruno, "Foresight: Its Logical Laws, Its Subjective Sources," Trans. Henry E. Kyburg, Jr. In Henry E. Kyburg, Jr. and Howard E. Smokler, *Studies in Subjective Probability*. New York: John Wiley, 1964, 93–158.

5. de Finetti, Bruno, "Methods for Discriminating Levels of Partial Knowledge Concerning a Test Item," *The British Journal of Mathematical and Statistical Psychology*, 18 (1965), 87–123.

6. Good, I. J., "Rational Decision," *Journal of the Royal Statistical Society*, Series B, 14 (1952), 107–14.

7. Good, Irving John, *The Estimation of Probabilities—An Essay on Modern Bayesian Methods*. Cambridge: The M.I.T. Press, 1965.

8. Marschak, Jacob, "Actual vs. Consistent Decision Behavior," *Behavioral Science*, 9 (1964), 103–10.

9. McCarthy, John, "Measures of the Value of Information," *Proceedings of the National Academy of Sciences*, 42 (1956), 654–55.

10. Phillips, Lawrence D., and Edwards, Ward, "Conservatism in a Simple Probability Inference Task," *Journal of Experimental Psychology*, 72 (1966), 346–54.

11. Roberts, Harry V., "Probabilistic Prediction," *Journal of the American Statistical Association*, 60 (1965), 50–62.

12. Roby, Thornton B., "Belief States and the Uses of Evidence," *Behavioral Science*, 10 (1965), 255–70.

13. Sanders, Frederick, "On Subjective Probability Forecasting," *Journal of Applied Meteorology*, 2 (1963), 191–201.

14. Savage, Leonard J., *The Foundations of Statistics*. New York: John Wiley, 1954.

15. Savage, Leonard J., et al., *The Foundations of Statistical Inference*. London: Methuen, 1962.

16. Shuford, Emir H., Jr., Albert, Arthur, and Massengill, H. Edward, "Admissible Probability Measurement Procedures," *Psychometrika*, 31 (1966), 125–45.

17. Toda, Masanao, "Measurement of Subjective Probability Distribution." State College, Pennsylvania: Report No. 3, Division of Mathematical Psychology, Institute for Research, 1963.

18. van Naerssen, Robert F., "A Scale for the Measurement of Subjective Probability," *Acta Psychologica*, 20 (1962), 159–66.

19. Winkler, Robert L., "The Assessment of Prior Distributions in Bayesian Analysis," *Journal of the American Statistical Association*, 62 (1967), 776–800.

10

Information and Capital Markets*

Eugene B. Fama
University of Chicago

Arthur B. Laffer
University of Chicago

I. Introduction

There has been much work documenting the speed of adjustment of security prices to new information.[1] So far, however, this "efficient markets" literature has had little to say about the process of information generation itself. That will be the topic of concern here.

We emphasize that the analysis will be far from complete. Many questions will be left not only unanswered but unmentioned. The goals are (i) to take a few beginning steps toward formalizing concepts in the economics of information generation in the capital market and (ii) to see what types of interesting (and perhaps surprising) results can be obtained from simple premises. The following assumptions are maintained throughout.

1. Individual firms are perfectly competitive in the markets for their products, and the capital market is perfect in the usual sense of zero transactions costs, costless access to whatever information is publicly available, and the existence of perfect substitutes for the securities of a firm.
2. Firms issue only a single type of security, common stock, and the goal of the firm is to maximize the market value of its stock.
3. Investors can trade in the market without identifying themselves or indi-

Reprinted by permission of the publisher and author from *The Journal of Business of the University of Chicago*, Vol. XLIV, No. 3, July 1971, © 1971. The University of Chicago.

*This research was supported by a grant from the National Science Foundation. After writing this paper we became aware of a paper by Jack Hirshleifer ("The Private and Social Value of Information and the Reward to Inventive Activity," Working Paper no. 158, Western Management Science Institute, University of California, Los Angeles, April 1970) which comes to many of the conclusions reached here, though from a completely different approach. We are happy to be in such company. We also wish to thank Profs. Merton H. Miller and Charles Nelson for their helpful comments.

1. An overview of this literature, along with references, can be found in Eugene F. Fama, "Efficient Capital Markets: A Review of Theory and Empirical Work," *Journal of Finance* 25 (1970): 383–417.

cating that they might have new information. Thus any person with private access to information can get the maximum benefits.

4.   Investors agree on the implications of any given information set for the equilibrium prices of securities. This assumption (usually called "homogeneous expectations") allows us to avoid the difficulties that arise in analyzing the information-generating process (or even defining the concept of information) when people disagree about the implications of events for current and future equilibrium prices. This is not to say that such problems are uninteresting or unimportant, but just that our analysis will abstract from them completely.

5.   There is no short selling of securities. Moreover, a seller of new information insists that the purchaser guarantee against resale of the information.

Given assumptions 1 and 3, the role of assumption 5 is to bound the potential gains from information generation. That is, in a perfect capital market an investor could purchase quantities of a security in excess of its total supply by inducing others to short sell. Other investors would be willing to short sell, since there are perfect substitutes for the security that they can purchase to neutralize their short positions. Likewise an investor could in principle short sell amounts of a security in excess of its total supply. In some rather special cases (in particular when there is a producer who faces no actual or potential competition in generating information about a firm) these possibilities lead to difficulties in bounding the potential gains from information. And the difficulties are compounded when information itself can be used and then resold in the market. These problems can be handled in more realistic ways (and in ways equally consistent with the general results to be derived below),[2] but the restrictions of assumption 5 on short sales and resale of information are the simplest.

As in any model, the general role of the assumptions is to provide an uncomplicated framework within which a theory can be developed. And as always, the hope is that in simplifying the analysis, the assumptions help to obtain useful insights about the real world.

II. The Nature of Information and Its Benefits

The analysis will concentrate entirely on information about individual firms, and the time sequence envisioned is as follows. Before information is generated, the anticipated result of a given amount of expenditures by a pro-

---

2. For example, the gains from information generation could be bounded (and perhaps more realistically) by imposing assumptions about the maximum number of transactions per unit time and the rate of unavoidable leakage of new information into the market. But these would lead to the same general conclusions as our simple approach.

ducer of information about a firm is a probability distribution of changes in the current market value of the firm. When the information is generated, the expenditure produces an implied change in market value which is just a drawing from this distribution. The actual change in market value then takes place when the information becomes known to the market.

We shall consider separately three different sources of benefits from information: (i) reduction of risk, (ii) improved operating decisions by the firm, and (iii) investor trading profits as a result of private access to new information. Most of the discussion will be concerned with potential trading profits.

Let us suppose that investors in general are risk-averse and that the market value of a firm's stock reflects a discount for the risk inherent in the firm's activities.[3] If information that has the effect of reducing estimates of the risk of a firm's activities is disclosed, then, other things equal, the market value of the firm's shares should rise by the value of the implied reduction in risk. If an investor generates risk-reducing information, he can buy all the firm's shares and then release the information to the market; or he can make the same gain by selling the information either to the firm or to other investors. If the firm generates the information, it can recoup all the gains for its shareholders by simply releasing the information to the market.

With more information a firm can always make operating decisions at least as good as those it would make with less. If information about the firm's activities indicates they are likely to be more profitable than was previously anticipated, then the firm should probably invest more in the activities or operate them more intensely. On the other hand, if the information indicates that the activities are likely to be less profitable than was anticipated, then the firm will probably want to invest less in them. In this case, the information brings about a savings in resources that would otherwise be unprofitably allocated to the activity.

Information that would improve a firm's operating decisions in general would also be risk reducing and have potential value for trading purposes. The rule for a producer of information to follow is clear: he should generate information to the point where its marginal value (to him) in all its uses is equal to its marginal cost.

Though we fully recognize that any information is likely to have potential value in all three uses, in the rest of the paper we shall be concerned with the economics of information when used for trading purposes. Thus it will be convenient to assume that investors are risk neutral, and that the information being considered has no effect on operating decisions. In essence we shall be concerned with information, as yet unavailable to the market, about decisions

---

3. To be complete we should specify the exact nature of risk and how its price is determined. (See, for example, Eugene F. Fama, "Risk, Return, and Equilibrium," *Journal of Political Economy* 79 [January–February 1971] : 30–56.) But this much detail is not necessary for our purposes.

already made. These assumptions, however, will not be critical to the results; they are only used to free the analysis from distracting and unnecessary encumbrances.[4]

We shall also assume that any potential producer of information about a firm knows the probability distributions of market-value changes associated with different levels of information expenditures. Thus should these distributions have a nonzero mean, this is costless information (that is, it is known without any expenditures).[5] It follows that if the costless information is always immediately utilized, market prices will be unbiased with respect to potential information generation by any producer. The result of going from zero to some positive level of expenditures is then a probability distribution of market-value changes that has a zero mean.

Nevertheless, positive information expenditures can still have positive expected trading profits. And we shall find that $E|\tilde{v}|$, the expected absolute value of the market-value change $\tilde{v}$, is always directly related to potential trading profits.[6] Thus $E|\tilde{v}|$ will be the natural measure of the information output of any producer. His output function, $E|\tilde{v}| = f(c)$, then tells the levels of $E|\tilde{v}|$ associated with expenditures c on information generation. Thus to assume (as we have done above) that any producer of information knows the probability distributions of market-value changes associated with different levels of expenditures implies that the producer knows his output function.

Moreover, $E|\tilde{v}|$ is the only measure of the output of information generation that we shall need. In particular, we need not specify the nature of the information that gives rise to the distribution of $\tilde{v}$. Note, however, that when we talk about producers competing to generate the same information, we mean that they are trying to produce the same type of information (e.g., about the firm's

---

4. And again we have chosen the simplest possible assumptions consistent with the analysis and conclusions to follow. For example, instead of assuming that investors are risk neutral and that information generated for trading purposes has no effect on operating decisions, nothing would change if we simply said that the costs of information used for trading purposes are measured net of whatever value accrues to the information producer because the information has value in reducing risk or improving operating decisions. In support of the simpler assumptions of the text, however, it is interesting to note that much of the funds spent on research by "money managers" (e.g., brokerage houses, banks, mutual funds, etc.) are specifically directed toward generating information for trading purposes. Though such information, when disclosed to the market, may lead to improved operating decisions by firms, this would not be considered by the "money managers" in their decisions about how much information to produce. This could, of course, be important for determining whether "socially optimal" quantities of information are produced.

5. Note that since a producer knows the probability distributions of market-value changes associated with different levels of his information expenditures, if one of these distributions has a nonzero mean, then logical consistency requires that all of them have the same nonzero mean.

6. The first absolute moment of the distribution of v is $E|v|$. The tilde ($\sim$) here denotes the fact that before the information is generated, the market-value change, v, is a random variable.

productive efficiency, or its research and development, or its marketing activities, etc.). The analysis of the economics of information will implicitly focus on a single type of information.

Finally, information that improves a firm's operating decisions or (if the market is risk averse) reduces the outstanding supply of risk is consistent with Pareto optimality. In one case information causes resources to be utilized more efficiently; in the other it reduces the supply of a good that has negative utility. But since the expected change in market value associated with positive expenditures on information generated for trading purposes is always zero, the expected effect of such information is just a redistribution of wealth among investors.[7] Thus if its production uses up real resources, this production is not consistent with Pareto optimality: that is, we shall show that there are always distributions of wealth among investors that are obtainable without information generation that dominate those obtained with information generation (in the sense that some investors would consider themselves better off, while none would consider themselves worse off).

Thus we shall argue that production of information for trading purposes is socially suboptimal. The rest of our analysis will be concerned with the conditions under which the production of such information exists and the conditions under which production is eliminated by natural market forces or by the effects of legal restrictions. The next section will be concerned with the economics of information generation for trading purposes under conditions of monopoly, competition, and partial monopoly. In the final section the results will be summarized and the role of a disclosure law will be studied.

III. Information for Trading Under Different Conditions of Production

A. Monopoly

A monopoly producer of information is one who either because of technology or timing has sole access to information. We shall consider two types of producers of information about a firm: the firm itself and independent out-

---

7. Remember that the capital market is assumed to be perfect, and producing firms are assumed to be perfectly competitive in the markets for their products. Thus information about a specific firm does not affect the consumption-investment opportunities of individuals except through its effects on their wealth. This would not be true, though, for a more macro-economic type information (e.g., information about a product or an industry or the economy as a whole) which is likely also to affect consumption-investment opportunities through its implications for changes in relative prices. But the social welfare effects of such changes are probably impossible to analyze without extreme simplifying assumptions about consumer tastes. In this paper we concentrate on types of information where such "substitution effects" are assumed to be negligible relative to "income" or "wealth effects."

siders. Following Hirshleifer (see unnumbered footnote, p. 289), we shall also consider two types of information: foreknowledge and discovery. Foreknowledge concerns events that will occur whether or not information about them is generated. Discovery, on the other hand, involves things that would not become known without information production.[8]

The independent producer of foreknowledge has the option of selling his output or using it for his own trading. If the producer must make an irreversible choice either to sell or to trade, the choice is not a matter of indifference. Since by assumption short selling is prohibited, if he can only trade on the information he can only make profits when the information turns out positive. Thus his expected profit is $\frac{1}{2}E|\tilde{v}| - c$, where c is the cost of producing the distribution of market-value changes with expected absolute value $E|\tilde{v}|$.[9] But if the information producer sells his information about the firm, he will be able to obtain $E|\tilde{v}|$ from the firm's shareholders (or from the firm itself, operating in behalf of its shareholders) if he guarantees exclusive access to his output. The price of $E|\tilde{v}|$ the shareholders would pay is the sum of (i) the expected trading gain of $\frac{1}{2}E|\tilde{v}|$—if the information is negative the shareholders will sell out at a price that is higher than the equilibrium price implied by this information—plus (ii) the savings of the expected losses of $\frac{1}{2}E|\tilde{v}|$—these losses would be incurred if other investors had exclusive access to the information, the information turned out positive, and these other investors bought out the shareholders at a price lower than the equilibrium price implied by the new information. Since their position is complementary to that of the shareholders, outsiders (that is nonshareholders) would likewise pay $E|\tilde{v}|$ for monopolistic access to the information. The price of $E|\tilde{v}|$ that outsiders would pay is the sum of expected trading gains of $\frac{1}{2}E|\tilde{v}|$ should the information turn out positive, plus avoidance of expected losses of $\frac{1}{2}E|\tilde{v}|$ that would be incurred if shareholders had exclusive access to the infor-

---

8. Though we do not wish to press the point, in general, information about a firm that has no effect on its operating decisions will be foreknowledge, while information that leads to improved operating decisions probably involves some amount of discovery. In the latter case the appropriate interpretation of "information for trading purposes" is that of footnote 4. That is, we recognize that the information might lead to improved operating decisions, but we choose to concentrate on the value of the information for trading purposes. To do so we measure the cost of the information net of its value (to the information producer) in improved operating decisions.

9. Since $E(\tilde{v}) = 0$, the expectation of all possible negative values of $\tilde{v}$ must be equal to the negative of the expectation of all possible positive values. Moreover,

$$E|\tilde{v}| = \left| \int_{-\infty}^{0} v dP(v) \right| + \int_{0}^{\infty} v dP(v), \tag{1}$$

where $P(v)$ is the distribution function of v. Since our arguments imply that the first term on the right side of the equality must be equal to the second, both must be equal to $\frac{1}{2}E|\tilde{v}|$. And the second term is, of course, the expected market-value change that is relevant to the monopolistic producer who will trade on his information.

mation and the information turned out negative.[10] Alternatively, shareholders and outsiders would separately pay $\frac{1}{2}E|\tilde{v}|$ each to neutralize the expected effects of the information by simply having it disclosed to both. Then neither shareholders nor outsiders have expected trading gains, but both will avoid the expected losses that would be incurred if the other had exclusive access to the information. And avoidance of expected losses is all they are paying for.[11]

When information is produced by a monopolistic outsider, the analysis of the economics of discovery information is identical with the analysis of foreknowledge. The price either shareholders or outsiders would be willing to pay for exclusive first access to the information is again $E|\tilde{v}|$, or separately they would pay $\frac{1}{2}E|\tilde{v}|$ each to prevent the other from having first access. The profit to the information producer from sales of the information would be $E|\tilde{v}| - c$, while again if he trades on the information himself, the expected profit is only $\frac{1}{2}E|\tilde{v}| - c$.

Thus an independent monopolistic producer of information will as a rule sell his output rather than use it for his own trading. And it is important to note that the restriction on short sales is not critical here. Rather the result arises from the fact that the producer can sell the information for the equivalent of what would be his own trading gains *plus* the expected losses purchasers would suffer if others had exclusive access to the information.

The independent monopolist will produce information to a point that maximizes his profit, $E|\tilde{v}| - c$, and the producer is the only one who has expected profits from information production. Investors as a whole would be better off (and the producer would be no worse off) if they could simply pay the monopolist his profits to induce him not to produce information, since then they would only pay $E|v| - c$ rather than $E|v|$. But in the absence of such side payments we have an equilibrium that is socially suboptimal (i.e., non-Pareto optimal).

The gains of the monopolist are at the expense of investors, including the shareholders of the firm about which information is being generated. Thus if the

---

10. In line with assumption 3 of the Introduction, the presumption here is that if anybody has exclusive access to information, this would be unknown to others. To the extent that this is not true, the monopoly returns from information will be lessened, which of course lessens the incentive to generate information.

11. For analytic convenience, we treat shareholders and outsiders as if they were two distinct groups. This is, of course, almost never the case. A shareholder who owns only part of the outstanding supply of a firm's shares is also an outsider to the extent that he would purchase information for the purpose of buying additional shares if the information indicated that the current price was too low. Our analytic device is simply to treat such an investor as two separate people. Treating shareholders and outsiders as groups does have a more important advantage, however. It allows us to avoid serious problems that arise in determining how information will be priced and distributed to different members of a given group.

firm itself is the monopolist it will consider the effects of its activities on its shareholders, and this will lead to a different information output decision than would be made by an independent monopolist operating under the same cost conditions. In fact, on the criterion of maximum net gain to its shareholders, in producing information the monopolistic firm will maximize $\frac{1}{2} E|\widetilde{v}| - c$. For example, in producing foreknowledge, since positive information would eventually come to light anyway, the firm's shareholders can only have net expected gains (vis-à-vis what they would have if no information were produced) from negative information (that is, being able to sell out before such information reaches the market).[12] The net expected gains from such negative foreknowledge information are $\frac{1}{2} E|\widetilde{v}| - c$. In the case of discovery information (which would not come to light in the absence of information production), the firm simply releases positive information (which has ex ante expected value $\frac{1}{2} E|\widetilde{v}|$), and either suppresses negative information or gives shareholders the opportunity to sell out before it reaches the market. The net expected gains to the shareholder (vis-à-vis what they would have if no information were produced) are again $\frac{1}{2} E|\widetilde{v}| - c$.

Thus the output of information for trading purposes will be less when the firm itself is the monopolistic producer than when the monopolist is an independent outsider. Moreover, the proposition that the firm would produce less information about itself than an independent outsider with the same output function does not depend on the existence of monopoly or on the restriction on short sales. Rather it arises from the fact that an independent producer simply maximizes profits, neglecting completely the effects of his activities on investors, whereas the firm at least considers the effects of its activities on its own shareholders.

Finally, though the output of information for trading purposes is less when the firm itself is the monopolistic producer, any such information production is again socially suboptimal. The firm's shareholders would be no worse off without information production if outsiders simply paid the firm the expected profits from information (i.e., $\frac{1}{2} E|\widetilde{v}| - c$). Outsiders would be better off, since net expected shareholder trading profits with information are less than expected losses to outsiders by the amount of the cost that the firm would incur in generating the information.

B. Information Generation Is Competitive

Suppose now that information generation is competitive in the sense that (i) there are always many potential producers of given amounts of information

---

11. For analytic convenience, we treat shareholders and outsiders as if they were two distinct groups. This is, of course, almost never the case. A shareholder who owns only part of the outstanding supply of a firm's shares can, of course, be treated as if he were to purchase information for the purpose of buying additional shares if the information indicates that the current share price was too low. Our device avoids this complexity by treating investors as two separate people. Treating shareholders and outsiders as groups does have a more important advantage, however. It allows us to avoid serious problems that arise in determining the incentive to generate information.

12. It is easy to show that when a firm is a monopolistic producer of information about itself, the policy of using the information for shareholder trading gains is optimal. That is, from the viewpoint of the shareholders it is at least as profitable as any policy involving sale of the information to outsiders.

at minimum cost, and (ii) it is always possible for one producer of information to react to the activities of another before trading on the basis of information takes place.

Nevertheless, in equilibrium there will only be one producer of given information about the firm. If there were multiple producers of the same information, it would always pay for them to merge, since by producing the information only once their combined costs are lowered, though their combined output is unaffected. On the other hand, with the production function of the one producer also available to others, potential entry ensures that the producer on average makes at most his costs.

As in the case of monopolistic production, when the producer of information about a firm is an independent outsider, an equilibrium will occur when output is at a point that maximizes $E|\tilde{v}| - c$. An independent producer of information about a firm will sell his output to both the firm's shareholders and outsiders. When both have the information neither will have positive expected profits. Shareholders will buy to avoid the expected losses (from positive information, and equal to $\frac{1}{2}E|\tilde{v}|$) that they would have if outsiders had sole access to the information, while outsiders will buy to avoid expected losses (from negative information, and equal to $\frac{1}{2}E|\tilde{v}|$) that they would have if shareholders had sole access to the information. Shareholders and outsiders together will pay marginal cost for an additional unit of output, as long as the marginal cost is not greater than the marginal benefit (that is, as long as $\frac{1}{2}dE|\tilde{v}|/dc + \frac{1}{2}dE|\tilde{v}|/dc \geqslant 1$). Thus equilibrium occurs when $dE|\tilde{v}|/dc = 1$.

On the other hand, suppose the firm is the producer of information about itself. Since its costs represent the reproduction costs of any outside producer, it can give its information output to its shareholders, recover its costs entirely from sales to outsiders, and still prevent entry by an independent producer, as long as it can persuade its shareholders never to purchase additional information from an outside producer. Outsiders will not pay more than marginal value for additional information, however, so that equilibrium output for the firm occurs at a point where $\frac{1}{2}dE|\tilde{v}|/dc = 1$.

Thus with competitive conditions of production (as with monopoly) the output of information for trading purposes is less when the producer is the firm itself rather than some independent outsider. And the reason in both cases is that the firm takes account of the effects of its actions on its shareholders while an independent producer simply maximizes his gains without regard to the losses he imposes on any investors.

Indeed it may happen that there is no level of information output for which the value of information to outsiders ($\frac{1}{2}E|\tilde{v}|$) is as great as the firm's production cost, c. Then the firm cannot cover costs from sales to outsiders, and its shareholders would be better off if no information were produced. In this case, the firm can cease production of information without fear of entry by outsiders if it behaves as follows. First, the firm tells the market that if an independent producer generates information, the firm will match his output and give it away to its shareholders. Then an independent producer would only be able to sell his output to outsiders. Given that the output is also available to the firm's shareholders, its value to outsiders is only $\frac{1}{2} E|\tilde{v}|$. But since the independent producer's costs of generating information are the same as the firm's, there will be no output at which an independent producer can cover costs, and so none will enter.

Finally, with competitive conditions of production, in equilibrium any information about a firm will be available both to its shareholders and outsiders, so no investors have expected trading gains from information. In fact, since investors as a group pay an information producer his costs, these costs are their net expected losses from information production. Since an information producer only covers costs, both he and investors would be better off if investors gave him some infinitesimally small positive amount to induce him not to produce. Thus with competitive conditions of production (as with monopoly), production of information for trading purposes is socially suboptimal (that is, non-Pareto optimal).

C. Partial Monopoly

Suppose now that there is a partial monopolist—that is a producer who can generate any given information about a firm more cheaply than other producers. If the partial monopolist is an outsider, he will sell to investors the information that would be generated by the next cheapest producer, charging the production costs of this next cheapest producer. Thus profit on this segment of his output will be the difference between the next cheapest producer's costs and his own. He will continue to produce information up to the point where marginal expected absolute value equals marginal cost (i.e., as long as $dE|\tilde{v}|/dc \geqslant 1$). On this segment of his output he will be a monopolist, selling the additional information for its expected absolute value.

But if the firm itself is the partially monopolistic information generator, it will take into account the effects of its activities on its shareholders and produce less information than would be produced by an independent partial monopolist with the same cost function. Like a partially monopolistic outsider, if the firm produces information, it will want to sell to investors the information that would be generated by the next cheapest profit-maximizing producer. The group of investors who will want access to this information includes it own shareholders. This then means that the most the firm can charge outsiders is the lesser of $\frac{1}{2} E|\tilde{v}|_o$, half the expected absolute value of the information, or c_o, the cost of generating the information to the cheapest outsider producer. Since outsiders also have access to the information, the expected gain to the firm's shareholders simply from having this segment of information freely available to them is zero. Thus the shareholders will only have net expected gains from production of this segment of information when revenues from sales to outsiders exceed total costs of production: and this need not be the case if the price to outsiders must be $\frac{1}{2}E|\widetilde{v}|_o$.

On the remainder of its output the firm will behave like a complete monopolist, generating additional information as long as $\frac{1}{2}\,dE|\widetilde{v}|/dc > 1$. The firm can then give the incremental information to its shareholders for their exclusive trading purposes. If expected profit to the firm's shareholders from this segment of its information output plus the profit or loss from sale of the initial segment to outsiders is negative, the firm's shareholders would be better off if no information were produced. As in the competitive case, the firm can cease production of information without fear of entry as long as independent producers understand the firm's incentives to produce any information that will be available about itself.

Throughout this section we have assumed that all information is firm specific. In many instances information may pertain to an entire group of firms, such as an industry. In these cases the analysis becomes somewhat more complicated and may be more like that for bilateral monopoly.

IV. Summary and the Effects of a Disclosure Law

A. Summary

We have, then, considered the economics of information generated for trading purposes when the information industry is monopolistic, competitive, or partially monopolistic. And in the course of the analysis some general conclusions have emerged.

First, when generating information for trading consumes real resources, such information is socially suboptimal. Investors could induce a producer to cease generating information by paying him the profits he would make from production. Since the necessary side payments would always be less (by at least the amount of the producer's costs) than investors would have to pay for (or expect to lose from) the firm's output, they would be better off and the information producer would be no worse off. But such side payments may be difficult to arrange, and then in general there will be some socially suboptimal information output.

Second, in equilibrium there is a single producer of a given type of information about a firm. And when the producer is an independent outsider, his profits can always be greater if he sells the information rather than using it for his own trading. Under competitive conditions of production, the only way an information producer can cover costs is through sales to investors, since if he does not offer to sell his output investors can obtain it from another producer and so negate any trading profits he might make. Under monopolistic conditions of production, information will as a rule be sold, since the information producer can charge purchasers for trading profits and for the expected losses they would incur if other investors had exclusive access to the information.

Third, when a firm is the producer of information about itself, it produces less than would an independent outsider with the same output function. Under all conditions of production, equilibrium output for the firm is at a point that maximizes $\frac{1}{2}E[v|v] - c$, whereas equilibrium for an outsider is at a point that maximizes $E[v|v] - c$. And in all cases, the result arises from the fact that, unlike the firm, the outsider does not consider the effects of his activities on the firm's shareholders or any other investors.

Finally, in the interests of its shareholders, the firm has strong incentives to have all the information that is to be available about itself produced at its discretion. In every situation considered, when the firm's shareholders buy information from an outside producer, the incentive is loss minimization rather than positive profits. Even though it may not be as efficient as the independent information producer, the shareholders will be better off if the firm produces the information, as long as the firm's losses are less than shareholder losses when the information is purchased from an outside producer. Moreover, when the firm has control over the production of information about itself, it will get to use any information produced to improve its operating decision. Thus the "net" cost to the firm of generating information for trading purposes is lower by the value of the information when used for the purpose of improved operating decisions. And in attempting to control the production of information about itself, the firm is not limited to direct competition with independent producers for sales to outsiders, since the costs to an outsider of producing information about a firm are likely to be somewhat in the firm's control.

B. Disclosure Laws

In some cases where the firm would be the producer of information about itself, a social optimum can be achieved by means of legal disclosure provisions (much like those already on the books in the United States). That is, the firm is restricted by law both from selling information about itself and from giving preferential treatment to either its shareholders or outsiders in releasing information. Such a law destroys the firm's incentive to generate information for trading purposes since (even neglecting costs of production) its expected value to the firm's shareholders is always zero. Thus the legal restrictions will lead to a social optimum (that is, absence of production of information for trading purposes) when the firm is a monopolist in the production of information about itself or when an outside producer (assumed to sell to both insiders and outsiders) must charge the firm's shareholders more for any information than the firm's costs of generating the same information. In the latter case the firm's shareholders will be better off if the firm produces the information and discloses it to the market. But as long as potential outside producers realize that the firm will act to destroy any profits they might make from information generation, the firm can cease production without fear of entry.

But we hasten to add that a disclosure law can lead to inefficiencies. It is easy to think of situations where an outsider produces information that the firm could produce more cheaply (or that the firm would produce less of) except that the presence of the disclosure law destroys the firm's incentive to produce.

11

The "True Probability" Problem

Lawrence D. Phillips
Brunel University, Middlesex, U.K.

Asking a person for his subjective probability regarding some event is all
very well, but how do we know he will give us his *true* probability? How
meaningful is the number he gives us? The contributors to this volume appear to
have found different answers to these questions: Rapoport prefers to observe
behaviour (in a dynamic decision task) rather than ask subjects for their probabilities; Pitz partially rejects probability as a meaningful response and seeks other
behavioural measures of uncertainty such as decision time; Murphy and Staël
von Holstein accept probability estimates but advocate use of scoring systems to
keep the estimator 'honest'; Kidd finds biases in his assessors' probabilities;
Wise shows that probabilities subjects give in their task obey the laws of probability theory, and so are meaningful in the sense of being consistent, a view that
would, I am sure, please de Finetti.

Behind these apparently differing viewpoints I sense a fundamental agreement about the basis of probability. In spite of differing views of probability
itself and of how probabilities can be used, most of us seemed to think that
underlying the behaviour of our subjects was some state of the person in which
he has a certain feeling of uncertainty. It is this feeling of uncertainty that we
were referring to when we used the term 'true probability'. Being subjectivists,
most of us were *not* using 'true probability' in the sense of 'real' or 'objective'
probability (often equated with relative frequency). Some of us to disagree,
however, on the inferential links between observed behaviour and unobserved
feelings of uncertainty.

It is well to remember at this point that a probability is a number between
0 and 1 inclusive. I find it difficult to believe that my feelings of uncertainty
register within me as numbers, to be detected, and, hopefully, reported honestly.
My feelings of uncertainty are feelings, not numbers, so they cannot be probabilities. Thinking or uttering probabilities must require translating feelings of uncertainty into degrees of belief, probabilities. Once this translation has occurred, it
makes sense to enquire about the correspondence between probabilities that
have been uttered and those that have not, but it is my impression that this is
not really the issue. It is the possible discrepancy between a person's feelings of

Reprinted by permission of the publisher and author from *Acta Psychologica*, Vol. 34
(1970), pp. 254–264. © North-Holland Publishing Company.

uncertainty and his assessed probabilities that worries many psychologists, statisticians and others.

My suggestion is that we accept probability assessments for what they are: verbal behaviour. The statistician, businessman or any decision maker may well wish to concentrate solely on the probabilities, devising whatever schemes are necessary to elicit probabilities that are consistent, or coherent, in the sense that they obey the probability axioms. But the investigator interested in understanding the process that leads to probabilities will wish to know what is behind those assessments, what factors influence probabilities. Probability exists only as a verbal response, the subjective correlate is a feeling of uncertainty, and many things can influence the feeling of uncertainty and the mechanisms that generate the response. It is to these influencing factors that I turn next.

Factors That Influence Probability

In a sense, what follows is nothing more than a catalogue of psychological functioning. Perhaps a more complete and comprehensive list could have been obtained if I had consulted the chapter headings in any introductory psychology textbook. But I shall go a little beyond a mere listing and suggest possible avenues for new research, for there are some glaring holes in current emphases.

Stimulus Characteristics

Most of the research to date on probability falls under this heading. Early work (reviewed by Peterson and Beach, 1967) concentrated on judgements of proportions or relative frequencies. This psycho-physical-like approach is currently found in experiments on probability when the sole basis for the probability judgement is thought by the experimenter to be a relative frequency or porportion. Then the experimenter looks at the shape of the function relating objective and subjective probability.

Notice that this approach assumes the experimenter's view of the world is 'objective', that he has correctly identified the stimulus characteristics that will go furthest in accounting for the subject's probabilities. Again, the psycho-physical approach is apparent. The experimenter has identified some reality in the world and he wishes to see how the subject perceives this reality.

But for a subjectivist, the assumption is wrong. Insofar as the functions obtained are not straight lines, the experiment succeeds in showing only that the subject and the experimenter view the world differently, not that the subject's view differs from some objective reality. The functions should be relabeled: subject's probability vs. experimenter's probability.

Most of the research on probability revision has been a search for relevant stimulus characteristics. We now know, for example, that the amount of probability revision in a variety of tasks depends on the prior probability, the likelihood ratio, sample size, the sequence in which the data are presented, and so forth. Research on man-computer systems for revising probabilities has also concentrated on stimulus characteristics and task variables.

My only quarrel with this research is that much of it assumes the existence of an 'objective' likelihood or likelihood ratio which can be entered into Bayes' theorem to provide posterior probabilities or odds that are then compared to subjects' assessments of probabilities or odds. In a bookbag-and-pokerchip experiment, the experimenter 'knows' what the 'correct' likelihood ratio is. He 'knows' in the sense that other experimenters would agree with him. But this agreement should not hide the subjective nature of the judgement, and we have no justification for calling the resulting posterior probabilities calculated from applying Bayes' theorem 'veridical' or 'objective' probabilities, as I once did (Phillips, 1966) and as others continue to do. A likelihood is a probability, and it is every bit as subjective as any other probability, even though the reasons for arriving at a particular value are so compelling that any reasonable man (not our subjects, of course!) would agree. Revision experiments that compare subjects' probabilities with 'objective' ones calculated from Bayes' theorem are subject to the same criticism I have just made about the psychophysical studies: we are not comparing subjects with an objective norm, we are comparing subjects' degree of revision with the experimenter's judgement about the amount of revision that he, as a reasonable man, would make. The only claim the experimenter can make to objectivity is that he has a calculator at hand to enable him to do the arithmetic correctly, while the subject doesn't. But that simply allows the experimenter to be consistent in his judgements, while the subject is forced into inconsistency by his limited ability to process information.

At this point I must disagree with those investigators who believe conservatism resides either in misaggregation of data or in misperception of the data-generating process or both (Phillips, 1966; Edwards, 1968). In these studies 'misperception' is usually applied to the likelihood, but as I have just noted, likelihoods are probabilities, the results of subjective judgement, and so cannot, by definition, be misperceived. Seen in this light 'misperception' really means 'differs from the experimenter's view of the world'. I don't doubt that different people see the world differently and that they would give different likelihoods from one another in identical circumstances, but we should not conclude then that conservatism in making inferences about the world is a result of misperception; better to say that differing amounts of conservatism result from different judgements about the size of the likelihood ratio (as well as from misaggregation of data). The emphasis shifts from an absolute statement about the source of conservatism to one concerning individual differences in conservatism.

Probabilities do not exist as characteristics of the physical world; they are a person's statement about his degrees of belief. Accordingly, experimenters should examine the influence of stimulus characteristics or task variables on judgements of probability, without trying to identify any particular characteristic as the 'objective' basis for judgement. Certainly Wise's contribution to this conference is in that spirit.

Cognitive Processes

When a person is asked for a probability he may engage different cognitive processes. If he is a probability assessor in a man-machine system for diagnosis, he may have to learn to attend only to those pieces of information that affect the likelihood ratio, ignoring irrelevant detail. If he is a businessman trying to assess the uncertainty in the market for a proposed product he may have to call up from memory experience that is relevant to the present situation. If he is a medical doctor making a probabilistic diagnosis, he may rely heavily on his knowledge of the etiology of a disease in trying to assess the probabilistic relationship between symptom and disease. An individual's feelings of uncertainty may be affected by his differential *attention* to his environment, by his *memory* of relevant information, and by the *logical processes* he employs to deal with information. I know of no systematic attempts to show how all these cognitive processes affect an individual's feelings of uncertainty or assessments of probability; here we are poor in both theory and data, though Pitz's paper in this volume is a start.

Prior Experience and Information

Lindley (1965) observes that two people giving different probabilities about the same events may do so because they do not share the same information. After all, if information brings about near agreement, through the application of Bayes' theorem, it follows that the initial disagreement resulted from different information.

How does prior information affect an individual's feelings of uncertainty? Gustafson (1969) obtained probabilities from experienced and inexperienced medical doctors and found that predictions based on the probabilities were more often true for the experienced men. It would be incorrect to say that the experienced men's *probabilities* were 'truer', for both groups of men probably made the best assessments they could in light of their own past experience. It would be fair to say that the probabilities of the experienced doctors were more meaningful for the purposes of prediction.

While it is reassuring to hear that probabilities given by experienced people are meaningful, this says little about how prior information affects feelings of uncertainty. Most research has concentrated on the effects of sample or experimental data on probabilities; the general finding is well known: people don't revise probabilities as much as they could. Their feelings of uncertainty are not very affected by experimental data. But just the opposite finding is reported by Schlaifer (1969) for the case where assessments are based on prior information rather than experimental data.

> The most important evidence for this proposition comes from a series of experiments which Howard Raiffa has conducted with nearly a thousand graduate students as subjects. The students were asked to assess their distributions of various uncertain quantities whose true values could be determined but were unknown to the students at the time they assessed their distributions; results were as follows. In 30% to 40% of all cases, the true value proved to lie either below the 0.01 fractile or above the 0.99 fractile of the assessed distribution; in 2/3 of all cases, the true value proved to lie outside the interquartile range. The only notable exceptions are typified by the case where the students were asked to assess their distributions of next week's Dow Jones average and the average turned out to have the same value that it had at the time of the assessment (p. 65).

Perhaps this finding explains the inconsistencies in the conservatism studies. Conservatism is always found in bookbag-and-pokerchip experiments; for these tasks most subjects have had very little prior experience with binomial data-generators. But in a task using normal data-generators DuCharme and Peterson (1968) found little conservatism. Possibly subjects' considerable experience with the normal distributions of heights of men and women leads them to be too certain, and this just balances out the conservatism associated with revision in the light of the data. This hypothesis could easily be checked using unfamiliar normal processes. Raiffa's observations also discredit a response bias explanation of conservatism; it would be a curious response bias that operates in one direction for judgements based on experimental data and in the opposite direction for assessments based only on past experience.

Another kind of past experience that may affect feelings of uncertainty is betting shop experience. Since coming to England, I have found that asking subjects in my experiments to express their degrees of belief in odds leads to confusion because people often have considerable experience with betting-shop odds. As everyone knows, these odds don't relate just to the events you are betting on, but also reflect the behaviour of other bettors. Thus, the feelings of uncertainty experienced by the skilled punter may be biased to take account of the betting behaviour of others, so when he is participating in an experiment his judgements of probability may be different than the estimates of a non-gambler purely because of his different past experience.

Scoring Rules

Are an assessor's feelings of uncertainty affected by a scoring rule, or does the rule influence primarily the decision process that enables a subject to translate his feelings of uncertainty into a number? Research to date is unclear on these questions. Beach and Phillips (1967) found very good agreement between probabilities estimated directly and probabilities inferred from choices among bets, where the judgements were based on a sequential display of relative frequencies. Beach and Wise (1969) obtained similar results in an inferential task where subjects were not simply making judgements based on a relative frequency display. It seems reasonable to conclude that since two very different kinds of responses, choices among bets and assessed probabilities, yield nearly identical results, they are both tapping the same feelings of uncertainty. Further, since the choices-among-bets condition in the Beach and Phillips study was basically the choice of a payoff from a proper scoring rule, it appears that the scoring rule had little if any effect on the subjects' feelings of uncertainty.

On the other hand, Phillips and Edwards (1966) found that subjects make different assessments under two different proper scoring rules, the quadratic and logarithmic. Is it possible that subjects' feelings of uncertainty were different under the two conditions even though the tasks were identical? Another possibility is that uncertainty was the same, but the decision processes were different. This is certainly a plausible possibility. The optimal response of a subject using a scoring rule is to choose the probability with the highest expected payoff. However, the expected payoff function in the vicinity of the subject's 'true' judgement is very flat, especially for a logarithmic payoff, so a subject can 'hedge' his choice in either direction from his 'true' feelings with little consequent loss in *expected* payoff, but with a noticeable change in real payoff. So, possibly the differences they noted say more about decision processes than feelings of uncertainty.

Winkler and Murphy's (1968) findings support this view. They report that assessors ranked according to their average scores achieve consistent ranks when making judgements under different proper scoring rules. Staël von Holstein has obtained similar results (1969). Although these findings appear to conflict with those of Phillips and Edwards it is difficult to say how sensitive the ranking procedure is to intra-individual differences when inter-individual differences are large, as is typically the case in these studies.

The matter is far from settled, but it appears that the presence of a scoring rule does not affect an assessor's feelings of uncertainty. But what effect does it have? A scoring rule is a payoff, and as Edwards (1961) has pointed out, payoffs are instructions. A scoring rule is another input to the individual, and while its presence or absence at any given moment probably does not affect the assessor's feelings of uncertainty, it can bring about, through its motivating and instructional function, changes in a person's feelings of uncertainty as he gains experience in the task. I do not believe the scoring rule necessarily keeps the assessor honest, nor does it enable the experimenter to determine the relative 'goodness' of different assessors. Let me report an anecdote to illustrate these points.

Some years ago I performed an unpublished experiment on short-term memory in which subjects had to classify each trigram in a long sequence as old or new. The task was made sufficiently difficult that subjects would feel some degree of uncertainty about each trigram's classification, so they responded on a 10-point probability scale extending from 'highly probable new' to 'highly probable old'. A proper scoring rule was associated with the scale, and pay for serving in the experiment was based solely on the total payoff score.

Two of the 20 subjects caught my interest; they almost always used the most or next-most extreme categories. I later asked the most extreme subject why he was always so sure of himself, especially in light of his less-than-perfect success rate (it was 66.7% overall). He replied that on each trial he felt quite sure he was correct. Now suppose he was telling the truth. Then, he was reporting his feelings of uncertainty as honestly as he could and so should qualify as a 'good' assessor. Yet his payoff-ranking (compared to the other subjects) was low, seventh from the bottom, so by Winkler and Murphy's standards 13 subjects were 'better' than he. Why, when he ranked fifth from the top in number of correct identifications, do we deem him a relatively poor assessor? Because he was too extreme in his judgements. But on what basis do we say he was too extreme, for he said he reported what he felt? Here is the crux of the problem: we, as onlookers, feel that he should have paid more attention to his record of successes. If he had, he wouldn't have been so sure of himself. But this assumption, and that is all it is, reveals our probability-is-relative-frequency upbringing. In other words, our standard of 'goodness' contains an implicit identification rule for probability that is not in the personalist tradition. In this case, relative frequency of correct identifications does not necessarily bear on the subject's assessment as he sees it. And, if that is the assessor's judgement, that is as it should be.

Social and Cultural Factors

Virtually no systematic work has been done to establish the effects of social and cultural factors on assessments of probability, so what I have to say can only be suggestive. John Kidd's contribution to this conference shows the possible influence of social norms on probability judgement. By comparing predicted with actual times of completion of overhauls, he found an optimism effect: his assessors were too sure that an overhaul would be completed by a certain date, so their probabilities were too extreme. I am not saying that their probabilities were wrong, for to a personalist that is possible only if assessments do not obey the probability laws. But it is possible to compare the diagnostic *system's* predictions with the actual duration of overhaul that eventually obtains. If a consistent discrepancy shows up, we may suspect that individual assessors were influenced in their probability judgements by factors other than those relating to the overhaul itself. Their assessments aren't wrong, they are just not related only to the task characteristics.

So what other factors account for this optimism effect? Kidd and Morgan (1969) report several types of distortion that may occur as information passes up the executive hierarchy; several may account for the optimism effect, but they all have a common characteristic: a subordinate passing information on to his boss has some idea of possible courses of action that may result, so he reports in a manner to minimize undesirable consequences to him or his men. In decision theory language, probabilities of events on a decision tree may not be judged independently of the utilities of the outcomes or end positions. In this case the subordinate may see the consequence of an overhaul's not being completed on time in terms of personal status, promotion and judged competence. Not wishing to lose face with his boss, he allows these factors to influence his probability judgement.

Discussions I have had with decision theorists from different countries and at universities with a substantial international subject pool lead me to suspect that not all cultures view probability in the same way. Chance factors in determining one's future play a more prominent role in some eastern cultures than they do in the west, for example. Possibly this non-deterministic view affects judgements of probability. Here is a rich area for research.

What other factors may influence probability assessments? Social class? Age? Roles? Pressures toward conformity? Norms? The area has hardly been touched.

Personality and Cognitive Style

Some of the large individual differences found in studies on probability assessment must be related to personality and cognitive style. For example, one of a person's subidentities may not allow for feelings of uncertainty. That seems to be the case for some business executives. Brown (1970) quotes a business consultant:

> Very few executives think of themselves as gamblers or of making the best kind of decisions in a gambling situation. They want, instead, to think of themselves as individuals whose greater grasp of the available information and whose greater insights remove the uncertainty from the situation.

Perhaps some executives who cannot face their feelings of uncertainty reduce such situations to cases of black and white. If this is so, then some relationship may exist between probability judgements and intolerance of ambiguity or dogmatism. But the nature of the relationship is probably complex, for it may well be mediated by the type of defense mechanisms employed by the person in coping with his unacceptable feelings of uncertainty. For example, note that in the quotation above the uncertainty is located in the situation, not in the person. Perhaps these executives project the unacceptable uncertainty to the situation where it can safely be dealt with in an 'objective' manner.

Another possibility: some people, afraid to act, may introduce uncertainty into a situation to justify their inaction and need for more information. Perhaps these are the people who change their opinions very little as they receive new information. Possibly 'levelers' find similar past occurrences more relevant to judging a probability in a new situation than 'sharpeners', who tend to differentiate more between situations. Almost nothing is known about the influence of these factors on probability judgements.

References

Beach, L.R. and L.D. Phillips, 1967. Subjective probabilities inferred from estimates and bets. J. exp. Psychol. 75, 354–359.

—— and J.A. Wise, 1969. Subjective probability and decision strategy. J. exp. Psychol. 79, 133–138.

Brown, R.V., 1970. Do managers find decision theory useful? Harvard Business Review, May–June, 78–89.

DuCharme, W.M. and C.R. Peterson, 1968. Intuitive inference about normally distributed populations. J. exp. Psychol. 78, 269–275.

Edwards, W., 1961. Costs and payoffs are instructions. Psychol. Rev. 68, 275–84.

——, 1968. Conservatism in human information processing. In: B. Kleinmuntz (ed.), Formal representation of human judgement. New York: Wiley.

Gustafson, D.H., 1969. Evaluation of probabilistic information processing in medical decision making. Organ. Behav. hum. Perform. 4, 20–34.

Kidd, J.B. and J.R. Morgan, 1969. A predictive information system for management. Opl. Res. Quar. 20, 149–170.

Lindley, D.V., 1965. Introduction to probability and statistics from a Bayesian viewpoint: Part 2, Inference. Cambridge: University Press.

Peterson, C. and L.R. Beach, 1967. Man as an intuitive statistician. Psychol. Bull. 68, 29–46.

Phillips, L.D., 1966. Some components of probabilistic inference. Technical Report No. 1, University of Michigan, Human Performance Center.

—— and W. Edwards, 1966. Conservatism in a simple probability inference task. J. exp. Psychol. 72, 346–54.

Schlaifer, R., 1969. Teacher's solutions manual to accompany analysis of decisions under uncertainty. New York: McGraw-Hill.

Staël von Holstein, C.-A. S., 1969. The assessment of discrete subjective probability distributions—an experimental study. Research Report No. 41, Institute of Mathematical Statistics, University of Stockholm.

Winkler, R.L. and A.H. Murphy, 1968. 'Good' probability assessors, J. appl. Meteorol. 7, 751–758.

References

Beach, L.R. and L.D. Phillips, 1967. Subjective probabilities inferred from estimates and bets. J. exp. Psychol. 75, 354–359.

—— and J.A. Wise, 1969. Subjective probability and decision strategy. J. exp. Psychol. 79, 133–138.

Brown, R.V., 1970. Do managers find decision theory useful? Harvard Business Review, May–June, 78–89.

DuCharme, W.M. and C.R. Peterson, 1968. Intuitive inference about normally distributed populations. J. exp. Psychol. 78, 269–275.

Edwards, W., 1961. Costs and payoffs are instructions. Psychol. Rev. 68, 275–84.

——, 1968. Conservatism in human information processing. In: B. Kleinmuntz (ed.), Formal representation of human judgement. New York: Wiley.

Gustafson, D.H., 1969. Evaluation of probabilistic information processing in medical decision making. Organ. Behav. hum. Perform. 4, 20–34.

Kidd, J.B. and J.R. Morgan, 1969. A predictive information system for management. Opl. Res. Quar. 20, 149–170.

Lindley, D.V., 1965. Introduction to probability and statistics from a Bayesian viewpoint: Part 2, Inference. Cambridge: University Press.

Peterson, C. and L.R. Beach, 1967. Man as an intuitive statistician. Psychol. Bull. 68, 29–46.

Phillips, L.D., 1966. Some components of probabilistic inference. Technical Report No. 1, University of Michigan, Human Performance Center.

—— and W. Edwards, 1966. Conservatism in a simple probability inference task. J. exp. Psychol. 72, 346–54.

Part IV
The Efficient Markets Hypothesis

12

Proof that Properly Anticipated Prices Fluctuate Randomly

Paul A. Samuelson
Massachusetts Institute of Technology

The Enigma Posed

"In competitive markets there is a buyer for every seller. If one could be sure that a price will rise, it would have already risen." Arguments like this are used to deduce that competitive prices must display price changes over time, $X_{t+1} - X_t$, that perform a random walk with no predictable bias.

Is this a correct fact about well-organized wheat or other commodity markets? About stock exchange prices for equity shares? About futures markets for wheat or other commodities, as contrasted to the movement of actual "spot prices" for the concrete commodity.

Or is it merely an interesting (refutable) hypothesis about actual markets that can somehow be put to empirical testing?

Or is it a valid deduction (like the Pythagorean Theorem applicable to Euclidean triangles) whose truth is as immutable as $2 + 2 = 4$? Does its truth follow from the very definition of "free, competitive markets?" (If so, can there fail to exist in New York and London actual stock and commodity markets with those properties; and must any failures of the "truism" that turn up be attributable to "manipulation," "thinness of markets," or other market imperfections?)

The more one thinks about the problem, the more one wonders what it is that could be established by such abstract argumentation. Is the fact that American stocks have shown an average annual rise of more than 5 per cent over many decades compatible with the alleged "fair game" (or martingale property) of an unbiased random walk? Is it an exception that spot wheat prices generally rise (presumably because of storage costs) from the July harvest time to the following spring and drop during June? Is the fact that the price of next July's future shows much less strong seasonal patterns a confirmation of the alleged truism? If so, what about the alleged Keynes-Hicks-Houthakker-Cootner pattern of "normal backwardation," in which next July's wheat future could be expected to rise in price a little from July harvest to, say, the following March (as a result of need of holders of the crop to coax out, at a cost, risk-disliking speculators with whom to make short-hedging transactions); and what about the Cootner

Reprinted by permission of the publisher and author from *Sloan Management Review*, Spring 1965, pp. 41–49.

167

pattern in which, once wheat stocks become low in March, processors wishing to be sure of having a minimum of wheat to process, seek short-selling speculators with whom to make long-hedging transactions, even at the cost of having the July quotation dropping a little in price in months like April and May?

Consideration of such prosaic and mundane facts raises doubt that there is anything much in celestial *a priori* reasoning from the axiom that what can be perceived about the future must already be "discounted" in current price quotations. Indeed, suppose that all the participants in actual markets are necessarily boobs when it comes to foreseeing the unforeseeable future. Why should "after-the-fact" price changes show *any* systematic pattern, such as non-bias? Are the very mathematical notions of probability of any relevance to actual market quotations? If so, how could we decide that this is indeed so?

Whatever the answers to these questions, I think we can suspect that there is no *a priori* necessity for actual Board of Trade grain prices to act in accordance with specific probability models. Perhaps it is a lucky accident, a boon from Mother Nature, so to speak, that so many actual price time series do behave like uncorrelated or quasi-random walks. Thus, Maurice Kendall[1] almost proves too much when he finds negligible serial correlation in spot grain prices. For reasons that I shall discuss, we would not be too surprised to find this property in futures price changes. But surely spot prices ought to vary with shifts in such supply and demand factors as weather, crop yields, and crop plantings; or population, income, and taste changes. Who says that the weather must itself display no serial correlation? A dry month does tend to be followed by a dryer-than-average month because of persistence of pressure patterns, etc. Perhaps it is true that prices depend on a summation of so many small and somewhat independent sources of variation that the result is like a random walk. But there is no necessity for this. And the fact, if it is one, is not particularly related to perfect competition or market anticipations. For consider a monopolist who sells (or buys) at fixed price. If the demand (or supply) curve he faces is the resultant of numerous independent, additive sources of variation each of which is limited or small, his resulting quantity $\{q_t\}$ may well behave like a random walk, showing variations like the normal curve of error.

At this point, the reader may feel inclined to doubt that the arguments of my first paragraph have even a germ of interest for the economist. But I hope to show that such a rejection goes too far.

By positing a rather general stochastic model of price change, I shall deduce a fairly sweeping theorem in which next-period's price differences are shown to be uncorrelated with (if not completely independent of) previous period's price differences. This martingale property of zero expected capital gain will then be replaced by the slightly more general case of a constant mean percentage gain per unit time.

---

1. See ref. [1].

You never get something for nothing. From a nonempirical base of axioms you never get empirical results. Deductive analysis cannot determine whether the empirical properties of the stochastic model I posit come at all close to resembling the empirical determinants of today's real-world markets. That question I shall not here investigate. I shall be content if I can, for once, find definite and unambiguous content to the arguments of the opening paragraph— arguments which have long haunted economists' discussions of competitive markets.

A General Stochastic Model of Price

Let $\left\{ \ldots, X_{t-1}, X_t, X_{t+1}, \ldots, X_{t+T}, \ldots \right\}$ represent the time sequence of prices—as for example the price of spot #2 wheat in Chicago (or it could be a vector of prices or even quantities of several different goods). Given knowledge of today's price and of past prices $[X_t, X_{t-1}, \ldots]$, suppose we cannot know with certainty tomorrow's price X_{t+1}, or any future price X_{t+T}. Suppose there is at best a probability distribution for any future price, whose form depends solely on the number of periods ahead over which we are trying to forecast prices, given by

$$\text{Prob}\left\{ X_{t+T} \leqslant X | X_t = x_0, X_{t-1} = x_1, \ldots \right\} = P(X, x_0, x_1, \ldots; T) \quad (1)$$

These P's are assumed not to depend on, or change with, historical calendar time. In that sense, I posit a "stationary" process (but one consistent with, say, chronic inflation).

From the fundamental logic of probability, we can relate these probabilities relevant to different future forecast spans: $T = 1, 2, \ldots$. All are ultimately deducible from the basic one-period $P(X, x_0, x_1, \ldots; 1)$. Thus, always

$$P(X, x_0, x_1, \ldots; 2) = \int_{-\infty}^{\infty} P(X, y, x_0, x_1, \ldots; 1) \, dP(y, x_0, x_1, \ldots; 1) \quad (2)$$

$$P(X, x_0, x_1, \ldots; T) = \int_{-\infty}^{\infty} P(X, y, x_0, x_1, \ldots; T-1) \, dP(y, x_0, x_1, \ldots; 1).$$

These general Stieltjes integrals include summation of finite (or countably-infinite) probabilities and ordinary integrals of probability densities; no real ambiguity concerning the variable over which dP is being integrated will usually arise.

In words, (2) merely says that the probability of an event's happening is the sum of the probabilities of the different mutually-exclusive ways by which it could happen. If $P(X, x_0, x_1, \ldots; 1)$ had the Markov property of being quite independent of $(x_1, x_2, \ldots)$, (2) would be the so-called Chapman-Kolmogorov equation. But I do not assume any special Markov property. The generality of (1) and (2) must be emphasized. Nothing necessarily Gaussian or normal is assumed about any $P(X, x_0, x_1, \ldots; T)$. It is possible, but not necessarily assumed, that an ergodic state for P will emerge in the limit as T goes to infinity. Thus,

$$\lim_{T \to \infty} P(X, x_0, x_1, \ldots; T) = P(X) \text{ independently of } (x_0, x_1, \ldots) \qquad (3)$$

would involve such an ergodic property.

Here are some examples of possible processes that define the P's. Suppose $\{X_t\}$ satisfies a Yule-Wold autoregressive linear equation of the type

$$X_{t+1} = aX_t + \{u_t\}, \ |a| < 1, \qquad (4)$$

with u_t independent drawings from the same table of random digits or of Gaussian variates.

Or suppose the X_t price can take on only the finite discrete values $[Q_1, Q_2, \ldots, Q_n]$; and let a_{ij}, the nonnegative coefficients of a Markov transitional-probability matrix, represent the probability that a price now observed to be Q_i will one period later be observed to be Q_j, where $\Sigma_j a_{ij} = 1$ for all i. If $[a_{ij}] = A$, the reader can verify that A^2 defines $P(X, x_0; 2)$ and A^T defines $P(X, x_0; T)$. If all $a_{ij} > 0$, A^∞ is a well-defined ergodic state, composed of the matrix $[a_j]$ with identical rows and hence independent of the initial observed Q_i value.

As a third possible model let $\{X_t\}$ take a random walk in the sense of doubling in the next period with probability 1/3 and halving with probability 2/3. This defines $P(X, x_0; 1)$, and the reader can verify that (2) gives for $P(X, x_0; 2)$ the property that X_{t+2}/X_t will be (4, 1, 1/4) with respective probabilities (1/9, 4/9, 4/9), and so on with the usual binomial distribution for each T and with the central-limit theorem showing that a normal distribution is approached for $\log(X_{t+T}/X_t)$ as $T \to \infty$. This is an instance of a multiplication Brownian motion applied to prices. Unlike the absolute or additive Brownian motion, it has the grace to avoid negative prices.

Specification of a Model Defining
Behavior of a Futures Price

Now consider today's "futures price quotation" for the actual spot price that will prevail T periods from now—i.e., the price quoted today at t for a contract requiring delivery of actual physical goods at time $t + T$. If the present time is t, with present spot price X_t, the relevant spot price that is to prevail later is given by X_{t+T}. The newly defined futures price, quoted today, for that future X_{t+T}, we might denote by $Y(T, t)$. When another period passes, we shall know $(X_{t+1}, X_t, X_{t-1}, \ldots)$ instead of merely $(X_t, X_{t-1}, \ldots)$; and the new quotation for the same futures price we have been talking about will be written as $Y(T - 1, t + 1)$. It in turn will be succeeded by the sequence $[Y(T - 2, T + 2), \ldots, Y(t - n, t + n), \ldots, Y(1, t + T - 1), Y(0, t + T)]$. After $t + T$, there is no problem of pricing this particular futures contract. Thus, the July, 1964, Chicago Wheat Contract for delivery of wheat became closed, ancient history after July, 1964; but for more than twelve months prior to that date, its quotation oscillated from period to period and could be read in the newspaper.

What relationship shall we posit between the sequence $\left\{ Y(T - n, t + n) \right\}$ and the sequence $\left\{ X_{t+1} \right\}$? When the due date for the futures contract arrives, arbitrage will ensure that

$$Y(0, t + T) = X_{t+T}, \text{commissions aside}. \tag{5}$$

A period earlier no one can know what X_{t+T} will turn out to be. If interest and risk-aversion can be ignored, it is tempting to assume that people in the market place make as full use as they can of the posited probability distribution $P(X_{t+T}, X_{t+T-1}, X_{t+T-2}, \ldots ; 1)$ of next-period's price and bid by supply and demand $Y(1, t + T - 1)$ to the mean or mathematically-expected level of tomorrow's price. That way neither short-sellers nor long-buyers stand to make a positive gain or loss. This constitutes the rationale of my first model of futures price, which is based on the following.

Axiom of Mathematically Expected Price Formation. If spot prices $\left\{ X_t \right\}$ are subject to the probability distribution of (1), a futures price is to be set by competitive bidding at the now-expected level of the terminal spot price. That is,

$$Y(T, t + T) = E[X_{t+T} | X_t, X_{t-1}, \ldots] , (T = 1, 2, \ldots)$$

$$= \int_{-\infty}^{\infty} X dP(X, X_t, X_{t-1}, \ldots ; T). \tag{6}$$

The Basic Theorem

Equations (1) and (6) completely determine the properties of the model. I can now derive from them the basic theorem at which I hinted in the usual vague arguments expressed in the opening paragraph. Let us observe numerous sequences of futures prices generated by this model, up until their terminal data. They will turn out, *on the average*, to have no upward or downward drift anywhere! (This will be true, regardless of the systematic seasonal patterns in X_t. This would be true, under our axiom, even in time of severe inflation or deflation of X_t itself—only remember, please, that the neglect of interest underlying our axiom would seem unwarranted in time of confidently-anticipated extreme inflation.)

Theorem of Fair-Game Futures Pricing. If spot prices $\{X_t\}$ are subject to the probability laws of (1) and (2), and the futures price sequence $\{Y(T, t+T);$ $Y(T-1, t+T-1), \ldots, Y(1, t+T-1), Y(0, t+T)\}$ is subject to the axiom of expected price as formulated in (5) and (6), then the latter sequence is a fair game (or martingale) in the sense of having unbiased price changes, or

$$E[Y(T-1, t+T-1)|X_t, X_{t-1}, \ldots] \equiv Y(T, t), \text{ or writing} \tag{7}$$

$$Y(T-1, t+T-1) - Y(T, t) = \Delta Y(T, t), E[\Delta Y(T, t)] \equiv 0; \tag{8}$$

from which it follows inductively that

$$E[\Delta^n Y(T, t)] \equiv 0 \qquad (n = 1, 2, \ldots, T). \tag{9}$$

This means that there is no way of making an expected profit by extrapolating past changes in the futures price, by chart or any other esoteric devices of magic or mathematics. The market quotation $Y(T, t)$ already contains in itself all that can be known about the future and in that sense has discounted future contingencies as much as is humanly possible (or inhumanly possible within the axiom of the model).

The theorem does not imply that the sequence of Y's perform a Brownian motion. It does not imply that $\Delta Y(T, t)$ is statistically *independent* of $\Delta Y(T+1, t-1)$; it implies only that given knowledge of $Y(T, t)$ the Pearsonian correlation coefficient between the above two Δ's will be zero. It is a source of comfort to the economist, rather than otherwise, that wheat prices should not perform a Brownian random walk. A Brownian walk, like the walk of a drunken sailor, wanders indefinitely far, listing with the wind.

Surely, economic law tells us that the price of wheat—whether it be spot $\{X_t\}$ or futures $\{Y(T, t)\}$—cannot drift sky-high or ground-low. It does have a rendezvous with its destiny of supply and demand, albeit our knowledge of future supply and demand trends becomes dimmer as the envisaged date T recedes farther into the future. We would expect people in the market place, in pursuit of avid and intelligent self-interest, to take account of those elements of future events that in a probability sense may be discerned to be casting their shadows before them. (Because past events cast *their* shadows after them, future events can be said to cast their shadows before them.)

Although the sequence $\{\Delta Y(T-n, t+n)\}$ has a zero first moment at all time periods $T-n$, there is no reason to suppose that the riskiness of holding a futures—in the sense of the second moment of variance, as measured by $E[\{\Delta Y(T-n, t+n)\}]$—should be the same when T is large and the terminal date far away as when $T - n$ is small and the futures contract about to expire. It is a well-known rule of thumb that nearness to expiration date involves greater variability or riskiness per hour or per day or per month than does farness. Partly this is due, I think, to factors not encompassed in the present model—for example, the real-life complications that make arbitrage equality shown in (5) hold only approximately. However, the present theory can contribute an elegant explanation of why we should expect far-distant futures to move more sluggishly than near ones. Its explanation does not lean at all on the undoubted fact that, during certain pre-harvest periods when stocks are normally low, changes in spot prices $\{\Delta X_t\}$ can themselves be expected to experience great volatility and second moment. Instead, it uses the contrary minor premise of posited *uniformity* through time of the distribution of $\{\Delta X_t\}$ —so that it constitutes a stationary time series—to deduce the law of increasing volatility of a maturing futures contract. Before deriving the result, I present a proof of the martingale theorem.

By definition

$Y(T, t) = \int_{-\infty}^{\infty} X dP(X, X_t, X_{t-1}, \ldots ; T)$, axiom of (6)

$Y(T - 1, t + 1)$

$= \int_{-\infty}^{\infty} X dP(X, X_{t+1}, X_t, X_{t-1}, \ldots ; T - 1)$, axiom of (6)

$= f(X_{t+1}, X_t, X_{t-1}, \ldots .) E[Y(T - 1, t + 1)|X_t, X_{t-1}, \ldots]$

$= \int_{-\infty}^{\infty} f(Z, X_t, X_{t-1}, \ldots .) dP(Z, X_t, X_{t-1}, \ldots ; 1)$

$= \int_{-\infty}^{\infty} [\int_{-\infty}^{\infty} X dP(X, Z, X_t, \ldots ; T - 1)] dP(Z, X_t, \ldots ; 1)$

$= \int_{-\infty}^{\infty} X d[\int_{-\infty}^{\infty} P(X, Z, X_t, \ldots ; T - 1) dP(Z, X_t, \ldots ; 1)]$

$= \int_{-\infty}^{\infty} X dP(X, X_t, \ldots ; T)$, by (2) $= Y(T, t)$ Q.E.D.   (10)

In thus proving (7), I have made permissible interchanges in the order of integration of the double Stieltjes intergrals.

The content of this general theorem can be illustrated by some specific stochastic processes.

(a) Thus, suppose $\{X_t\}$ represents a simple Brownian motion without bias. Then $Y(T, t)$ becomes nothing but X_t itself. Since $\{X_t\}$ is a fair-game with $E[\Delta X] = 0$, then so must $E[\Delta Y] = 0$.

(b) Going beyond this simple case, suppose $\{X_t\}$ is a random walk with biased drift so that $E[\Delta X] = \mu \neq 0$. Then $Y(T, t) = X_t + \mu T$ and $E[\Delta Y] = E[\Delta X] + \mu(T - 1 - T) = \mu - \mu = 0$, as the theorem requires.

(c) Now let $\{X_t\}$ satisfy an autoregressive stochastic relation

$$X_{t+1} = aX_t + \{u_t\}, E(u_t) = \mu,$$

where $\{u_t\}$ is an unserially correlated random variable with distribution $P(U)$. Then

$$Y(T, t) = a^T X_t + \mu T$$

$$E[\Delta Y] = \int_{-\infty}^{\infty} a^{T-1}(aX_t + U_t)\, dP(U_t) + \mu(T - 1) - a^T X_t - \mu T$$

$$= 0 + \mu - \mu = 0.$$

(d) Finally, let $A = [a(i,j)]$ be a finite Markov transition-probability matrix giving

$$\text{Prob}\{X_{t+1} = Q_i | X_t = Q_j\}.$$

Write $A^T = [a_{ij}{}^T]$, and

$Y(T, t) = [Q_1, \ldots, Q_n]$ times the jth column of A^T, by Axiom

$$= \sum_i Q_i a_{ij}{}^T, \text{ denoted by } Y(T|Q_j).$$

Then

$$E[Y(T - 1), t + 1 | X_t = Q_j] = \sum_k Y(T - 1)|Q_k) a_{kj}, \text{ by definition}$$

$$= \sum_i Q_i a_{ij}{}^{T-1} a_{kj}$$

$$= \sum_i Q_i a_{ij}{}^T, \text{ since } A^{T-1}A = A^T$$

$$= Y(T, t) \qquad \text{Q.E.D.}$$

The theorem is so general that I must confess to having oscillated over the years in my own mind between regarding it as trivially obvious (and almost trivially vacuous) and regarding it as remarkably sweeping. Such perhaps is characteristic of basic results. And actually the empirical question of the applicability of the model to economic reality must be kept distinct from the logical problem of what is the model's implied content.

Figure 1 should help to explain the theorem. It supposes $\{X_t\}$ is generated by (4)'s autoregressive model with $a = 1/2$. Random shocks $\{u_t\}$ aside, if price is once perturbed above (or below) its normal value (set at zero by convention), in each period it will return one-half way back to zero.

Generalizing the Theorem

If money has to be tied up in holding the $Y(T, t)$ contract and if there is a positive safe rate of interest, the process—being a fair game—does not stand to earn even the opportunity-cost of foregone safe interest. If, in addition, people have risk aversion (so that the utility whose expected value they seek to maximize is a strictly concave function of money wealth or income), the contract will probably have to promise a positive percentage yield per unit time, R, where $1 + R = \lambda > 1 +$ safe interest.

Therefore, we replace the simple axiom of mean expected value by a slightly more general axiom.

Axiom of Present-Discounted Expected Value: At each point of time t for a future price, we posit

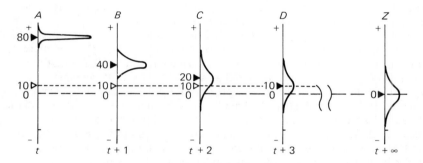

Figure 1A. At time t, we know $X_t = 80$ with certainty. We can expect, from (4) with $a = 1/2$ and u_t approximately normally distributed, that X_{t+t} be distributed as shown, with $E[X_{t+t} | X_t = 80] = 40$; for X_{t+2} the distributions are becoming slightly more dispersed, with means drifting downward like $80(2^{-2})$, $80(2^{-3})$; because $a = 1/2 < 1$, there is a limiting ergodic state for $t + \infty$, much as shown, with $E[X_{t+x} | X_t] = 0$ independently of X_t. At time t, the futures price X_{t+3} is evaluated at 10, as shown by the white arrow at A, which merely reflects what can now be known about the distribution and mean of the spot price three periods from now. Now ask yourself the question. What do I think at this time t will be the likely distribution of this futures price $Y(3, t)$ at the next period when it will have become $Y(2, t + 1)$? It will be distributed around 1/4 of next period's spot price X_{t+1} in exactly the same way that C shows X_{t+2} distributed around 1/4 of the period's spot price X_t. You do not today know where tomorrow's X_{t+1} will fall; but B does give you its probability distribution. Combining these bits of information, Figure 1B below plots (with enlarged vertical scale) what you *now* are entitled to regard as the probability distribution for $Y(3, t)$, $Y(2, t +1)$, $Y(1, t + 2)$, $Y(0, t + 3) = X_{t+3}$.

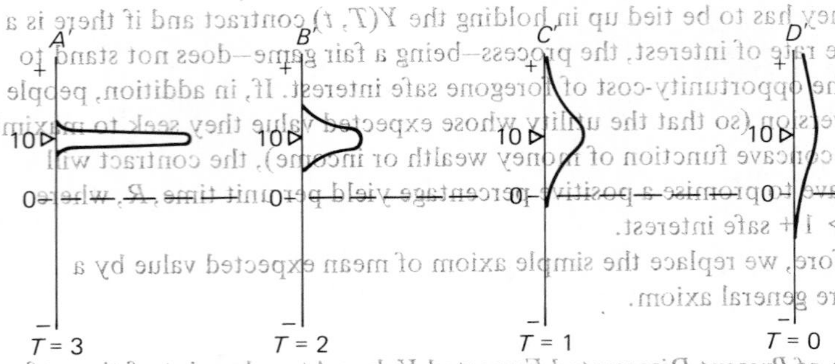

Generalizing the Theorem

$$A' \qquad B' \qquad C' \qquad D'$$

$$10\triangleright \qquad 10\triangleright \qquad 10\triangleright \qquad 10\triangleright$$

$$T = 3 \qquad T = 2 \qquad T = 1 \qquad T = 0$$

Figure 1B. A', B', C', and D' give the probability distributions you are entitled to envisage on the basis of today's certain knowledge of $[X_t, X_{t+1}, \ldots$ and $Y(3, t)]$ for next periods' $[Y(2, t + 1), Y(1, t + 2), Y(0, t + 3) = X_{t+3}]$. Note that all have the same mean of 10 but that your cone of uncertainty widens as the time in which new unknown, independent disturbances $\{u_{t+1}\}$ can intervene. Note that after one period passes, both diagrams will have to be redrawn: A and A' will be irrelevant; a particular point on B and B' will become the new present, and the new (C, C') and (D, D') will bear the same relation to (B, B') that now (C, C') and (B, B') bear respectively to (A, A'). If the stochastic variables u_{t+1}, u_{t+3} were identically zero, the futures price would show no variability, staying always at 10. $Y(3, t)$ and $Y(2, t + 1)$ are likely to be more alike with a less volatile difference ΔY than can $Y(2, t + 1)$ and $Y(1, t + 2)$. (For equation (4), the variance of $\Delta Y(t - n, t + n)$ is proportional to a^{T-n}, diminishing as $T - n$ becomes large.) Why? Because the first pair stand to have (u_{t+2}, u_{t+3}) in common and differ only in that the first of the pair also has u_t as a source of variation. The fact that this pair has two out of three elements of variation in common is stabilizing on their difference ΔY in comparison with the second pair which have only u_{t+3} out of the possible (u_{t+2}, u_{t+3}) in common. A far-distant future will not change much in the next month since so few of the disturbances upon which its fate depends will change in this month; it stays close to the general level given by the so-called law of averages. At the other extreme, $Y(1, t + 2)$ and $Y(0, t + 3) = X_{t+3}$ will differ because of the single unknowable u_{t+3}, and this sudden-death kind of situation will subject their difference to great variance without any cushioning from the law of large numbers. A striking way of seeing this is to disregard the varying means and to think of the passage of one period as leaving us at the left of the diagram subtracting the last (rather than the first, as when we shift the present from A to B) of the vertical axes. Precisely because D approaches an ergodic state, C and D differ less than do A and B in Figure 1A. So losing the last axis, which is like making C become the new D, gives less of a change than would shifting B to A.

$$Y(T,t) = \lambda^{-T} E[X_{t+T}|X_t, X_{t-1}, \ldots]$$

or, slightly more generally, since the variability of Y may be slightly different for each value of T, we may expect a different $(\lambda_1, \lambda_2, \ldots, \lambda_T)$ yield for which people hold out if they are to hold for the next period a futures contract with T years to go. The present-discounted expectation becomes

$$Y(T,t) = \lambda_1^{-1} \lambda_2^{-1} \cdots \lambda_T^{-1} E[X_{t+T}|X_t, X_{t-1}, \ldots].$$

Just as the simple axiom of expected gain led to the theorem of unbiased price change, the new general axiom leads to the theorem on "normal backwardation".

Theorem of Mean Percentage Price Drift. If spot prices $\{X_t\}$ are determined by the stipulated general stochastic process $P(X_{t+T}, X_t, X_{t-1}, \ldots; T)$ and we define the sequence $\{Y(T,t), Y(T-1, t+1), \ldots, Y(1, t+T-1), Y(0, t+T)\}$ by

$$Y(T,t) = \lambda_T^{-1} E[X_{t+T}|X_t, X_{t-1}, \ldots] = \lambda_T^{-1} \int_{-\infty}^{\infty} X \, dP(X, X_t, X_{t-1}, \ldots; T),$$

it follows that

$$E[Y(T-n, t+n)|X_t, X_{t-1}, \ldots] = \lambda_T^{-1} \cdots \lambda_{T-n+1}^{-1} Y(T,t)$$

$$\equiv \lambda^{-n} Y(T,t) \text{ if } \lambda_1 \equiv \lambda.$$

In words, this says that the futures price will rise in each period by the percentage $\lambda - 1$ (or $\lambda_T - 1$, where presumably $\lambda_1 > \lambda_2 > \ldots > \lambda_T$ if people abhor the extra riskiness inherent in a futures contract as it matures). This theorem provides rational account of the Keynes-Houthakker-Cootner[2] doctrine of "normal backwardation". It says that, within the defined model, all chart methods attempting to read out of the past sequence of known prices $[X_t, X_{t-1}, \ldots, Y(T,t), Y(T+1, t-1), \ldots]$ any profitable pattern of prediction is doomed to failure. So to speak, the market has already, by our axiom, discounted all knowable future information so that the present-discounted variable $(\lambda_T \cdots \lambda_1)^{-1} Y$ sequence is itself a fair-game martingale.

Re-examining the proof of the simple theorem, we see that the same interchange of order of integration in the relevant double integral gives an immediate proof of the theorem.

---

2. See refs. [2], [3], [4], [5], and [6].

Finally, examining the proof shows that a still more general theorem is valid. Wherever we have had X_{t+T} in $E[X_{t+T}|X_t, X_{t-1}, \ldots]$ or X in the double integral, we could have put in any function of X, say $g(X)$ or $g(X_{t+T})$ and still preserved the martingale properties. This is important because, as mentioned, we may want to interpret X_t as a vector—as e.g. with components (soft wheat price, hard wheat price, corn price, midwest rainfall, national income, etc.). Then the scalar $g(X_{t+T})$ might be the selection of soft wheat price, the deliverable goods for the futures contract in question. Only a deluded chartist would think that extraneous variables, such as rainfall, can be excluded from an optimal *probability* description of future soft wheat prices; and yet it is true that, after speculators have taken such variables into account in implementing the axiom of expected gain, the resulting Y sequence tells its own (simple!) story.

Still one more bargain in cheap generality can be garnered. As far as the theorem's proof is concerned, $g(X_{t+T})$ could just as well be a function also of all present known data and be written as $g(X_{t+T}, X_t, X_{t-1}, \ldots)$, without affecting its general martingale property. It would even be possible to put now-known values of $Y(T + k, t - k)$ as variables in g, but there would seem to be no need to do this since ultimately all known Y's should be reducible to functions of the X_{t-k} inputs. Still there is no harm in so including the Y's, and in some cases the form of the function might be much simplified by including such Y's (and even the Y's of other terminal date). To illustrate how one might want X_t in $g(X_{t+T}, X_t, \ldots)$, suppose that either number 1 or number 2 grades of soft wheat are deliverable on the July, 1965, contract. Let the vector X_t contain as elements price data on both grades; and suppose that if one of these is now known to be much cheaper than the other, one can be pretty sure that this cheaper grade will be the grade actually delivered on the contract at the terminal date; and hence for certain value of the elements of the vector X_t, $g(\ldots)$ will be the expected price of one grade rather than of the other.

Conclusion

A result of some generality has now been established. Anyone who thinks it obvious should reflect on the following fact: if instead of taking an expected value or mean value of X_{t+T}, we set $Y(T, t)$ at, say, its median value, then it will not necessarily be true that expected value of ΔY is zero. Nor is it true that the median of ΔY so defined is zero. For example, let $P(X_{t+1}, X_t, 1) = P(X_{t+1}/X_t)$ with $P(1) > \frac{1}{2} = P(m)$, $0 < m < 1$. Then $Y(T, t) = mX_t$, $Y(T + 1, t + 1) = mX_{t+1}$. For median $\Delta Y = 0$, we require

$$\text{Prob}\left\{Y_{t+1} \leqslant Y_t\right\} = \text{Prob}\left\{mX_{t+1} \leqslant mX_t\right\} = \text{Prob}\left\{X_{t+1} - X_t\right\} = \frac{1}{2}.$$

But actually,

$$\text{Prob}\left\{X_{t+1} \leqslant X_t\right\} = \text{Prob}\left\{\frac{X_{t+1}}{X_t} \leqslant 1\right\} = P(1) > \tfrac{1}{2}.$$

Hence, ΔY is more likely to be negative than positive—even if $P(X/x)$ defines a fair game with $E(X/x) = x$.

One should not read too much into the established theorem. It does not prove that actual competitive markets work well. It does not say that speculation is a good thing or that randomness of price changes would be a good thing. It does not prove that anyone who makes money in speculation is *ipso facto* deserving of the gain or even that he has accomplished something good for society or for anyone but himself. All or none of these may be true, but that would require a different investigation.

I have not here discussed where the basic probability distributions are supposed to come from. In whose minds are they *ex ante*? Is there any *ex post* validation of them? Are they supposed to belong to the market as a whole? And what does that mean? Are they supposed to belong to the "representative individual," and who is he? Are they some defensible or necessitous compromise of divergent expectation patterns? Do price quotations somehow produce a Pareto-optimal configuration of *ex ante* subjective probabilities? This paper has not attempted to pronounce on these interesting questions.

References

1. Kendall, Maurice G., "The Analysis of Economic Time-Series—Part I: Prices," *Journal of the Royal Statistical Society* 96, Part I (1953), pp. 11–25; also pp. 85–99 in Cootner, Paul H. (editor), *The Random Character of Stock Market Prices*. Cambridge: The M.I.T. Press, 1964.
2. Keynes, J.M., *A Treatise on Money*, Vol. II: *The Applied Theory of Money*. London: Macmillan & Company, 1930.
3. Houthakker, H., "The Scope and Limits of Futures Trading," pp. 134–159 in Abramovitz, Moses (editor), *Allocation of Economic Resources*.
4. Houthakker, H., "Systematic and Random Elements in Short-Term Price Movements," *American Economic Review* 51 (1961), pp. 164–172.
5. Cootner, Paul H., "Returns to Speculators: Telser vs. Keynes," *Journal of Political Economy* 68 (1960), pp. 396–404.
6. Cootner, Paul H., "Rejoinder," *Journal of Political Economy* 68 (1960), pp. 415–418.

13

The Pricing of Options and Corporate Liabilities

Fischer Black
University of Chicago

Myron Scholes
University of Chicago

Introduction

An option is a security giving the right to buy or sell an asset, subject to certain conditions, within a specified period of time. An "American option" is one that can be exercised at any time up to the date the option expires. A "European option" is one that can be exercised only on a specified future date. The price that is paid for the asset when the option is exercised is called the "exercise price" or "striking price." The last day on which the option may be exercised is called the "expiration date" or "maturity date."

The simplest kind of option is one that gives the right to buy a single share of common stock. Throughout most of the paper, we will be discussing this kind of option, which is often referred to as a "call option."

In general, it seems clear that the higher the price of the stock, the greater the value of the option. When the stock price is much greater than the exercise price, the option is almost sure to be exercised. The current value of the option will thus be approximately equal to the price of the stock minus the price of a pure discount bond that matures on the same date as the option, with a face value equal to the striking price of the option.

On the other hand, if the price of the stock is much less than the exercise price, the option is almost sure to expire without being exercised, so its value will be near zero.

If the expiration date of the option is very far in the future, then the price of a bond that pays the exercise price on the maturity date will be very low, and the value of the option will be approximately equal to the price of the stock.

On the other hand, if the expiration date is very near, the value of the option will be approximately equal to the stock price minus the exercise price, or zero, if the stock price is less than the exercise price. Normally, the value of

Reprinted by permission of the publisher and authors from *Journal of Political Economy*, Vol. 81, No. 3 (May/June 1973), pp. 637–54. © 1973 The University of Chicago Press.

The inspiration for this work was provided by Jack L. Treynor (1961*a*, 1961*b*). We are grateful for extensive comments on earlier drafts by Eugene F. Fama, Robert C. Merton, and Merton H. Miller. This work was supported in part by the Ford Foundation.

an option declines as its maturity date approaches, if the value of the stock does not change.

These general properties of the relation between the option value and the stock price are often illustrated in a diagram like figure 1. Line A represents the maximum value of the option, since it cannot be worth more than the stock. Line B represents the minimum value of the option, since its value cannot be negative and cannot be less than the stock price minus the exercise price. Lines T_1, T_2, and T_3 represent the value of the option for successively shorter maturities.

Normally, the curve representing the value of an option will be concave upward. Since it also lies below the 45° line, A, we can see that the option will be more volatile than the stock. A given percentage change in the stock price, holding maturity constant, will result in a larger percentage change in the option value. The relative volatility of the option is not constant, however. It depends on both the stock price and maturity.

Most of the previous work on the valuation of options has been expressed in terms of warrants. For example, Sprenkle (1961), Ayres (1963), Boness (1964), Samuelson (1965), Baumol, Malkiel, and Quandt (1966), and Chen (1970) all produced valuation formulas of the same general form. Their formulas, however, were not complete, since they all involved one or more arbitrary parameters.

For example, Sprenkle's formula for the value of an option can be written as follows:

$$kxN(b_1) - k^*cN(b_2)$$

$$b_1 = \frac{\ln kx/c + \frac{1}{2}v^2(t^* - t)}{v\sqrt{(t^* - t)}}$$

$$b_2 = \frac{\ln kx/c - \frac{1}{2}v^2(t^* - t)}{v\sqrt{(t^* - t)}}$$

In this expression, x is the stock price, c is the exercise price, t^* is the maturity date, t is the current date, v^2 is the variance rate of the return on the stock,[1] ln is the natural logarithm, and $N(b)$ is the cumulative normal density function. But k and k^* are unknown parameters. Sprenkle (1961) defines k as the ratio of the expected value of the stock price at the time the warrant matures to the current stock price, and k^* as a discount factor that depends on the risk of the

---

1. The variance rate of the return on a security is the limit, as the size of the interval of measurement goes to zero, of the variance of the return over that interval divided by the length of the interval.

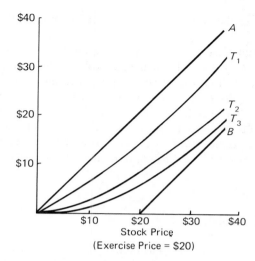

Figure 1. The relation between option value and stock price

stock. He tries to estimate the values of k and k^* empirically, but finds that he is unable to do so.

More typically, Samuelson (1965) has unknown parameters α and β, where α is the rate of expected return on the stock, and β is the rate of expected return on the warrant or the discount rate to be applied to the warrant.[2] He assumes that the distribution of possible values of the stock when the warrant matures is log-normal and takes the expected value of this distribution, cutting it off at the exercise price. He then discounts this expected value to the present at the rate β. Unfortunately, there seems to be no model of the pricing of securities under conditions of capital market equilibrium that would make this an appropriate procedure for determining the value of a warrant.

In a subsequent paper, Samuelson and Merton (1969) recognize the fact that discounting the expected value of the distribution of possible values of the warrant when it is exercised is not an appropriate procedure. They advance the theory by treating the option price as a function of the stock price. They also recognize that the discount rates are determined in part by the requirement that investors be willing to hold all of the outstanding amounts of both the stock and the option. But they do not make use of the fact that investors must hold other assets as well, so that the risk of an option or stock that affects its discount rate is only that part of the risk that cannot be diversified away. Their final formula

2. The rate of expected return on a security is the limit, as the size of the interval of measurement goes to zero, of the expected return over that interval divided by the length of the interval.

depends on the shape of the utility function that they assume for the typical investor.

One of the concepts that we use in developing our model is expressed by Thorp and Kassouf (1967). They obtain an empirical valuation formula for warrants by fitting a curve to actual warrant prices. Then they use this formula to calculate the ratio of shares of stock to options needed to create a hedged position by going long in one security and short in the other. What they fail to pursue is the fact that in equilibrium, the expected return on such a hedged position must be equal to the return on a riskless asset. What we show below is that this equilibrium condition can be used to derive a theoretical valuation formula.

The Valuation Formula

In deriving our formula for the value of an option in terms of the price of the stock, we will assume "ideal conditions" in the market for the stock and for the option:

a)   The short-term interest rate is known and is constant through time.
b)   The stock price follows a random walk in continuous time with a variance rate proportional to the square of the stock price. Thus the distribution of possible stock prices at the end of any finite interval is log-normal. The variance rate of the return on the stock is constant.
c)   The stock pays no dividends or other distributions.
d)   The option is "European," that is, it can only be exercised at maturity.
e)   There are no transaction costs in buying or selling the stock or the option.
f)   It is possible to borrow any fraction of the price of a security to buy it or to hold it, at the short-term interest rate.
g)   There are no penalties to short selling. A seller who does not own a security will simply accept the price of the security from a buyer, and will agree to settle with the buyer on some future date by paying him an amount equal to the price of the security on that date.

Under these assumptions, the value of the option will depend only on the price of the stock and time and on variables that are taken to be known constants. Thus, it is possible to create a hedged position, consisting of a long position in the stock and a short position in the option, whose value will not depend on the price of the stock, but will depend only on time and the values of known constants. Writing $w(x, t)$ for the value of the option as a function of the stock price x and time t, the number of options that must be sold short against one share of stock long is:

$$1/w_1(x,t). \tag{1}$$

In expression (1), the subscript refers to the partial derivative of $w(x,t)$ with respect to its first argument.

To see that the value of such a hedged position does not depend on the price of the stock, note that the ratio of the change in the option value to the change in the stock price, when the change in the stock price is small, is $w_1(x,t)$. To a first approximation, if the stock price changes by an amount Δx, the option price will change by an amount $w_1(x,t)\,\Delta x$, and the number of options given by expression (1) will change by an amount Δx. Thus, the change in the value of a long position in the stock will be approximately offset by the change in value of a short position in $1/w_1$ options.

As the variables x and t change, the number of options to be sold short to create a hedged position with one share of stock changes. If the hedge is maintained continuously, then the approximations mentioned above become exact, and the return on the hedged position is completely independent of the change in the value of the stock. In fact, the return on the hedged position becomes certain.[3]

To illustrate the formation of the hedged position, let us refer to the solid line (T_2) in figure 1 and assume that the price of the stock starts at $15.00, so that the value of the option starts at $5.00. Assume also that the slope of the line at that point is ½. This means that the hedged position is created by buying one share of stock and selling two options short. One share of stock costs $15.00, and the sale of two options brings in $10.00, so the equity in this position is $5.00.

If the hedged position is not changed as the price of the stock changes, then there is some uncertainty in the value of the equity at the end of a finite interval. Suppose that two options go from $10.00 to $15.75 when the stock goes from $15.00 to $20.00, and that they go from $10.00 to $5.75 when the stock goes from $15.00 to $10.00. Thus, the equity goes from $5.00 to $4.25 when the stock changes by $5.00 in either direction. This is a $.75 decline in the equity for a $5.00 change in the stock in either direction.[4]

In addition, the curve shifts (say from T_2 to T_3 in fig. 1) as the maturity of the options changes. The resulting decline in value of the options means an increase in the equity in the hedged position and tends to offset the possible losses due to a large change in the stock price.

Note that the decline in the equity value due to a large change in the stock price is small. The ratio of the decline in the equity value to the magnitude of

---

3. This was pointed out to us by Robert Merton.
4. These figures are purely for illustrative purposes. They correspond roughly to the way figure 1 was drawn, but not to an option on any actual security.

the change in the stock price becomes smaller as the magnitude of the change in the stock price becomes smaller.

Note also that the direction of the change in the equity value is independent of the direction of the change in the stock price. This means that under our assumption that the stock price follows a continuous random walk and that the return has a constant variance rate, the covariance between the return on the equity and the return on the stock will be zero. If the stock price and the value of the "market portfolio" follow a joint continuous random walk with constant covariance rate, it means that the covariance between the return on the equity and the return on the market will be zero.

Thus the risk in the hedged position is zero if the short position in the option is adjusted continuously. If the position is not adjusted continuously, the risk is small, and consists entirely of risk that can be diversified away by forming a portfolio of a large number of such hedged positions.

In general, since the hedged position contains one share of stock long and $1/w_1$ options short, the value of the equity in the position is:

$$x - w/w_1. \tag{2}$$

The change in the value of the equity in a short interval Δt is:

$$\Delta x - \Delta w/w_1. \tag{3}$$

Assuming that the short position is changed continuously, we can use stochastic calculus[5] to expand Δw, which is $w(x + \Delta x, t + \Delta t) - w(x,t)$, as follows:

$$\Delta w = w_1 \Delta x + \tfrac{1}{2} w_{11} v^2 x^2 \Delta t + w_2 \Delta t. \tag{4}$$

In equation (4), the subscripts on w refer to partial derivatives, and v^2 is the variance rate of the return on the stock.[6] Substituting from equation (4) into expression (3), we find that the change in the value of the equity in the hedged position is:

$$- (\tfrac{1}{2} w_{11} v^2 x^2 + w_2) \Delta t/w_1. \tag{5}$$

Since the return on the equity in the hedged position is certain, the return must be equal to $r\Delta t$. Even if the hedged position is not changed continuously, its risk is small and is entirely risk that can be diversified away, so the expected return on the hedged position must be at the short term interest rate.[7] If this

---

5. For an exposition of stochastic calculus, see McKean (1969).

6. See footnote 1.

7. For a thorough discussion of the relation between risk and expected return, see Fama and Miller (1972) or Sharpe (1970). To see that the risk in the hedged position can be

were not true, speculators would try to profit by borrowing large amounts of money to create such hedged positions, and would in the process force the returns down to the short term interest rate.

Thus the change in the equity (5) must equal the value of the equity (2) times $r\Delta t$.

$$- (\tfrac{1}{2} w_{11} v^2 x^2 + w_2) \, \Delta t / w_1 = (x - w/w_1) r \Delta t. \tag{6}$$

Dropping the Δt from both sides, and rearranging, we have a differential equation for the value of the option.

$$w_2 = rw - rxw_1 - \tfrac{1}{2} v^2 x^2 w_{11}. \tag{7}$$

Writing t^* for the maturity date of the option, and c for the exercise price, we know that:

$$w(x,t^*) = x - c, \qquad x \geqslant c$$

$$= 0 \qquad x < c. \tag{8}$$

There is only one formula $w(x,t)$ that satisfies the differential equation (7) subject to the boundary condition (8). This formula must be the option valuation formula.

To solve this differential equation, we make the following substitution:

$$w(x,t) = e^{r(t-t^*)} y \, [(2/v^2) \, (r - \tfrac{1}{2} v^2) \, \ln x/c - (r - \tfrac{1}{2} v^2) \, (t - t^*)],$$

$$- (2/v^2) \, (r - \tfrac{1}{2} v^2)^2 \, (t - t^*)]. \tag{9}$$

With this substitution, the differential equation becomes:

$$y_2 = y_{11}, \tag{10}$$

---

diversified away, note that if we don't adjust the hedge continuously, expression (5) becomes:

$$-(\tfrac{1}{2} w_{11} \Delta x^2 + w_2 \Delta t / w_1). \tag{5'}$$

Writing Δm for the change in the value of the market portfolio between t and $t + \Delta t$, the "market risk" in the hedged position is proportional to the covariance between the change in the value of the hedged portfolio, as given by expression (5'), and Δm: $-\tfrac{1}{2} w_{11} \, \text{cov} \, (\Delta x^2, \Delta m)$. But if Δx and Δm follow a joint normal distribution for small intervals Δt, this covariance will be zero. Since there is no market risk in the hedged position, all of the risk due to the fact that the hedge is not continuously adjusted must be risk that can be diversified away.

and the boundary condition becomes:

$$y(u,0) = 0, \qquad\qquad\qquad\qquad u < 0$$

$$= c\left[e^{u(\frac{1}{2}v^2)/(r-\frac{1}{2}v^2)} - 1\right], \qquad u \geqslant 0. \qquad (11)$$

The differential equation (10) is the heat-transfer equation of physics, and its solution is given by Churchill (1963, p. 155). In our notation, the solution is:

$$y(u,s) = 1/\sqrt{2\pi} \int_{-u/\sqrt{2s}}^{\infty}$$

$$c\left[e^{(u+q\sqrt{2s},)\,(\frac{1}{2}v^2)/(r-\frac{1}{2}v^2)} - 1\right]e^{-q^2/2}\,dq. \qquad (12)$$

Substituting from equation (12) into equation (9), and simplifying, we find:

$$w(x,t) = xN(d_1) - ce^{r(t-t^*)}\,N(d_2)$$

$$d_1 \quad = \frac{\ln x/c + (r + \frac{1}{2}v^2)\,(t^* - t)}{v\sqrt{t^* - t}}$$

$$d_2 \quad = \frac{\ln x/c + (r - \frac{1}{2}v^2)\,(t^* - t)}{v\sqrt{t^* - t}} \qquad (13)$$

In equation (13), $N(d)$ is the cumulative normal density function.

Note that the expected return on the stock does not appear in equation (13). The option value as a function of the stock price is independent of the expected return on the stock. The expected return on the option, however, will depend on the expected return on the stock. The faster the stock price rises, the faster the option price will rise through the functional relationship (13).

Note that the maturity $(t^* - t)$ appears in the formula only multiplied by the interest rate r or the variance rate v^2. Thus, an increase in maturity has the same effect on the value of the option as an equal percentage increase in both r and v^2.

Merton (1973) has shown that the option value as given by equation (13) increases continuously as any one of t^*, r, or v^2 increases. In each case, it approaches a maximum value equal to the stock price.

The partial derivative w_1 of the valuation formula is of interest, because it determines the ratio of shares of stock to options in the hedged position as in expression (1). Taking the partial derivative of equation (13), and simplifying, we find that:

$$w_1(x,t) = N(d_1). \qquad (14)$$

In equation (14), d_1 is as defined in equation (13).

From equations (13) and (14), it is clear that xw_1/w is always greater than one. This shows that the option is always more volatile than the stock.

An Alternative Derivation

It is also possible to derive the differential equation (7) using the "capital asset pricing model." This derivation is given because it gives more understanding of the way in which one can discount the value of an option to the present, using a discount rate that depends on both time and the price of the stock.

The capital asset pricing model describes the relation between risk and expected return for a capital asset under conditions of market equilibrium.[8] The expected return on an asset gives the discount that must be applied to the end-of-period value of the asset to give its present value. Thus, the capital-asset pricing model gives a general method for discounting under uncertainty.

The capital-asset pricing model says that the expected return on an asset is a linear function of its β, which is defined as the covariance of the return on the asset with the return on the market, divided by the variance of the return on the market. From equation (4) we see that the covariance of the return on the option $\Delta w/w$ with the return on the market is equal to xw_1/w times the covariance of the return on the stock $\Delta x/x$ with the return on the market. Thus, we have the following relation between the option's β and the stock's β:

$$\beta_w = (xw_1/w)\beta_x. \tag{15}$$

The expression xw_1/w may also be interpreted as the "elasticity" of the option price with respect to the stock price. It is the ratio of the percentage change in the option price to the percentage change in the stock price, for small percentage changes, holding maturity constant.

To apply the capital-asset pricing model to an option and the underlying stock, let us first define a as the rate of expected return on the market minus the interest rate.[9] Then the expected return on the option and the stock are:

$$E(\Delta x/x) = r\Delta t + a\beta_x \Delta t, \tag{16}$$

---

8. The model was developed by Treynor (1961b), Sharpe (1964), Lintner (1965), and Mossin (1966). It is summarized by Sharpe (1970), and Fama and Miller (1972). The model was originally stated as a single-period model. Extending it to a multi-period model is, in general, difficult. Fama (1970), however, has shown that if we make an assumption that implies that the short-term interest rate is constant through time, then the model must apply to each successive period in time. His proof also goes through under somewhat more general assumptions.

9. See footnote 2.

$$E(\Delta w/w) = r\Delta t + a\beta_w \Delta t. \tag{17}$$

Multiplying equation (17) by w, and substituting for β_w from equation (15), we find:

$$E(\Delta w) = rw\Delta t + axw_1\beta_x \Delta t. \tag{18}$$

Using stochastic calculus,[10] we can expand Δw, which is $w(x + \Delta x, t + \Delta t) - w(x,t)$, as follows:

$$\Delta w = w_1 \Delta x + \tfrac{1}{2} w_{11} v^2 x^2 \Delta t + w_2 \Delta t. \tag{19}$$

Taking the expected value of equation (19), and substituting for $E(\Delta x)$ from equation (16), we have:

$$E(\Delta w) = rxw_1 \Delta t + axw_1\beta_x \Delta t + \tfrac{1}{2} v^2 x^2 w_{11} \Delta t + w_2 \Delta t. \tag{20}$$

Combining equation (18) and (20), we find that the terms involving a and β_x cancel, giving:

$$w_2 = rw - rxw_1 - \tfrac{1}{2}v^2 x^2 w_{11}. \tag{21}$$

Equation (21) is the same as equation (7).

More Complicated Options

The valuation formula (13) was derived under the assumption that the option can only be exercised at time t^*. Merton (1973) has shown, however, that the value of the option is always greater than the value it would have if it were exercised immediately $(x - c)$. Thus, a rational investor will not exercise a call option before maturity, and the value of an American call option is the same as the value of a European call option.

There is a simple modification of the formula that will make it applicable to European put options (options to sell) as well as call options (options to buy). Writing $u(x,t)$ for the value of a put option, we see that the differential equation remains unchanged.

$$u_2 = ru - rxu_1 - \tfrac{1}{2} v^2 x^2 u_{11}. \tag{22}$$

The boundary condition, however, becomes:

---

10. For an exposition of stochastic calculus, see McKean (1969).

$$u(x,t^*) = 0, \qquad x \geqslant c$$

$$= c - x, \qquad x < c. \tag{23}$$

To get the solution to this equation with the new boundary condition, we can simply note that the difference between the value of a call and teh value of a put on the same stock, if both can be exercised only at maturity, must obey the same differential equation, but with the following boundary condition:

$$w(x,t^*) - u(x,t^*) = x - c. \tag{24}$$

The solution to the differential equation with this boundary condition is:

$$w(x,t) - u(x,t) = x - ce^{r(t-t^*)}. \tag{25}$$

Thus the value of the European put option is:

$$u(x,t) = w(x,t) - x + ce^{r(t-t^*)}. \tag{26}$$

Putting in the value of $w(x,t)$ from (13), and noting that $1 - N(d)$ is equal to $N(-d)$, we have:

$$u(x,t) = -xN(-d_1) + ce^{-rt^*} N(-d_2). \tag{27}$$

In equation (27), d_1 and d_2 are defined as in equation (13).

Equation (25) also gives us a relation between the value of a European call and the value of a European put.[11] We see that if an investor were to buy a call and sell a put, his returns would be exactly the same as if he bought the stock on margin, borrowing $ce^{r(t-t^*)}$ toward the price of the stock.

Merton (1973) has also shown that the value of an American put option will be greater than the value of a European put option. This is true because it is sometimes advantageous to exercise a put option before maturity, if it is possible to do so. For example, suppose the stock price falls almost to zero and that the probability that the price will exceed the exercise price before the option expires is negligible. Then it will pay to exercise the option immediately, so that the exercise price will be received sooner rather than later. The investor thus gains the interest on the exercise price for the period up to the time he would otherwise have exercised it. So far, no one has been able to obtain a formula for the value of an American put option.

If we relax the assumption that the stock pays no dividend, we begin to get

---

11. The relation between the value of a call option and the value of a put option was first noted by Stoll (1969). He does not realize, however, that his analysis applies only to European options.

into some complicated problems. First of all, under certain conditions it will pay to exercise an American call option before maturity. Merton (1973) has shown that this can be true only just before the stock's ex-dividend date. Also, it is not clear what adjustment might be made in the terms of the option to protect the option holder against a loss due to a large dividend on the stock and to ensure that the value of the option will be the same as if the stock paid no dividend. Currently, the exercise price of a call option is generally reduced by the amount of any dividend paid on the stock. We can see that this is not adequate protection by imagining that the stock is that of a holding company and that it pays out all of its assets in the form of a dividend to its shareholders. This will reduce the price of the stock and the value of the option to zero, no matter what adjustment is made in the exercise price of the option. In fact, this example shows that there may not be any adjustment in the terms of the option that will give adequate protection against a large dividend. In this case, the option value is going to be zero after the distribution, no matter what its terms are. Merton (1973) was the first to point out that the current adjustment for dividends is not adequate.

Warrant Valuation

A warrant is an option that is a liability of a corporation. The holder of a warrant has the right to buy the corporation's stock (or otehr assets) on specified terms. The analysis of warrants is often much more complicated than the analysis of simple options, because:

a)   The life of a warrant is typically measured in years, rather than months. Over a period of years, the variance rate of the return on the stock may be expected to change substantially.

b)   The exercise price of the warrant is usually not adjusted at all for dividends. The possibility that dividends will be paid requires a modification of the valuation formula.

c)   The exercise price of a warrant sometimes changes on specified dates. It may pay to exercise a warrant just before its exercise price changes. This too requires a modification of the valuation formula.

d)   If the company is involved in a merger, the adjustment that is made in the terms of the warrant may change its value.

e)   Sometimes the exercise price can be paid using bonds of the corporation at face value, even though they may at the time be selling at a discount. This complicates the analysis and means that early exercise may sometimes be desirable.

f)   The exercise of a large number of warrants may sometimes result in a significant increase in the number of common shares outstanding.

In some cases, these complications can be treated as insignificant, and equation (13) can be used as an approximation to give an estimate of the warrant value. In other cases, some simple modifications of equation (13) will improve the approximation. Suppose, for example, that there are warrants outstanding, which, if exercised, would double the number of shares of the company's common stock. Let us define the "equity" of the company as the sum of the value of all of its warrants and the value of all of its common stock. If the warrants are exercised at maturity, the equity of the company will increase by the aggregate amount of money paid in by the warrant holders when they exercise. The warrant holders will then own half of the new equity of the company, which is equal to the old equity plus the exercise money.

Thus, at maturity, the warrant holders will either receive nothing, or half of the new equity, minus the exercise money. Thus, they will receive nothing or half of the difference between the old equity and half the exercise money. We can look at the warrants as options to buy shares in the equity rather than shares of common stock, at half the stated exercise price rather than at the full exercise price. The value of a share in the equity is defined as the sum of the value of the warrants and the value of the common stock, divided by twice the number of outstanding shares of common stock. If we take this point of view, then we will take v^2 in equation (13) to be the variance rate of the return on the company's equity, rather than the variance rate of the return on the company's common stock.

A similar modification in the parameters of equation (13) can be made if the number of shares of stock outstanding after exercise of the warrants will be other than twice the number of shares outstanding before exercise of the warrants.

Common Stock and Bond Valuation

It is not generally realized that corporate liabilities other than warrants may be viewed as options. Consider, for example, a company that has common stock and bonds outstanding and whose only asset is shares of common stock of a second company. Suppose that the bonds are "pure discount bonds" with no coupon, giving the holder the right to a fixed sum of money, if the corporation can pay it, with a maturity of 10 years. Suppose that the bonds contain no restrictions on the company except a restriction that the company cannot pay any dividends until after the bonds are paid off. Finally, suppose that the company plans to sell all the stock it holds at the end of 10 years, pay off the bond holders if possible, and pay any remaining money to the stockholders as a liquidating dividend.

Under these conditions, it is clear that the stockholders have the equivalent of an option on their company's assets. In effect, the bond holders own the company's assets, but they have given options to the stockholders to buy the assets back. The value of the common stock at the end of 10 years will be the value of the company's assets minus the face value of the bonds, or zero, whichever is greater.

Thus, the value of the common stock will be $w(x,t)$, as given by equation (13), where we take v^2 to be the variance rate of the return on the shares held by the company, c to be the total face value of the outstanding bonds, and x to be the total value of the shares held by the company. The value of the bonds will simply be $x - w(x,t)$.

By subtracting the value of the bonds given by this formula from the value they would have if there were no default risk, we can figure the discount that should be applied to the bonds due to the existence of default risk.

Suppose, more generally, that the corporation holds business assets rather than financial assets. Suppose that at the end of the 10 year period, it will re-capitalize by selling an entirely new class of common stock, using the proceeds to pay off the bond holders, and paying any money that is left to the old stockholders to retire their stock. In the absence of taxes, it is clear that the value of the corporation can be taken to be the sum of the total value of the debt and the total value of the common stock.[12] The amount of debt outstanding will not affect the total value of the corporation, but will affect the division of that value between the bonds and the stock. The formula for $w(x,t)$ will again describe the total value of the common stock, where x is taken to be the sum of the value of the bonds and the value of the stock. The formula for $x - w(x,t)$ will again describe the total value of the bonds. It can be shown that, as the face value c of the bonds increases, the market value $x - w(x,t)$ increases by a smaller percentage. An increase in the corporation's debt, leeping the total value of the corporation constant, will increase the probability of default and will thus reduce the market value of one of the corporation's bonds. If the company changes its capital structure by issuing more bonds and using the proceeds to retire common stock, it will hurt the existing bond holders, and help the existing stockholders. The bond price will fall, and the stock price will rise. In this sense, changes in the capital structure of a firm may affect the price of its common stock.[13] The price changes will occur when the change in the capital structure becomes certain, not when the actual change takes place.

Because of this possibility, the bond indenture may prohibit the sale of additional debt of the same or higher priority in the event that the firm is re-capitalized. If the corporation issues new bonds that are subordinated to the existing bonds and uses the proceeds to retire common stock, the price of the existing bonds and the common stock price will be unaffected. Similarly, if the

12. The fact that the total value of a corporation is not affected by its capital structure, in the absence of taxes and other imperfections, was first shown by Modigliani and Miller (1958).

13. For a discussion of this point, see Fama and Miller (1972, pp. 151–52).

company issues new common stock and uses the proceeds to retire completely the most junior outstanding issue of bonds, neither the common stock price nor the price of any other issue of bonds will be affected.

The corporation's dividend policy will also affect the division of its total value between the bonds and the stock.[14] To take an extreme example, suppose again that the corporation's only assets are the shares of another company, and suppose that it sells all these shares and uses the proceeds to pay a dividend to its common stockholders. Then the value of the firm will go to zero, and the value of the bonds will go to zero. The common stockholders will have "stolen" the company out from under the bond holders. Even for dividends of modest size, a higher dividend always favors the stockholders at the expense of the bond holders. A liberalization of dividend policy will increase the common stock price and decrease the bond price.[15] Because of this possibility, bond indentures contain restrictions on dividend policy, and the common stockholders have an incentive to pay themselves the largest dividend allowed by the terms of the bond indenture. However, it should be noted that the size of the effect of changing dividend policy will normally be very small.

If the company has coupon bonds rather than pure discount bonds outstanding, then we can view the common stock as a "compound option." The common stock is an option on an option on . . . an option on the firm. After making the last interest payment, the stockholders have an option to buy the company from the bond holders for the face value of the bonds. Call this "option 1." After making the next-to-the-last interest payment, but before making the last interest payment, the stockholders have an option to buy option 1 by making the last interest payment. Call this "option 2." Before making the next-to-the-last

---

14. Miller and Modigliani (1961) show that the total value of a firm, in the absence of taxes and other imperfections, is not affected by its dividend policy. They also note that the price of the common stock and the value of the bonds will not be affected by a change in dividend policy if the funds for a higher dividend are raised by issuing common stock or if the money released by a lower dividend is used to repurchase common stock.

15. This is true assuming that the liberalization of dividend policy is not accompanied by a change in the company's current and planned financial structure. Since the issue of common stock or junior debt will hurt the common shareholders (holding dividend policy constant), they will normally try to liberalize dividend policy without issuing new securities. They may be able to do this by selling some of the firm's financial assets, such as ownership claims on other firms. Or they may be able to do it by adding to the company's short-term bank debt, which is normally senior to its long-term debt. Finally, the company may be able to finance a higher dividend by selling off a division. Assuming that it receives a fair price for the division, and that there were no economies of combination, this need not involve any loss to the firm as a whole. If the firm issues new common stock or junior debt in exactly the amounts needed to finance the liberalization of dividend policy, then the common stock and bond prices will not be affected. If the liberalization of dividend policy is associated with a decision to issue more common stock or junior debt than is needed to pay the higher dividends, the common stock price will fall and the bond price will rise. But these actions are unlikely, since they are not in the stockholders' best interests.

interest payment, the stockholders have an option to buy option 2 by making that interest payment. This is "option 3." The value of the stockholders' claim at any point in time is equal to the value of option $n + 1$, where n is the number of interest payments remaining in the life of the bond.

If payments to a sinking fund are required along with interest payments, then a similar analysis can be made. In this case, there is no "balloon payment" at the end of the life of the bond. The sinking fund will have a final value equal to the face value of the bond. Option 1 gives the stockholders the right to buy the company from the bond holders by making the last sinking fund and interest payment. Option 2 gives the stockholders the right to buy option 1 by making the next-to-the-last sinking fund and interest payment. And the value of the stockholders' claim at any point in time is equal to the value of option n, where n is the number of sinking fund and interest payments remaining in the life of the bond. It is clear that the value of a bond for which sinking fund payments are required is greater than the value of a bond for which they are not required.

If the company has callable bonds, then the stockholders have more than one option. They can buy the next option by making the next interest or sinking fund and interest payment, or they can exercise their option to retire the bonds before maturity at prices specified by the terms of the call feature. Under our assumption of a constant short-term interest rate, the bonds would never sell above face value, and the usual kind of call option would never be exercised. Under more general assumptions, however, the call feature would have value to the stockholders and would have to be taken into account in deciding how the value of the company is divided between the stockholders and the bond holders.

Similarly, if the bonds are convertible, we simply add another option to the package. It is an option that the bond holders have to buy part of the company from the stockholders.

Unfortunately, these more complicated options cannot be handled by using the valuation formula (13). The valuation formula assumes that the variance rate of the return on the optioned asset is constant. But the variance of the return on an option is certainly not constant: it depends on the price of the stock and the maturity of the option. Thus the formula cannot be used, even as an approximation, to give the value of an option on an option. It is possible, however, that an analysis in the same spirit as the one that led to equation (13) would allow at least a numerical solution to the valuation of certain more complicated options.

Empirical Tests

We have done empirical tests of the valuation formula on a large body of call-option data (Black and Scholes 1972). These tests indicate that the actual prices at which options are bought and sold deviate in certain systematic ways from the values predicted by the formula. Option buyers pay prices that are consistently higher than those predicted by the formula. Option writers, however, receive prices that are at about the level predicted by the formula. There are large transaction costs in the option market, all of which are effectively paid by option buyers.

Also, the difference between the price paid by option buyers and the value given by the formula is greater for options on low-risk stocks than for options on high-risk stocks. The market appears to underestimate the effect of differences in variance rate on the value of an option. Given the magnitude of the transaction costs in this market, however, this systematic misestimation of value does not imply profit opportunities for a speculator in the option market.

References

Ayres, Herbert F. "Risk Aversion in the Warrants Market." *Indus. Management Rev.* 4 (Fall 1963): 497–505. Reprinted in Cootner (1967), pp. 497–505.

Baumol, William J.; Malkiel, Burton G.; and Quandt, Richard E. "The Valuation of Convertible Securities." *Q.J.E.* 80 (February 1966): 48–59.

Black, Fischer, and Scholes, Myron. "The Valuation of Option Contracts and a Test of Market Efficiency." *J. Finance* 27 (May 1972): 399–417.

Boness, A. James. "Elements of a Theory of Stock-Option Values." *J.P.E.* 72 (April 1964): 163–75.

Chen, Andrew H.Y. "A Model of Warrant Pricing in a Dynamic Market." *J. Finance* 25 (December 1970): 1041–60.

Churchill, R.V. *Fourier Series and Boundary Value Problems,* 2d ed. New York: McGraw-Hill, 1963.

Cootner, Paul A. *The Random Character of Stock Market Prices.* Cambridge, Mass.: M.I.T. Press, 1967.

Fama, Eugene F. "Multiperiod Consumpton-Investment Decisions." *A.E.R.* 60 (March 1970): 163–74.

Fama, Eugene F., and Miller, Merton H. *The Theory of Finance.* New York: Holt, Rinehart & Winston, 1972.

Lintner, John. "The Valuation of Risk Assets and the Selection of Risky Investments in Stock Portfolios and Capital Budgets." *Rev. Econ. and Statis.* 47 (February 1965): 768–83.

McKean, H.P., Jr. *Stochastic Integrals.* New York: Academic Press, 1969.

Merton, Robert C. "Theory of Rational Option Pricing." *Bell J. Econ. and Management Sci.* (1973): in press.

Miller, Merton H., and Modigliani, Franco. "Dividend Policy, Growth, and the Valuation of Shares." *J. Bus.* 34 (October 1961): 411–33.

Modigliani, Franco, and Miller, Merton H. "The Cost of Capital, Corporation Finance and the Theory of Investment." *A.E.R.* 48 (June 1958): 261–97.

Mossin, Jan. "Equilibrium in a Capital Asset Market." *Econometrica* 34 (October 1966): 768–83.

Samuelson, Paul A. "Rational Theory of Warrant Pricing." *Indus. Management*

Rev. 6 (Spring 1965): 13–31. Reprinted in Cootner (1967), pp. 506–32.

Samuelson, Paul A., and Merton, Robert C. "A Complete Model of Warrant Pricing that Maximizes Utility." *Indus. Management Rev.* 10 (Winter 1969): 17–46.

Sharpe, Willian F. "Capital Asset Prices: A Theory of Market Equilibrium Under Conditions of Risk." *J. Finance* 19 (September 1964): 425–42.

——. *Portfolio Theory and Capital Markets:* New York: McGraw-Hill, 1970.

Sprenkle, Case. "Warrant Prices as Indications of Expectations." *Yale Econ. Essays* 1 (1961): 179–232. Reprinted in Cootner (1967), 412–74.

Stoll, Hans R. "The Relationship Between Put and Call Option Prices." *J. Finance* 24 (December 1969): 802–24.

Thorp, Edward O., and Kassouf, Sheen T. *Beat the Market.* New York: Random House, 1967.

Treynor, Jack L. "Implications for the Theory of Finance." Unpublished memorandum, 1961. (*a*)

——. "Toward a Theory of Market Value of Risky Assets." Unpublished memorandum, 1961. (*b*)

**Part V
The Time–State Preference
Valuation Framework**

14

The Role of Securities in the Optimal Allocation of Risk-Bearing[1]

Kenneth J. Arrow
Harvard University

1. Introduction

The theory of the optimal allocation of resources under conditions of certainty is well-known. In the present note, an extension of the theory to conditions of subjective uncertainty is considered.

Attention is confined to the case of a pure exchange economy; the introduction of production would not be difficult. We suppose I individuals and S possible states of nature. In the sth state, amount x_{sc} of commodity c ($c = 1$, ..., C) is produced. It is assumed that each individual acts on the basis of subjective probabilities as to the states of nature; let π_{is} be the subjective probability of state s according to individual i. Further, let x_{isc} be the amount of commodity claimed by individual i if state s occurs. These claims are, of course, limited by available resources, so that

$$\sum_{i=1}^{I} x_{isc} = x_{sc},\tag{1}$$

assuming the absence of saturation of individuals' desires.

The problem of optimal allocation of risk-bearing is that of choosing the magnitudes x_{isc}, subject to restraints (1), in such a way that no other choice will make every individual better off. In Section 2, it is briefly argued that, if there exist markets for claims on all commodities, the competitive system will lead to an optimal allocation under certain hypotheses.

However, in the real world the allocation of risk-bearing is accomplished by claims payable in money, not in commodities. In Section 3, it is shown that the

Reprinted by permission of the publisher and author from *Review of Economic Studies*, 1964, pp. 91–96.

1. This paper was originally read at the Colloque sur les Fondements et Applications de la Théorie du Risque en Econometrie of the Centre Nationale de la Recherche Scientifique, Paris, France, on May 13, 1952 and appeared in French in the proceedings of the colloquium, published by the Centre Nationale under the title, *Econometrie*, 1953. The research was carried out under contract Nonr–225 (50) of the U.S. Office of Naval Research at Stanford University.

Von Neumann-Morgenstern theorem enables us to conclude that, under certain hypotheses, the allocation of risk-bearing by competitive securities markets is in fact optimal.

In Section 4, it is shown that the hypotheses used in Sections 2 and 3 contain an important implication: that the competitive allocation of risk-bearing is guaranteed to be viable only if the individuals have attitudes of risk-aversion.[2]

2. Allocation of risk-bearing by commodity claims

Let $V_i(x_{i11}, \ldots, x_{i1C}, x_{i21}, \ldots, x_{iSC})$ be the utility of individual i if he is assigned claims of amount x_{isc} for commodity c if state s occurs ($c = 1, \ldots, C$; $s = 1, \ldots, S$). This is exactly analogous to the utility function in the case of certainty except that the number of variables has increased from C to SC. We may therefore achieve any optimal allocation of risk-bearing by a competitive system. Let x_{isc}^* ($i = 1, \ldots, I; s = 1, \ldots, S; c = 1, \ldots, C$) be any optimal allocation; then there exist a set of money incomes y_i for individual i, and prices $\bar{p}_{sc}$ for a unit claim on commodity c if state s occurs, such that if each individual i chooses values of the variables x_{isc} ($s = 1, \ldots, S; c = 1, \ldots, C$) subject to the restraint

$$\sum_{s=1}^{S} \sum_{c=1}^{C} \bar{p}_{sc} x_{isc} = y_i \tag{2}$$

taking prices as given, the chosen values of the x_{isc}'s will be the given optimal allocation x_{isc}^* ($i = 1, \ldots, I; s = 1, \ldots, S; c = 1, \ldots, C$).

The argument is a trivial reformulation of the usual one in welfare economics.[3] However, there is one important qualification; the validity of the theorem depends on the assumption (not always made explicitly) that the indifference surfaces are convex to the origin, or, to state the condition equivalently, that $V_i(x_{i11}, \ldots, x_{iSC})$ is a *quasi-concave* function of its arguments. [The function $f(x_1, \ldots, x_n)$ is said to be quasi-concave if for every pair of points $(x_1^1, \ldots, x_n^1)$ and $(x_1^2, \ldots, x_n^2)$ such that $f(x_1^1, \ldots, x_n^1) \geqslant f(x_1^2, \ldots, x_n^2)$ and every real number α,

$$0 \leqslant \alpha \leqslant 1;$$

---

2. Note added for this translation. Since the above was written I have come to the conclusion that this statement needs very severe qualification as explained in footnote 4.

3. See, for a simple exposition, O. Lange, "The Foundation of Welfare Economics" *Econometrica*, Volume 10, 1942, pp. 215–28, or P.A. Samuelson, *Foundations of Economic Analysis*, Chapter VIII.

$$f(\alpha x_1^1 + (1 - \alpha)x_1^2, \ldots, \alpha x_n^1 + (1 - \alpha)x_n^2) \geqslant f(x_1^2, \ldots, x_n^2).$$

It is easy to see geometrically the equivalence between this definition and the convexity of the indifference surfaces.]

Theorem 1. If $V_i(x_{i11}, \ldots, x_{iSC})$ is quasi-concave for every i, then any optimal allocation of risk-bearing can be realized by a system of perfectly competitive markets in claims on commodities.

The meaning of the hypothesis of Theorem 1 will be explored in Section 4.

3. Allocation of risk-bearing by securities

In the actual world, risk-bearing is not allocated by the sale of claims against specific commodities. A simplified picture would rather be the following: securities are sold which are payable in money, the amount depending on the state s which has actually occurred (this concept is obvious for stocks; for bonds, we have only to recall the possibility of default if certain states s occur); when the state s occurs, the money transfers determined by the securities take place, and then the allocation of commodities takes place through the market in the ordinary way, without further risk-bearing.

It is not difficult to show that any optimal allocation of risk-bearing can be achieved by such a competitive system involving securities payable in money. For the given optimal allocation, x_{isc}^*, let the prices $\bar{p}_{sc}$ and the incomes y_i be determined as in the previous section. For simplicity, assume there are precisely S types of securities, where a unit security of the sth type is a claim paying one monetary unit if state s occurs and nothing otherwise. Any security whatever may be regarded as a bundle of the elementary types just described.

Let q_s be the price of the sth security and p_{sc} the price of commodity c if state s occurs. Choose them so that

$$q_s p_{sc} = \bar{p}_{sc}. \tag{3}$$

An individual confronted with these prices has the same range of alternatives available as he did under the system described in Section 2, taking $q_s p_{sc}$ as equivalent to the price of a claim on commodity c in state s. He will plan to acquire the same claims, and therefore, on the market for securities of the sth type, individual i will purchase sufficient securities of type s to realize the desired purchase of commodities if state s occurs, i.e., he will purchase

$$y_{is}^* = \sum_{c=1}^{C} p_{sc} x_{isc}^* \tag{4}$$

units of the sth type of security. His purchase of securities of all types is restricted by the restraint

$$\sum_{s=1}^{S} q_s y_{is} = y_i;$$

the allocation $y_{is}^*(s = 1, \ldots, S)$ satisfies this restraint, as can be seen from (2), (3), and (4).

The total monetary stock available is $\Sigma_{i=1}^{I} y_i = y$. The net volume of claims payable when any state s occurs must therefore be precisely y or

$$\sum_{i=1}^{I} y_{is} = y \qquad (s = 1, \ldots, S). \tag{5}$$

Substitute (4) into (5) and multiply both sides by q_s/y, then, from (3),

$$q_s = \frac{\displaystyle\sum_{i=1}^{I} \sum_{c=1}^{C} \bar{p}_{sc} x_{isc}^* \cdot (s = 1, \ldots, S)}{y} \tag{6}$$

The prices p_{sc} are then determined from (3).

With the prices q_s and p_{sc} thus determined, and the incomes y_i, the competitive system, operating first on the securities markets and then on the separate commodity markets, will lead to the allocation x_{isc}^*. For, as we have already seen, individual i will demand y_{is}^* of security s. Suppose state s occurs. He then has income y_{is}^* to allocate among commodities with prices $\bar{p}_{sc}$. Let $U_i(x_{is1}, \ldots, x_{isC})$ be a utility function of individual i for commodities, then he chooses a bundle so as to maximize U_i subject to the restraint

$$\sum_{c=1}^{C} p_{sc} x_{isc} = y_{is}^*. \tag{7}$$

Let x_{isc}^+ ($c = 1, \ldots, C$) be the chosen commodity amounts. Since by (4), the quantities x_{isc}^* satisfy (7), it follows from the definition of a maximum that,

$$U_i(x_{is1}^+, \ldots, x_{isC}^+) \geq U_i(x_{is1}^*, \ldots, x_{isC}^*). \tag{8}$$

The quantities x_{isc}^+ are defined for all s.

By the Von Neumann-Morgenstern theorem, the function U_i may be chosen so that

$$V_i(x_{i11}, \ldots, x_{isC}) = \sum_{s=1}^{S} \pi_{is} U_i(x_{is1}, \ldots, x_{isC}).$$ (9)

Suppose that in (8), the strict inequality holds for at least s for which $\pi_{is} > 0$. Then by (9),

$$V_i(x_{i11}^+, \ldots, x_{isC}^+) > V_i(x_{i11}^*, \ldots, x_{isC}^*).$$ (10)

On the other hand, if we multiply in (7) by q_s and sum over s, it is seen that the bundle of claims $(x_{i11}^+, \ldots, x_{isC}^+)$ satisfies restraint (2). But by construction the bundle $(x_{i11}^*, \ldots, x_{isC}^*)$ maximizes V_i subject to (2); hence (10) is a contradiction, and the equality holds in (8) for all states with positive subjective probability. If the *strict* quasi-concavity of U_i is assumed, as usual, the equality implies that $x_{isc}^+ = x_{isc}^*$ for all c and all i and s for which $\pi_{is} > 0$. If $\pi_{is} = 0$, then obviously $x_{isc}^* = 0$ $(c = 1, \ldots, C)$, which implies that $y_{is}^* = 0$ and therefore $x_{isc}^+ = 0$ $(c = 1, \ldots, C)$. Hence, once the state s occurs, individual i will in fact purchase the bundle prescribed under the optimal allocation.

Theorem 2. If

$$\sum_{s=1}^{S} \pi_{is} U_i(x_{is1}, \ldots, x_{isC})$$

is quasi-concave, in all its variables, then any optimal allocation of risk-bearing can be achieved by perfect competition on the securities and commodity markets, where securities are payable in money.

Socially, the significance of the theorem is that it permits economizing on markets; only $S + C$ markets are needed to achieve the optimal allocation, instead of the SC markets implied in Theorem 1.

One might wonder if any loopholes have been left through arbitrage between securities and hold of money; in the allocation of securities, an individual has the option of holding cash instead and using the hoarding in the commodity allocation.

If we sum over s in (6) and use (2),

$$\sum_{s=1}^{S} q_s = \frac{\sum_{i=1}^{I} \sum_{s=1}^{S} \sum_{c=1}^{C} \bar{p}_{sc} x^*_{isc}}{y} = \frac{\sum_{i=1}^{I} y_i}{y} = 1. \qquad (11)$$

A monetary unit is equivalent to a bundle of S unit securities, one of each type; to avoid arbitrage, then, such a bundle should have a unit price. This is insured by (11).

4. Risk-aversion and the competitive allocation of risk-bearing

What is the economic significance of the hypothesis that the utility-functions:

$$V_i = \sum_{s=1}^{S} \pi_{is} U_i \qquad (12)$$

be quasi-concave? The easiest case to consider is that in which

$$S = 2, \qquad \pi_{is} = 1/2 \qquad (s = 1, 2).$$

Theorem 3. If $\frac{1}{2} [f(x_1, \ldots, x_C) + f(x_{C+1}, \ldots, x_{2C})]$ is quasi-concave in all its variables, then $f(x_1, \ldots, x_C)$ is a concave function.
    $[f(x_1, \ldots, x_C)$ will be said to be concave if for every pair of points $(x^1_1, \ldots, x^1_C)$ and $(x^2_1, \ldots, x^2_C)$,

$$f(\tfrac{1}{2}x^1_1 + \tfrac{1}{2}x^2_1, \ldots, \tfrac{1}{2}x^1_C + \tfrac{1}{2}x^2_C)$$

$$\geq \tfrac{1}{2} [f(x^1_1, \ldots, x^1_C) + \tfrac{1}{2} f(x^2_1, \ldots, x^2_C)].$$

It is well known that a concave function is always quasi-concave but not conversely.]

Proof: Suppose $f(x_1, \ldots, x_C)$ is not concave. Then for some pair of points, $(x^1_1, \ldots, x^1_C)$ and $(x^2_1, \ldots, x^2_C)$,

$$f\left(\frac{x^1_1 + x^2_1}{2}, \ldots, \frac{x^2_C + x^2_C}{2}\right) < \tfrac{1}{2} f(x^1_1, \ldots, x^1_C) + \tfrac{1}{2} f(x^2_1, \ldots, x^2_C).$$

Let

$$g(x_1, \ldots, x_{2C}) = \tfrac{1}{2}[f(x_1, \ldots, x_C) + f(x_{C+1}, \ldots, x_{2C})]. \qquad (13)$$

Then obviously

$$g(x_1^1, \ldots, x_C^1, x_1^2, \ldots, x_C^2) = g(x_1^2, \ldots x_C^2, x_1^1, \ldots, x_C^1).$$

By the hypothesis that g is quasi-concave, then

$$g\left(\frac{x_1^1 + x_1^2}{2}, \ldots, \frac{x_C^1 + x_C^2}{2}, \frac{x_1^2 + x_1^1}{2}, \ldots, \frac{x_C^2 + x_C^1}{2}\right) \qquad (14)$$

$$\geqslant g(x_1^1, \ldots, x_C^1, x_1^2, \ldots, x_C^2).$$

But from (13) and (12),

$$g\left(\frac{x_1^1 + x_1^2}{2}, \ldots, \frac{x_C^1 + x_C^2}{2}, \frac{x_1^2 + x_1^1}{2}, \ldots, \frac{x_C^2 + x_C^1}{2}\right)$$

$$= \tfrac{1}{2}\left[f\left(\frac{x_1^1 + x_1^2}{2}, \ldots, \frac{x_C^1 + x_C^2}{2}\right) + f\left(\frac{x_1^2 + x_1^1}{2}, \ldots, \frac{x_C^2 + x_C^1}{2}\right)\right]$$

$$= f\left(\frac{x_1^1 + x_1^2}{2}, \ldots, \frac{x_C^1 + x_C^2}{2}\right)$$

$$< \tfrac{1}{2}[f(x_1^1, \ldots, x_C^1) + f(x_1^2, \ldots, x_C^2)]$$

$$= g(x_1^1, \ldots, x_C^1, x_1^2, \ldots, x_C^2),$$

which contradicts (14). Hence, $f(x_1, \ldots, x_C)$ must be concave.

In terms of the allocation of risk-bearing, Theorem 3 implies that if one wishes to insure the viability of the competitive allocation for all possible assignments of probabilities π_{is}, it must be assumed that the individual utility functions U_i must be concave. This condition, in turn, is obviously equivalent to the assumption of risk aversion; for the conditions

$$U_i\left(\frac{x_1^1 + x_1^2}{2}, \ldots, \frac{x_C^1 + x_C^2}{2}\right)$$

$$\geqslant \tfrac{1}{2}[U_i(x_1^1, \ldots, x_C^1) + U_i(x_1^2, \ldots, x_C^2)]$$

means that an even gamble as between two bundles is never preferred to the arithmetic mean of those bundles.

The hypothesis of quasi-concavity of the utility function has here only been indicated as a sufficient, not a necessary condition for the viability of competitive allocation. However, without the assumption of quasi-concavity, some optimal allocations cannot be achieved by competitive means, and in general, there would be only very special cases in which any competitive equilibrium is achievable. Consider the following simple examples:

There are one commodity, two individuals, and two states. Both individuals have the same utility function.

$$U_i(x) = x^2 \qquad (i = 1, 2); \tag{15}$$

this function is monotonic and hence quasi-concave, but not concave, since it implies risk-preference. Assume further that $\pi_{is} = \frac{1}{2}$ ($i = 1, 2; s = 1, 2$) then

$$V_i(x_{i11}, x_{i21}) = \frac{1}{2}(x_{i11}^2 + x_{i21}^2) \qquad (i = 1, 2). \tag{16}$$

Finally, suppose that

$$x_{11} = 1, \qquad x_{21} = 2. \tag{17}$$

It is easy to see that for any fixed set of prices on claims under alternative states, each individual will buy all of one claim or all of the other. Hence any optimal allocation in which both individuals possess positive claims in both states is unachievable by competitive means. Such optimal allocations do exist; we have only to choose the variables x_{is1} ($i = 1, 2; s = 1, 2$) so as to maximise V_1 subject to the restraints, implied by (17),

$$x_{111} + x_{211} = 1, \qquad x_{121} = 2,$$

and the restraint V_2 = constant. If, for example, we fix $V_2 = \frac{1}{2}$, we have the optimal allocation,

$$x_{111} = \frac{\sqrt{5}-1}{\sqrt{5}}, \qquad x_{121} = \frac{2\sqrt{5}-2}{\sqrt{5}},$$

$$x_{211} = \frac{1}{\sqrt{5}}, \qquad x_{221} = \frac{2}{\sqrt{5}}.$$

In fact, for the functions given by (16), a competitive equilibrium usually does not exist. Let $y_i(i = 1, 2)$ be the incomes of the two individuals. Let p be the price of a unit claim for state 1, taking the unit claim in state 2 as *numeraire*. Then in a competitive market, individual maximises V_i subject to

$$px_{i11} + x_{i21} = y_i.$$

He will then choose $x_{i11} = y_i/p$, $x_{i21} = 0$ if $p < 1$ and choose $x_{i11} = 0$, $x_{i21} = y_i$ if $p > 1$. Hence, if $p \neq 1$, there will be zero demand, and hence disequilibrium, on one market. If $p = 1$, each individual will be indifferent between the bundles $(y_i, 0)$ and $(0, y_i)$. Except in the special case where $y_1 = 1$, $y_2 = 2$ (or *vice versa*), there is again no possible way of achieving equilibrium.[4]

Appendix

The previous discussion has been confined to the case of pure consumption. It is possible to introduce production decisions in a framework of essentially the same character. If we assume that the production takes place under random condition, for example, those induced by weather or by accident we can, in linear programming terminology, represent each activity by a vector whose components are the outputs or inputs of all commodities for all possible states of nature. If, as before, we substitute commodity options for commodities, the vector describing any particular activity can be formally identified with the commodity vector. An interesting point to be made is that under these circumstances production decisions of a firm do not depend on the probability judgments or utilities of the owners of the firms. Let q_s be the price of a security which promises \$1.00 in state s and nothing otherwise. Let p_{sc} be the price of commodity c in state s. Then among all the possible values of the variables x_{sc} available to the firm under its conditions of production the firm chooses so as to maximize,

$$\sum_{s=1}^{S} q_s \sum_{c=1}^{C} p_{sc} x_{sc}.$$

The values q_s might be interpreted as the market evaluation of the probability of

---

4. Though there is nothing wrong formally with the analysis of this last section, I now consider it misleading. If there are a large number of consumers, the income of each being relatively small, it has now been established by the important work of Farrell and Rothenberg, that the quasi-concavity of the indifference curves is unnecessary to the existence of competitive equilibrium; see M.J. Farrell, "The Convexity Assumption in the Theory of Competitive Markets", *Journal of Political Economy*, Volume 67, 1959, pp. 377–91, and J. Rothenberg, "Non-Convexity, Aggregation and Pareto Optimality", *Ibid.*, Volume 68, 1960, pp. 435–68.

state s. Then the rule for the firm is to compute for each possible state of nature the profit to be obtained from any given production plan, and weight these various profits for any given plan by the market evaluations of probabilities of that state of nature. The owners of the firm, if their evaluations of probabilities differ from that of the market, will be led to engage in other operations on the security market but their decisions as to production will not be affected by these judgments.

However, the definition of a commodity is seriously affected on the production side by the nature of the theory of uncertainty. For two units to be regarded as part of the same commodity, they must have the same role of production for any possible state of nature. Let us consider two identical machines with independent probabilities of breakdown. There are from this point of view four possible states of nature: one where both machines are in action, one where machine 1 is in action while machine 2 is out, one where machine 2 is in action and machine 1 is out and one where both are out of action. Since the two machines are not substitutable for each other in every state of nature, they must be regarded as different commodities. The number of commodities thus becomes enormously greater than is ordinarily supposed and indivisibility becomes a much more prevalent phenomenon. If there are a great many units of a commodity, even though each unit is indivisible, the indivisibilities may be regarded as so small compared to the total flow that they can be disregarded. This is not so, if each machine, for example, has to be regarded as a separate commodity. Hence the usual theory of allocation which presupposes convexity of the production structure will become inapplicable and the theorems of welfare economics and competitive allocation will become false. Consider for example the following situation which is greatly simplified from a case studied by a Swedish engineer Palm. Suppose we have two machines, each with a fifty-fifty chance of breakdown, and one man. To operate, a machine has to be in action and have a man assigned to it. If neither machine has broken down, then only one machine can be used. Hence it is clear one machine will be in operation with probability 3/4 and 0 machines will be in operation with probability 1/4 so that the expected output is 3/4 of the potential output of one machine. Now suppose there are four machines and two men and again assume that each machine will break down with probability 1/2; then 0 machines will be in action with probability 1/16, one machine with probability 1/4 and two machines with probability 11/16. The expected output will therefore be 13/8 of the potential output of a single machine which is more than twice as much. In other words, by doubling the number of men and doubling the number of machines we have more than doubled the expected output. An analysis shows that this increasing return arises out of the consideration of indivisibility just advanced. Such increasing returns are, of course, incompatible with the competitive allocation of risk-bearing. Other difficulties arise with the competitive allocation of risk-bearing in the case where some members of society have a preference for risk. Also the spread of information which may alter subjective probabilities creates some difficulties in the whole theory. These topics need more explanation than can be given to them here.

To conclude, we have seen that it is possible to set up formal mechanisms which under certain conditions will achieve an optimal allocation of risk by competitive methods. However, the empirical validity of the conditions for the optimal character of competitive allocation are considerably less likely to be fulfilled in the case of uncertainty than in the case of certainty and, furthermore, many of the economic institutions which would be needed to carry out the competitive allocation in the case of uncertainty are in fact lacking.

15

Problems in the Theory of Markets Under Uncertainty*

Roy Radner
University of California, Berkeley

Introduction

One of the notable intellectual achievements of economic theory during the past twenty years has been the rigorous elaboration of the Walras-Pareto theory of value; that is, the theory of the existence and optimality of competitive equilibrium. Although many economists and mathematicians contributed to this development, the resulting edifice owes so much to the pioneering and influential work of Arrow and Debreu that in this paper I shall refer to it as the "Arrow-Debreu theory." (For a comprehensive treatment, together with references to previous work, see [6].)

The Arrow-Debreu theory was not originally put forward for the case of uncertainty, but an ingenious device introduced by Arrow [1], and further elaborated by Debreu [5], enabled the theory to be reinterpreted to cover the case of uncertainty about the availability of resources and about consumption and production possibilities. (See [6, Chap. 7] for a unified treatment of time and uncertainty.)

In the present paper I take the Arrow-Debreu theory as a starting point and discuss certain extensions, limitations, and possible new departures. In particular, I: (1) show how the theory can be extended to account explicitly for differences in information available to different economic agents, and for the "production" of information; (2) present a critique of the (extended) theory, especially its failure to explain or take account of money, stock markets, and the presence in the real world of active markets at every date; (3) argue for the consideration of a theory of a sequence of markets and suggest several concepts of equilibrium that might be appropriate to such a theory; and (4) present some results on the existence of an equilibrium of plans, prices, and price expectations in a sequence of markets.

The main features of the Arrow-Debreu theory have been available in the literature for more than a decade and were even discussed at a meeting of this Association six years ago [12]. Nevertheless, it seemed to me wise to begin the paper with a brief review of the elements of the theory, although I fear that the

Reprinted by permission of the publisher and author from *American Economic Review*, May 1970, pp. 454–60.
*This paper is based on research supported in part by the National Science Foundation.

review may be too brief to be intelligible to those who are not already familiar with the material!

The consideration of a sequence of markets under conditions of uncertainty is not new in economics but does not seem to have received much attention from value theorists since the publication of Hicks's *Value and Capital* [11]. I would therefore have felt more comfortable presenting this paper in a session entitled, "Old Ideas in Pure Theory," but as far as I know, no such session has been organized for the current meetings.

I. Review of the Arrow-Debreu Model of a Complete Market for Present and Future Contingent Delivery

In this section I review the approach of Arrow [1] and Debreu [6] to incorporating uncertainty about the environment into a Walrasian model of competitive equilibrium. The basic idea is that commodities are to be distinguished, not only by their physical characteristics and by the location and dates of their availability and/or use, but also by the environmental event in which they are made available and/or used. For example, ice cream made available (at a particular location on a particular date) if the weather is hot may be considered to be a different commodity from the same kind of ice cream made available (at the same location and date) if the weather is cold. We are thus led to consider a list of "commodities" that is greatly expanded by comparison with the corresponding case of certainty about the environment. The standard arguments of the theory of competitive equilibrium, applied to an economy with this expanded list of commodities, then require that we envisage a "price" for each commodity in the list, or, more precisely, a set of price ratios specifying the rate of exchange between each pair of commodities.

Just what institutions could, or do, effect such exchanges is a matter of interpretation that is, strictly speaking, outside the model. I shall present one straightforward interpretation, and then comment briefly on an alternative interpretation.

First, however, it will be useful to give a more precise account of the concepts of environment and event that I shall be employing. The description of the "physical world" is decomposed into three sets of variables: (1) decision variables, which are controlled (chosen) by economic agents; (2) environmental variables, which are not controlled by any economic agent; and (3) all other variables, which are completely determined (possibly jointly) by decisions and environmental variables. A state of the environment is a complete specification (history) of the environmental variables from the beginning to the end of the economic system in question. An event is a set of states; for example, the event "the weather is hot in New York on July 1, 1970" is the set of all possible histories of the environment in which the temperature in New York during the day of July 1, 1970, reaches a high of at least (say) 75°F. Granting that we cannot know the future with certainty, at any given date, there will be a family of elementary observable (knowable) events, which can be represented by a partition of the set of all possible states (histories) into a family of mutually exclusive subsets. It is natural to assume that the partitions corresponding to successive dates are successively finer, which represents the accumulation of information about the environment.

We shall imagine that a "market" is organized before the beginning of the physical history of the economic system. An elementary contract in this market will consist of the purchase (or sale) of some specified number of units of a specified commodity to be delivered at a specified location and date, if and only if a specified elementary event occurs. Payment for this purchase is to be made now (at the beginning), in "units of account," at a specified price quoted for that commodity-location-date-event combination. Delivery of the commodity in more than one elementary event is obtained by combining a suitable set of elementary contracts. For example, if delivery of one quart of ice cream (at a specified location and date) in hot weather costs $1.50 (now) and delivery of one quart in non-hot weather costs $1.10, then sure delivery of one quart (i.e., whatever be the weather) costs $1.50 + $1.10 = $2.60.

There are two groups of economic agents in the economy: producers and consumers. A producer chooses a production plan, which determines his input and/or output of each commodity at each date in each elementary event. (I shall henceforth suppress explicit reference to location, it being understood that the location is specified in the term commodity.) For a given set of prices, the present value of a production plan is the sum of the values of the inputs minus the sum of the values of the outputs. Each producer is characterized by a set of production plans that are (physically) feasible for him: his production possibility set.

A consumer chooses a consumption plan, which specifies his consumption of each commodity at each date in each elementary event. Each consumer is characterized by: (1) a set of consumption plans that are (physically, psychologically, etc.) feasible for him, his consumption possibility set; (2) preferences among the alternative plans that are feasible for him; (3) his endowment of physical resources, i.e., a specification of the quantity of each commodity, e.g., labor, at each date in each event with which he is exogenously endowed; and (4) his shares in producers' profits, i.e., a specification for each producer, of the fraction of the present value of that producer's production plan that will be credited to the consumer's account. (For any one producer, the sum of the consumers' shares is unity.) For given prices and given production plans of all the producers, the present net worth of a consumer is the total value of his resources plus the total value of his shares of the present values of producers' production plans.

An equilibrium of the economy is a set of prices, a set of production plans (one for each producer), and a set of consumption plans (one for each consumer), such that (a) each producer's plan has maximum present value in his production possibility set; (b) each consumer's plan maximizes his preferences within his consumption possibility set, subject to the additional (budget) constraint that the present cost of his consumption plan not exceed his present net worth; (c) for each commodity at each date in each elementary event, the total demand equals the total supply; i.e., the total planned consumption equals the sum of the total resource endowments and the total planned net ouput (where inputs are counted as negative outputs).

Notice that (1) producers and consumers are "price takers"; (2) for given prices there is no uncertainty about the present value of a production plan or of given resource endowments, nor about the present cost of a consumption plan; (3) therefore, for given prices and given producers' plans, there is no uncertainty about a given consumer's present net worth; (4) since a consumption plan may specify that, for a given commodity at a given date, the quantity consumed is to vary according to the event that actually occurs, a consumer's preferences among plans will reflect not only his "tastes" but also his subjective beliefs about the likelihoods of different events and his attitude towards risk [16].

It follows that beliefs and attitudes towards risk play no role in the assumed behaviour of producers. On the other hand, beliefs and attitudes towards risk do play a role in the assumed behavior of consumers, although for given prices and production plans each consumer knows his (single) budget constraint with certainty.

I shall call the model just described an "Arrow-Debreu" economy. One can demonstrate, under "standard conditions": (1) the existence of an equilibrium, (2) the Pareto optimality of an equilibrium, and (3) that, roughly speaking, every Pareto optimal choice of production and consumption plans is an equilibrium relative to some price system for some distribution of resource endowments and shares [6, Chaps. 5 and 6] [7].

In the above interpretation of the Arrow-Debreu economy, all accounts are settled before the history of the economy begins, and there is no incentive to revise plans, reopen the market or trade in shares. There is an alternative interpretation, which will be of interest in connection with the rest of this paper but which corresponds to exactly the same formal model. In this second intrepretation, there is a single commodity at each date—let us call it "gold"—that is taken as a numeraire at that date. A "price system" has two parts: (1) for each date and each elementary event at that date, there is a price, to be paid in gold at date 1, for one unit of gold to be delivered at the specified date and event; (2) for each commodity, date, and event at that date, there is a price, to be paid in gold at that date and event, for one unit of the commodity to be delivered at that same date and event. The first part of the price system can be interpreted as "insurance premiums" and the second part as "spot prices" at the given date and event. The insurance interpretation is to be made with some reservation, however, since there is no real object being insured and no limit to the amount of insurance that an individual may take out against the occurence of a given event. For this reason, the first part of the price system might be better interpreted as reflecting a combination of betting odds and interest rates.

Although the second part of the price system might be interpreted as spot prices it would be a mistake to think of the determination of the equilibrium values of these prices as being deferred in real time to the dates to which they refer. The definition of equilibrium requires that the agents have the access to the complete system of prices when choosing their plans. In effect, this requires that at the beginning of time all agents have available a (common) forecast of the equilibrium spot prices that will prevail at every future date and event.

II. Extension of the Arrow-Debreu Model to the Case in Which Different Agents Have Different Information

In an Arrow-Debreu economy, at any one date each agent will have incomplete information about the state of the environment, but all the agents will have the same information. This last assumption is not tenable if we are to take good account of the effects of uncertainty in an economy. I shall now sketch how, by a simple reinterpretation of the concepts of production possibility set and consumption possibility set, we can extend the theory of the Arrow-Debreu economy to allow for differences in information among the economic agents.[1]

For each date, the information that will be available to a given agent at that date may be characterized by a partition of the set of states of the environment. To be consistent with our previous terminology, we should assume that each such information partition must be at least as coarse as the partition that describes the elementary events at that date; i.e., each set in the information partition must contain a set in the elementary event partition for the same date.

For example, each set in the event partition at a given date might specify the high temperature at that date, whereas each set in a given agent's information partition might specify only whether this temperature was higher than 75°F. or not. Or the event partition at a given date might specify the temperature at each date during the past month, whereas the information partition might specify only the mean temperature over the past month.

An agent's information restricts his set of feasible plans in the following manner. Suppose that at a given date the agent knows only that the state of the environment lies in a specified set A (one of the sets in his information partition

---

1. This section is based upon [14, Sections 2-6].

at that date), and suppose (as would be typical) that the set A contains several of the elementary events that are in principle observable at that date. Then any action that the agent takes at that date must necessarily be the same for all elementary events in the set A. In particular, if the agent is a consumer, then his consumption of any specified commodity at that date must be the same in all elementary events contained in the information set A; if the agent is a producer, then his input or output of any specified commodity must be the same for all events in A. (I am assuming that consumers know what they consume and producers what they produce at any given date.)

Let us call the sequence of information partitions for a given agent his information structure and let us say that this structure is fixed if it is given independent of the actions of himself or any other agent. Furthermore, in the case of a fixed information structure, let us say that a given plan (consumption or production) is compatible with that structure if it satisfies the conditions described in the previous paragraph, at each date.

Suppose that the consumption and production possibility sets of the Arrow-Debreu economy are interpreted as characterizing, for each agent, those plans that would be feasible if he had "full information" (i.e., if his information partition at each date coincided with the elementary event partition at that date). The set of feasible plans for any agent with a fixed information structure can then be obtained by restricting him to those plans in the full information possibility set that are also compatible with his given information structure.

From this point on, all of the machinery of the Arrow-Debreu economy (with some minor technical modifications) can be brought to bear on the present model. In particular, we get a theory of existence and optimality of competitive equilibrium relative to fixed structures of information for the economic agents. I shall call this the "extended Arrow-Debreu economy."[2]

III. Choice of Information

There is no difficulty in principle in incorporating the choice of information structure into the model of the extended Arrow-Debreu economy. I doubt, however, that it is reasonable to assume that the technological conditions for the acquisition and use of information generally satisfy the hypotheses of the standard theorems on the existence and optimality of competitive equilibrium.

The acquisition and use of information about the environment typically require the expenditure of goods and services; i.e., of commodities.

If one production plan requires more information for its implementation than another (i.e., requires a finer information partition at one or more dates),

---

2. This terminology is not in any way meant to imply that either Arrow or Debreu approve of this way of incorporating information into their model!

then the list of (commodity) inputs should reflect the increased inputs for information. In this manner a set of feasible production plans can reflect the possibility of choice among alternative information structures.

Unfortunately, the acquisition of information often involves a "set-up cost"; i.e. the resources needed to obtain the information may be independent of the scale of the production process in which the information is used. This set-up cost will introduce a nonconvexity in the production possibility set, and thus one of the standard conditions in the theory of the Arrow-Debreu economy will not be satisfied [14, Sec. 9].

There is another interesting class of cases in which an agent's information structure is not fixed, namely, cases in which the agent's information at one date may depend upon production or consumption decisions taken at previous dates, but all actions can be scaled down to any desired size. Unfortunately space limitations prevent me from discussing this class in the present paper.

IV. Critique of the Extended
Arrow-Debreu Economy

If the Arrow-Debreu model is given a literal interpretation, then it clearly requires that the economic agents possess capabilities of imagination and calculation that exceed reality by many orders of magnitude. Related to this is the observation that the theory requires in principle a complete system of insurance and futures markets, which appears to be too complex, detailed, and refined to have practical significance. A further obstacle to the achievement of a complete insurance market is the phenomenon of "moral hazard" [2].

A second line of criticism is that the theory does not take account of at least three important institutional features of modern capitalist economies: money, the stock market, and active markets at every date.

These two lines of criticism have an important connection, which suggests how the Arrow-Debreu theory might be improved. If, as in the Arrow-Debreu model, each production plan has a sure unambiguous present value at the beginning of time, then consumers have no interest in trading in shares, and there is no point in a stock market. If all accounts can be settled at the beginning of time, then, there is no need for money during the subsequent life of the economy; in any case, the standard motives for holding money do not apply.

On the other hand, once we recognize explicitly that there is a sequence of markets, one for each date, and no one of them complete (in the Arrow-Debreu sense), then certain phenomena and institutions not accounted for in the Arrow-Debreu model become reasonable. First, there is uncertainty about the prices that will hold in future markets, as well as uncertainty about the environment.

Second, producers do not have a clear-cut natural way of comparing net revenues at different dates and states. Stockholders have an incentive to establish a stock exchange, since it enables them to change the way their future revenues depend on the states of the environment. As an alternative to selling his shares in a particular enterprise, a stockholder may try to influence the management of the enterprise in order to make the production plan conform better to his own subjective probabilities and attitude towards risk.

Third, consumers will typically not be able to discount all of their "wealth" at the beginning of time, because (*a*) their shares of producers' future (uncertain) net revenues cannot be so discounted and (*b*) they cannot discount all of their future resource endowments. Consumers will be subject to a sequence of budget constraints, one for each date (rather than to a single budget constraint relating present cost of his consumption plan to present net worth, as in the Arrow-Debreu economy).

Fourth, economic agents may have an incentive to speculate on the prices in future markets, by storing goods, hedging, etc. Instead of storing goods, an agent may be interested in saving part of one date's income, in units of account, for use on a subsequent date, if there is an institution that makes this possible. There will thus be a demand for "money" in the form of demand deposits.

Fifth, agents will be interested in forecasting the prices in markets at future dates. These prices will be functions of both the state of the environment and the decisions of (in principle, all) economic agents up to the date in question.

V. Equilibrium of Plans, Prices, and Price Expectations in a Sequence of Markets

Consider now a sequence of markets at successive dates. Suppose that no market at any one date is complete in the Arrow-Debreu sense; i.e., at every date and for every commodity there will be some future dates and some events at those future dates for which it will not be possible to make current contracts for future delivery contingent on those events. In such a model, several types of "equilibrium" concept suggest themselves. First, we may think of a sequence of "momentary" equilibria in which the current market is cleared at each date. The prices at which the current market is cleared at any one date will depend upon (among other things) the expectations that the agents hold concerning prices in future markets (to be distinguished from future prices on the current market!). We can represent a given agent's expectations in a precise manner as a function (schedule) that indicates what the prices will be at a given future date in each elementary event at that date. This includes, in particular, the representation of future prices as random variables, if we admit that the uncertainty of the agent about future events can be scaled in terms of subjective probabilities [16].

In the evolution of a sequence of momentary equilibria, each agent's expectations will be successively revised in the light of new information about the environment and about current prices. Therefore, the evolution of the economy will depend upon the rules or processes of expectation formation and revision used by the agents. In particular, there might be interesting conditions under which such a sequence of momentary equilibria would converge, in some sense, to a (stochastic) steady state. This steady state, e.g., stationary probability distribution of prices, would constitute a second concept of equilibrium.

I am not aware of any systematic general theory of markets under uncertainty, incorporating one or both of these two concepts of equilibrium, that has appeared since Hicks's *Value and Capital,* and I don't think that we can rest satisfied with Hicks's treatment in terms of "certainty equivalents" and "elasticities of expectation." The desirability of having a better theory and the importance of the role of expectations are well recognized, of course [3]. In the further development of such a theory, we shall no doubt have to face some of the difficult problems that have appeared in recent work on sequences of momentary equilibria under conditions of certainty [10] [17] [18].

A third concept of equilibrium emerges if we investigate the possibility of consistency among the expectations and plans of the various agents. I shall say that the agents have common expectations if they associate the same (future) prices to the same events. (Note that this does not necessarily imply that they agree on the joint probability distribution of future prices, since different agents might well assign different subjective probabilities to the same event.) I shall say that the plans of the agents are consistent if for each commodity, each date, and each event at that date the planned supply of that commodity at that date in that event equals the planned demand and if a corresponding condition holds for the stock markets. An equilibrium of plans, prices, and price expectations is a set of prices on the current market, a set of common expectations for the future, and a consistent set of individual plans, one for each agent, such that, given the current prices and price expectations, each individual agent's plan is optimal for him, subject to an appropriate sequence of budget constraints.

Of the three concepts of optimality, the last is perhaps the closest in spirit to the Arrow-Debreu theory. How far do the conclusions of the Arrow-Debreu theory (existence and optimality of equilibrium) extent to this new situation? Concerning existence, for particular definitions of "individual optimality" and specifications of the agents' "budget constraints," one can prove the following theorem. Before stating the existence theorem I must define what I shall call a pseudo-equilibrium.

The definition of pseudo-equilibrium is obtained from the definition of equilibrium by replacing the requirement of consistency of plans by the condition that at each date and each event the difference between total saving and total investment (by consumers) is smaller at the pseudo-equilibrium prices than at any other prices.[3]

---

3. This second condition will be automatically satisfied at an equilibrium. It should be noted that at each date the set of current prices is normalized; e.g., by taking the sum to be unity.

One can prove [15] that under assumptions about technology and consumer preferences similar to those used in the Arrow-Debreu theory: (1) there exists a pseudo-equilibrium; (2) if in a pseudo-equilibrium the current and future prices on the stock market are all strictly positive, then the pseudo-equilibrium is an equilibrium; (3) in the case of a pure exchange economy, there exists an equilibrium.

The crucial difference between this theorem and the corresponding one in the Arrow-Debreu theory seems to be due to the form take by Walras' law, which in this model can be paraphrased by saying that saving must be at least equal to investment at each date in each event. This form derives from the replacement of a single budget constraint (in terms of present value) by a sequence of budget constraints, one for each date.

With regard to optimality, there is little that can be said at this time. The main difficulty in investigating this question seems to be in characterizing the set of states of the economy that are attainable, given the restrictions on the set of allowable contracts at each date.

VI. Unsolved Problems

I can only list here a few unsolved problems that I personally find interesting and promising for further research.

I have already mentioned the question of the optimality properties (if any) of an equilibrium of plans, prices, and price expectations. One possible approach is to consider more explicitly the information that the observation of prices provides for agents in the economy. One might hope to show that an equilibrium is an optimum relative to the set of states of the economy that could be attained with just the same information that is provided by the equilibrium prices (in addition, of course, to the information structures originally available to the individual agents). Notice that since the equilibrium price expectations are self-fulfilling, the observation of the prices in any current market provides information about the true state of the environment (i.e., the specification of the values of particular prices defines an "event" in the set of possible states of the environment). An approach of this kind was tried in a two-period model [13], which was further complicated, however, by allowing agents to make contracts for future delivery contingent on the values taken on by future prices. (An example of such a contract would be a wage contract with a cost-of-living excalation clause.) It was shown that in this model, if the introduction of such contracts enabled all the agents to discount future receipts and costs back to the initial date (i.e., if all uncertainty about the environment could be reflected in some corresponding uncertainty about future prices), then an equilibrium would be an optimum in the above sense. Unfortunately, the existence of an equilibrium in such a model was not demonstrated, and indeed there might be important economic phenomena that would rule out the existence of equilibrium in such a model [13].

I have also already mentioned the unsatisfactory state of the theory of the evolution of momentary equilibria in a sequence of markets and the question of possible convergence of momentary equilibria to a (stochastic) steady state.

In all of these (potential) theories of a sequence of markets we shall need a more detailed theory of the firm than that used in the Arrow-Debreu model. Simple profit maximization is not well defined if future profits are uncertain and cannot fully be discounted back to the present. The model of Section V essentially begged this question by assuming that each producer maximizes a utility function whose arguments are his future net revenues in different events Such an assumption fails to relate the behavior of the firm to the preferences of the stockholders or potential stockholders. (It is rather an expression of the "divorce of ownership from management"!) An alternative candidate that has been discussed is the assumption that at each date a producer maximizes the current stock market value of his firm. (Note that in the Arrow-Debreu model, profit maximization is equivalent to maximization of the value of the stock.) However, except in the context of a special example considered by Diamond [8], I have not seen a formulation of this hypothesis that enables the producer to act as a price-taker; i.e., that does not imply that the producer is able to calculate the effect of his actions on the equilibrium prices.

We shall also want to incorporate into our theories the process of entry and exit of firms. In particular, the results described in Section V on the relationship between equilibrium and pseudo-equilibrium suggest that the possibility of exit may be important in assuring the existence of such an equilibrium.

Finally, I mention the old problem of incorporating a theory of money and credit in a Walrasian model of general equilibrium [9]. In a sense, the model of Section V allows "secured" loans that are backed either by physical collateral or by contracts for future delivery of commodities. The theory also provides a framework for explaining the holding of "commodity money." The model does not, however, describe any institutions for carrying over "units of account" from one date to the next. the introduction of such institutions seems a natural next step and one for which the model seems to me to be well suited.

References

1. K.J. Arrow, "Le Rôle de Valeurs Boursières pour la Répartition la Meilleure des Risques," *Econométrie,* 1953 (Centre National de la Recherche Scientifique), pp. 41–48; or see the translation "The Role of Securities in the Optimal Allocation of Risk Bearing," *Rev. of Econ. Studies,* 1961, pp. 91–96.

2. ——, *Aspects of the Theory of Risk-Bearing* (Helsinki: Yrjo Jahnsson Lecture Series, 1965).

3. M.J. Bowman, ed., *Expectations, Uncertainty, and Business Behavior* (S.S.R.C., 1958).

4. D. Cass and J.E. Stiglitz, "The Implication of Alternative Saving and Expectations Hypotheses for Choices of Technique and Patterns of Growth," *J.P.E.,* July-Aug., 1969, pp. 586–627.

5. G. Debreu, "Une Economie de l'Incertain" (Paris, 1953, Electricité de France) (mimeographed).

6. ——, *Theory of Value* (Wiley, 1959).

7. ——, "New Concepts and Techniques for Equilibrium Analysis," *Int. Econ. Rev.,* 1962, pp. 257–73.

8. P. Diamond, "The Role of a Stock Market in a General Equilibrium Model with Technological Uncertainty," *A.E.R.,* Sept., 1967, pp. 759–76.

9. F.H. Hahn, "On Some Problems of Proving the Existence of an Equilibrium in a Monetary Economy," in Hahn and Brechling, eds., *The Theory of Interest Rates* (London: Macmillan, 1965).

10. ——, "Equilibrium Dynamics with Heterogeneous Capital Goods," *Q.J.E.,* Nov., 1966.

11. J.R. Hicks, *Value and Capital* (Clarendon Press, 1939).

12. J. Hirshleifer, "Efficient Allocation of Capital in an Uncertain World," *A.E.R.,* May, 1964, pp. 77–85.

13. R. Radner, "Equilibre des Marchés à Terme et au Comptant en Cas d'Incertitude," *Cahiers d'Econométrie* (Paris: Centre National de la Recherche Scientifique, 1967).

14. ——, "Competitive Equilibrium under Uncertainty," *Econometrica,* Jan., 1968, pp. 31–58.

15. ——, "Equilibrium of Plans, Prices, and Price-Expectations in a Sequence of Markets" (1969, unpublished).

16. L.J. Savage, *The Foundations of Statistics* (Wiley, 1954).

17. K. Shell and J.E. Stiglitz, "The Allocation of Investment in a Dynamic Economy," *Q.J.E.,* Nov., 1967, pp. 592–609.

18. H. Uzawa, "Market Allocation and Optimum Growth," *Australian Economic Papers,* June, 1968, pp. 17–27.

16

A Time–State–Preference Model of Security Valuation*

Stewart C. Myers
Alfred P. Sloan School of Management
Massachusetts Institute of Technology

I. Introduction and Summary

Determining the market values of streams of future returns is a task common to many sorts of economic analysis. The literature on this subject is extensive at all levels of abstraction. However, most work has not take uncertainty into account in a meaningful way.

This paper presents a model of security valuation in which uncertainty takes the central role. The model is based on the requirements for equilibrium in a world in which uncertainty is described by a set of possible event-sequences, or states of nature. This "time-state-preference" framework is a generalized version of that used in articles by Arrow, Debreu, and Hirshleifer, as well as in several more recent studies.[1]

The valuation formulas presented here are, of course, imperfect. They cannot be represented as handy empirical tools. On the theoretical front, moreover, new results and new problems seem always to arrive hand in hand. Although the problems are duly noted, the time-state-preference model will be defended as a plausible approximation and a useful analytical tool.

The paper is organized as follows. The basic time-state-preference model is

Reprinted by permission of the publisher and author from *Journal of Financial and Quantitative Analysis*, March 1968, pp. 1–33.

*This paper is a further development of my doctoral dissertation [20], which was submitted to the Graduate School of Business, Stanford University, in 1967. I am indebted for good advice and apt suggestions to my dissertation committee, Professors Alexander Robichek, Gert von der Linde, and Ezra Solomon. Also, Professor Kenneth Arrow was kind enough to read and comment on the entire dissertation. I wish also to thank Professors Jack Hirshleifer, Avraham Beja, Paul Cootner, and Peter Diamond, as well as this paper's referees, for helpful comments.

My research was supported by a Ford Foundation Doctoral Fellowship and a Ford Foundation Grant to the Sloan School for research in business finance. Neither the Ford Foundation nor the persons cited above are responsible for my opinions or mistakes.

1. The framework is due to Arrow [2] and has been extended and expounded by Debreu [5], Ch. VII, and Hirshleifer [9] [10] [11]. See also Radner [24], Drèze [7], Pye [23], Diamond [4], and Beja [3] for examples of related work. Lancaster [14] has used a similar analytical framework in recent discussions of theory of consumer choice.

derived in Section II. This requires careful statement of the assumed market characteristics and the constraints on investors' strategies: although the general characteristics of the formulas obtained are intuitively appealing, their precise form is sensitive to the range of trading opportunities open to investors. The Kuhn-Tucker conditions are used to obtain the necessary conditions for equilibrium. In Section III, the special case discussed by other authors is related to my more general model. Some implications are considered in Section IV.

Finally, I consider the possible effects of "the interdependence of investors' strategies," which arise whenever the value of a security to an investor depends on other investors' beliefs and market strategies. This interdependence leads to price uncertainty, which greatly complicates the necessary conditions for equilibrium. Thus, it is difficult to evaluate its systematic effect, if any, on the structure of security prices. It is possible, however, to make qualitative comments on the nature of the problem and its possible effects.

The main contributions of this paper are as follows:

1.   It is a general description of how markets for risky assets would work under a variety of conditions. Although it is more exploratory than definitive, this should not be surprising: work in the area has a relatively short history, and has concentrated mostly on issues that are even broader than those considered here. This paper is one of the first detailed investigations of a particular market under uncertainty.

2.   It is widely agreed that the time-state-preference framework as developed by Arrow, Debreu, and Hirshleifer[2] is an important addition to the economist's theoretical tool-kit. This paper shows that the framework is amenable to considerable generalization, and that it allows explicit statement of the effects of certain "imperfections"—e.g., restrictions on short selling or borrowing.

3.   The model was originally developed as a contribution to the theory of corporate financial management. Although details are not included here, it has already proved useful in this context.[3] Thus it should be worthwhile to set out the logic of the model in detail as a basis for further work.

II. The Basic Time-State-Preference Model

One way of describing uncertainty about conditions in a future period[4] is to say that one of a set of possible states of nature will occur at that time. Definition of a set of states, in turn, provides a means of describing risk character-

---

2. In the articles already cited.

3. See Myers [20] [21], Robichek and Myers [25], and Hirshleifer [10], esp. pp. 264–68.

4. The most common alternative is to specify the mean, variance and possibly other statistical measures of risk and return. See Sharpe [26] and Lintner [16] [17], for formal models using a mean-variance framework, and Hirshleifer [11] for a detailed comparison of the two approaches.

istics of securities, since any security can be regarded as a contract to pay an amount which depends on the state which actually occurs.

For instance, we might regard a share of stock as a contract to pay an x dollar dividend if state 1 occurs at $t = 1$, a y dollar dividend if state 2 occurs at $t = 1$, etc. Let the dividend paid be $R(s,t)$ and suppose 100 states of nature are being considered for $t = 1$. Then the set $\{R(s,1)\} = \{R(1,1), R(2,1), \ldots, R(100,1)\}$ specifies the particular bundle of *contingent payments* which the investor obtains for $t = 1$ by purchasing one share. In this case, $R(1,1) = x$, $R(2,1) = y$, and so on.

The following model relates the present value of a security to the present value of the contingent returns the security may pay to its owner. This relationship will be derived from the *necessary* conditions of security market equilibrium. First, however, the assumed characteristics of the market must be carefully specified.

Assumptions

1. *States of Nature*—A state of nature which may occur at time τ is defined as a particular *sequence of events* during the time span from $t = 1$ to $t = \tau$. Constructing a set of possible states is simply a means of identifying the possible event-sequences relevant to present decisions.

   The concept of an event-sequence is ambiguous, however, if "event" is left undefined, since a possibility that is relevant in one context may not be in another. A benchmark can be established by imagining a set of states defined in such great detail that the knowledge of the state that will occur at any time t would allow specification of every characteristic of the future world from the present to time t. Let this set be S. The sets of states which would be considered relevant to actual decisions may be regarded as *partitions* of S. Thus, if an investor finds it useful to identify a state by "GM's dividend is increased at $t = 1$," the state refers to that subset of S for which this "event" takes place.

   In the model presented here, it is assumed that investors agree on a particular partition,[5] which defines a set of states $\{(s,t)\}$. The set is assumed to apply to the time span from $t = 1$ to $t = T$.[6] Conditions at $t = 0$ are known

---

5. The choice of a particular partition is arbitrary. An even coarser partition than that used here would undoubtedly be more "realistic," since investors would in practice regard computational efforts as a scarce resource. The intuitive meaning of a still finer partition is difficult to pin down, if only because no one person is likely to be *interested* in more than a small subset of the additional event-sequences which could be defined.

The interpretation of time-state-preference models given coarser partitions than $\{(s,t)\}$ is discussed in Section IV, below.

6. The horizon $t = T$ is introduced for analytical convenience; it is not a "planning horizon" in the usual sense of the phrase. There is some error because of the lack of explicit analysis of events subsequent to the horizon, but the effect of any such errors on the market's valuation of securities at $t = 0$ may be considered negligible if the horizon is far enough distant in time.

with certainty. The set $\{(s,t)\}$ is sufficiently detailed that, if state s occurs at time t, then returns on every security are uniquely specified for period t and all previous periods. Also, the set of states is finite and exhaustive with respect to possible sequences of security returns.[7]

Given these conditions, a security's contingent returns $\{R(s,t)\}$ are not random variables; the return $R(s,t)$ is *certain* to be paid in period t *if* state s occurs. However, it is important to remember that the set $\{(s,t)\}$ does not catalogue all possible future events. Even if it could be known that a particular state (s,t) is to occur, an investor would still face a residual uncertainty about his health, tastes, family status, employment, etc.

2.   *The Economy*—We will imagine an economy split into real and financial sectors. For present purposes, "financial sector" and "security markets" are synonymous.

It is clearly meaningless to speak of the equilibrium of security markets except in relation to a particular set of conditions in the real sector. Accordingly, the following items are taken as given:

a.   The set of states $\{(s,t)\}$.

b.   Investors' assessments of the probabilities that the various states will occur.

c.   The (sequences of) security returns contingent on each state (s,t).

Also, it is assumed that investors have given endowments of wealth available for allocation among securities and other uses, which will be referred to collectively as "consumption."

3.   *Available Securities*—Taking conditions in the economy's real sector as given necessitates a restriction on the types of securities that may be issued (or retired) in response to security prices at $t = 0$. There is no need to hold supplies of all securities constant; however, it is not consistent to admit changes in the supply of securities that are part and parcel of changes in the allocation of resources within the real sector.

To illustrate, suppose that interest rates fall at $t = 0$. In response, a firm issues bonds to finance purchases of additional plant and equipment. Because the additional real assets enable the firm to pay higher returns in some or all future contingencies, a link is created between current interest rates and the bundle of contingent returns which the firm offers to present investors. This is unacceptable if the analysis is to be limited to conditions for equilibrium in the financial sectors.

If, on the other hand, the firm uses the bond issue to retire a portion of its outstanding common stock, conditions in the real sector may be considered unchanged. The substitution of debt for equity in a firm's capital

---

7. The assumption is that security returns may take specific, discrete values. Continuous variables could just as well be used—e.g., $R_k(s,t)$ could be regarded as a continuous function of s and t. Diamond's argument [4] is cast in this form.

structure is a financing decision, and changes in the firm's real assets or investment strategy are not a necessary consequence.[8]

To generalize, changes in the supply of securities, or the issue of new types of securities, are not ruled out in what follows. It is assumed, however, that such adjustments are not of the sort that imply changed conditions in the real sector. It has already been noted that the concept "equilibrium of security markets" is meaningful only if conditions in the real sector are given.

4. *Market Characteristics*—Markets are assumed to be perfect.
5. *Reinvestment of Contingent Returns*—Investment in securities amounts to the purchase of bundles of contingent returns, which may, in general, be either consumed or reinvested when and if they are realized. For this model, however, we will effectively rule out reinvestment by assuming that investors hold their original portfolios unchanged at least until $t = T$. (This assumption is reconsidered in Section V below.) Accordingly, a security's return in (s,t) will be interpreted as the *cash* payment (i.e., dividend, interest, or principal payment) which its owner receives in (s,t). Capital gains or losses will not be considered, except that the price of the security in the most distant future time period under consideration will be treated as if it were a liquidating dividend.[9]

For stocks, this assures that market value is determined solely by the present value of future dividends.
6. *Utility Functions*—Investors choose portfolios which we assume maximize the expected utility of future returns on the portfolio. In addition, the total expected utility associated with any portfolio is a linear function of utility functions defined for each state. Specifically, if $\pi(s,t)$ is an investor's judgment of the probability of occurrence of contingency (s,t) and $U(s,t)$ is the utility of returns to be received in (s,t), then the overall utility of a portfolio's contingent returns will be given by

$$\psi = \sum_{s,t} \pi(s,t)\, U(s,t). \tag{1}$$

8. It is true that the contingent returns received by stock- and bond-holders are affected if the firm replaces equity with debt. However, the bundles of contingent returns offered by the firm's securities can still be clearly specified within the set of states $\{(s,t)\}$, provided that (a) there is no change in the total contingent returns paid by the firm on all its outstanding securities and (b) investors are certain about how the firm's total payout is to be divided among stock- and bondholders in every possible contingency. Although these conditions may not always hold in practice (see Robichek and Myers [25], esp. pp. 15–19) they are a reasonable approximation for present purposes.

9. However, there is no requirement that all securities offer contingent returns in all time periods from $t = 1$ to $t = T$. Bonds, in particular, will often mature before the horizon period.

The notation $\Sigma_{s,t}$ denotes summation over all states in the set $\{(s,t)\}$, $t = 1, 2, \ldots, T$.

Further, we assume that each utility function $U(s,t)$ is defined only in terms of returns to be received in (s,t). That is, if an investor holds a portfolio yielding y in (s,t), then the utility of y is independent of the utility of returns in all other contingencies, and vice versa.

This assumption would not be reasonable without our proviso that contingent returns on securities are consumed, rather than reinvested. If, say, the amount y were invested in real assets, the investor's income in subsequent contingencies would be increased. As a consequence, the marginal utility of income in these contingencies would not be the same, in general, as it would be if y were consumed.

In this framework $U'(s,t)$, the marginal utility of income in a given contingency, may be high for either or both of two reasons:[10]

a.   Assuming that the investor is risk-averse, $U'(s,t)$ will be relatively high to the extent that the total income to be received in (s,t) is low.

b.   The utility of a given amount of money income may differ from state to state, since the utility *functions* $U'(s,t)$ are not necessarily the same for each contingency.

One class of reasons why the functions $U(s,t)$ may depend on (s,t) is fairly obvious: differences can arise, for instance, if commodity prices differ from state to state and over time, or if the investor's need for income depends on, say, his age at (s,t).

Another kind of reason follows from the way we have set up the problem. The set $\{(s,t)\}$ assumed for purposes of analysis is exhaustive in the sense that it offers a complete catalogue of possible future returns on *securities,* but it does not catalogue *all* future events exhaustively. The risks inherent in these "uncatalogued" contingencies will not, in general, be independent of the state being considered. An investor will perhaps be less certain of the amount of income he will receive from sources other than securities in wartime, but the occurrence of a war will also effect returns on securities. The functions $U(s,t)$ will reflect such interrelationships.

Formally, then, the phrase "utility of a contingent return A in (s,t)" must be taken to mean "the *expected* utility to the investor of the (certain) amount A at time t given that state s occurs." We thus consider only a part of the investor's overall decision problem: the possible incremental effects on his future income of his portfolio choice at $t = 0$.

The Basic Model

We begin by considering N different securities which investors can purchase at $t = 0$. These securities may have been issued at $t = 0$, or they may be "left

---

10. As noted by Hirshleifer [11], pp. 523–34.

over" from previous periods. The word "share" will be used to refer to a single unit of investment in a given security.

For the kth security, the set $\{R_k(s,t)\}$ of contingent returns per share will be written in vector form, and referred to as R_k, where

$$R_k = [R_k(0), \ldots, R_k(s,t), \ldots]$$

for $s = 1, 2, \ldots, m(t)$, and for each period $t = 1, 2, \ldots, T$. The "state" $s = 0$ refers to the present—i.e., to $t = 0$—and for each security $R_k(0) = -P_k$, where P_k is the ex-dividend market price per share of the kth security at $t = 0$.

We define a dummy security $k = 0$ to be "consumption" at $t = 0$, with

$$R_0 = [1, 0, \ldots, 0].$$

That is, purchasing one share of security zero is interpreted as the consumption of one dollar at $t = 0$. P_0, the "price" of consumption, is likewise one dollar.

Consider the portfolio selection problem of a particular investor. Let h_k be the number of shares of the kth security which he purchases. His decision problem at $t = 0$ is to choose $[h_0, h_1, \ldots, h_N]$ to maximize expected utility ψ, where

$$\psi = \sum_{s,t} \pi(s,t) U(s,t) + U(0), \tag{1}$$

with

$$U(s,t) = f\left[\sum_{k=1}^{N} h_k R_k(s,t)\right] \quad \text{and}$$

$$U(0) = f[h_o].$$

The variables $\pi(s,t)$ represent the investor's assessments of the probabilities that the states (s,t) actually will occur. (Note that we have made no assumption ruling out disagreement among investors on the probabilities $\pi(s,t)$.)

In addition, the investor is constrained in that he has only a given amount of wealth, W, available for allocation among consumption and investment. The constraint is

$$\phi = \sum_{k=0}^{N} h_k P_k - W = 0. \tag{2}$$

Since consumption and investment in securities are the only available uses for this wealth, Equation (2) is necessarily an equality.

If no short selling or borrowing is permitted, then $h_k \geq 0$ for all k. In this case, maximizing Equation (1) subject to the stated constraint is a problem in non-linear programming. The necessary conditions for the maximum may be inferred from the Kuhn-Tucker conditions.[11] If a maximum exists, we know from these conditions that we can assign a positive number $\lambda(\phi)$ to the constraint Equation (2).[12] Maximizing utility implies that

$$\frac{\delta \psi}{\delta h_k} - \lambda(\phi) \frac{\delta \phi}{\delta h_k} \leq 0, \tag{3}$$

for $k = 0, 1, \ldots, N$. The left hand side of Equation (3) is zero if $h_k > 0$.

Note that

$$\frac{\delta \phi}{\delta h_k} = P_k \qquad \text{for } k > 0, \qquad \text{and}$$

$$\frac{\delta \phi}{\delta h_o} = 1.$$

Substituting in Equation (3) for security $k = 0$ (i.e., consumption at $t = 0$), we obtain

$$\lambda(\phi) = U'(0), \tag{4}$$

where $U'(0)$ is the marginal utility of income used for present consumption.

Using these results, we can rewrite Equation (3) as

$$\delta \psi / \delta h_k - U'(0) P_k \leq 0,$$

---

11. Kuhn and Tucker [13]. Also, see Dorfman, Samuelson, and Solow [6], Ch. VII, for the exposition which prompted my use of the conditions. Rémember that the conditions to be presented are not sufficient for equilibrium. For instance, one necessary condition not mentioned is that the utility functions $U(s,t)$ be convex—i.e., risk-averse. See Arrow [2], p. 95. Also, in the absence of any direct or indirect restraints on the ability of investors to *sell* single contingent payments, we must require that $\pi_i(s,t) > 0$ for all investors (indexed by i) and all (s,t). If an investor really believes that the contingency (s,t) is impossible, he will be willing to sell contingent payments in (s,t) in unlimited amounts. This latter point was mentioned to me by Avraham Beja. For a detailed treatment of the *existence* of equilibrium, see Debreu [5].

12. Since, from the nature of the problem, the constraint Equation (2) must be satisfied exactly, $\lambda(\phi)$ cannot be zero.

or

$$P_k \geq 1/U'(0) \, [\delta\psi/\delta h_k] .$$

Since, for $k \neq 0$, $\delta\psi/\delta h_k = \Sigma_{s,t} \, \pi(s,t) \, U'(s,t) \, R_k(s,t)$, we have the fundamental result

$$P_k \geq \sum_{s,t} q(s,t) \, R_k(s,t), \tag{5}$$

where

$$q(s,t) = \pi(s,t) \frac{U'(s,t)}{U'(0)} . \tag{6}$$

Equation (5) is the basic valuation formula for the time-state-preference framework. In words, it tells us that when an investor maximizes the expected utility of his portfolio, the price of each security is at least equal to the expectation of the marginal utility associated with a small increment in his holdings of that security, when the utility of money in future contingencies is measured in terms of the utility of money used for present consumption. If the investor actually holds that security in his portfolio, then its price is exactly equal to the expectation of the marginal utility associated with the security. The terms $q(s,t)$ thus indicate the present value to this investor of an incremental dollar of portfolio return to be received at time t if state (s,t) occurs.

A necessary condition for equilibrium is that Equation (5) holds for all securities from the point of view of each investor. In effect, it establishes a lower bound on the price of each security, expressed in terms of investors' marginal valuations of contingent returns. For if P_k were less than the right hand side of Equation (5) from the point of view of any investor, then that investor could increase the total expected utility of returns to his portfolio by purchasing security k in at least marginal amounts. Equilibrium cannot exist until all such opportunities are exhausted.

Borrowing

The introduction of investors' borrowing opportunities does not change the necessary conditions for equilibrium given by Equation (5). Borrowing is simply the purchase of a particular type of security. If the jth security is a borrowing contract open to an investor, then its contingent cash "returns" can be written in the same format used above:

$$R_j = [R_j(0), \ldots, R_j(s,t), \ldots].$$

The vector R_j is unusual only in that $R_j(0) > 0$ and $R_j(s,t) \leqslant 0$.

Selling Short

Selling short can be most conveniently analyzed within the present framework by regarding the short sale of security k as the purchase of a dummy security $k*$ with a vector of contingent returns R_k* derived from R_k. The vector R_k* will be roughly a mirror image of R_k. If there are no margin requirements, then $R_k* = -R_k$, in which case selling security k short is algebraically equivalent to purchasing negative amounts of security k, assuming $k*$ is held to time $t = T$.[13]

It is entirely feasible to incorporate dummy securities such as $k*$ in the investor's portfolio problem wherever short sales make sense. The necessary conditions for the maximum imply a result comparable to Equation (5) for each dummy security—that is,

$$P_k* \geqslant \sum_{s,t} q(s,t) R_k*(s,t). \tag{7}$$

This holds with an equality if $h_k* > 0$.

For the case in which there are no margin requirements, comparison of Equations (5) and (7) leads to an interesting result. As we have observed, for this case $R_k* = -R_k$, implying that $P_k* = -P_k$ and that $R_k*(s,t) = -R_k(s,t)$ for all (s,t). Substituting in Equation (7),

$$P_k* \leqslant \sum_{s,t} q(s,t) R_k(s,t). \tag{8}$$

Equations (5) and (8) taken together require[14]

---

13. Given the distant horizon T, the short sale becomes a promise to pay security k's dividends from period $t = 1$ to $t = T$ to the lender of the security. The payments include the security's price at $t = T$, which we have interpreted as a liquidating dividend. Thus selling short is the sale of future contingent returns. That we do not actually find short sales undertaken as long-term commitments is apparently due to uncertainty about whether any particular investor could fulfill such a contract. Margin requirements are a reaction to this uncertainty.

14. In words, the argument is this. If the investor's total expected utility is reduced by selling a marginal amount of security k short, he will necessarily be better off by purchasing a marginal amount of k long. Conversely, if the investor's total expected utility is reduced by purchasing a marginal amount of security k, then it will pay him to sell security k short.

$$P_k = \sum_{s,t} q(s,t)\, R_k(s,t). \tag{9}$$

Note that Equation (9) implies that all investors agree, at the margin, on the equilibrium values of all securities, although not necessarily on the value of any particular contingent return. Because each investor is willing to "take a position" in each security, there can be no such thing as a "clientele effect." That is, investors holding a particular security will *not* value it more highly than other investors do.

On the other hand, Equation (5) *is* in itself consistent with a clientele effect. Any such effect must therefore be ascribed to restricted trading opportunities, not to the existence of uncertainty or differences in investors' expectations.

Other Constraints

The frictions and imperfections which exist in actual markets have, for the most part, been left out of the above analysis. However, those which impose constraints on investors' portfolio choices can be analyzed with relative ease if portfolio choice is viewed as a problem of non-linear programming.

For example, suppose the investor must invest at least $100b$ percent of his funds in securities from the set K. Now the objective function must be maximized subject to two constraints:

$$\phi_1 = \sum_{k=0}^{N} h_k P_k - W = 0, \tag{10}$$

$$\phi_2 = bW - \sum_{k \in K} h_k P_k \leq 0.$$

For securities not included in the set K, $\delta\phi_2/\delta h_k = 0$. Here the constraint $\phi_2 = 0$ is irrelevant, and Equation (5) holds. For $k \in K$, however, the Kuhn-Tucker conditions are:

$$\frac{\delta\psi}{\delta h_k} - \lambda(\phi_1)\frac{\delta\phi_1}{\delta h_k} - \lambda(\phi_2)\frac{\delta\phi_2}{\delta h_k} \leq 0. \tag{11}$$

Therefore, *each* investor at equilibrium will be willing to hold at least marginal amounts of *each* security either long or short in his portfolio. Only if this condition is satisfied will Equations (5) and (8) be consistent.

Computing $\lambda(\phi_1)$ and the partial derivatives, and solving for P_k, we have:

$$P_k = \frac{1}{U'(\phi) - \lambda(\phi_2)} \sum_{s,t} \pi(s,t)\, U'(s,t)\, R_k(s,t), \qquad (12)$$

assuming that k is actually included in the investor's optimal portfolio. The variable $\lambda(\phi_2)$ is the expected utility lost (at the margin) by investing one dollar in a security $k \in K$ instead of consuming the dollar.[15]

III. A Special Case

We now return to the main thread of the argument. A necessary condition for equilibrium if short sales are permitted, and if there are no margin requirements or other imperfections, is that Equation (9) hold for each investor and each security. For the ith investor, then,

$$P_k = \sum_{s,t} q_i(s,t)\, R_k(s,t), \qquad (9)$$

$k = 1, 2, \ldots, N$. In other words, if there are N securities, equilibrium requires that N equations of this form hold for each investor. The "unknowns" are the variables $q_i(s,t)$, since security prices and contingent returns are taken as given by investors in a perfect market. The set $\{q_i(s,t)\}$ represents the present values of contingent returns to the ith investor, given by Equation (6).

In general, there is no requirement that investors agree on the present value of contingent returns. However, consider the special case in which $N \geqslant M$, where M is the number of future states, and M of the vectors R_k are linearly independent. Here the equations may be solved to yield a unique set of *prices* $\{q_i(1,1)$, $\ldots, q_i(s,t), \ldots\}$. Moreover, since P_k and R_k are the same for all investors, *the set must be identical for all investors.* Given the structure of security prices at equilibrium, we can thus infer an entirely objective set of prices $\{q(s,t)\}$, where $q(s,t)$ is the price at $t = 0$ of one dollar to be paid contingent on the occurrence of (s,t). We have, therefore:

$$P_k = \sum_{s,t} q(s,t)\, R_k(s,t), \qquad (13)$$

with $q(s,t) = q_i(s,t)$ for all i and all (s,t).[16]

---

15. It is given by $\lambda(\phi_2) = U'(0) - \sum_{s,t} \pi(s,t)\, U'(s,t)\, [R_k(s,t)/P_k]$.

16. This result *may* hold even if short sales are restricted. But this requires that (a) the vectors of returns of available securities—including borrowing and any "dummy securities"

In reality, of course, the number of securities is likely to be much less than the number of states. Nevertheless, this simplest possible case is important in several respects.

1. It is customarily argued that, since investors will disagree in their subjective evaluations of the size and risk of streams of future returns, their estimates of the value of these streams will also differ. This may well be true in fact, but Equation (13) establishes that any such disagreement is not a necessary consequence of either (a) the existence of uncertainty, or (b) differences in investors' expectations. In fact, Equation (13) implies that all investors would agree on the value of any conceivable bundle of contingent returns, no matter how bizzare, which could be specified in terms of the catalogue of contingencies $\{(s,t)\}$.

2. Equation (13) is closely related to (and, in fact, depends on) the ability of any investor to achieve any desired *pattern* of contingent returns from his portfolio. To be specific, let the vector X_p represent the desired pattern:

$$X_p = [X_p(1,1), \ldots, X_p(s,t), \ldots] = \frac{1}{\sum_{s,t} R_p(s,t)} R_p. \qquad (14)$$

Here $R_p(s,t)$ is the return of the portfolio in (s,t) and R_p is the vector of these returns. The numbers $X_p(s,t)$ represent the pattern of the contingent returns $R_p(s,t)$. Because $1/\Sigma s,t\ R_p(s,t)$ adjusts for the *scale* of the portfolio's returns, $\Sigma s,t\ X_p(s,t) = 1$. The pattern of returns for a security can be described similarly:

$$X_k = [X_k(1,1), \ldots, X_k(s,t), \ldots] = \frac{1}{\sum_{s,t} R_k(s,t)} R_k. \qquad (15)$$

Since, in this special case, there are M securities with linearly independent vectors X_k, and there are no margin requirements for short sales, the vectors span the M-dimensional space defined by the catalogue of M states. The portfolio vector X_p lies in this same space. It follows that any vector X_p can be obtained by a linear combination of the vectors X_k.

To put this another way, we have established that an investor can adjust

---

used to describe types of trading different from simple purchases—span a cone equivalent to the M-dimensional space created by the set $\{(s,t)\}$, and (b) that Equation (5) holds with an equality for all securities and all investors. In this case the number of securities would have to be substantially *more* than the number of states.

his portfolio to change a particular contingent return $R_p(s,t)$, while leaving returns in all other contingencies unchanged. In effect, he can buy or sell returns for any contingency. It is as if there were a separate forward market for dollars to be delivered in each future state. Viewed in this light, it is not surprising that a unique set of prices $\{q(s,t)\}$ is a necessary condition for equilibrium.

3.   Previous time-state-preference models have, without significant exception, confined their analysis to this special case. In fact, it is usually assumed that trading of contingent returns takes place in explicit markets, rather than implicitly, via portfolio adjustments. Arrow and Hirshleifer, for instance, have assumed markets for "primitive securities":[17] the primitive security for (s,t) pays one dollar contingent on (s,t), but nothing in any other state. Thus the equilibrium price of such a security would be simply $q(s,t)$.[18]

Without denying the theoretical productivity of this special case,[19] it is important to recognize that the time-state-preference framework can be generalized and adopted to particular market characteristics.

Some Implications

This section notes some implications of the time-state-preference model of security valuation. First, the conventional valuation formulas are briefly re-examined. Observations follow on the implications of individual risk aversion for market prices, the interpretation of time-state-preference models if the catalogue of states is not exhaustively defined, and the concept of a risk-equivalent class of securities.

Conventional Formulas

Consider the ith investor, who holds at least one share of the kth stock. Then Equation (11) holds at equilibrium:

$$P_k = \sum_{s,t} q_i(s,t) R_k(s,t). \tag{9}$$

---

17. See Arrow [2]. Hirshleifer calls these primitive securities "time-state claims." [11], p. 527, and *passim*.

18. The set of primitive securities and the M normal securities considered above are simply alternative bases for the vector space defined in terms of $\{(s,t)\}$.

19. For instance, the special case has generated considerable insight into the problem of determining optimal capital structure for corporations. See Robichek and Myers [25] and Hirshleifer [10], pp. 264–68.

This investor may or may not agree with others on the present value of contingent returns. For simplicity's sake, however, we will drop the subscript i in what follows.

The formulas normally used are:

$$P_k = \sum_{t=1}^{T} \frac{\bar{R}_k(t)}{(1+r)^t} = \sum_{t=1}^{T} \frac{C_k(t)}{(1+i)^t} , \qquad (16)$$

where $\bar{R}_k(t)$ is the investor's expected return in t; r is his required rate of return; $C_k(t)$ is the certainty equivalent of $\bar{R}_k(t)$, and i is the riskless rate of interest. These formulas may be regarded as simplifications of Equation (9). Thus the size of r or $C_k(t)$ depends on (1) the pattern across states of stock k's contingent dividends, (2) the investor's valuations of contingent returns, and (3) his probability assessments. Specifically,[20]

$$C_k(t) = Z_k(t)Q'(t)D_k(t), \qquad (17)$$

where

$$D_k(t) = \sum_{s=1}^{m(t)} R_k(s,t),$$

a measure of the *scale* of the bundle of contingent returns for period t, and $Z_k(t)$ and $Q(t)$ are $1 \times m(t)$ row vectors:

$$Z_k(t) = \frac{1}{D_k(t)} \; [R_k(1,t) \ldots R_k(m(t),t)]$$

$$Q(t) = \frac{1}{\displaystyle\sum_{s=1}^{m(t)} q(s,t)} \; [q(1,t) \ldots q(m(t),t)] .$$

The variables $\bar{R}_k(t)$ and $C_k(t)$ are related as follows:[21]

---

20. This is purely algebraic juggling. Note that $Z_k(t) D_k(t)$ is equivalent to the vector $[R_k(1, t) \ldots R_k(m(t), t)]$. Also, $Q(t) = [1/ \Sigma_s q(s,t)] \, [q(1,t) \ldots q(m(t), t)] = (1 + i)^t \, [q(1, t) \ldots q(m(t),t)]^s$. That is, $\Sigma_s q(s,t)$ is the value to the investor of one dollar to be delivered with certainty in period t.

21. This is obtained by multiplying $C_k(t)$ as given by Equation (17) by

$$C_k(t) = \alpha(t)\bar{R}_k(t) = \frac{Z_k(t)Q'(t)}{Z_k(t)\pi'(t)} \; \bar{R}_k(t). \tag{18}$$

Here $\pi(t)$ is a row vector of the investor's probability assessments $\pi(s,t)$ for period t.

There is, of course, no guarantee that investors will agree on the appropriate size for $C_k(t)$, $\bar{R}_k(t)$, $\alpha(t)$ or r.

Equations (16) are two among many ways of simplifying the more basic valuation formula, Equation (9). Alternative forms based on continuous compounding and exponential growth are often seen, as are rules of thumb using price-earnings ratios or "multipliers." Given a little algebraic ingenuity, the possible formats are endless.

Consequently, it is pointless to say that any particular simplification is *the* correct way to represent present value.

Risk Aversion

The next few paragraphs investigate the implications of investors' risk aversion for the structure of security prices. The conclusions are generally consistent with those obtained elsewhere.[22] I repeat them because they serve as a basis for discussing implications of coarse partitions of states, and because of the persistence of the notion that security prices are adequately explained by simply considering the characteristics of individual investors' utility functions.

It is generally accepted that most investors are risk averse. From this, it is often inferred that "the market" should be risk averse, in the sense that the certainty equivalent of an uncertain return should always be no more than the expectation of the return. In other words, the prediction would be that $\alpha(t) \leqslant 1$, or that $r \geqslant i$, where i is the pure rate of interest.

Actually, it is always possible to construct patterns of contingent returns for which $\alpha(t) > 1$ for all t,—i.e., such that $r < i$. Note that the numerator and denominator of Equation (18) are weighted averages of relative prices and probabilities, respectively. In general, the relative price for (s,t) may be more or

$$\frac{\bar{R}_k(t)}{\bar{R}_k(t)} = \frac{\bar{R}_k(t)}{Z_k(t)\,\pi'(t)\,D_k(t)} = 1.$$

Confidence in the theoretical appropriateness of certainty equivalents may be somewhat increased by finding that they can be conveniently expressed in a time-state-preference framework. Unfortunately, the required rate r cannot be conveniently expressed—a fact which corroborates Lintner's view that r is not a "primary" variable for theoretical uses. See Lintner [19], pp. 27–28.

22. See, for instance, Drèze [7], pp. 36–38; Lintner [17], pp. 22–23.

less than $\pi(s,t)$. By changing the weights $Z_k(t)$, therefore, we can always[23] assure that $Z_k(t)Q(t)' > Z_k(t)\,\pi\,(t)'$, or that $\alpha(t) > 1$. The economic meaning of this manipulation is that a bundle of contingent returns will be relatively more valuable if it pays higher returns in states in which contingent returns have a high value.

On the other hand, suppose the weights $Z_k(t)$ are chosen randomly, subject to the condition that the elements of $Z_k(t)$ sum to one. The expected result of this experiment is that[24]

$$E[C_k(t)] = E[Z_k(t)\,Q'(t)\,D_k(t)] = \frac{D_k(t)}{m(t)}. \tag{19}$$

That is, period t's bundle of contingent returns is on the average, exactly as valuable as a *certain* return $[D_k(t)]/[m(t)]$. Securities constructed in this manner would tend to be no more or less valuable than riskless securities with the same scale of returns.[25]

These mental experiments indicate that rewards for risk bearing are not explained by uncertainty per se, but by some systematic relationship between the relative sizes of the returns $R_k(s,t)$ and the "prices" $q(s,t)$. In actual markets, the relationship seems to be that returns on most available securities are positively correlated, so that securities tend to pay high returns precisely when most portfolio returns are high and low returns in times of scarcity. The normal risk premium is thus explained, given the inverse relationship between supplies of contingent returns and their present values.

Interpretation of the Model Given Coarse Partitions of States

The application of the time-state-preference model within a relatively coarse partition of the set S of possible event-sequences is entirely feasible, given attention to several complicating factors. One of these is that investors will not, in general, adopt identical partitions, so that agreement among investors on the

---

23. If $\pi(t) = Q(t)$, $\alpha(t) = 1$ for any pattern on contingent returns. This is improbable.

24. That is, the expected value of each of the elements of $Z_k(t)$ is $1/[m(t)]$. $m(t)$ is the number of states defined for period t.

25. Unfortunately it would not be correct to predict that, on the average, such securities would be priced so that investors would anticipate an *expected* rate of return equal to the riskless rate of interest. Although $E[Z_k(t)\,Q'(t)] = E[Z_k(t)\,\pi'(t)]$, it is *not* true that

$$E[\alpha_t] = E\left[\frac{Z_k(t)\,Q'(t)}{Z_k(t)\,\pi'(t)}\right] = 1.$$

risk characteristics of securities cannot be taken for granted. Nevertheless, postu-lating agreement will often prove to be appropriate.

Another problem is that our previous definition of contingent returns will no longer serve. Given a partition $\{(\sigma,t)\}$ which is coarser than $\{(s,t)\}$, the returns contingent on (σ,t) are the *random* variables $R_k(\sigma,t)$. They cannot be used in the same sense as the variables $R_k(s,t)$—which are *certain* returns, given (s,t)—without further explanation.

Adopting the partition $\{(\sigma,t)\}$, the investor's decision problem is to maximize

$$\psi = \sum_{\sigma,t} \pi(\sigma,t)\, E[U(\sigma,t)] + U(0), \tag{20}$$

subject to a wealth constraint, where

$$E[U(\sigma,t)] = E\left[U\left(\sum_{k=1}^{N} h_k \widetilde{R}_k(\sigma,t)\right)\right]. \tag{21}$$

The value of $E[U(\sigma,t)]$ could be computed readily if the investor had specified the returns $R_k(s,t)$, the probabilities $\pi(s,t)$, given (σ,t), and the functions $U(s,t)$; but he does not have this information. A reasonable heuristic tool is to rewrite his decision problem as:

$$\psi = \sum_{\sigma,t} \pi(\sigma,t)\, U^*(\sigma,t) + U(0), \tag{20a}$$

$$U^*(\sigma,t) = U\left(\sum_{k=1}^{N} h_k C_k(\sigma,t)\right). \tag{21a}$$

Here $C_k(\sigma,t)$ is the certainty equivalent of $\widetilde{R}_k(\sigma,t)$—that is, if state (σ,t) occurs, the investor is indifferent to receiving $\widetilde{R}_k(\sigma,t)$ or a certain amount $C_k(\sigma,t)$. The investor is assumed to act as if he is certain to receive a portfolio return of

$$\sum_{k=1}^{N} h_k C_k(\sigma,t)$$

if (σ,t) occurs.

The decision problem shown as Equations (20a) and (21a) may be solved by exactly the same procedure used in Section II to derive the basic time-state-preference model. However, this provides an easy way out only if the certainty equivalent can itself be explained without undue complication. Various simple relationships might be assumed if the partition represented by the set (σ, t) is not too coarse.[26]

One interesting thing is that the special case discussed in Section III is less unlikely when a coarse partition of states is used. The coarser $\{(\sigma, t)\}$, the smaller the number of states, and the more likely it is that the available vectors of security returns will span the vector space associated with $\{(\sigma, t)\}$. It would not be entirely unreasonable, therefore, to attempt to measure the price of one dollar to be delivered (with certainty) at $t = 1$ contingent on, say, an increase in GNP of more than five percent.[27]

"Risk Classes" as a Consequence of
Coarse Partitions

In a time-state-preference framework, the risk characteristics of the kth security are determined by its pattern of returns across the possible states of nature. The vector X_k, defined by Equation (15), is one way to describe this pattern.

Unfortunately, it is not very helpful to say that securities j and k are in the same risk class if $X_j = X_k$, for this requires the return $R_k(s, t)$ to be the same proportion of $R_j(s, t)$ in every contingency. If this is true, there is little point in calling j and k different securities. The use of such a definition would thus require creating a risk class for every security, and it implies that no two securities can be considered perfect substitutes.

This is not surprising, considering that individuals are assumed to have made the computational investment necessary to evaluate securities within the set of states $\{(s, t)\}$. A small computational effort yields a coarser partition, and a corresponding reduction in the investor's ability to distinguish among the risk

---

26. If, for instance, the partition is fine enough to describe all systematic interrelationships among returns, then the returns $\tilde{R}_k(\sigma, t)$ of the N securities are independent random variables. So long as the states (s, t) are not explicitly considered, the securities' returns can be distinguished only by summary measures of the residual uncertainty—e.g., by $\mathrm{Var}[\tilde{R}_k(\sigma, t)]$. Consequently, a relation such as $C_k(\sigma, t) = E[\tilde{R}_k(\sigma, t)] - A\, \mathrm{Var}[\tilde{R}_k(\sigma, t)]$ could be assumed. The result would be a hybrid model, in which a security's price is related to (a) the pattern of its returns across the states (σ, t) and (b) the mean and variability of its contingent returns. It might even be fruitful to set $A = 0$, on the grounds that most of the uncertainty about security returns is resolved by the occurrence of a state (σ, t), and that diversification can eliminate most of the residual variance. Note that the covariance of $R_j(\sigma, t)$ and $\tilde{R}_k(\sigma, t)$ would be zero for all $j \neq k$.

27. This would also establish the market price of the certainty equivalent of a random return to be delivered contingent on this event.

characteristics of securities. If computation is costly, it is perfectly conceivable that an investor will consider the jth and k^{th} securities to be perfect substitutes, knowing that $X_j \neq X_k$, but not being able to specify the differences among the two (because of a coarse partition of future states) in any way which would allow a choice among them.[28] Thus the concept of a class of securities with homogeneous risk characteristics—found useful by Modigliani and Miller, for instance[29]—is not unreasonable if computational effort is a scarce resource.

V. The Interdependence of Investors' Strategies

The model of security valuation presented in this paper is not descriptive in any strict sense. On the other hand, the assumptions used are mostly familiar ones; few readers will be surprised to encounter such abstractions as the Perfect Market or the Rational Investor.

One novel assumption is that all investors purchase portfolios at $t = 0$ with the certain intention of holding them unchanged at least until period $t = T$. This proviso insures that investors' portfolio choices are *independent,* in the sense that the expected utility of any investor's portfolio depends only on the cash returns of the securities included, and in no way on possible future actions of other investors.

It takes only cursory observations of actual security markets to see that this assumption of a "one-shot" portfolio choice is inaccurate. Investors' strategies are clearly interdependent, for instance, if securities are purchased partly for anticipated capital gains. Here, the return realized by any particular investor depends not only on the state (s,t) occurring, but also on what other investors will think the security is worth.

The interdependence of investors' strategies is a matter of considerable theoretical interest and uncertain practical importance. It is discussed briefly and qualitatively in this section.

Why Investors Revise Their Portfolios

There are two sorts of reasons why an investor may sell securities from his original portfolio.

---

28. However, because of the general benefits of diversification, the investor may hold both securities in his portfolio.

29. See Modigliani and Miller [18]. These comments are not meant to imply that the concept of a risk class is necessary to the proof of Modigliani and Miller's Proposition I—that the market value of the firm is independent of financial leverage in the absence of taxes on corporate income. The proposition can be readily proved given the detailed partition defined by $\left\{ (s,t) \right\}$, in which no two securities can be said to belong to the same risk class. See Hirshleifer [10], pp. 264–68, and Robichek and Myers [25].

1. *To provide funds for consumption*—An investor may sell securities if the cash returns on his portfolio do not sustain his "desired" consumption expenditures. Some of these consumption needs, such as retirement income, are fairly predictable, but others are not: security investment serves in part as a cushion or reserve source of funds which may be needed unexpectedly for other uses.

It is important, however, to look one step behind this proximate cause of the sale of securities. Our previous assumption of a one-shot investment decision is *not necessarily* inconsistent with an investor's providing exactly for a large contingent cash payment, since there may be some portfolio with a pattern of returns across the set of states which is appropriate. If this pattern lies within the cone spanned by the vectors X_k of available securities, then the investor can purchase a portfolio now to meet these contingent needs precisely.

However, such opportunities do not generally exist for all types of consumption needs, since the actual number of securities is too small to span more than a small portion of the different patterns of portfolio returns which may be desired. Moreover, the problem is only partially solved by postulating the "special case" in which an investor can obtain any conceivable pattern in the vector space defined by the set of states $\{(s,t)\}$. Suppose, for instance, that an investor perceives the possibility of a personal emergency at $t = 1$. He will not be able to provide for the emergency situation by his portfolio choice unless securities exist which give different returns *contingent on the occurrence of the emergency.* Unless this event is related in some way to economic conditions on a broader scale, this will not be the case. One would not expect to find securities offering different returns contingent on the occurrence of an event of purely personal interest.[30] Even in this special case, therefore, an investor's need for a large amount of money income contingent on a personal event cannot always be met without portfolio adjustments when the event occurs.

2. *Portfolio choice is a sequential decision problem*[31]—Whereas the contingent

---

30. It may be possible for an investor to issue securities which are differentiated in this regard. We see this in practice as insurance. But many risks are not insurable, so that we can count on some emergencies remaining.

The reasons why investors usually cannot issue securities to cover all contingent needs have been discussed by Radner [27] and Arrow [1], pp. 45–56. Transaction costs are an obvious reason. Another is the difficulty of writing a contract in which the duties of the parties depend on which state of nature actually occurs, when the catalogue of states is not exhaustively defined and agreed upon. A third reason is that the very existence of a contract may change the subsequent actions of the parties to it, in turn affecting the probabilities of occurrence of the states on which the contract is contingent. As Arrow [1] notes (p. 55) this problem arises in practice when insurance policies may make the issuing company vulnerable to a "moral hazard."

31. One of the referees remarked: "The discussion of portfolio choice over time is very weak. The introduction of opportunities developing between t and T means that (s,t) can never be completely specified, which is a good part of what uncertainty is about. Further-

needs just discussed are needs for funds to be consumed, investors may also wish to *reinvest* these funds in other securities. In this case, formal analysis requires explicit treatment of portfolio choice as a *sequential* decision problem. The nature of the problem may be indicated by noting that, in our model, the marginal utility to an investor of money in (s,t) is dependent only on his portfolio choice at $t = 0$, since the returns yielded by the portfolio are determined solely by this choice. In general, however, the return received in (s,t) also depends on (a) the opportunities which develop before time t and (b) the investor's strategy in pursuing these opportunities. In this more general case, the marginal utility of income in (s,t) cannot be deduced solely from consideration of the initial portfolio choice. The result is that this variable cannot be derived and used to evaluate contingent returns in (s,t) without further analysis.

Treatment of These Problems in the Literature of Finance

The problems raised by the interdependence of investors' strategies have been recognized, but not emphasized, in the literature. In essence, what has been done is to assume that these problems have no systematic effect on the valuation process.

Suppose we begin by comparing (a) an investor's valuation of an incremental share of a security on the assumption that he will hold the share until time T to (b) his valuation of this share, assuming that it is to be sold in some period $t < T$. The bundle of contingent returns he receives in case (b) differs from (a) in the substitution of the security's price at t for the contingent dividends paid by the firm between t and T. Since the level and risk characteristics of the security's price at time t are closely associated with those of the security's bundle of contingent returns subsequent to that time, it is a reasonable first approximation to assume that the present value of the price at t and the bundle of subsequent returns is the same. Given this assumption, the value of any security can be expressed solely as a function of its contingent cash returns.

This argument, which has been widely used in the literature,[32] *also justifies any of the results which can be obtained by use of the basic time-state-preference model presented above.*

The difficulty is that the risk characteristics of a security price at some

---

more, information processing is central to what goes on in portfolio management (the sequential problem). In fact, information is of the essence."

The referee is absolutely right. The only defense available is that my model is no weaker in this regard than other formal security valuation models. The tools available are clearly less powerful than we would like; we must do what we can with what we have.

32. For example, see Gordon [8], pp. 131–32, Porterfield [22], p. 19, Lintner [17]. Lintner uses a slight variant of this assumption in another paper. See [15], p. 69.

future date t are also dependent on all investors' demands for this security at that time. Therefore, the investor who may sell a security at time t is exposed to uncertainty about other investors' future demands *in addition to* the uncertainty inherent in its bundle of subsequent contingent returns. This *price uncertainty* is precisely why the interdependence of investors' strategies is potentially important to any theory of security valuation. Its actual importance cannot be determined here, but the next subsection considers a situation in which it is likely to be relevant.

Commitments to Future Sale or Purchase of Securities

Interesting theoretical problems are not always empirically relevant. Could we improve a prediction of the structure of security prices by taking the interdependence of investors' strategies into account? Such an improvement could take place only if (a) securities differ in ways not reflected in their sets of contingent cash returns and (b) these differences are relevant to the investor because of the interdependence of investors' strategies.

The *commitment* to buy or sell a security at a future date (or in a particular state of nature) clearly increases an investor's exposure to price uncertainty; the extent of the increase depends on the extent of the commitment. Therefore, security prices should be affected by the interdependence of investors' strategies where strong commitments are common. It should suffice here to cite two examples.

The many studies of the term structure of interest rates have investigated the effects, if any, of price uncertainty. The liquidity premium found by most such studies is interpreted as an extra payment made by holders of short-term bonds for protection from price uncertainty. It may not be clear, however, how a commitment to buy or sell bonds is involved.

If an investor "needs" a certain amount of funds in ten years, we might refer to $t = 10$ as his "preferred habitat."[33] since a bond maturing at that time would be ideal for him. Higher anticipated yields on bonds of different maturities may lure him from his habitat, but if he does so, he is exposed to price uncertainty. If the "need" is in fact given, purchasing a five-year bond now commits him to buy another bond at $t = 5$, and bond yields at that time are uncertain. On the other hand, buying a fifteen-year bond effectively commits him to selling, at an uncertain price, at $t = 10$. Thus an investor can be said to commit himself to future sales or purchases when he forsakes his habitat. These commitments are one consideration which may explain the liquidity premiums just noted.[34]

---

33. The term is Modigliani and Sutch's [19].

34. They are not sufficient explanations. For instance, see Modigliani and Sutch [19], pp. 183–84.

A second type of implied commitment is found in much corporate borrow-ing, evidenced by the frequent refinancing of corporate issues. Most firms borrow for relatively short periods, compated with the *de facto* maturities of their assets. When this is done, the firm commits itself to refinancing when the borrowed funds are due.[35] If new borrowing is to be undertaken, the firm's shareholders are indirectly exposed to the price uncertainty reflected in uncertainty about the level and term structure of interest rates.

To be sure, the commitment to borrow is not absolute, since the share-holders always have the option of providing additional future financing them-selves. This may be done by retention of earnings or by issue of new securities. Unfortunately, the effects of price uncertainty are not avoided in either case. If refinancing by shareholders is anticipated, ownership of the firm's shares implies a commitment to make an additional investment in some future period or con-tingencies. In general, there is no guarantee that such an investment is consistent with portfolios which would otherwise be optimal at that time.[36] If it is not con-sistent, we would expect an adverse effect on the present price of the firm's shares. The magnitude of the effect would depend on the firm's debt-equity ratio and the disparity between the maturity structures of its assets and liabilities.

VI. Concluding Note

Hirshleifer has remarked that "one surprising aspect of the time-and-state preference model is that it leads to a theory of decision under uncertainty while entirely excluding the 'vagueness' we usually associate with uncertainty."[37] It should now be clear that such precision is not a necessary characteristic of all time-state-preference models, but only of the special case Hirshleifer was con-cerned with. Given a limited number of securities, restrictions on short sales, the possible effects of the interdependence of investors' strategies, etc., a certain amount of vagueness—i.e., indetermination—seems unavoidable. It should not be surprising that Equation (5), the most basic valuation formula, is an inequality. I do not find this particularly discouraging. Such properties seem to be character-istic of actual problems, not of the models we invent to solve them.

To be sure, it will often be sufficient to assume that prices are determined as if the world were perfectly precise. But we have shown that the usefulness of time-state-preference models does not rest on this assumption.

35. Robichek and Myers [25] discuss how the necessity to refinance may effect the optimal degree of leverage for highly leveraged firms.

36. In the "special case" discussed in Section IV above, however, the investor could always offset the effect of the additional investment by short sales and/or sale of other securities in his portfolio. Thus the commitment to invest additional amounts does not constrain his portfolio choice. In less idealized worlds, the commitment may be binding.

37. Hirshleifer [11], p. 534.

References

1. Arrow, Kenneth J., *Aspects of the Theory of Risk-Bearing* (Helsinki: Yrjö Jahnsson Lectures, 1965).
2. ——, "The Role of Securities in the Optimal Allocation of Risk-Bearing," *Review of Economic Studies,* XXXI (1963–1964), pp. 91–96.
3. Beja, Avraham, "A General Framework for the Analysis of Capital Markets and Some Results for Equilibrium," (Unpublished manuscript, Stanford University, 1966).
4. Diamond, Peter A., "The Role of a Stock Market in a General Equilibrium Model with Technological Uncertainty," *American Economic Review,* LVII (September 1967), pp. 759–778.
5. Debreu, Gerard, *The Theory of Value* (New York: John Wiley & Sons, Inc., 1959).
6. Dorfman, Robert, Paul A. Samuelson, and Robert M. Solow, *Linear Programming and Economic Analysis* (New York: McGraw-Hill Book Co., Inc., 1958).
7. Drèze, Jacques H., "Market Allocation Under Uncertainty," (Preliminary draft of paper presented at the First World Congress of the Econometric Society, Rome, September 9–14, 1965).
8. Gordon, Myron J., *The Investment, Financing, and Valuation of the Corporation* (Homewood, Ill.: Richard D. Irwin, Inc., 1962).
9. Hirshleifer, J., "Efficient Allocation of Capital in an Uncertain World," *American Economic Review,* LIV (May 1964), pp. 77–85.
10. ——, "Investment Decision Under Uncertainty: Application of the State-Preference Approach," *Quarterly Journal of Economics,* LXXX (May 1966), pp. 252–77.
11. ——, "Investment Decision Under Uncertainty: Choice-Theoretic Approaches," *Quarterly Journal of Economics,* LXXIX (November 1965), pp. 509–36.
12. ——, "On the Theory of Optimal Investment Decision," *Journal of Political Economy,* LXVI (August 1958), pp. 329–52.
13. Kuhn, H.W., and A.W. Tucker, "Nonlinear Programming," in U. Neyman (ed.), *Proceedings of the Second Berkeley Symposium of Mathematical Statistics and Probability* (Berkeley: University of California Press, 1951).
14. Lancaster, Kevin, "Change and Innovation in the Technology of Consumption," *American Economic Review,* LVI (May 1966), pp. 14–23.
15. Lintner, John, "Optimal Dividends and Corporate Growth Under Uncertainty," *Quarterly Journal of Economics,* LXXVII (February 1964), pp. 49–95.
16. ——, "Security Prices, Risk and Maximal Gains from Diversification," *Journal of Finance,* XX (December 1965), pp. 587–616.
17. ——, "The Valuation of Risk Assets and the Selection of Risky Investments," *Review of Economics and Statistics,* XLVII (February 1967), pp. 13–37.
18. Modigliani, Franco, and M.H. Miller, "The Cost of Capital Corporation

Finance and the Theory of Investment," *American Economic Review,* XLVIII (June 1958), pp. 261–97.

19. ——, and Richard Sutch, "Innovations in Interest Rate Policy," *American Economic Review,* LVI (May 1966), pp. 178–197.

20. Myers, Stewart C., *Effects of Uncertainty on the Valuation of Securities and the Financial Decisions of the Firm* (Unpublished Doctoral Dissertation, Stanford University, 1967).

21. ——, "Procedures for Capital Budgeting Under Uncertainty," Massachusetts Institute of Technology, Sloan School of Management Working Paper 257–67 (mimeo).

22. Porterfield, James T.S., *Investment Decisions and Capital Costs* (Englewood Cliffs, N. J.: Prentice-Hall, Inc., 1965).

23. Pye, Gordon, "Portfolio Selection and Security Prices," *Review of Economics and Statistics,* XLIX (February 1967), pp. 111–115.

24. Radner, Roy, "Competitive Equilibrium Under Uncertainty," Technical Report No. 20, Prepared Under Contract Nonr–222(77) for the Office of Naval Research, Center for Research in Management Science (Berkeley, California: University of California, 1967) (mimeo).

25. Robichek, Alexander A., and Stewart C. Myers, "Problems in the Theory of Optimal Capital Structure," *Journal of Financial and Quantitative Analysis,* I (June 1966), pp. 1–35.

26. Sharpe, William F., "Capital Asset Prices: A Theory of Market Equilibrium Under Conditions of Risk," *Journal of Finance,* XIX (September 1964), pp. 425–42.

Part VI
The Capital Growth Portfolio Criterion

17 Portfolio Choice and the Kelly Criterion*

Edward O. Thorp
University of California, Irvine

1. Introduction

The Kelly (or capital growth) criterion is to maximize the expected value $E \log X$ of the logarithm of the wealth random variable X. Logarithmic utility has been widely discussed since Daniel Bernoulli introduced it about 1730 in connection with the Petersburg game [3, 28]. However, it was not until certain mathematical results were proven in a limited setting by Kelly in 1956 and then in much more general setting by Breiman in 1960 and 1961 that logarithmic utility was clearly distinguished *by its properties* from other utilities as a guide to portfolio selection. (See also [2, 4, 15], and the very significant paper of Hakansson [11].

Suppose for each time period ($n = 1, 2, \ldots$) there are k investment opportunities with results per unit invested denoted by the family of random variables $X_{n,1}, X_{n,2}, \ldots, X_{n,k}$. Suppose also that these random variables have only finitely many distinct values, that for distinct n the families are independent of each other, and that the joint probability distributions of distinct families (as subscripted) are identical. Then Breiman's results imply that portfolio strategies Λ which maximize $E \log X_n$, where X_n is the wealth at the end of the n-th time period, have the following properties:

Property 1. (Maximizing $E \log X_n$ asymptotically maximizes the rate of asset growth.) If, for each time period, two portfolio managers have the same family of investment opportunities or investment universes, and one uses a strategy Λ^* maximizing $E \log X_n$ whereas the other uses an "essentially different" (i.e., $E \log X_n(\Lambda^*) - E \log X_n(\Lambda) \to \infty$) strategy Λ, then $\lim X_n(\Lambda^*)/X_n(\Lambda) \to \infty$ almost surely (a. s.).

Property 2. The expected time to reach a fixed preassigned goal x is, asymptotically as x increases, least with a strategy maximizing $E \log X_n$.

The qualification "essentially different" conceals subtleties which are not generally appreciated. For instance if $x_j = X_j/X_{j-1}$, then even though $E \log x_j$

Reprinted by permission of the author from the *1971 Business and Economics Statistics Section Proceedings of the American Statistical Association*, p. 215–224.

*This research was supported in part by the Air Force Office of Scientific Research under Grant AF–AFOSR 1870A. An expanded version of this paper will be submitted for publication elsewhere.

> 0 for all j it need not be the case that $P(\lim X_n = \infty) = 1$. In fact, we can have (just as in the case of Bernoulli trials and $E \log x_j = 0$; see [26]) $P(\lim \sup X_n = \infty) = 1$ and $P(\lim \inf X_n = 0) = 1$ (contrary to [11, p. 522, eq. (18)] and following assertions). Similarly, when $E \log x_j < 0$ for all j we can have these alternatives instead of $P(\lim X_n = 0) = 1$ (contrary to [11, p. 522, eq. (17)] and the following statements; footnote 1 is also incorrect.)

Note [6] that with the preceding assumptions, there is a fixed fraction strategy Λ which maximizes $E \log X_n$. A fixed fraction strategy is one in which the fraction of wealth $f_{n,j}$ allocated to investment $X_{n,j}$ is independent of n.

We emphasize that Breiman's results can be extended to cover many if not most of the more complicated situations which arise in real world portfolios. Specifically, the number and distribution of investments can vary with the time period, the random variables need not be finite or even discrete, and a certain amount of dependence can be introduced between the investment universes for different time periods. We have used such extensions in certain applications (e.g., [25; 26, p. 287]).

We consider almost surely having more wealth than if an "essentially different" strategy were followed, as the desirable objective for most institutional portfolio managers. (It also seems appropriate for wealthy families who wish mainly to accumulate and whose consumption expenses are only a small fraction of their total wealth.) Property 1 says that maximizing $E \log X_n$ is a recipe for approaching this goal asymptotically as n increases. This is our principal justification for selecting $E \log X$ as the guide to portfolio selection.

In any real application n is finite, the limit is not reached, and we have $P(X_n(\Lambda^*)/X_n(\Lambda) > 1 + M) = 1 - \epsilon(n, \Lambda, M)$ where $\epsilon \to 0$ as $n \to \infty$, $M > 0$ is given, Λ^* is the strategy which maximizes $E \log X_n$ and Λ is an "essentially different' strategy. Thus in any application is is important to have an idea of how rapidly $\epsilon \to 0$. Work needs to be done on this in order to reduce $E \log X$ to a guide that is useful (not merely valuable) for portfolio managers. Some illustrative examples for $n = 6$ appear in [11].

Property 2 shows us that maximizing $E \log X$ also is appropriate for individuals who have a set goal (e.g., to become a millionaire).

Appreciation of the compelling properties of the Kelly criterion may have been impeded by certain misunderstandings about it that persist in the literature of mathematical economics.

The first misunderstanding involves failure to distinguish among kinds of utility theories. We compare and contrast three types of utility theories: (1) *descriptive,* where data on observed behavior is fitted mathematically. Many different utility functions might be needed, corresponding to widely varying circumstances, cultures, or behavior types[1] ; (2) *predictive,* which "explains"

---

1. Information on descriptive utility is sparse; how many writers on the subject have even been able to determine for us their own personal utility?

observed data: fits for observed data are deduced from hypotheses, with the hope future data will also be found to fit. Many different utility functions may be needed, corresponding to the many sets of hypotheses that may be put forward; (3) *prescriptive* (also called *normative*), which is a guide to behavior, i.e., a recipe for optimally achieving a stated goal. It is not necessarily either descriptive or predictive nor is it intended to be so.

We use logarithmic utility in this last way, and much of the misunderstanding of it comes from those who think it is being proposed as a descriptive or a predictive theory. The $E \log X$ theory is a prescription for allocating resources so as to (asymptotically) maximize the rate of growth of assets.

Another "objection" voiced by some economists to $E \log X$ and, in fact to all unbounded utility functions, is that it doesn't resolve the (generalized) Petersburg paradox. The rebuttal is blunt and pragmatic: The generalized Petersburg paradox does not arise in the real world because any one real world random variable is bounded (as is any finite collection). Thus in any real application the paradox does not arise.

To insist that a utility function resolve the paradox is an artificial requirement, certainly permissible, but obstructive and tangential to the goal of building a theory which is also a practical guide.

2. Samuelson's Objections to Logarithmic Utility

Samuelson [21, pp. 245–6; 22, pp. 4–5] says that repeatedly authorities [5, 6, 14, 15, 30] ". . . have proposed a drastic simplification of the decision problem whenever T [the number of investment periods] [2] is large.

Rule: Act in each period to maximize the geometric mean or the expected value of $\log x_t$.
The plausibility of such a procedure comes from the recognition of the following valid asymptotic result.

Theorem: Acting to maximize the geometric mean at every step will if the period is "sufficiently long," "almost certainly"[3] result in higher terminal wealth and terminal utility than from any other decision rule." . . .

"From this indisputable fact, it is apparently tempting to believe in the truth of the following false corollary:

False corollary: If maximizing the geometric mean almost certainly leads to a better outcome, then the expected value utility of its outcomes exceeds that of any other rule, provided T is sufficiently large."

---

2. Parenthetical explanation added since we have used n.
3. "Almost certainly" and "almost surely" are synonymous.

Samuelson then gives counter examples to the corollary. We heartily agree that the corollary is false. In fact we had already shown this for one of the utilities Samuelson uses, for we noted [26] that in the case of Bernoulli trials with probability $1/2 < p < 1$ of success, one should commit a fraction $w = 1$ of his capital at each trial to maximize expected final gain $E\,X_n$ (page 283; the utility is $U(x) = x$) whereas to maximize $E \log X_n$ he should commit $w = 2p - 1$ of his capital at each trial (page 285, Theorem 4).

The statements which we have seen in print supporting this "false corollary" are by Latané [15, p. 151, fn. 13] as discussed in [21, p. 245, fn. 8], and Markowitz [16, pp. ix-x]. Latané may not have fully supported this corollary for he adds the qualifier ". . . (in so far as certain approximations are permissible) . . .".

That there were or are adherents of the "false corollary" seems puzzling in view of the following formulation. Consider a T stage investment process. At each stage we allocate our resources among the available investments. For each sequence A of allocations which we choose, there is a corresponding terminal probability distribution F_T^A of assets at the completion of stage T. For each utility function $U(\cdot)$, consider those allocations $A^*(U)$ which maximize the expected value of terminal utility $\int U(x)\,dF_T^A(x)$. Assume sufficient hypotheses on U and the set of F_T^A so that the integral is defined and that furthermore the maximizing allocation $A^*(U)$ exists. Then Samuelson says that $A^*(\log)$ is not in general $A^*(U)$ for other U. This seems intuitively evident.

Even more seems strongly plausible: that if U_1 and U_2 are inequivalent utilities then $\int U_1(x)\,dF_T^A(x)$ and $\int U_2(x)\,dF_T^A(x)$ will in general be maximized for different F_T^A. (Two utilities U_1 and U_2 are equivalent if and only if there are constants a and b such that $U_2(x) = aU_1(x) + b$, $a > 0$; otherwise U_1 and U_2 are inequivalent.) In this connection we have proved:

Theorem: Let U and V be utilities defined and differentiable on $(0, \infty)$, with $U'(x)$ and $V'(x)$ positive and strictly decreasing as x increases. Then if U and V are inequivalent, there is a one period investment setting such that U and V have distinct optimal strategies.[4]

All this is in the nature of an aside for Samuelson's correct criticism of the "false corollary" does not apply to our use of logarithmic utility. Our point of view is: if your goal is property 1 or property 2, then a recipe for achieving either goal is to maximize $E \log X$. These properties distinguish log from the prolixity of utility functions in the literature. Furthermore, we consider these goals appropriate for many (*but not all*) investors. Investors with other utilities, or with goals incompatible with logarithmic utility, will of course, find it inappropriate.

Property 1 implies that if Λ^* maximizes $E \log X_n(\Lambda)$ and Λ' is "essentially different," then $X_n(\Lambda^*)$ tends almost certainly to be better than $X_n(\Lambda')$ as

---

4. The proof of this theorem, and some further results obtained with R. Whitley, will appear elsewhere.

$n \to \infty$. Samuelson [21, p. 246], apparently referring to this, says after refuting the "false corollary": "Moreover, as I showed elsewhere [20, p. 4], the ordering principle of selecting between two actions in terms of which has the greater probability of producing a higher result does not even possess the property of being transitive. . . . we could have w^{***} better than w^{**}, and w^{**} better than w^*, and also have w^* better than w^{***}."

For some entertaining examples, see the discussion of non-transitive dice in [9]. (Consider the dice with equiprobable faces numbered as follows: $X = (3, 3, 3, 3, 3, 3); Y = (4, 4, 4, 4, 1, 1); Z = (5, 5, 2, 2, 2, 2)$. Then $P(Z > Y) = 5/9, P(Y > X) = 2/3, P(X > Z) = 2/3$.) What Samuelson does *not* tell us is that the property of producing a higher result *almost certainly*, as in property 1, is transitive. If we have $w^{***} > w^{**}$ almost certainly, and $w^{**} > w^*$ almost certainly, then we must have $w^{***} > w^*$ almost certainly.

One might object [20, p. 6] that in a real investment sequence the limit as $n \to \infty$ is not reached. Instead the process stops at some finite N. Thus we do not have $X_N(\Lambda^*) > X_n(\Lambda')$ almost certainly. Instead we have $P(X_n(\Lambda^*) > X_n(\Lambda')) = 1 - \epsilon_N$ where $\epsilon_N \to 0$ as $N \to \infty$, and transitivity can be shown to fail.

This is correct. But an approximate form of transitivity does hold: Let X, Y, Z be random variables with $P(X > Y) = 1 - \epsilon_1, P(Y > Z) = 1 - \epsilon_2$. Then $P(X > Z) \geqslant 1 - (\epsilon_1 + \epsilon_2)$. To prove this, let A be the event $X > Y$, B be the event $Y > Z$, and C be the event $X > Z$. Then $P(A) + P(B) = P(A \cup B) + P(A \cap B) \leqslant 1 + P(A \cap B)$. But $A \cap B \subset C$ so $P(C) \geqslant P(A \cap B) \geqslant P(A) + P(B) - 1$, i.e., $P(X > Z) \geqslant 1 - (\epsilon_1 + \epsilon_2)$.

Thus our approach is not affected by the various Samuelson objections to the uses of logarithmic utility.

Markowitz [16, pp. ix-x] says ". . . in 1955-56, I concluded . . . that the investor who is currently reinvesting everything for "the long run" should maximize the expected value of the logarithm of wealth." (This assertion seems to be regardless of the investor's utility and so indicates belief in the "false corollary.") Mossin [18] and Samuelson [20] ". . . have each shown that this conclusion is not true for a wide range of [utility] functions . . . The fascinating Mossin-Samuelson result, combined with the straightforward arguments supporting the earlier conclusions, seemed paradoxical at first. I have since returned to the view of Chapter 6 (concluding that: for large T, the Mossin-Samuelson man acts absurdly, . . ." Markowitz says here, in effect, that alternate utility functions (to log) are absurd. This position is unsubstantiated and unreasonable.

He continues ". . . like a player who would pay an unlimited amount for the St. Petersburg game . . ." If you agree with us that the St. Petersburg game is not realizable and may be ignored when fashioning utility theories for the real world, then his continuation ". . . the terminal utility function must be bounded to avoid this absurdity; . . ." does not follow.

Finally, Markowitz says ". . . and the argument in Chapter 6 applies when utility of terminal wealth is bounded." If he means by this that the "false corollary" holds if we restrict ourselves to bounded utility functions, then he is mistaken. Mossin [18] already showed that the optimal strategies for $\log x$ and x^{γ}/γ, $\gamma \neq 0$, are fixed fraction for these and only these utilities. Thus any bounded utility besides x^{γ}/γ, $\gamma < 0$, will have optimal strategies which are *not* fixed fraction, hence not optimal for $\log x$. Samuelson [22] gives counter-examples which include the bounded utilities x^{γ}/γ, $\gamma < 0$. Since Mossin assumes U'' exists and our theorem only assumes that U' exists, it provides additional counterexamples.

3. An outline of the theory of logarithmic utility as applied to portfolio selection

The simplest case is Bernoulli trials with probability p of success, $0 < p < 1$. The unique strategy which maximizes $E \log X_n$ is to bet at trial n the fixed fraction $f^* = p - q$ of total current wealth X_{n-1} if $p > 1/2$ and to bet nothing otherwise.

To maximize $E \log X_n$ is equivalent to maximizing $E \log [X_n/X_o]^{1/n} \equiv G(f)$, which we call the (exponential) rate of growth (per time period). It turns out that for $p > 1/2$, $G(f)$ has a unique positive maximum at f^* and that there is a critical fraction f_c, $0 < f^* < f_c < 1$, such that $G(f) = 0$, $G(f) > 0$ if $0 < f < f_c$, $G(f) < 0$ if $f_c < f \leq 1$ (we assume "no margin"; the case with margin is similar). If $f < f_c$, $X_n \to \infty$ a.s.; if $f = f_c$, $\lim \sup X_n = +\infty$ a.s., and $\lim \inf X_n = 0$ a.s.; if $f > f_c$, $X_n \to \infty$ a.s.; if $f = f_c$, $\lim \sup X_n = +\infty$ a.s., and $\lim \inf X_n = 0$ a.s.; if $f > f_c$, $\lim X_n = 0$ a.s. ("ruin").

Bernoulli trials exhibit many of the features of the following more general case. Suppose we have at each trial $n = 1, 2, \ldots$ the k investment opportunities $X_{n,1}, X_{n,2}, \ldots, X_{n,k}$ and that the conditions of property 1, section 1 are satisfied. This means that the joint distributions of $\{X_{n,i_1}, X_{n,i_2}, \ldots, X_{n,i_j}\}$ are the same for all n, for each subset of indices $1 \leq i_1 < i_2 < \ldots < i_j \leq k$. Furthermore $\{X_{m,1}, \ldots, X_{m,k}\}$ and $\{X_{n,1}, \ldots, X_{n,k}\}$ are independent when $m \neq n$, and all random variables $X_{i,j}$ have only a finite number of distinct values. Thus we have in successive time periods repeated independent trials of "the same" investment universe.

Since Breiman has shown that there is for this case an optimal fixed fraction strategy $\Lambda^* = (f_1^*, \ldots, f_k^*)$, we will have an optimal strategy if we find a strategy which maximizes $E \log X_n$ in the class of fixed fraction strategies.

Let $\Lambda = (f_1, \ldots, f_k)$ be any fixed fraction strategy. We assume that $f_1 + \ldots + f_k \leq 1$ so there is no borrowing, or margin. The margin case is similar (the approach resembles [23]). Using the concavity of the logarithm, it is easy to show (see below) that the exponential rate of growth $E \log [X_n(\Lambda)/X_o]^{1/n} = G(f_1, \ldots, f_k)$ is a concave function of $(f_1, \ldots, f_k)$, just as in the Bernoulli trials case. The domain of $G(f)$ in the Bernoulli trials case was the interval $[0, 1]$

with $G(f) \searrow -\infty$ as $f \to 1$. The domain in the present instance is analogous. First, it is a subset of the k dimensional simplex $S_k = \{(f_1, \ldots, f_k): f_1 + \ldots + f_k \leqslant 1; f_1 \geqslant 0, \ldots, f_k \geqslant 0\}$.

To establish the analogy further, let $R_j = X_{n,j} - 1, j = 1, \ldots, k$, be the return per unit on the i-th investment opportunity at an arbitrary time period n. Let the range of R_j be $\{r_{j,1}; \ldots; r_{j,ij}\}$ and let the probability of the outcome $[R_1 = r_{1,m_1}$ and $R_2 = r_{2,m_2}$ and $\ldots$ and $R_k = r_{k,m_k}]$ be $p_{m_1,m_2,\ldots,m_k}$. Then $E \log X_n/X_{n-1} = G(f_1, \ldots, f_k) = \Sigma \{p_{m_1,\ldots,m_k} \log (1 + f_1 r_{1,m_1} + \ldots + f_k r_{k,m_k}): 1 \leqslant m_1 \leqslant i_1; \ldots; 1 \leqslant m_k \leqslant i_k\}$, from which the concavity of $G(f_1, \ldots, f_k)$ can be shown. Note that $G(f_1, \ldots, f_k)$ is defined if and only if $1 + f_1 r_{1,m_1} + \ldots + f_k r_{k,m_k} > 0$ for each set of indices $m_1, \ldots, m_k$. Thus the domain of $G(f_1, \ldots, f_k)$ is the intersection of all these open half-spaces with the k-dimensional simplex S_k. Note that the doman is convex and includes all of S_k in some neighborhood of the origin. Note too that the doman of G is all of S_k if (and only if) $R_j > -1$ for all j, i.e., if there is no probability of total loss on any investment. The domain of G includes the interior of S_k if $R_j \geqslant -1$. Both domains are particularly simple and most cases of interest are included.

If $f_1, \ldots, f_k$ are chosen so that $1 + f_1 r_{1,m_1} + \ldots + f_k r_{k,m_k} \leqslant 0$ for some $m_1, \ldots, m_k$, then $P(f_1 X_{n,1} + \ldots + f_k X_{n,k} \leqslant 0) = \epsilon > 0$ for all n and ruin occurs with probability 1.

Computational procedures for finding an optimal fixed fraction strategy (generally unique in our present setting) are based on the theory of concave (dually, convex) functions [29] and will be presented elsewhere. (As Hakansson [11, p. 552] has noted, ". . . the computational aspects of the capital growth model are [presently] much less advanced" than for the Markowitz model.)

The theory may be extended to more general random variables and to dependence between different time periods. Most important, we may include the case where the investment universe changes with the time period, provided only that there be some mild regularity conditions on the $X_{i,j}$, such as that they be uniformly a.s. bounded and that they do not tend to 0 uniformly as i $\to \infty$. (See [15], and the generalization of the Bernoulli trials case as applied to blackjack in [26].) The techniques rely heavily on those used to generalize the law of large numbers.

Transactions costs, the use of margin, and the effect of taxes can be incorporated into the theory. Bellman's dynamic programming method is used here.

The general procedure for developing the theory into a practical tool imitates Markowitz [16]. Markowitz requires as inputs estimates of the expectations, standard deviations, and covariances of the $X_{i,j}$. We require joint probability distributions. This would seem to be a much more severe requirement, but in practice does not seem to be so [16, pp. 193-4, 198-201].

Among the actual inputs which Markowitz chose were (1) past history [16, ex., 8-20], (2) probability beliefs of analysts (pp. 26-33), and (3) models,

most notably regression models, to predict future performance from past data
(p. 33, pp. 99-100). In each instance one can get enough additional information
to estimate $E \log (X_n/X_{n-1})$.

There are, however, two great difficulties which all theories of portfolio
selection have, including ours and that of Markowitz. First, there seems to be no
established method for generally predicting security prices which gives an edge
of even a few per cent. The random walk is the best model for security prices
today. (See [7, 10].)

The second difficulty is that for portfolios with many securities the volume
of inputs called for is prohibitive: for 100 securities, Markowitz requires 100
expectations and 4950 covariances; and our theory requires somewhat more
information. Although considerable attention has been given to finding con-
densed inputs that can be used instead, this aspect of portfolio theory still seems
unsatisfactory.

In the fifth section we will show how both these difficulties were overcome
in practice by an institutional investor. That investor, guided by the Kelly criterion, then outperformed for the year 1970 every one of the approximately 400
Mutual Funds listed by the S & P stock guide!

But first we relate our theory to that of Markowitz.

4. Relation to the Markowitz theory;
solution to problems therein

The most widely used guide to portfolio selection today is probably the
Markowitz theory. The basic idea is that a portfolio P_1 is superior to a portfolio
P_2 if the expectation ("gain") is at least as great, i.e., $E(P_1) \geq E(P_2)$ and the
standard deviation ("risk") is no greater, i.e., $\sigma(P_1) \leq \sigma(P_2)$, with at least one
inequality. This partially orders the set $\mathcal{P}$ of portfolios. A portfolio such that no
portfolio is superior (i.e., a maximal portfolio in the partial ordering) is called
efficient. The goal of the portfolio manager is to determine the set of efficient
portfolios, from which he then makes a choice based on his needs.

This is intuitively very appealing: It is based on standard quantitites for the
securities in the portfolio, namely expectation, standard deviation, and covariance (needed to compute the variance of the portfolio from that of the component securities). It also gives the portfolio manager "choice."

As Markowitz [16, Chapter 6] has pointed out, the optimal Kelly portfolio
is approximately one of the Markowitz efficient portfolios under certain circumstances. If $E = E(P)$ and $R = P - 1$ is the return per unit of the portfolio P, let
$\log P = \log (1 + R) = \log ((1 + E) + (R - E))$. Expanding in Taylor's series about
$1 + E$ gives $\log P = \log (1 + E) + (R - E)/(1 + E) - (R - E)^2/2(1 + E)^2$ + higher
order terms. Taking expectations and neglecting higher order terms gives $E \log P$
$= \log (1 + E) - \sigma^2(P)/2(1 + E)^2$.

This leads to a simple pictorial relationship with the Markowitz theory. Consider the $E - \sigma$ plane, and plot $(E(P), \sigma(P))$ for the efficient portfolios. The locus of efficient portfolios is a convex non-decreasing curve which includes its endpoints (Figure 1).

Then constant values of the growth rate $G = E \log P$ approximately satisfy $G = \log (1 + E) - \sigma^2(P)/2(1 + E)^2$. This family of curves is illustrated in Figure 1 and the (efficient) portfolio which maximizes logarithmic utility is (approximately) the one which lies on the greatest G curve. Because of the convexity of

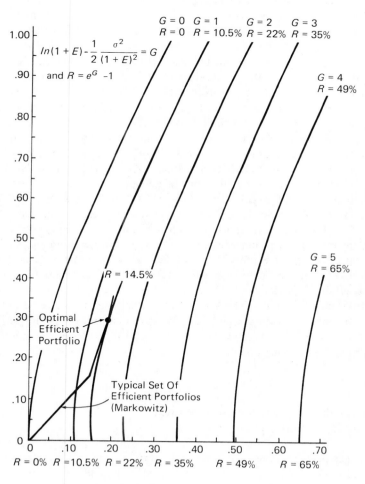

Figure 1. Growth Rate G (Return Rate R) in the $E - \sigma$ Plane Assuming the Validity of the Power Series Approximation

the curve of efficient portfolios and the concavity of the G curves, the (E, σ) value where this occurs is unique.

The approximation to G breaks down badly in some significant practical settings, including that of the next section. But for portfolios with large numbers of "typical" securities, the approximation for G will generally provide an efficient portfolio which approximately maximizes asset growth. This solves the portfolio manager's problem of which efficient portfolio to choose. Also, if he repeatedly chooses his portfolio in successive time periods by this criterion he will tend to maximize the rate of growth of his assets, i.e., maximize "performance." We see also that in this instance the problem is reduced to that of finding the efficient portfolios plus the easy step of using Figure 1. Thus if the Markowitz theory can be applied in practice in this setting, so can our theory.

We have already remarked on the ambiguity of the set of efficient portfolios, and how our theory resolves them. To illustrate further that such ambiguity represents a defect in the Markowitz theory, let X_1 be uniformly distributed over $[1,3]$, let X_2 be uniformly distributed over $[10,100]$, let cor $(X_1, X_2) = 1$, and suppose these are the only securities. Then X_1 and X_2 are both efficient with $\sigma_1 < \sigma_2$ and $E_1 < E_2$ so Markowitz' theory does not choose between them. Yet "everyone" would choose X_2 over X_1 because the worst outcome with X_2 is far better than the best outcome from X_1. (We present this example in [26]. Hakansson [11] presents further examples and an extended analysis. He formalizes the idea by introducing the notion of stochastic dominance: S stochastically dominates Y if $P(X \geqslant Y) = 1$ and $P(X > Y) > 0$. It is easy to prove the Lemma: An $E \log X$ optimal portfolio is never stochastically dominated. Thus our portfolio theory does nto have this defect.)

There are investment universes $(X_1, \ldots, X_n)$ such that a unique portfolio P maximizes $E \log P$ yet P is not efficient in the sense of Markowitz. Hence choosing P in repeated independent trials will outperform any strategy limited to choosing efficient portfolios. In addition, the optimal Kelly strategy gives positive growth rate, yet some of the Markowitz-efficient strategies give negative growth rate and ruin after repeated trials. We gave such an example in [26] and another appears in [11]. See also [11, pp. 553–4] for further discussion of defects in the Markowitz model.

5. The theory in action: results for a real institutional portfolio

The elements of a practical profitable theory of convertible hedging were published in [27]. Thorp and Kassouf indicated an annualized return on investments of the order of 25% per year. Since then the theory has been greatly extended and refined with most of these new results thus far unpublished.

The historical data which has been used to develop the theory includes well over 100,000 observations of convertibles.

A convertible hedge transaction generally involves *two* securities, one of which is convertible into the other. Mathematical price relationships exist between pairs of such securities. When one of the pair is comparatively underpriced, a profitable convertible hedge may be set up by buying the relatively underpriced security and selling short an appropriate amount of the relatively overpriced security.

The purpose of selling short the overpriced security is to reduce the risk in the position. Typically, one sells short in a single hedge from 50% to 125% as much stock (in "share equivalents") as is held long. The exact proportions depend on the analysis of the specific situation; the quantity of stock sold short is selected to minimize risk. The risk (i.e., change in asset value with fluctuations in market prices) in a suitable convertible hedge should be much less than in the usual stock market long positions.

The securities involved in convertible hedges include common stock, convertible bonds, convertible preferreds, and common stock purchase warrants. Options such as puts, calls, and straddles may replace the convertible security. For this purpose, the options may be either written or purchased.

The theory of the convertible hedge is highly enough developed so that the probability characteristics of a single hedge can be worked out based on an assumption for the underlying distribution of the common. (Sometimes even this can almost be dispensed with! (See [27, App. C].) A popular and plausible assumption is that the future price of the common is lognormally distributed about its' current price, with a trend and a variance proportional to the time. Plausible estimates of these parameters are readily obtained. Furthermore, it turns out that the return from the hedge is comparatively insensitive to changes in the estimates for these parameters.

Thus with convertible heding we fulfill two important conditions for the practical application of our (or any other) theory of portfolio choice: (1) We have identified investment opportunities which are markedly superior to the usual ones. Compare the return rate of 20%–25% per year with the long term rate of 8% or so for listed common stocks. Further, it can be shown that the risks tend to be much less. (2) The probability inputs are available for computing $G(f_1, \ldots, f_n)$.

On November 3, 1969, a private institutional investor decided to commit all its resources to convertible hedging and to use the Kelly criterion to allocate its assets. The performance record appears in the Table.

The market period covered included one of the sharpest falling markets as well as one of the sharpest rising markets (up 50% in 11 months) since World War II. The gain was +16.3% for the year 1970, which outperformed all of the approximately 400 Mutual Funds Listed in the S & P stock guide. Unaudited figures show that gains were achieved during every single month.

Table 17-1
Performance Record

Date	Change To Date (%)	Elapsed Time (months)	Growth Rate To Date (%)[++]	Closing DJIA[+]	DJIA Chg. (%)[++]	Starting Even With DJIA[+]	Gain Over DJIA (%)
11– 3-69	0.0	0	–	855	0.0	855	0.0
12-31-69	+ 4.0	2	+26.8	800	– 6.3	889	+10.3
9– 1-70	+14.0	10	+17.0	758	–11.3	974	+25.3
12-31-70	+21.0	14	+17.7	839	– 1.8	1034	+22.8
6–30-71*	+39.9	20	+22.3	891	+ 4.2	1196	+35.7

Assets on 7-1-71 were 5.2 million.

* Preliminary-unaudited.
[+]DJIA = Dow Jones Industrial Average.
[++]Compound growth rate, annualized.

The unusually low risk in the hedged positions is also indicated by the results for the 200 completed hedges. There were 190 winners, 6 break-evens, and 4 losses. The losses as a per cent of the long side of the specific investment ranged from 1% to 15%

A characteristic of the Kelly criterion is that as risk decreases and expectation rises, the optimal fraction of assets to be invested in a single situation may become "large." On several occasions, the institution discussed above invested up to 30% of its assets in single hedge. Once it invested 150% of its assets in a single arbitrage. This characteristic of Kelly portfolio strategy is not part of the behavior of most portfolio managers.

To indicate the techniques and problems, we consider a simple portfolio with just one convertible hedge. We take as our example Kaufman and Broad common stock and warrants. A price history is indicated in Figure 2.

Price data shows that $W = .455S$ is a reasonable fit for $S \leq 38$ and that $W = S - 21.67$ is a reasonable fit for $S \geq 44$. Between $S = 38$ and $S = 44$ we have the line $W = .84S - 15.5$. For simplicity of calculation we replace this in our illustrative analysis by $W = .5S$ if $S \leq 44$ and $W = S - 22$ if $S \geq 44$. The lines are also indicated in Figure 2.

Past history at the time the hedge was instituted in late 1970 supported the fit for $S \leq 38$. The converson feature of the warrant ensured $W \geq S - 21.67$ until the warrant expires. Thus $W = S - 21.67$ for $S \geq 44$ underestimates the price of the warrant in this region. Extensive historical studies of warrants [12, 13, 24, 27] show that the past history fit would probably be maintained until about two years before expiration, i.e., until about March, 1972. Thus it is plausible to assume for the next 1.3 years S may be roughly approximated by $W = .5S$ for $S \leq 44$ and $W = S - 22$ for $S \geq 44$.

Next we assume that S_t, the stock price at time $t > 0$ years after the hedge was initiated, is lognormally distributed with density $f_{S_t}(x) = (x\sigma\sqrt{2\pi})^{-1} \exp [-(\log x - \mu)^2/2\sigma^2]$, hence mean $E(S_t) = \exp(\mu + \sigma^2/2)$ and standard deviation $\sigma(S_t) = E(S_t)(e^{\sigma^2} - 1)^{1/2}$. The functions $\mu \equiv \mu(t)$ and $\sigma \equiv \sigma(t)$ depend on the stock and on the time t. If t is the time in years until S_t is realized, it is plausible to assume $\mu(t) = \log S_o + mt$ and $\sigma(t)^2 = a^2 t$, where S_o is the present stock price and m and a are constants depending on the stock. For a detailed discussion, see [1, 19].

Then $E(S_t) = S_o \exp[(m + a^2/2)t]$ and a mean increase of 10%/year is approximated by setting $m + a^2/2 = .1$. If we estimate a^2 from past price changes we can solve for m. In the case of Kaufman and Broad it is plausible to take $\sigma \doteq .45$ whence $a^2 = \sigma^2 \doteq .20$. This yields $m \doteq 0$. We then find $\sigma(S_t) \doteq .52S_o$.

It is by no means established that the log-normal model is the appropriate one for stock price series [7, 10]. However, once we clarify certain general principles by working through our example on the basis of the lognormal model, it can be shown that the results are substantially unchanged by choosing instead any distribution that roughly fits observation!

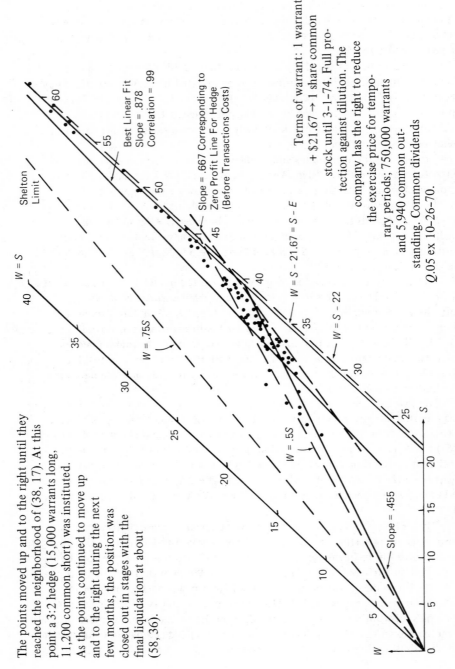

The points moved up and to the right until they reached the neighborhood of (38, 17). At this point a 3:2 hedge (15,000 warrants long, 11,200 common short) was instituted. As the points continued to move up and to the right during the next few months, the position was closed out in stages with the final liquidation at about (58, 36).

Terms of warrant: 1 warrant + $21.67 → 1 share common stock until 3-1-74. Full protection against dilution. The company has the right to reduce the exercise price for temporary periods; 750,000 warrants and 5,940 common outstanding. Common dividends Q.05 ex 10-26-70.

Best Linear Fit
Slope = .878
Correlation = .99

Shelton Limit

Slope = .667 Corresponding to Zero Profit Line For Hedge (Before Transactions Costs)

$W = S$

$W = .75S$

$W = S - 21.67 = S - E$

$W = S - 22$

$W = .5S$

Slope = .455

Figure 2. Price History of Kaufman and Broad Common, S, Versus the Warrants, W

For a time of one year, a computation shows the return $R(S)$ on the stock to be +10.5%, the return $R(W)$ on the warrant to be +34.8%, $\sigma(S) = .52$, $\sigma(W) = .92$, and the correlation coefficient cor $(S, W) = .99$. The difference in $R(S)$ and $R(W)$ shows that the warrant is a much better buy than the common. Thus a hedge long warrants and short common has a substantial positive expectation. The value cor $(S, W) = .99$ shows that a hedge corresponding to the best linear fit of W to S has a standard deviation of approximately $(1 - .99)^{\frac{1}{2}} = .1$ which suggests that $\sigma(P)$ for the optimal hedged portfolio is probably going to be close to .1. The high return and low risk for the hedge will remain, it can be shown, under wide variations in the choice of m and a.

To calculate the optimal mix of warrants long to common short we maximize $G(f_1,f_2) = E \log (1 + f_1 S + f_2 W)$. The detailed computational procedures are too lengthy and involved to be presented here. We plan to present them elsewhere.

Our institutional investor considered positions already held, some of which might have to be closed out to release assets, and also other current candidates for investment. The decision was made to short common and buy warrants in the ratio of three shares to four. The initial market value of the long side was about 14% of assets and for the short side about 20% of assets. The net profit, in terms of the initial market value of the long side, was about 20% in six months. This resulted from a move in the common from about 40 to almost 60.

6. Concluding remarks

As remarked above, we do not propose logarithmic utility as descriptive of actual investment behavior, nor do we believe any one utility function could suffice. It would be of interest, however, to have empirical evidence showing areas of behavior which are characterized adequately by logarithmic utility. Neither do we intend logarithmic utility to be predictive; again, it would be of interest to know what it does predict.

We only propose the theory to be normative or prescriptive, and only for those institutions, groups, or individuals whose overriding current objective is maximization of the rate of asset growth. Those with a different "prime directive" may find that another utility function is a better guide.

We have found $E \log X$ to be valuable as a qualitative guide and suggest that this could be its most important use. Once familiarity with its properties is gained, many investment decisions can be guided by it without complex supporting calculations.

What sort of economic behavior can be expected from followers of $E \log X$? Insurance is "explained," i.e., even though it is a negative expectation investment for the insured and we assume both insurer and insured have the same probability information, it is often optimal for him (as well as for the insurance company) to insure [3]. It usually turns out that insurance against large losses is indicated and insurance against small losses is not. (Don't insure an old car for collision, take $200 deductible, not $25, etc.)

We find that if all parties to a security transaction are followers of $E \log X$ they will often find it mutually optimal to trade. This may be true whether the transactions be two party (no brokerage), or three party (brokerage), and whether or not the parties have the same probability information about the security involved, or even about the entire investment universe.

Maximizing logarithmic utility excludes portfolios which have positive probability of total loss of assets. Yet it can be argued that an impoverished follower of $E \log X$ might in some instances risk "everything." This agrees with some observed behavior, but is not what we might at first expect in view of the prohibition against positive probability of total loss. But consider each individual as a piece of capital equipment with an assignable monetary value. Then if he risks and loses all his cash assets, he hasn't really lost everything [3].

All of us behave as though death itself does not have infinite negative utility. Since the risk of death, although generally small, is ever present, a negative infinite utility for death would make all expected utilities negative infinite and utility theory meaningless. In the case of logarithmic utility as applied to the extended case of the (monetized) individual plus all his resources, death should be assigned a finite, though large and negative, utility. The value of this "death constant" is an additional arbitrary assumption for the enlarged theory of logarithmic utility.

In the case of investors who behave according to $E \log X$ (or other utilities unbounded below), it might be possible to discover their tacit "death constants."

Hakansson [11, p. 551] observes that logarithmic utility exhibits decreasing absolute risk aversion in agreement with deductions of Arrow and others on the qualities of "reasonable" utility functions. Hakansson says, "What the relative risk aversion index [given by $-xU''(x)/U'(x)$] would look like for a meaningful utility function is less clear . . . In view of Arrow's conclusion that '. . . broadly speaking, the relative risk aversion must hover around 1, being, if anything, somewhat less for low wealths and somewhat higher for high wealths . . .' the optimal growth model seems to be on safe ground." As he notes, for $U(x) = \log x$, the relative risk aversion is precisely 1. However, in both the extension to valuing the individual as capital equipment, and the further extension to include the death constant, we are led to $U(x) = \log (x + c)$ where c is positive. But then the relative risk aversion index is $x/(x + c)$ which behaves strikingly like Arrow's description. See also the discussion of $U(x) = \log (x + c)$ in [8, p. 103, p. 112].

Morgenstern [17] has forcefully observed that assets are random variables, not numbers, and that economic theory generally does not incorporate this. To replace assets by their expected utility in valuing companies, portfolios, property and the like, allows for comparisons when asset values are given as random

variables. We think logarithmic utility will often be appropriate for such valuation.
    I wish to thank James Bicksler for several stimulating and helpful conversations.

References

1. Ayres, Herbert F., "Risk Aversion in the Warrant Markets," S.M. Thesis, M.I.T., *Industrial Management Review* 5:1 (1963), 45–53. Reprinted in Cootner, pp. 479–505.
2. Bellman, R. and Kalaba, R., "On the Role of Dynamic Programming in Statistical Communication Theory," *IRE Transactions of the Professional Group on Information Theory*, IT–3:3 (1957), 197–203.
3. Bernoulli, Daniel, "Exposition of a New Theory on the Measurement of Risk," *Econometrica*, XXII (January 1954), 23–36, trans. Louise Sommer.
4. Borch, Karl H., *The Economics of Uncertainty*, Princeton University Press, 1968.
5. Breiman, Leo, "Investment Policies for Expanding Businesses Optimal in a Long Run Sense," *Naval Research Logistics Quarterly*, 7:4 (1960), 647–651.
6. Breiman, Leo, "Optimal Gambling Systems for Favorable Games," *Fourth Berkeley Symposium on Probability and Statistics*, I, (1961), 65–78.
7. Cootner, P.H., ed., *The Random Character of Stock Market Prices*, The M.I.T. Press, 1964.
8. Freimer, Marshall and Gordon, Myrson S., "Investment Behavior With Utility a Concave Function of Wealth," in K. Borch and J. Mossin, eds., *Risk and Uncertainty*, New York: St. Martin's Press, 1968, 94–115.
9. Gardner, Martin, "Mathematical Games: The Paradox of the Non-Transitive Dice and the Elusive Principle of Indifference," *Scientific American* (December 1970), 110.
10. Granger, Clive and Morgenstern, Oskar, *Predictability of Stock Market Prices*, Lexington, Massachusetts: D.C. Heath and Company, 1970.
11. Hakansson, Nils, "Capital Growth and the Mean-Variance Approach to Portfolio Selection," *Journal of Finance and Quantitative Analysis* (January 1971), 517–557.
12. Kassouf, Sheen T., "A Theory and an Econometric model for common stock purchase warrants," Thesis, Columbia University, 1965; New York: Analytic Publishers Company, 1965. A regression model statistical fit of normal price curves for warrants. There are large systematic errors in the model due to faulty (strongly biased) regression techniques. The average mean square error in the fit is large. Thus, it is not safe to use the model in practice as a predictor of warrant prices. However, the model and the methodology are valuable as a first *qualitative* description of warrant behavior and as a guide to a more precise analysis.
13. Kassouf, Sheen T., "An econometric model for option price with implications for investors' expectations and audacity," *Econometrica*, 37:4 (1969), 685–694. Based on the thesis. The variance of residuals is given as .248, or a

standard deviation of about .50 in y, the normalized warrant price, and a standard error of about .34. The mid-range of y varies from 0 to .5 and is never greater, thus the caveat about not using the model for practical predictions!

14. Kelly, J.L., "A New Interpretation of Information Rate," *Bell System Technical Journal*, 35 (1956), 917–926.

15. Latané, Henry A., "Criteria for Choice Among Risky Ventures," *Journal of Political Economy*, 67 (1959), 144–155.

16. Markowitz, H., *Portfolio Selection*, New York: John Wiley and Sons, Inc., 1959. See also the preface to the second printing of the Yale University Press, 1970 reprint.

17. Morgenstern, Oskar, *On the Accuracy of Economic Observations*, 2nd ed. revised, Princeton University Press, 1963.

18. Mossin, Jan. "Optimal Multiperiod Portfolio Policies," *Journal of Business* (April 1968).

19. Osborne, M.F.M., "Brownian Motion in the Stock Market," *Operations Research*, 7 (1959), 145–173. Reprinted in Cootner, pp. 100–128.

20. Samuelson, Paul A., "Risk and Uncertainty: A Fallacy of Large Numbers," *Scientia*, 6th Ser., 57th Yr., (April–May 1963).

21. Samuelson, Paul A., "Lifetime Portfolio Selecton by Dynamic Stochastic Programming," *The Review of Economics and Statistics* (August 1969), 239–246.

22. Samuelson, Paul A., "The 'Fallacy' of Maximizing the Geometric Mean in Long Sequences of Investing or Gambling," Unpublished preliminary preprint, 1971.

23. Schrock, Nicholas W., "The Theory of Asset Choice: Simultaneous Holding of Short and Long Positions in the Futures Market," *Journal of Political Economy*, 79:2 (1971), 270–293.

24. Shelton, John P., "The Relation of the Price of a Warrant to Its Associated Common Stock," *Financial Analysts Journal*, 23:3 (1967), 143–151; and *Financial Analysts Journal*, 23:4 (1967), 88–99.

25. Thorp, Edward, "A Winning Bet in Nevada Baccarat," *Journal of the American Statistical Association*, 61, Part I (1966), 313–328.

26. Thorp, Edward, "Optimal Gambling Systems for Favorable Games," *Review of the International Statistical Institute*, 37:3 (1969), 273–293.

27. Thorp, E. and Kassouf, S., *Beat the Market*, New York: Random House, 1967.

28. Todhunter, I., *A History of the Mathematical Theory of Probability*, 1st ed., Cambridge, 1865, as reprinted by Chelsea, New York, 1965. (See pp. 213 ff. for details on Daniel Bernoulli's use of logarithmic utility.)

29. Wagner, Harvey M., *Principles of Operations Research, With Application to Managerial Decisions*, New Jersey: Prentice-Hall, 1969.

30. Williams, J.B., "Speculation and the Carryover," *Quarterly Journal of Economics*, 50, (May 1936), 436–455.

18

The "Fallacy" of Maximizing the Geometric Mean in Long Sequences of Investing or Gambling

Paul A. Samuelson
Massachusetts Institute of Technology

Background

Suppose one begins with initial wealth, X_0, and after a series of decisions one is left with terminal wealth, X_T, subject to a conditional probability distribution

$$\text{prob}\left\{X_T \leqslant X | X_0 = A\right\} = P_T(X, A) \tag{1}$$

Then an "expected utility" maximizer, by definition, will choose his decisions to

$$\max E\left\{u(X_T)\right\} = \max \int_{-\infty}^{\infty} u(X) P_T(dX, A), \tag{2}$$

where E stands for the "expected value" and where $u(x)$ is a specified utility function that is unique except for arbitrary scale and origin parameters, b and a, in $a + bu(x), b > 0$.

In a portfolio, or gambling situation, at each period one can make investments or bets proportional to wealth at the beginning of that period, X_t, so that the outcome of wealth for the next period is the random variable

$$X_{t+1} = X_t\left\{w_1 Y_1 + \ldots + w_n Y_n\right\}, \quad \sum_1^n w_j = 1 \tag{3}$$

where the w's are the proportions decided upon for investment in the different securities (or gambling games). The returns per dollar invested in each alternative, respectively, are subject to known probability distributions.

$$\text{prob}\left\{Y_1 \leqslant y_1, \ldots, Y_n \leqslant y_n\right\} = F(y_1, \ldots, y_n), \tag{4}$$

where for simplicity the vector outcomes at any t are assumed each to be independent of outcomes at any other time periods, and to remain the same

Reprinted by permission of the author from *Proceedings of the National Academy of Sciences*, Vol. 68, No. 10 (October 1971), pp. 2493–96.

distribution over all time periods. Usually Y_i is restricted to being nonnegative to avoid bankruptcy. A complete decision involves selecting over the interval of time $t = 1, 2, \ldots, T$, all the vectors $[w_j(t)]$, which will be nonnegative if short-selling and bankruptcy are ruled out.

In particular, if the same strategy is followed at all times, so that $w_j(t) \equiv w_j$, the variables become

$$X_1 = X_0 x_1, X_2 = X_1 x_2 = X_0 x_1 x_2$$

$$X_t = X_{t-1} x_t = X_0 x_1 x_2 \cdots x_t \tag{5}$$

and all x_i are independently distributed according to the same distribution, which we may write as

$$\text{prob} \left\{ x_t \leqslant x \right\} = \text{II}(x). \tag{6}$$

Of course, $\text{II}(x)$ will depend on the w strategy chosen, and is short for $\text{II}(x; w_1, \ldots, w_n)$ in this particular case, and on the assumed $F(y_1, \ldots, y_n)$ function. It can be easily shown that

$$\text{prob } X_t \leqslant X | X_0 = Z = P_t(X, Z)$$

$$P_t(X, Z) = P_t(X/Z, 1)$$

$$= P_t(X/Z) \text{ for short} \tag{7}$$

and

$$P_1(x) \equiv \text{II}(x)$$

$$P_2(x) = \int_{-\infty}^{\infty} P_1(x/s) dP_1(s)$$

. . . .

$$P_T(x) = \int_{-\infty}^{\infty} P_{T-1}(x/s) dP_1(s) \tag{8}$$

Exact Solutions

For general $u(.)$ functions, a different decision-vector $[wl(t)]$ is called for at each intermediate time period, $t = 1, 2, \ldots, T - 1$. This is tedious, but both inevitable and feasible. It is well known that for one, and only one, family of utility functions, namely

$$u(x;\gamma) = x^\gamma/\gamma \qquad \gamma \neq 0$$

$$= \log x \qquad \gamma = 0 \tag{9}$$

it is optimal to use the same repeated strategy. For this case the common optimal strategy is that of a $T = 1$ period problem, namely

$$X_0{}^\gamma \max_{w_i} Ex^\gamma/\gamma = X_0{}^\gamma \max_{w_i} \int_0^\infty (x^\gamma/\gamma)dP_1(x;w_1,\ldots,w_n) \tag{10}$$

The $\log x$ case is included in this formulation, since as $\gamma \to 0$, the indeterminate form is easily evaluated.

Proposed Criterion

Often in probability problems, as the number of variables becomes large, $T \to \infty$. In this case, certain asymptotic simplifications become feasible. Repeatedly, authorities (1–3) have proposed a drastic simplification of the decision problem whenever T is large.

Rule. Act in each period to maximize the geometric mean or the expected value of $\log x_t$.

The plausibility of such a procedure comes from recognition of the following valid asymptotic result.

Theorem. If one acts to maximize the geometric mean at every step, if the period is "sufficiently long," "almost certainly" higher terminal wealth and terminal utility will result than from any other decision rule.

To prove this obvious truth, one need only apply the central-limit theorem, or even the weaker law of large numbers, to the sum of independent variables

$$\log X_T = \log X_0 + \sum_1^n \log x_t \tag{11}$$

We may note the following fact about $P_T(x; \max \text{ g.m.}) = Q_T{}^*(x)$ and $P_T(x; \text{other rule}) = Q_T(x)$.

$$Q_T{}^*(x) < Q_T(x) \qquad \text{for } T > M(x) \tag{12}$$

The crucial point is that M is a function of x that is unbounded in x.

From this indisputable fact, it is tempting to believe in the truth of the following false corollary:

False Corollary. If maximizing the geometric mean almost certainly leads to a better outcome, then the expected utility of its outcomes exceeds that of any other rule, provided T is sufficiently large.

The temptation to error is compounded by the consideration that both distributions approach asymptotically log normal distributions.

$$\lim_{T \to \infty} Q_T{}^*(x) \cong \frac{1}{\sqrt{2\pi}\sigma^* T^{\frac{1}{2}}} \quad \int_{-\infty}^{\log x} \left\{ \exp - \frac{1}{2}[s - u^*T]^2/(\sigma^*)^2 T \right\} ds = L_T{}^*(x)$$

$$\lim_{T \to \infty} Q_T(x) \cong \frac{1}{\sqrt{2\pi}\sigma T^{\frac{1}{2}}} \quad \int_{-\infty}^{\log x} \left\{ \exp - \frac{1}{2}[s - \mu T]^2/\sigma^2 T \right\} ds = L_T(x) \quad (13)$$

Since $\mu^* > \mu$ by hypothesis, it follows at once that, for T large enough $L_T{}^*(x)$ can be made smaller than $L_T(x)$ for *any* x. From this it is thought, apparently, that one can validly deduce that

$$\int_0^\infty u(x)dQ_T{}^* > \int_0^\infty u(x)dQ_T(x).$$

Falsity of Corollary

A single example can show that the needed corollary is not generally valid. Suppose $\gamma = 1$, and one acts, in the fashion recommended by Pascal, to maximize expected money wealth itself. Let the gambler-investor face a choice between investing completely in safe cash, Y_1, or completely in a "security" that yields for each dollar invested, $2.70 with probability $\frac{1}{2}$ or only $0.30 with probability $\frac{1}{2}$. To maximize the geometric mean, one must stick only to cash, since $[(2.7)(.3)]^{\frac{1}{2}} = .9 < 1$. But, Pascal will always put all his wealth into the risky gamble.

Isn't he a fool? If he wins and loses an equal number of bets, and in the long run that will be his median position, he ends up with

$$(2.7)^T (.3)^T = (.9)^T \to 0 \text{ as } T \to \infty \quad (14)$$

"Almost certainly," he will be "virtually ruined" in a "long enough" sequence of play.

No, Pascal is not a fool according to *his* criterion. In those rare long sequences (and remember *all* sequences are *finite*, albeit very large) when he does experience relatively many wins, he makes more than enough to compensate him, according to the max EX_T criterion, for the more frequent times when he is ruined.

Actually,

$$E\{X_T\} = E\left\{X_0 \prod_1^T x_i\right\}$$

$$= X_0 \prod_1^n E\{x_t\}, \text{ for independent variates}$$

$$= X_0 \{Ex_1\}^T$$

$$= X_0 1.5^T > X_0 1^T \text{ for } \textit{all } T \tag{15}$$

But, you may say, Pascal is foolish to court ruin just for a large money gain. A dollar he wins is surely worth less in utility than the dollar he loses. Very well, as with eighteenth-century writers on the St. Petersburg Paradox, let us assume a concave utility-function, $u(x)$, with $u''(x) < 0$. Let us now test the false corollary for $u(x) = x^\gamma/\gamma$, $1 > \gamma \neq 0$. Let the decision according to the geometric mean rule lead to

$$E\{\log x_1{}^*\} > E \log x_1 \tag{16}$$

But let the alternative decision produce

$$E\{x_1{}^\gamma/\gamma\} > E\{x_1{}^{*\gamma}/\gamma\} \tag{17}$$

Then, as before, except for the changed value of the γ exponent

$$E\{X_T{}^\gamma/\gamma\} > E\{X_T{}^{*\gamma}/\gamma\}, \tag{18}$$

since

$$E\{X_T{}^\gamma/\gamma\} = X_0{}^\gamma \prod_1^T E\{x_t{}^\gamma/\gamma\}$$

$$= X_0{}^\gamma [E\{x_1{}^\gamma/\gamma\ ]^T\}$$

$$> X^\gamma [E\{x_1{}^{*\gamma}/\gamma\ ]^T\} = EX_T{}^{*\gamma}/\gamma \tag{19}$$

This strong inequality holds for all T, however large. Thus, the false corollary is seen to be invalid in general, even for concave utilities.

Bounded Utilities

Most geometric-mean maximizers are convinced by this reasoning (5). But not all. Thus, Markowitz, in the new 1971 preface to the reissue of his classic work on portfolio analysis (4), says that "boundedness" of the utility function will save the geometric-mean rule. For $\gamma < 0, u = x^\gamma/\gamma$ will be bounded from above, and a run of favorable gains will not bring the decision maker a utility gain of more than a finite amount. But, as the case $\gamma = -1$ shows, that cannot save the false corollary. For in all cases when $\gamma < 0$, the false rule leads to *over*-riskiness, just as for $\gamma > 0$ it leads to *under*-riskiness. Those few times, and they will happen for all T, however large, with a positive (albeit diminishing probability), whenever the false rule brings you closer to zero terminal wealth (or ruin), the unboundedness of u as $x \to 0$ and $u \to -\infty$ puts a prohibitive penalty against the false rule.

What about the case where utility is bounded above and is finite at $X_T = 0$ or ruin? It is easy to show that *no* uniform decision rule can be optimal for such a case, where

$$-\infty < u(0) \leqslant u(X) \leqslant M < \infty \tag{20}$$

But suppose we choose among all suboptimal uniform strategies that have the property of "limited liability," so that each x_t is confined to the range of nonnegative numbers. Then the following theorem, which seems to contain the germ of truth the geometric mean maximizers are groping for, is valid.

Theorem. For $u(x)$ bounded above and below in the range of nonnegative numbers, the uniform rule of maximizing the geometric mean $E\{\log X_T{}^*\}$, will asymptotically outperform any other uniform strategy's result, $E\{u(X_T)\}$, in the following sense

$$E\{u(X_T{}^*)\} > E\{u(X_T)\}, T > \bar{T}(X_0) \tag{21}$$

The limited worth of this theorem is weakened a bit further by the consideration that an infinite number of blends of a suboptimal strategy with the geometric mean rule, of the form $vx* + (1 - v)x$, v sufficiently small and positive, will do negligibly worse as $T \to \infty$.

Thus for all X_0,

$$\lim_{T \to \infty} E\left\{ u(X_T*) \right\} = (0) \text{ or } M = \sup_X u(X), \qquad (22)$$

depending upon whether

$$E(\log x_1*) \leqslant 0 \text{ or} > 0$$

For a range of v's, the same utility level will be approached as $T \to \infty$.

Optimal Nonuniform Strategy

To illustrate that no uniform strategy can be optimal when utility is bounded, consider the well-known case of $u = -e^{-bx}$. Suppose X_t can be invested at each stage into Z_t dollars of a risky Y_2 such that $E\left\{ Y_2 \right\} > 1$, or into $X_t - Z_t$ dollars of safe cash. Under "limited liability," if the lowest Y_2 could get were r, Z_t could not exceed $X_t/(1 - r)$.

First, disregard limited liability and permit negative X_T. Then a well-known result of Pfansangl (6) shows that at every stage, it is optimal to set $Z_t = Z*$, where

$$\max_z \int_{-\infty}^{\infty} - \exp[- b(X - Z) - bY_2 Z] dF_2(Y_2)$$

$$= - [\exp - b(X - Z*)] \int_{-\infty}^{\infty} \exp - [bY_2 Z*] dF_2(Y_2) \qquad (23)$$

Then optimally

$$X_T = X_0 - TZ* + (Y_2^{(1)} + Y_2^{(2)} + \ldots + Y_2^{(T)})Z* \qquad (24)$$

As $T \to \infty$, X_T approaches a normal distribution, not a log-normal distribution as in the case of uniform strategies. However, the utility level itself will approach a log-normal distribution.

$$U_t \equiv \exp - b[X_0 - TZ*] \prod_1^T (\exp - bY_2^{(t)}Z*)$$

$$\lim_{T \to \infty} E\left\{ U_T \right\} = 0 = M \qquad (25)$$

For this option of cash or a risky asset with positive return, it will necessarily be the case that

$$\max_{w} E\left\{\log[w + (1 - w)Y_2]\right\} > 1 \lim_{T \to \infty} E\left\{U_T{}^*\right\} = 0 = M$$

Nonetheless, at every wealth level, above or below a critical number, the optimal policy will generally differ from that of maximum geometric mean.

When we reintroduce limited liability in the problem and never permit an investor to take a position that could leave him bankrupt with negative wealth, the optimal strategy at each X_t will be to put min (X_t, Z^*) into the risky asset and an exact solution becomes more tedious. But clearly the optimal strategy is nonuniform and will outperform any and all uniform strategies, including that of the geometric-mean maximizer.

Maximizing Expected Average Compound Growth

Hakansson (7) has presented an analysis with a bearing on geometric-mean maximization by the long-run investor. Defining the rate of return in any period as x_t and the average compound rate of return as $(x_1 x_2 \ldots x_t{}^{1/T})$, one can propose as a criterion of portfolio selection maximizing the expected value of this magnitude. After the conventional scaling-factor T is introduced, this gives

$$\max_{w_i} TX_0 E(x_1 x_2 \ldots x_T)^{1/T} = X_0 \left\{\max_{w_i} E[x_j{}^{1/T}/(1/T)]\right\}^T \tag{26}$$

This problem we have already met in (19) for $\gamma = 1/T$. For finite T, this new criterion leads to slightly more risk-taking than does geometric-mean or expected-logarithm maximizing: for $T = 1$, it leads to Pascal's maximizing of expected money gain; for $T = 2$, it leads to the eighteenth century square-root utility function proposed by Cramer to resolve the St. Petersburg Paradox.

However, as $T \to \infty$ and $\gamma = 1/T \to 0$,

$$\lim_{\gamma \to 0} x^\gamma / \gamma = \log x \tag{27}$$

and we asymptotically approach the geometric-mean maximizing.

Thus, one wedded psychologically to a utility function $-x^{-1}$ will find the new criterion leads to rash investing. Example: modify the numerical example of (14) above so that 2.7 and .3 are replaced by 2.4 and .6. Because the geometric mean of these numbers equals $1.2 > 1$, none in cash is better for such an investor than is all in cash. But, since the harmonic means of these numbers equals

.96 $<$ 1, our hypothesized investor would prefer to satisfy his own pyschological tastes and choose to invest all in cash rather than none in cash—no matter how great T is and in the full recognition that he is violating the new criterion. The few times that following that criterion leads him to comparative losses are important enough in his eyes to scare him off from use of that criterion.

Indeed, if commissions were literally zero, then no matter how short were T in years, the number of transaction periods would become indefinitely large: Hence, with $\gamma = 0$, the novel criterion would lead to geometric-mean maximization, not just asymptotically for long-lived investors, but for any T. To be sure, as one shortens the time period between transactions, my assertion of independence of probabilities between periods might become unrealistic. This opens a Pandora's Box of difficulties. Fortuitously, the utility function $\log x$ is the one case that is least complicated to handle when probabilities are intertemporally dependent. This makes $\log x$ an attractive candidate for Santa Claus examples in textbooks, but will not endear it to anyone whose psychological tastes deviate significantly from $\log x$. (For what it is worth, I may mention that I do not fall into that category, but that does not affect the logic of the problem.)

These remarks critical of the criterion of maximum expected average compound growth do not deny that this criterion, arbitrary as it is, still avoids some of the even greater arbitrariness of conventional mean-variance analysis. Its essential defect is that it attempts to replace the pair of "asymptotically sufficient parameters" $[E \{\log x_i\}$, Variance $\{\log x_i\}]$ by the first of these alone, thereby gratuitously ruling out arbitrary γ in the family $u(x) = x^\gamma/\gamma$ in favor of $u(x) = \log x$. This diagnosis can be substantiated by the valuable discussion in the cited Hakansson paper of the efficiency properties of the pair $[E \{$average-compound-return$\}$, Variance$\{$average-compound-return$\}]$, which are asymptotically surrogates for the above sufficient parameters.

Financial aid from the National Science Foundation and editorial assistance from Mrs. Jillian Pappas are gratefully acknowledged. I have benefited from conversations with H.M. Markowitz, H.A. Latané, and L.J. Savage, but cannot claim that they would hold my views. N.H. Hakansson has explicitly warned that the purpose of his paper was not to favor maximizing the expected average-compound-return criterion.

References

1.   Williams, J.B., "Speculation and Carryover," *Quarterly Journal of Economics*, 50, 436–455 (1936).
2.   Kelley, J.L., Jr., "A New Interpretation of Information Rate," *Bell System Technical Journal*, 917–926 (1956).
3.   Latané, H.A., "Criteria for Choice Among Risky Ventures," *Journal of*

Political Economy, 67, 144–155 (1956); Kelley, J.L., Jr., and L. Breiman, "Investment Policies for Expanding Business Optimal in a Long-Run Sense," *Naval Research Logistics Quarterly*, 7 (4), 647–651 (1960); Breiman, L., "Optimal Gambling Systems for Favorable Games," ed. J. Neyman, *Proceedings of the Fourth Berkeley Symposium on Mathematical Statistics and Probability* (University of California Press, Berkeley, Calif., 1961).

4. Markowitz, H.M., *Portfolio Selection. Efficient Diversification of Investments* (John Wiley & Sons, New York, 1959), Ch. 6.

5. Samuelson, P.A., "Lifetime Portfolio Selection by Dynamic Stochastic Programming," *Review of Economics and Statistics*, 51, 239–246 (1969).

6. Pfanzangl, J., "A General Theory of Measurement-Applications to Utility," *Naval Research Logistics Quarterly*, 6, 283–294 (1959).

7. Hakansson, N.H., "Multi-period Mean-variance Analysis: Toward a General Theory of Portfolio Choice," *Journal of Finance*, 26, 4 (September, 1971).

Part VII
The Two-Parameter
Pricing Model

19

Risk, Return, and Equilibrium: Some Clarifying Comments

Eugene F. Fama*

University of Chicago

Sharpe [12] and Lintner [7] have recently proposed models directed at the following questions: (a) What is the appropriate measure of the risk of a capital asset? (b) What is the equilibrium relationship between this measure of the asset's risk and its one-period expected return?[1] Lintner contends that the measure of risk derived from his model is different and more general than that proposed by Sharpe. In his reply to Lintner, Sharpe [13] agrees that their results are in some ways conflicting and that Lintner's paper supersedes his.

This paper will show that in fact there is no conflict between the Sharpe-Lintner models. Properly interpreted they lead to the same measure of the risk of an individual asset and to the same relationship between an asset's risk and its one-period expected return. The apparent conflicts discussed by Sharpe and Lintner are caused by Sharpe's concentration on a special stochastic process for describing returns that is not necessarily implied by his asset pricing model. When applied to the more general stochastic processes that Lintner treats, Sharpe's model leads directly to Lintner's conclusions.

I. Equilibrium in the Sharpe Model

The Sharpe capital asset pricing model is based on the following assumptions:

(a) The market for capital assets is composed of risk averting investors, all of whom are one-period expected-utility-of-terminal-wealth maximizers (in the von Neumann-Morgenstern [16] sense) and find it possible to make optimal portfolio decisions solely on the basis of the means and standard deviations of the probability distributions of terminal wealth associated with the various

Reprinted by permission of the publisher and author from *Journal of Finance*, March 1968, pp. 29–40.

*In preparing this paper I have benefited from discussions with members of the Workshop in Finance of the Graduate School of Business. The comments of M. Blume, P. Brown, M. Jensen, M. Miller, H. Roberts, R. Roll, M. Scholes and A. Zellner were especially helpful. The research was supported by a grant from the Ford Foundation.

1. The terms "capital asset" and "one-period return" will be defined below.

available portfolios.[2] If the one-period return on an asset or portfolio is defined as the change in wealth during the horizon period divided by the initial wealth invested in the asset or portfolio, then the assumption implies that investors can make optimal portfolio decisions on the basis of means and standard deviations of distributions of one-period portfolio returns.[3]

(b) All investors have the same decision horizon, and over this common horizon period the means and variances of the distributions of one-period returns on assets and portfolios exist.

(c) Capital markets are perfect in the sense that all assets are infinitely divisible, there are no transactions costs or taxes, information is costless and available to everybody, and borrowing and lending rates are equal to each other and the same for all investors.

(d) Expectations and portfolio opportunities are "homogenous" throughout the market. That is, all investors have the same set of portfolio opportunities, and view the expected returns and standard deviations of return[4] provided by the various portfolios in the same way.

Assumption (a) places the analysis within the framework of the Markowitz [10] one-period mean-standard deviation portfolio model. Tobin [15] shows that the mean-standard deviation framework is appropriate either when probability distributions of portfolio returns are normal or Gaussian[5] or when investor utility of return functions are well-approximated by quadratics. In either case the optimal portfolio for a risk averter will be a member of the mean-standard deviation efficient set, where an efficient portfolio must satisfy the

---

2. In the one-period expected utility of terminal wealth model, the objects of choice for the investor are the probability distributions of terminal wealth provided by each asset and portfolio. Each "portfolio" represents a complete investment strategy covering all assets (e.g., bonds, stocks, insurance, real estate, etc.) that could possibly affect the investor's terminal wealth. That is, at the beginning of the horizon period the investor makes a single portfolio decision concerning the allocation of his investable wealth among the available terminal wealth producing assets. All terminal wealth producing assets are called capital assets.

3. The one-period return defined in this way is just a linear transformation of the units in which terminal wealth is measured; an investor's utility function can be defined in terms of one-period return just as well as in terms of terminal wealth. Note that the one-period return involves no compounding; it is just the ratio of the change in terminal wealth to initial wealth, even though the horizon period may be very long.

Though the remainder of the analysis will be in terms of the one-period return, we should keep in mind that the objects being priced in the market are the probability distributions of terminal wealth associated with each of the available capital assets.

4. Henceforth the terms "return" and "one-period return" will be used synonomously.

5. Tobin claims (and properly so) that the mean-standard deviation framework is appropriate whenever distributions of returns on all assets and portfolios are of the same type and can be fully described by two parameters. If the distribution of the return on a portfolio is always of the same type as the distributions of the returns on the individual assets in the portfolio, then that distribution must be a member of the stable (or stable Paretian) class. But the only stable distribution whose variance exists is the normal.

following criteria: (1) If any other portfolio provides lower standard deviation of one-period return, it must also have lower expected return; and (2) if any other portfolio has greater expected return, it must also have greater standard deviation of return.[6]

Assumptions (b), (c) and (d) of the Sharpe model standardize the picture of the portfolio opportunity set available to each investor. Assumption (b) implies that the portfolio decisions of all investors are made at the same point in time, and the horizon considered in making these decisions is the same for all. Assumptions (c) and (d) standardize both the set of available portfolios and investors' evaluations of the combinations of expected return and standard deviation provided by each member of the set.[7]

The situation facing each investor can be represented as in Figure 1. The horizontal axis of the figure measures expected return $E(R)$ over the common horizon period, while the vertical axis measures standard deviation of return, $\sigma(R)$. If attention is restricted to portfolios involving only risky assets, Sharpe [12] shows that the set of mean-standard deviation efficient portfolios will fall along a curve convex to the origin, like LMO in Figure 1.[8]

The model assumes, however, that in addition to the opportunities pre-

---

6. The mean-standard deviation model presupposes, of course, the existence of means and variances for all distributions of one-period returns. The work of Mandelbrot [9], Fama [2], and Roll [11] suggests, however, that this assumption may be inappropriate, at least with respect to the standard deviation. Distributions of returns on common stocks and bonds apparently conform better to members of the stable or stable Paretian family for which the variance does not exist than to the normal distribution (the only member of the family for which the variance does exist). This does not mean that mean-standard deviation portfolio models are useless. Fama [3] has shown that insights into the effects of diversification on dispersion of return that are derived from the mean-standard deviation model remain valid when the model is generalized to include the entire stable family. In a later paper [4] it is shown that much of the Sharpe-Lintner mean-standard deviation capital asset pricing model can also be generalized to include the non-normal members of the stable family. Thus it is not inappropriate to reconsider the Sharpe-Lintner models, since resolution of the apparent conflicts between them has implications for the more general model of [4].

7. Lintner [7, pp. 600–01] considers an extension of the asset pricing model to the case where investors disagree on the expected returns and standard deviations provided by portfolios. The results are essentially the same as those derived under the assumption of "homogenous expectations." Since Lintner's criticism of Sharpe does not depend on this part of his work, our discussion will use the simpler "homogeneous expectations" version of the model. Most of Lintner's discussion is also within this framework, and in all other respects his assumptions are identical to those of Sharpe.

It is important to emphasize that the Sharpe-Lintner asset pricing models, like the Markowitz-Tobin portfolio models, present one-period analyses. For a more complete discussion of the on-period framework see [4].

8. Strictly speaking this result presupposes that there are at least two portfolios in the efficient set. That is, there is no portfolio which has both higher expected return and lower standard deviation of return than *any* other portfolio. In a market of risk averters with "homogeneous expectations" this is not a strong presumption.

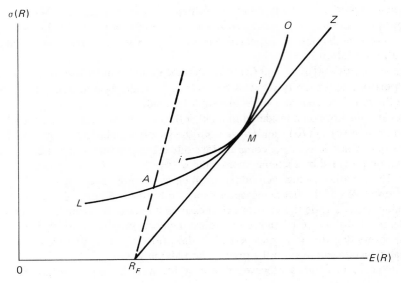

Figure 1

sented by portfolios of risky assets, there is a riskless asset F which will provide the sure return R_F over the common horizon period; it is assumed that the investor can both borrow and lend at the riskless rate R_F. Consider portfolios C involving combinations of the riskless asset F and an arbitrary portfolio A of risky assets. The expected return and standard deviation of return provided by such combinations are

$$E(R_C) = x\,R_F + (1-x)\,E(R_A) \qquad x \leqslant 1, \tag{1}$$

$$\sigma(R_C) = (1-x)\,\sigma(R_A), \tag{2}$$

where x is the proportion of available funds invested in the riskless asset F, so that $(1-x)$ is invested in A. Applying the chain rule,

$$\frac{d\,\sigma(R_C)}{d\,E(R_C)} = \frac{d\,\sigma(R_C)}{dx} \cdot \frac{dx}{d\,E(R_C)} = \frac{\sigma(R_A)}{E(R_A) - R_F}. \tag{3}$$

This implies that the combinations of expected return and standard deviation provided by portfolios involving F and A must fall along a straight line through R_F and A in Figure 1.

It is now easy to determine the effects of borrowing-lending opportunities on the set of efficient portfolios. In Figure 1 consider the line $R_F MZ$, touching

LMO at *M*. This line represents the combinations of expected return and standard deviation associated with portfolios where the proportion $x(x \leqslant 1)$ is invested in the riskless asset *F* and $1 - x$ in the portfolio of risky assets *M*. At the point $R_F, x = 1$, while at the point $M, x = 0$. Points below *M* along $R_F MZ$ correspond to lending portfolios $(x > 0)$, while points above *M* correspond to borrowing portfolios $(X < 0)$. At given levels of $\sigma(R)$ there are portfolios along $R_F MZ$ which provide higher levels of $E(R)$ than the corresponding portfolios along *LMO*. Thus (except for *M*) the portfolios along *LMO* are dominated by portfolios along $R_F MZ$, which is now the efficient set.

The conditions necessary for equilibrium in the asset market can now be stated. Since all investors have the same horizon and view their portfolio opportunities in the same way, the Sharpe model implies that everybody faces the same picture of the set of efficient portfolios. If the relevant picture is Figure 1, then all efficient portfolios for all investors will lie along $R_F MZ$. More risky efficient portfolios involve borrowing $(x < 0)$ and investing all available funds (including borrowings) in the risky combination *M*. Less risky efficient portfolios involve lending $(x > 0)$ some funds at the rate R_F and investing remaining funds in *M*. The particular portfolio that an investor chooses will depend on his attitudes toward risk and return, but optimum portfolios for all investors will involve some combination of the riskless asset *F* and the portfolio of risky assets *M*.[9] There will be no incentive for anyone to hold risky assets not included in *M*. If *M* does not contain all the risky assets in the market, or if it does not contain them in exactly the proportions in which they are outstanding, then there will be some assets that no one will hold. This is inconsistent with equilibrium, since in equilibrium all assets must be held.

Thus, if Figure 1 is to represent equilibrium, *M* must be the market portfolio; that is, *M* consists of all risky assets in the market, each weighted by the ratio of its total market value to the total market value of all assets.[10] In addi-

---

9. As noted earlier, Tobin [15] shows that the mean-standard deviation portfolio model is appropriate either when probability distributions of returns on portfolios are normal or when investor utility of return functions are well approximated by quadratics. In either case the indifference curves (i.e., loci of constant expected utility) of a risk averter will be positively sloping and concave to the origin in the $E(R)$, $\sigma(R)$ plane of Figure 1, with expected utility increasing as we move on to indifference curves further to the right in the plane. Since the efficient set of portfolios is linear, equilibrium for the investor (i.e., the point of maximum attainable expected utility) will occur at a point of tangency between an indifference curve and the efficient set or at the point R_F. The degree of the investor's risk aversion will determine whether this will be a point above or below *M* along $R_F MZ$ in Figure 1.

10. Figure 1 itself does not tell us that the market portfolio *M* is the only combination of risky assets with expected return and standard deviation $E(R_M)$ and $\sigma(R_M)$. Suppose there is another portfolio *G* such that $E(R_G) = E(R_M)$ and $\sigma(R_G) = \sigma(R_M)$. Consider portfolios *C* where the proportion $x, (0, < x < 1)$, is invested in *G* and $(1 - x)$ in *M*. Then

tion, the riskless rate R_F must be such that net borrowing in the market is 0; that is, at the rate R_F the total quantity of funds that people want to borrow is equal to the quantity that others want to lend.

As a description of reality, this view of equilibrium has an obvious short-coming. In particular, all investors hold only combinations of the riskless asset F and M. The market portfolio M is the only efficient portfolio of all risky assets.[11] This result follows from the assumed existence of the opportunity to borrow or lend indefinitely at the riskless rate R_F. Fortunately, in [4] it is shown that the measure of the risk of an individual asset and the equilibrium relationship between risk and expected return derived from the capital asset pricing model will be essentially the same whether or not it is assumed that such riskless borrowing-lending opportunities exist.

$$E(R_C) = x\, E(R_G) + (1-x)\, E(R_M) = E(R_M)$$

$$\sigma(R_C) = [x^2 \sigma^2(R_G) + (1-x)^2 \sigma^2(R_M) + 2x(1-x)\, \text{corr}\,(R_G, R_M)\, \sigma(R_G)\sigma(R_M)]^{1/2}.$$

It follows that $\sigma(R_C) < \sigma(R_M)$ unless corr$(R_G, R_M) = 1$, that is, unless the returns on portfolios G and M are perfectly correlated. The condition $\sigma(R_C) < \sigma(R_M)$ is inconsistent with equilibrium, since in equilibrium M must be a member of the efficient set. Thus, if there is a portfolio with the same expected return and standard deviation as the market portfolio M, its returns must be *perfectly* correlated with those of M, an unlikely situation. In any case, such a portfolio would be a perfect substitute for M.

11. Sharpe [12] himself proposes a slightly different version of equilibrium, one which does not imply that the market portfolio M is the *only* efficient portfolio of risky assets. He argues that in equilibrium an entire segment of the right boundary of the set of feasible risky portfolios may be tangent to a straight line through R_F. He further shows that the returns on all portfolios along such a segment must be perfectly correlated. Since ex post returns on portfolios of different risky assets are never perfectly correlated, it is unlikely that investors will expect them to be perfectly correlated ex ante, and so multiple tangencies would seem to represent an uninteresting case.

Note, though, that if a segment of the right boundary of the set of feasible risky portfolios is tangent to a line through R_F, to be consistent with equilibrium the market portfolio M must be one of the tangency points along the segment. This is an implication of the fact that when the portfolios of individuals are aggregated, the aggregate is just the market portfolio with zero net borrowing. Thus, it must be possible to obtain the market portfolio by taking weighted combinations of portfolios along the tangency segment.

In sum, given the assumptions of the Sharpe model, equilibrium can be associated (a) with a situation where the market portfolio is the only efficient combination of risky assets or (b) with a situation where there are many efficient combinations of risky assets, one of which is the market portfolio. Fortunately, Sharpe shows that in using the portfolio model to develop the relationship between risk and expected return on individual assets, it does not matter which of these representations of equilibrium is adopted. Because it simplifies the exposition of the model and also seems to be more realistic, we shall con-centrate on the case where the market portfolio is the only efficient combination of risky assets. This is also the case dealt with by Lintner [7].

II. The Measurement of Risk and the
Relationship Between Risk and Return

We consider now the major problems of the Sharpe capital asset pricing model; that is, (a) determination of a measure of risk consistent with the portfolio and expected utility models, and (b) derivation of the equilibrium relationship between risk and expected return. It is important to note that the development of the Sharpe model to this point is completely consistent with Lintner [7]. In particular, the two models are based on the same set of assumptions, and the resulting views of equilibrium are the same. Thus it seems unlikely that the implications of the two models for the measurement of risk and the relationship between risk and return can be different. In fact it will now be shown that Sharpe's approach leads to exactly the same conclusions as Lintner's. The "conflicts" which they find in their respective results will be shown to arise from the fact that both misinterpret the implications of the Sharpe model.

For any risky asset i there will be a curve, like $i M i'$ in Figure 1, which shows the combinations of $E(R)$ and $\sigma(R)$ that can be attained by forming portfolios of asset i and the market portfolio M. If x is the proportion of available funds invested in asset i, the returns on such portfolios (C) can be expressed as[12]

$$R_C = x R_i + (1 - x)R_M \qquad (x \leq 1). \qquad (4)$$

Now consider portfolios (D) where the proportion x is invested in the riskless asset F and $(1 - x)$ in the market portfolio M. The returns on such portfolios will be given by

$$R_D = x R_F + (1 - x)R_M. \qquad (5)$$

As noted earlier, the combinations of expected return and standard deviation of return provided by such portfolios fall along the efficient set line $R_F MZ$ in Figure 1. It is easy to show that the functions underlying $i M i'$ and LMO are both differentiable at the point M. Since $R_F MZ$ is the efficient set, $i M i'$ and LMO must be tangent at M. That is,

$$\frac{d \, \sigma(R_C)}{d \, E(R_C)} = \frac{d \, \sigma(R_D)}{d \, E(R_D)}, \text{ when } x = 0. \qquad (6)$$

---

12. When $0 \leq x \leq 1$ portfolios along $i M i'$ between i and M are obtained. At $x = 0$, the market portfolio M is obtained. Since M contains asset i, even when $x = 0$ the portfolio C will contain some of i. When $x < 0$, so that there is a short position in asset i, portfolios along the segment $M i'$ are obtained.

Though the discussion in the text is phrased in terms of individual assets, the analysis applies directly to the case where i is a portfolio.

The economic interpretation of (6) is familiar. $d\,\sigma(R_D)/d\,E(R_D)$ is the marginal rate of exchange of standard deviation for expected return along the efficient set $R_F MZ$. Since all investors have the same view of the efficient set, $d\,\sigma(R_D)/d\,E(R_D)$ is in fact the market rate of exchange. On the other hand, $d\,\sigma(R_C)/d\,E(R_C)$ is the marginal rate of exchange of standard deviation for expected return in the market portfolio as the proportion of asset i in the market portfolio is changed. In equilibrium excess demand for asset i must be 0. But this will only be the case if when $x = 0$ in (4), the expected return on asset i is such that the marginal rate of exchange $d\,\sigma(R_C)/d\,E(R_C)$ is equal to the market rate of exchange $d\,\sigma(R_D)/d\,E(R_D)$.

Sharpe's insight was in noting that the equilibrium condition (6) implies both a measure of the risk of asset i and the equilibrium relationship between the risk and the expected return on the asset. Using the chain rule to derive expressions for $d\,\sigma(R_C)/d\,E(R_C)$ and $d\,\sigma(R_D)/d\,E(R_D)$,[13] and then evaluating these derivatives at $x = 0$, (6) becomes

$$\frac{\mathrm{cov}(R_i, R_M) - \sigma^2(R_M)}{[E(R_i) - E(R_M)]\,\sigma(R_M)} = \frac{\sigma(R_M)}{E(R_M) - R_F}. \tag{7}$$

To get an expression for the expected return on asset i, it suffices to solve (7) for $E(R_i)$, leading to

$$E(R_i) = R_F + \frac{[E(R_M) - R_F]}{\sigma^2(R_M)}\,\mathrm{cov}(R_i, R_M), \qquad i = 1, 2, \ldots, N, \tag{8}$$

where N is the total number of assets in the market. Alternatively, the "risk premium" in the expected return on asset i is

$$E(R_i) - R_F = \left[\frac{E(R_M) - R_F}{\sigma^2(R_M)}\right]\mathrm{cov}(R_i, R_M) = \lambda\,\mathrm{cov}(R_i, R_M),$$

$$i = 1, 2, \ldots, N. \tag{9}$$

Now (9) applies to each of the N assets in the market, and the value of λ, the ratio of the risk premium in the expected return on the market portfolio to the variance of this return, will be the same for all assets. Thus the differences between the risk premiums on different assets depend entirely on the covariance term in (9). The coefficient λ can be thought of as the market price per unit

---

13. That is,

$$\frac{d\,\sigma(R_C)}{d\,E(R_C)} = \frac{d\,\sigma(R_C)}{dx} \cdot \frac{dx}{d\,E(R_C)}, \text{ and } \frac{d\,\sigma(R_D)}{d\,E(R_D)} = \frac{d\,\sigma(R_D)}{dx} \cdot \frac{dx}{d\,E(R_D)}.$$

of risk so that the appropriate measure of the risk of asset i is $\text{cov}(R_i, R_M)$. Thus this term certainly deserves closer study. In the process we shall find that (9), which is just a rearrangement of the last expression in Sharpe's [12] footnote 22, is exactly Lintner's [7] expression for the risk premium.

Note that by definition R_M, the return on the market portfolio, is just the weighted average of the returns on all the individual assets in the market. That is,

$$R_M = \sum_{j=1}^{N} X_j R_j, \tag{10}$$

where X_j is the proportion of the total market value of all assets that is accounted for by asset j. It follows that

$$\text{cov}(R_i, R_M) = E\left\{ [R_M - E(R_M)] \ [R_i - E(R_i)] \right\}$$

$$= E\left\{ \sum_{j=1}^{N} X_j \ [R_j - E(R_j)] \ [R_i - E(R_i)] \right\}$$

$$= \sum_{j=1}^{N} X_j \ \text{cov}(R_j, R_i). \tag{11}$$

Substituting (11) into (9) yields

$$E(R_i) - R_F = \lambda \sum_{j=1}^{N} X_j \ \text{cov}(R_j, R_i) \qquad i = 1, 2, \ldots, N, \tag{12}$$

which is exactly Lintner's [7, p. 596] equation (11) but derived from Sharpe's model.[14]

---

14. Lintner [7, 8] makes much of the fact that

$$\text{cov}(R_i, R_M) = \Sigma X_j \ \text{cov}(R_j, R_i) + X_i \ \sigma^2(R_i) \tag{14}$$
$$j \neq i$$

contains a term for the variance of asset i. He stresses the importance of the variance term in empirical studies concerned with measuring the riskiness of an individual asset. Recall, however, that X_i is the total market value of all outstanding units of asset i divided by the total market value of *all* assets. Thus the variance term in (14) is likely to be trivial relative to the weighted sum of covariances—a familiar result in portfolio models.

Within the context of the Sharpe model (12) is quite reasonable. From (10)

$$\sigma^2(R_M) = \sum_{k=1}^{N} \sum_{j=1}^{N} X_k X_j \, \text{cov}(R_j, R_k) = \sum_{k=1}^{N} X_k \sum_{j=1}^{N} X_j \, \text{cov}(R_j, R_k).$$

$$(13)$$

Now the term for $k = i$ in (13) is just

$$X_i \sum_{j=1}^{N} X_j \, \text{cov}(R_j, R_i) = X_i \, \text{cov}(R_i, R_M).$$

Thus $X_i \, \text{cov}(R_i, R_M)$ measures the contribution of asset i to the variance of the return on the market portfolio. Since this contribution is proportional to $\text{cov}(R_i, R_M)$ and since the market portfolio is the only stochastic component in all efficient portfolios, it is not unreasonable that the risk premium on asset i is proportional to $\text{cov}(R_i, R_M)$.

Note that (9) and (12) allow us to rank the risk premiums in the expected returns on different assets, but they provide no information about the magnitudes of the premiums. These depend on the difference $E(R_M) - R_F$, which in turn depends on the attitudes of all the different investors in the market toward risk and return. Without knowing more about attitudes toward risk, all we can say is that $E(R_M) - R_F$ must be such that in equilibrium all risky assets are held and the borrowing-lending market is cleared.

Thus, properly interpreted, the models of Sharpe and Lintner lead to identical conclusions concerning the appropriate measure of the risk of an individual asset and the equilibrium relationship between the risk of the asset and its expected return. What, then, is the source of the "conflict" between the two models which both authors apparently feel exists? Unfortunately Sharpe puts the major results of his paper in his footnote 22 [12, p. 438]; in the text he concentrates on applying these results to the market or "diagonal" model of the behavior of asset returns which he proposed in an earlier paper [14]. But the market model that he uses contains inconsistent constraints which lead to misinterpretation of the capital asset pricing model. Lintner, in his turn, does not appreciate the generality of Sharpe's results, and accepts (and in some ways misinterprets) Sharpe's treatment of the market model.

III. The Relationship Between Risk and
Return in the Market Model

In the "market model" which Sharpe [12, pp. 438–42] uses to illustrate his asset pricing model, it is assumed that there is a linear relationship between the one-period return on an individual asset and the return on the market portfolio M. That is,

$$R_i = \alpha_i + \beta_i R_M + \epsilon_i \qquad i = 1, 2, \ldots, N, \tag{15}$$

where α_i and β_i are parameters specific to asset i. It is further assumed that the random disturbances ϵ_i have the properties,

$$E(\epsilon_i) \qquad = 0 \qquad i = 1, 2, \ldots, N \tag{16a}$$

$$\text{cov}(\epsilon_i, \epsilon_j) \quad = 0 \qquad i, j = 1, 2, \ldots, N; \qquad i \neq j \tag{16b}$$

$$\text{cov}(\epsilon_i, R_M) = 0. \qquad i = 1, 2, \ldots, N. \tag{16c}$$

Thus the assumption is that the only relationships between the returns on individual risky assets arise from the fact that the return on each is related to the return on the market portfolio M via (15).

Applying the market model of (15) and (16) to the equivalent risk premium expressions (9) and (12) will allow us to pinpoint the apparent source of conflict between the results of Sharpe and Lintner. From (15) and (16)

$$\text{cov}(R_i, R_M) = E\left\{(\beta_i [R_M - E(R_M)] + \epsilon_i)(R_M - E(R_M))\right\} \tag{17a}$$

$$= \beta_i \sigma^2(R_M) + \text{cov}(\epsilon_i, R_M) \tag{17b}$$

$$= \beta_i \sigma^2(R_M). \tag{17c}$$

Substituting (17c) into (9) yields

$$E(R_i) - R_F = \lambda \beta_i \sigma^2(R_M) = [E(R_M) - R_F] \beta_i,$$

$$i = 1, 2, \ldots, N. \tag{18}$$

Thus when the stochastic process generating returns is as described by the market model of (15) and (16), the risk premium in the expected return on a given asset is proportional to the slope coefficient β for that asset. The more sensitive the asset is to the return on the market portfolio, the larger its risk premium.

In discussing the implications of his capital asset pricing model Sharpe concentrates on (18). But it is important to remember that the market model assumes a very special stochastic process for asset returns which was not assumed in the derivation of the general expressions (9) and (12) for the risk premium in the capital asset pricing model. The asset pricing model itself, as summarized by expressions (9) and (12), applies to much more general stochastic processes than those assumed in the market model and thus in (18). This point is especially crucial since we shall now see that the market model, as defined by (15) and (16), is inconsistent.

Expression (18) was obtained by applying the market model to (9). Since (12) and (9) are equivalent expressions for the risk premium in the expected return on asset i, it should be possible to apply the market model to (12) and obtain (18):

$$E(R_i) - R_F = \lambda \sum_{j=1}^{N} X_j \, \text{cov}(R_j, R_i) \qquad (19)$$

$$= \lambda \left\{ \beta_i \sum_{j=1}^{N} X_j \, \beta_j \, \sigma^2(R_M) + X_i \, \sigma^2(\epsilon_i) \right\}, \qquad (20)$$

which is exactly Lintner's [7, p. 605] expression (24). It will presently be shown that the market model implies $\Sigma \, X_j \beta_J = 1$. Thus (20) reduces to

$$E(R_j) - R_F = \lambda [\beta_i \, \sigma^2(R_M) + X_i \, \sigma^2(\epsilon_i)] \qquad (21)$$

or

$$E(R_i) - R_F = [E(R_M) - R_F)] \left[\beta_i + \frac{X_i \, \sigma^2(\epsilon_i)}{\sigma^2(R_M)} \right]. \qquad (22)$$

But (22) includes a term involving $\sigma^2(\epsilon_i)$ which does not appear in (18), and this is the major source of controversy between Lintner and Sharpe. In applying the asset pricing model to the market model, Sharpe arrives at (18) while Lintner derives (20) or its equivalent (22). Lintner [7, pp. 607–08] presumes that Sharpe is considering the case where all residual variances [the $\sigma^2(\epsilon_i)$] are 0. But Sharpe clearly did not intend to impose this restriction on his model.[15] In addition, (18) is derived directly from (9), (15), and (16), and there is no presumption in the derivation that the residual variances are 0.

In fact the discrepancy between (18) and (22) arises from an inconsistency in the specification of the market model; neither of these expressions for the risk premium is correct. Note that (10) and (15) together imply

$$R_M = \sum_{j=1}^{N} X_j R_j = \sum_{j=1}^{N} X_j [\alpha_j + \beta_j R_M + \epsilon_j]. \tag{23}$$

Thus, since ϵ_j is one of the terms in R_M, (16c) is inconsistent with the remaining assumptions of the market model. Since (16c) is used in deriving both (18) and (22), these are both incorrect expressions for the risk premium in the market model.

Unfortunately, (16c) is not the only inconsistency in the market model of (15), (16) and (23); it is also easy to show that (15), (16b) and (23) cannot hold simultaneously. Recalling that α_j and β_j are constants, (23) implies

$$\sum_{j=1}^{N} X_j \alpha_j = 0, \sum_{j=1}^{N} X_j \beta_j = 1, \tag{24a}$$

$$\sum_{j=1}^{N} X_j \epsilon_j = 0. \tag{24b}$$

The constraints of (24a) pose no problem; (24b), however, is inconsistent with (16b)—we cannot assume that the disturbances are independent and then constrain their weighted sum to be 0.

One possible specification of the market model which does not lead to the problems discussed above is as follows.

$$R_i = \alpha_i + \beta_i r_M + \epsilon_i \quad i = 1, 2, \ldots, N; \tag{25a}$$

---

15. Cf., Sharpe [12, pp. 438–39]. "The response of R_i to changes in R_g (our R_M) (and variations in R_g itself) account for much of the variation of R_i. It is this component of the asset's total risk which we term the *systematic* risk. The remainder, being uncorrelated with R_g, is the unsystematic component." Though Sharpe does not explicitly specify the version of the market model he is considering, it seems clear from this quotation and the remainder of his discussion that, for his purposes, (15) and (16) represent the relevant model.

$$E(\epsilon_i) \qquad = 0 \qquad\qquad\qquad i \;= 1, 2, \ldots, N; \qquad\qquad\qquad (25b)$$

$$\mathrm{cov}(\epsilon_i, \epsilon_j) \quad = 0 \qquad\qquad\qquad i,j = 1, 2, \ldots, N: \qquad i \neq j; \qquad (25c)$$

$$\mathrm{cov}(\epsilon_i, r_M) \;= 0 \qquad\qquad\qquad i \;= 1, 2, \ldots, N. \qquad\qquad\qquad (25d)$$

In this model r_M is interpreted as a common underlying market factor which affects the returns on all assets. The relationship between r_M and the return on the market portfolio is then

$$R_M = \sum_{j=1}^{N} X_j R_j = \sum_{j=1}^{N} X_j [\alpha_j + \beta_j r_M + \epsilon_j]. \qquad (26)$$

From either (9) or (12) it follows that in this model the risk premium on asset i is

$$E(R_i) - R_F \;= \lambda \sum_{j=1}^{N} X_j \,\mathrm{cov}(R_j, R_i)$$

$$= \lambda \sum_{j=1}^{N} X_j \, E\{(\beta_j [r_M - E(r_M)] + \epsilon_j) \,(\beta_i [r_M$$

$$- E(r_M)] + \epsilon_i)\}$$

$$E(R_i) - R_F \;= \lambda \left\{ \beta_i \sum_{j=1}^{N} X_j \beta_j \, \sigma^2(r_M) + X_i \, \sigma^2(\epsilon_i) \right\} \qquad (27)$$

which is equivalent to Lintner's [7, equation (23)] expression for the risk premium in this more general version of the market model. But it is again important to note that Lintner's results follow directly from (9) and (12), the general expressions for the risk premium developed in Sharpe's model.

Finally, though the issues discussed above are certainly interesting from a theoretical viewpoint, from a practical viewpoint (18), (22) and (27) are nearly equivalent expressions for the risk premium in the market model. The empirical evidence of King [6] and Blume [1] suggests that, on average, $\sigma^2(\epsilon_i)$ and $\sigma^2(R_M)$ in (22) are about equal. Thus the size of the residual term in (22) will be determined primarily by X_i, the proportion of the total value of all assets accounted for by asset i, which will usually be quite small relative to β_i (which is on average 1). The risk premiums given by (18) and (22), then, will be nearly equal.

Next note that it is always possible to scale r_M in (26) so that $\Sigma\, X_j\, \alpha_j = 0$ and $\Sigma\, X_j\, \beta_j = 1$. Then

$$\sigma^2(R_M) = \sigma^2(r_M) + \sum_{j=1}^{N} X_j^2\, \sigma^2(\epsilon_j). \tag{28}$$

But again the weighted sum of residual variances will be small relative to $\sigma^2(r_M)$ so that $\sigma^2(R_M) \cong \sigma^2(r_M)$, which implies that the risk premiums given by (22) and (27) are almost equal.

IV. Conclusions

In sum, then, there are no real conflicts between the capital asset pricing models of Sharpe [12] and Lintner [7, 8]. When they apply their general results to the market model, both make errors which turn out to be unimportant from a practical viewpoint. The important point is that their general models represent equivalent approaches to the problem of capital asset pricing under uncertainty.

References

1. Marshall E. Blume. "The Assessment of Portfolio Performance," unpublished Ph.D. dissertation, Graduate School of Business, University of Chicago, 1967.
2. Eugene F. Fama. "The Behavior of Stock-Market Prices," *Journal of Business* (January, 1965), pp. 34–105.
3. ——. "Portfolio Analysis in a Stable Paretian Market," *Management Science* (January, 1965), pp. 404–19.
4. ——. "Risk, Return, and Equilibrium in a Stable Paretian Market," unpublished manuscript (October, 1967).
5. Michael Jensen. "Risk, the Pricing of Capital Assets, and the Evaluation of Investment Portfolios," unpublished Ph.D. dissertation, Graduate School of Business, University of Chicago, 1967.
6. Benjamin F. King. "Market and Industry Factors in Stock Price Behavior," *Journal of Business*, Supplement (January, 1966), pp. 139–90.
7. John Lintner. "Security Prices, Risk, and Maximal Gains from Diversification," *Journal of Finance* (December, 1965), pp. 587–615.
8. ——. "The Valuation of Risk Assets and the Selection of Risky Investments

in Stock Portfolios and Capital Budgets," *Review of Economics and Statistics* (February, 1965), pp. 13–37.

9. Benoit Mandelbrot. "The Variation of Certain Speculative Prices," *Journal of Business* (October, 1963), pp. 394–419.

10. Harry Markowitz. *Portfolio Selection: Efficient Diversification of Investments.* New York: John Wiley and Sons, Inc., 1959.

11. Richard Roll. "The Efficient Market Model Applied to U.S. Treasury Bill Rates" unpublished Ph.D. thesis, Graduate School of Business, University of Chicago, 1968.

12. William F. Sharpe. "Capital Asset Prices: A Theory of Market Equilibrium under Conditions of Risk," *Journal of Finance* (September, 1964), pp. 425–42.

13. ———. "Security Prices, Risk, and Maximal Gains from Diversification: Reply," *Journal of Finance* (December, 1966), pp. 743–44.

14. ———. "A Simplified Model for Portfolio Analysis," *Management Science* (January, 1963), pp. 277–93.

15. James Tobin. "Liquidity Preference as Behavior Towards Risk," *Review of Economic Studies* (February, 1958), pp. 65–86.

16. John von Neumann and Oskar Morgenstern. *Theory of Games and Economic Behavior*, Princeton: Princeton University Press, third edition, 1953.

20

Capital Market Equilibrium with Restricted Borrowing*

Fischer Black
University of Chicago

Introduction

Several authors have contributed to the development of a model describing the pricing of capital assets under conditions of market equilibrium.[1] The model states that under certain assumptions the expected return on any capital asset for a single period will satisfy

$$E(\widetilde{R}_i) = R_f + \beta_i [E(\widetilde{R}_m) - R_f] . \tag{1}$$

The symbols in equation (1) are defined as follows: $\widetilde{R}_i$ is the return on asset i for the period and is equal to the change in the price of the asset, plus any dividends, interest, or other distributions, divided by the price of the asset at the start of the period; $\widetilde{R}_m$ is the return on the market portfolio of all assets taken together; R_f is the return on a riskless asset for the period; β_i is the "market sensitivity" of asset i and is equal to the slope of the regression line relating $\widetilde{R}_i$ and $\widetilde{R}_m$. The market sensitivity β_i of asset i is defined algebraically by

$$\beta_i = \mathrm{cov}(\widetilde{R}_i, \widetilde{R}_m)/\mathrm{var}(\widetilde{R}_m). \tag{2}$$

The assumptions that are generally used in deriving equation (1) are as follows: (*a*) All investors have the same opinions about the possibilities of various end-of-period values for all assets. They have a common joint probability distribution for the returns on the available assets. (*b*) The common probability distribution describing the possible returns on the available assets is joint normal (or joint stable with a single characteristic exponent). (*c*) Investors choose portfolios that maximize their expected end-of-period utility of wealth, and all

Reprinted by permission of the publisher and author from *The Journal of Business of the University of Chicago*, Vol. 45, No. 3, July 1972. © 1972 by the University of Chicago.

*Some of the basic ideas in this paper, and many helpful comments, were provided by Eugene Fama, Michael Jensen, John Lintner, John Long, Robert Merton, Myron Scholes, William Sharpe, Jack Treynor, and Oldrich Vasicek. This work was supported in part by Wells Fargo Bank and the Ford Foundation.

1. A summary of the development of the model may be found in William F. Sharpe, *Portfolio Theory and Capital Markets* (New York: McGraw-Hill Book Co., 1970).

investors are risk averse. (Every investor's utility function on end-of-period wealth increases at a decreasing rate as his wealth increases.) (*d*) An investor may take a long or short position of any size in any asset, including the riskless asset. Any investor may borrow or lend any amount he wants at the riskless rate of interest.

The length of the period for which the model applies is not specified. The assumptions of the model make sense, however, only if the period is taken to be infinitesimal. For any finite period, the distribution of possible returns on an asset is likely to be closer to lognormal than normal; in particular, if the distribution of returns is normal, then there will be a finite probability that the asset will have a negative value at the end of the period.

Of these assumptions, the one that has been felt to be the most restrictive is (*d*). Lintner has shown that removing assumption (*a*) does not change the structure of capital asset prices in any significant way,[2] and assumptions (*b*) and (*c*) are generally regarded as acceptable approximations to reality. Assumption (*d*), however, is not a very good approximation for many investors, and one feels that the model would be changed substantially if this assumption were dropped.

In addition, several recent studies have suggested that the returns on securities do not behave as the simple capital asset pricing model described above predicts they should. Pratt analyzes the relation between risk and return in common stocks in the 1926–60 period and concludes that high-risk stocks do not give the extra returns that the theory predicts they should give.[3] Friend and Blume use a cross-sectional regression between risk-adjusted performance and risk for the 1960–68 period and observe that high-risk portfolios seem to have poor performance, while low-risk portfolios have good performance.[4] They note that there is some bias in their test, but claim alternately that the bias is so small that it can be ignored, and that it explains half of the effect they observe.[5] In fact, the bias is serious. Miller and Scholes do an extensive analysis of the nature of the bias and make corrections for it.[6] Even after their corrections, however, there is a negative relation between risk and performance.

Black, Jensen, and Scholes analyze the returns on portfolios of stocks at

---

2. John Lintner, "The Aggregation of Investors' Diverse Judgments and Preferences in Perfectly Competitive Security Markets," *Journal of Financial and Quantitative Analysis* 4 (December 1969): 347–400.

3. Shannon P. Pratt, "Relationship between Viability of Past Returns and Levels of Future Returns for Common Stocks 1926–1960," memorandum (April 1967).

4. Irwin Friend and Marshall Blume, "Measurement of Portfolio Performance under Uncertainty," *American Economic Review* 60 (September 1970): 561–75.

5. Ibid., p. 568. Compare the text with n. 15.

6. Merton H. Miller and Myron Scholes, "Rates of Return in Relation to Risk: A Re-Examination of Some Recent Findings," in *Studies in the Theory of Capital Markets*, ed. Michael C. Jensen (New York: Praeger Publishing Co., in press).

different levels of β_i in the 1926–66 period.[7] They find that the average returns on these portfolios are not consistent with equation (1), especially in the postwar period 1946–66. Their estimates of the expected returns on portfolios of stocks at low levels of β_i are consistently higher than predicted by equation (1), and their estimates of the expected returns on portfolios of stocks at high levels of β_i are consistently lower than predicted by equation (1).

Black, Jensen, and Scholes also find that the behavior of well-diversified portfolios at different levels of β_i is explained to a much greater extent by a "two-factor model" than by a single-factor "market model."[8] They show that a model of the following form provides a good fit for the behavior of these portfolios:

$$\widetilde{R}_i = a_i + b_i \widetilde{R}_m + (1 - b_i)\widetilde{R}_z + \widetilde{\epsilon}_i. \tag{3}$$

In equation (3), $\widetilde{R}_z$ is the return on a "second factor" that is independent of the market (its β_i is zero), and $\widetilde{\epsilon}_i, i = 1, 2, \ldots, N$ are approximately mutually independent residuals.

This model suggests that in periods when R_z is positive, the low β_i portfolios all do better than predicted by equation (1), and the high β_i portfolios all do worse than predicted by equation (1). In periods when R_z is negative, the reverse is true: low β_i portfolios do worse than expected, and high β_i portfolios do better than expected. In the postwar period, the estimates obtained by Black, Jensen, and Scholes for the mean of $\widetilde{R}_z$ were significantly greater than zero.

One possible explanation for these empirical results is that assumption (d) of the capital asset pricing model does not hold. What we will show below is that the relaxation of assumption (d) can give models that are consistent with the empirical results obtained by Pratt, Friend and Blume, Miller and Scholes, and Black, Jensen and Scholes.

Equilibrium with No Riskless Asset

Let us start by assuming that investors may take long or short positions of any size in any risky asset, but that there is no riskless asset and that no borrowing or lending at the riskless rate of interest is allowed. This assumption is not realistic, since restrictions on short selling are at least as stringent as restrictions on borrowing. But restrictions on short selling may simply add to the effects that

---

7. Fischer Black, Michael C. Jensen, and Myron Scholes, "The Capital Asset Pricing Model: Some Empirical Tests," in *Studies in the Theory of Capital Markets*, ed. Michael C. Jensen (New York: Praeger Publishing Co., in press).

8. One form of market model is defined in Eugene F. Fama, "Risk, Return, and Equilibrium," *Journal of Political Economy* 79 (January/February 1971): 34.

we will show are caused by restrictions on borrowing. Under these assumptions, Sharpe shows that the efficient set of portfolios may be written as a weighted combination of two basic portfolios, with different weights being used to generate the different portfolios in the efficient set.[9] In his notation, the proportion X_i of asset i in the efficient portfolio corresponding to the parameter λ satisfies (4), where K_i and k_i are constants:

$$X_i = K_i + \lambda k_i \qquad i = 1, 2, \ldots, N. \tag{4}$$

Thus the weights on the stocks in the two basic portfolios are $K_i, i = 1, 2, \ldots, N$, and $k_i, i = 1, 2, \ldots, N$. The weights satisfy (5), so the sum of the weights X_i is always equal to 1.

$$\sum_{i=1}^{N} K_i = 1; \qquad \sum_{i=1}^{N} k_i = 0. \tag{5}$$

Sharpe also shows that the variance of return on an efficient portfolio is a quadratic function of its expected return.

Similarly, Lintner shows that a number of relations can be derived when there is no riskless asset.[10] His equation (16c) can be interpreted, in the case where all investors agree on the joint distribution of end-of-period values for all assets, as saying that even when there is no riskless asset, every investor holds a linear combination of two basic portfolios. And his equation (18) can be interpreted as saying that the prices of assets in equilibrium are related in a relatively simple way even without a riskless asset.

Cass and Stiglitz show that if the returns on securities are not assumed to be joint normal, but are allowed to be arbitrary, then the set of efficient portfolios can be written as a weighted combination of two basic portfolios only for a very special class of utility functions.[11]

Using a notation similar to that used by Fama, we can show that every efficient portfolio consists of a weighted combination of two basic portfolios as follows. An efficient portfolio is one that has maximum expected return for given variance, or minimum variance for given expected return. Thus the efficient portfolio held by individual k is obtained by choosing proportions $x_{ki}, i = 1, 2, \ldots, N$, invested in the shares of each of the N available assets, in order to

---

9. Sharpe, pp. 59–69.

10. Lintner, pp. 373–84.

11. David Cass and Joseph E. Stiglitz, "The Structure of Investor Preferences and Asset Returns, and Separability in Portfolio Allocation: A Contribution to the Pure Theory of Mutual Funds," *Journal of Economic Theory* 2 (June 1970): 122–60.

$$\text{Minimize:} \quad \text{var}(\widetilde{R}_k) = \sum_{i=1}^{N} \sum_{j=1}^{N} x_{ki} x_{kj} \, \text{cov}(\widetilde{R}_i, \widetilde{R}_j); \tag{6}$$

$$\text{Subject to:} \quad E(\widetilde{R}_k) = \sum_{j=1}^{N} x_{kj} E(\widetilde{R}_j); \tag{7}$$

$$\sum_{j=1}^{N} x_{kj} = 1. \tag{8}$$

Using Lagrange multipliers S_k and T_k, this can be expressed as

$$\text{Minimize:} \quad \sum_{i=1}^{N} \sum_{j=1}^{N} x_{ki} x_{kj} \, \text{cov}(\widetilde{R}_i, \widetilde{R}_j)$$

$$- 2S_k \left[\sum_{j=1}^{N} x_{kj} E(\widetilde{R}_j) - E(\widetilde{R}_k) \right]$$

$$- 2T_k \left[\sum_{j=1}^{N} x_{kj} - 1 \right]. \tag{9}$$

Taking the derivative of this expression with respect to x_{ki}, we have

$$\sum_{j=1}^{N} x_{kj} \, \text{cov}(\widetilde{R}_i, \widetilde{R}_j) - S_k E(\widetilde{R}_i) - T_k = 0. \tag{10}$$

This set of equations, for $i = 1, 2, \ldots, N$, determines the values of x_{ki}. If we write D_{ij} for the inverse of the covariance matrix $\text{cov}(\widetilde{R}_i, \widetilde{R}_j)$, then the solution to this set of equations may be written

$$x_{ki} = S_k \sum_{j=1}^{N} D_{ij} E(\widetilde{R}_j) + T_k \sum_{j=1}^{N} D_{ij}. \tag{11}$$

Note that the subscript k, referring to the individual investor, appears on the right-hand side of this equation only in the multipliers S_k and T_k. Thus every investor holds a linear combination of two basic portfolios, and every efficient portfolio is a linear combination of these two basic portfolios. In equation (11), there is no guarantee that the weights on the individual assets in the two portfolios sum to one. If we normalize these weights, then equation (11) may be written

$$x_{ki} = w_{kp} x_{pi} + w_{kq} x_{qi}.$$ (12)

In equation (12), the symbols are defined as follows:

$$w_{kp} = S_k \sum_{i=1}^{N} \sum_{j=1}^{N} D_{ij} E(\widetilde{R}_j);$$

$$w_{kq} = T_k \sum_{i=1}^{N} \sum_{j=1}^{N} D_{ij};$$

$$x_{pi} = \sum_{j=1}^{N} D_{ij} E(\widetilde{R}_j) / \sum_{i=1}^{N} \sum_{j=1}^{N} D_{ij} E(\widetilde{R}_j);$$

$$x_{qi} = \sum_{j=1}^{N} D_{ij} / \sum_{i=1}^{N} \sum_{j=1}^{N} D_{ij}.$$ (13)

Thus we have

$$\sum_{i=1}^{N} x_{pi} = 1;$$

$$\sum_{i=1}^{N} x_{qi} = 1;$$

$$w_{kp} + w_{kq} = 1 \qquad k = 1, 2, \ldots, L.$$ (14)

The last equation in (14) follows from the fact that the x_{ki}'s must also sum to one.

Equation (12), then, shows that the efficient portfolio held by investor k consists of a weighted combination of the basic portfolios p and q. Note, however, that the two basic portfolios are not unique. Suppose that we transform the basic portfolios p and q into two different portfolios u and v, using weights w_{up}, w_{uq}, w_{vp}, and w_{vq}. Then we have

$$x_{ui} = w_{up} x_{pi} + w_{uq} x_{qi},$$

$$x_{vi} = w_{vp} x_{pi} + w_{vq} x_{qi}. \tag{15}$$

Normally, we will be able to solve equations (15) for x_{pi} and x_{qi}. Let us write the resulting coefficients w_{pu}, w_{pv}, w_{qu}, and w_{qv}. Then we will have

$$x_{pi} = w_{pu} x_{ui} + w_{pv} x_{vi},$$

$$x_{qi} = w_{qu} x_{ui} + w_{qv} x_{vi}. \tag{16}$$

Substituting equations (16) into equation (12), we see that we can write the efficient portfolio k as a linear combination of the new basic portfolios u and v as follows:

$$x_{ki} = w_{ku} x_{ui} + w_{kv} x_{vi}. \tag{17}$$

In equation (17), the weights w_{ku} and w_{kv} sum to one.

Thus the basic portfolios u and v can be any pair of different portfolios that can be formed as weighted combinations of the original pair of basic portfolios p and q. Every efficient portfolio can be expressed as a weighted combination of portfolios u and v, but they need not be efficient themselves.

Portfolios p and q must have different β's, if it is to be possible to generate every efficient portfolio as a weighted combination of these two portfolios. But if they have different β's, then it will be possible to generate new basic portfolios u and v with arbitrary β's, but choosing appropriate weights. In particular, let us choose weights such that

$$\beta_u = 1; \qquad \beta_v = 0. \tag{18}$$

Multiplying equation (12) by the fraction x_{mk} of total wealth held by investor k, and summing over all investors ($k = 1, 2, \ldots, L$), we obtain the weights x_{mi} of each asset in the market portfolio:

$$x_{mi} = \left(\sum_{k=1}^{L} x_{mk} w_{kp} \right) x_{pi} + \left(\sum_{k=1}^{L} x_{mk} w_{kq} \right) x_{qi}. \tag{19}$$

Since the market portfolio is a weighted combination of portfolios p and q, and since β_m is one, portfolio u must be the market portfolio. Thus we can rename the portfolios u and v specified by (18) portfolios m and z, for the market portfolio and the zero-β basic portfolio. When we write the return on an efficient portfolio k as a weighted combination of the returns on portfolios m and z, the coefficient of the return on portfolio m must be β_k. Thus we can write

$$\tilde{R}_k = \beta_k \tilde{R}_m + (1 - \beta_k)\tilde{R}_z. \tag{20}$$

Taking expected values of both sides of equation (20), and rewriting slightly, we have

$$E(\tilde{R}_k) = E(\tilde{R}_z) + \beta_k [E(\tilde{R}_m) - E(\tilde{R}_z)]. \tag{21}$$

Equation (21) says that the expected return on an efficient portfolio k is a linear function of its β_k. From (1), we see that the corresponding relationship when there is a riskless asset and riskless borrowing and lending are allowed is

$$E(\tilde{R}_k) = R_f + \beta_k [E(\tilde{R}_m) - R_f]. \tag{22}$$

Thus the relation between the expected return on an efficient portfolio k and its β_k is the same whether or not there is a riskless asset. If there is, then the intercept of the relationship is R_f. If there is not, then the intercept is $E(\tilde{R}_z)$.

We can now show that equation (21) applies to individual securities as well as to efficient portfolios. Subtracting equation (10) from itself after permuting the indexes, we get

$$\text{cov}(\tilde{R}_i, \tilde{R}_k) - \text{cov}(\tilde{R}_j, \tilde{R}_k) = S_k [E(\tilde{R}_i) - E(\tilde{R}_j)]. \tag{23}$$

Since the market is an efficient portfolio, we can put m for k, and since i and j can be taken to be portfolios as well as assets, we can put z for j. Then equation (23) becomes

$$\text{cov}(\tilde{R}_i, \tilde{R}_m) = S_m [E(\tilde{R}_i) - E(\tilde{R}_z)]. \tag{24}$$

Equation (24) may be rewritten as

$$E(\tilde{R}_i) = E(\tilde{R}_z) + [\text{var}(\tilde{R}_m)/S_m]\beta_i. \tag{25}$$

Putting m for i in equation (25), we find

$$\text{var}(\tilde{R}_m)/S_m = E(\tilde{R}_m) - E(\tilde{R}_z). \tag{26}$$

So equation (25) becomes

$$E(\widetilde{R}_i) = E(\widetilde{R}_z) + \beta_i[E(\widetilde{R}_m) - E(\widetilde{R}_z)].$$ (27)

Thus the expected return on every asset, even when there is no riskless asset and riskless borrowing is not allowed, is a linear function of its β. Comparing equation (27) with equation (1), we see that the introduction of a riskless asset simply replaces $E(\widetilde{R}_z)$ with R_f.

Now we can derive another property of portfolio z. Equation (27) holds for any asset and thus for any portfolio. Setting $\beta_i = 0$, we see that every portfolio with β equal to zero must have the same expected return as portfolio z. Since the return on portfolio z is independent of the return on portfolio m, and since weighted combinations of portfolios m and z must be efficient, portfolio z must be the minimum-variance zero-β portfolio.

Fama comes close to deriving equation (27). His equation (27) says that the expected return on an asset is a linear function of its risk, measured relative to an efficient portfolio containing the asset. Lintner also derives a linear relationship (eq. [18]) between the expected return on an asset and its risk. It is possible to derive equation (27) from either Fama's or Lintner's equations in a relatively small number of steps.

Fama, however, goes on to introduce the concept of a new kind of financial intermediary that he calls a "portfolio sharing company." In the absence of riskless borrowing or lending opportunities, he says that this fund can purchase units of the market portfolio, and sell shares in its return to different investors. He says that an investor can specify the proportion of the return on this fund that he will receive *per unit of his own funds invested*. Writing β_k for this proportion, Fama claims that

$$\widetilde{R}_k = \beta_k \widetilde{R}_m.$$ (28)

But this is not consistent with market equilibrium. Assuming that $E(R_z)$ is positive, shares in this fund will be less attractive than direct holdings of efficient portfolios with β_k less than one, as given by equation (2). If $E(\widetilde{R}_z)$ is negative, shares in this fund will be less attractive than direct holdings of efficient portfolios with β_k greater than one. So there is no way that the fund can sell all of its shares, except, of course, that it can determine a number R_f such that when the return on the holdings of investor k is defined by equation (29), all of the fund's shares can be sold:

$$\widetilde{R}_k = R_f + \beta_k (\widetilde{R}_m - R_f).$$ (29)

But this is just an implicit way of creating borrowing and lending opportunities.

So the concept of portfolio sharing does not cast any light on market equilibrium in the absence of riskless borrowing and lending opportunities.

Starting with equation (23), we can now show one final property of portfolio z. Let p and q be two efficient portfolios and let w_{zp} and w_{zq} be the weights that give portfolio z when applied to portfolios p and q. Putting m for j and p for k to give one equation, and putting m for j and q for k to give another, we have

$$\text{cov}(\widetilde{R}_i, \widetilde{R}_p) - \text{cov}(\widetilde{R}_m, \widetilde{R}_p) = S_p\,[E(\widetilde{R}_i) - E(\widetilde{R}_m)]\;;$$

$$\text{cov}(\widetilde{R}_i, \widetilde{R}_q) - \text{cov}(\widetilde{R}_m, \widetilde{R}_q) = S_q\,[E(\widetilde{R}_i) - E(\widetilde{R}_m)]\,. \tag{30}$$

Multiplying the equations by w_{zp} and w_{zq}, respectively, and adding them—noting that $\text{cov}(\widetilde{R}_m, \widetilde{R}_z)$ is zero—we have

$$\text{cov}(\widetilde{R}_i, \widetilde{R}_z) = (w_{zp}S_p + w_{zq}S_q)\,[E(\widetilde{R}_i) - E(\widetilde{R}_m)]\,. \tag{31}$$

Substituting for $E(\widetilde{R}_i)$ from equation (27), we obtain

$$\text{cov}(\widetilde{R}_i, \widetilde{R}_z) = (1 - \beta_i)\,(w_{zp}S_p + w_{zq}S_q)\,[E(\widetilde{R}_z) - E(\widetilde{R}_m)]\,. \tag{32}$$

Thus we see that the covariance of the return on any asset i with the return on portfolio z is proportional to $1 - \beta_i$.

In sum, we have shown that when there is no riskless asset, and no riskless borrowing or lending, every efficient portfolio may be written as a weighted combination of the market portfolio m and the minimum-variance zero-β portfolio z. The covariance of the return on any asset i with the return on portfolio z is proportional to $1 - \beta_i$. The expected return on any asset or portfolio i depends only on β_i, and is a linear function of β_i.

Prohibition of borrowing and lending, then, shifts the intercept of the line relating $E(R_i)$ and β_i from R_f to $E(\widetilde{R}_z)$. Since this is the effect that complete prohibition would have, it seems likely that partial restrictions on borrowing and lending, such as margin requirements, would also shift the intercept of the line, but less so. Thus it is possible that restrictions on borrowing and lending would lead to a market equilibrium consistent with the empirical model expressed in equation (3) and developed by Black, Jensen, and Scholes.

Equilibrium with No Riskless Borrowing

Let us turn now to the case in which there is a riskless asset available, such as a short-term government security, but in which investors are not allowed to take short positions in the riskless asset. We will continue to assume that investors may take short positions in risky assets.

Vasicek has shown that in this case the principal features of the equilibrium with no riskless borrowing or lending are preserved.[12] The expected return on any asset i continues to be a function only of its β. The function is still linear. The efficient set of portfolios now has two parts, however. One part consists of weighted combinations of portfolios m and z, and the other part consists of weighted combinations of the riskless asset with a single portfolio of risky assets that we can call portfolio t.

We can show this, in our notation, as follows. Since the restriction on borrowing applies only to the riskless asset, there will be only two kinds of efficient portfolios, those that contain the riskless asset and those that do not. Let us call the riskless asset number $N + 1$.

For those efficient portfolios that do not contain the riskless asset, equations (6)–(18) of the previous section apply. Each such efficient portfolio can be expressed as a weighted combination of portfolios u and v, where β_u is one and β_v is zero.

For those efficient portfolios that do contain the riskless asset, we can extend equation (10) to $N + 1$ assets. The covariance term for $j = N + 1$ vanishes, so we have

$$\sum_{j=1}^{N} x_{kj} \, \text{cov}(\widetilde{R}_i, \widetilde{R}_j) - S_k E(\widetilde{R}_i) - T_k = 0. \tag{33}$$

For $i = 1, 2, \ldots, N$, this set of equations determines values for $x_{ki}, i = 1, 2, \ldots, N$, as before. Thus we see that the risky portions of these investors' portfolios are weighted combinations of portfolios u and v. For $i = N + 1$, equation (33) becomes

$$-S_k R_f - T_k = 0 \qquad k = 1, 2, \ldots, L. \tag{34}$$

This means that every investor places the same relative weights S_k and T_k on portfolios u and v. Let us write t for the portfolio of risky assets containing relative weights S_k and T_k of portfolios u and v. Then every investor who holds the riskless asset holds a weighted combination of the riskless asset and portfolio t.

Since the risky part of every investor's portfolio, whether he holds the riskless asset or not, consists of a weighted combination of portfolios u and v,

---

12. Oldrich A. Vasicek, "Capital Market Equilibrium with No Riskless Borrowing," memorandum (March 1971); available from the Wells Fargo Bank.

the sum of all investors' risky holdings, which is the market portfolio, must be a weighted combination of portfolios u and v. Using arguments parallel to those used in the last section, we can show that portfolio u must be the market portfolio, and portfolio v must be the minimum-variance zero-β portfolio of risky assets.

Equation (33) is the same as equation (10), so we can see that it holds for all risky assets i, $i = 1, 2, \ldots, N$, and all efficient portfolios k. Equations (23)–(27) go through as before, and we see that equation (27) applies to all risky assets even when there are riskless lending opportunities.

Now we can derive some additional properties of portfolios z and t. Let us write w_{km}, w_{kz}, and w_{kf} for the weights on portfolios m, z, and the riskless asset in efficient portfolio k. Since the return on portfolio z is independent of the return on portfolio m, the expected return and variance of portfolio k will be

$$E(\widetilde{R}_k) = w_{km} E(\widetilde{R}_m) + w_{kz} E(\widetilde{R}_z) + w_{kf} R_f; \tag{35}$$

$$\text{var}(\widetilde{R}_k) = w_{km}^2 \, \text{var}(\widetilde{R}_m) + w_{kz}^2 \, \text{var}(\widetilde{R}_z). \tag{36}$$

The weights must also satisfy constraints (37) and (38):

$$w_{km} + w_{kz} + w_{kf} = 1; \tag{37}$$

$$w_{kf} \geqslant 0. \tag{38}$$

We can see immediately that $E(\widetilde{R}_z)$ must satisfy

$$R_f < E(\widetilde{R}_z) < E(\widetilde{R}_m). \tag{39}$$

If $E(\widetilde{R}_z)$ is less than or equal to R_f, then we can increase w_{kf} and decrease w_{kz} by the same amount, and we will reduce the variance of portfolio k and increase or leave unchanged its expected return. But if this is possible, it means that portfolio k is not efficient.

When portfolio k is the market portfolio, w_{km} must be one, and w_{kz} must be zero. If $E(\widetilde{R}_z)$ is greater than or equal to $E(\widetilde{R}_m)$, then we can decrease w_{km} by a very small amount and increase w_{kz} by the same amount, and we will reduce the variance of portfolio k and increase or leave unchanged its expected return. But if this is possible, it means that the market portfolio is not efficient. Thus the inequality (39) must hold.

When w_{kf} is greater than zero, portfolio k is a mixture of portfolio t and the riskless asset. We can incorporate equation (37) in equation (35) as follows:

$$E(\widetilde{R}_k - R_f) = w_{km} [E(\widetilde{R}_m - R_f] + w_{kz} [E(\widetilde{R}_z - R_f)]. \tag{40}$$

Equation (36) may be written equivalently as

$$\text{var}(\widetilde{R}_k - R_f) = w_{km}^{\;2}\,\text{var}(\widetilde{R}_m - R_f) + w_{kz}^{\;2}\,\text{var}(\widetilde{R}_z - R_f). \tag{41}$$

Since equations (40) and (41) hold for any portfolio containing the riskless asset, they must hold also for portfolio t. Since portfolio t is efficient, it must maximize (40) subject to (41). But the solution to that problem is the same as the solution to

$$\text{Maximize:} \qquad E(\widetilde{R}_k - R_f)/\sigma(\widetilde{R}_k - R_f). \tag{42}$$

But when the efficient portfolios are plotted on a graph with $E(\widetilde{R}_k - R_f)$ on the y-axis, and $\sigma(\widetilde{R}_k - R_f)$—which is the same as $\sigma(\widetilde{R}_k)$—on the x-axis, the value of k that satisfies (42) is the value of k that maximizes the slope of a line drawn from the origin to point k. So portfolio t is the "tangent portfolio" to the efficient set.

In sum, the introduction of riskless lending opportunities changes the nature of the market equilibrium in just one way. There are now two kinds of efficient portfolios. The less risky efficient portfolios are mixtures of portfolio t and the riskless asset. The more risky efficient portfolios continue to be mixtures of portfolios m and z. Portfolio t itself is a mixture of portfolios m and z. The expected return on portfolio z must now be greater than the return on the riskless asset. The expected return on a security continues to be a linear function of its β.

Thus the empirical results reported by Black, Jensen, and Scholes are consistent with a market equilibrium in which there are riskless lending opportunities, as well as with an equilibrium in which there are no riskless borrowing or lending opportunities. The general approach used in this section can be used to obtain similar results when every individual has a limit on the amount he can borrow that may be greater than zero. Thus we can say that the empirical results are consistent with an equilibrium in which borrowing at the riskless interest rate is either fully or partially restricted.

Conclusions

We have explored the nature of capital market equilibrium under two assumptions that are more restrictive than the usual assumptions used in deriving the capital asset pricing model. First, we have assumed that there is no riskless asset and that no riskless borrowing or lending is allowed. Then we have assumed that there is a riskless asset and that long positions in the riskless asset are allowed but that short positions in the riskless asset (borrowing) are not allowed. In both cases, we have assumed that an investor can take unlimited long or short positions in the risky assets.

In both cases, we find that the expected return on any risky asset is a linear function of its β, just as it is without any restrictions or borrowing. If there is a riskless asset, then the slope of the line relating the expected return on a risky asset to its β must be smaller than it is when there are no restrictions on borrowing. Thus a model in which borrowing is restricted is consistent with the empirical findings reported by Black, Jensen, and Scholes.

In both cases, the risky portion of every portfolio is a weighted combination of portfolios m and z, where portfolio m is the market portfolio, and portfolio z is the minimum-variance zero-β portfolio. Portfolio z has a covariance with risky asset i proportional to $1 - \beta_i$. If there is a riskless asset, then the efficient portfolios that contain the riskless asset are all weighted combinations of the riskless asset and a single risky portfolio t. Portfolio t is the efficient portfolio of risky assets with the highest ratio of the expected difference between the return on the portfolio and the return on the riskless asset to the standard deviation of the return on the portfolio. The line relating the expected return on an efficient portfolio to its β is composed of two straight line segments, where the segment for the lower-risk portfolios has a greater slope than the segment for the higher-risk portfolios.

21

Risk, Return, and Disequilibrium: An Application to Changes in Accounting Techniques

Ray Ball*
University of Chicago

Changes in accounting techniques are commonly believed to mislead the stock market. The income of a firm can increase or decrease because of changes in "real" events affecting its operations or, alternatively, because it adopts a new technique for measuring income. If the stock market cannot distinguish the two sources of income change, then it might be mislead. That is, it might react to income changes due to underlying events and accounting changes in a similar fashion. Prior research indicates that market prices generally respond to changes in reported income;[1] it is undetermined whether prices respond to income changes that are due to changes in accounting techniques.[2] This paper aims at developing the research methodology to make that determination.[3]

I. Measuring the Market's Reaction

The market's response to new data, such as an income report, is a disequilibrium phenomenon. Understanding disequilibrium requires some notion of equilibrium. For example, the disequilibrium which is associated with a stock split must be measured relative to the behavior which "would" have occurred if the split (and correlated events) had not taken place. The "market model" of Fama, Fisher, Jensen and Roll [13] is one technique of measuring what "would" have occurred.

The theme of this paper is that one has to carefully consider the nature of equilibrium before attempting to identify market responses to new data. Sources of disequilibrium are not only many, but they can occur simultaneously. Further, it is not obvious that existing models can handle some types of disequilibria, especially changes in risks.

Reprinted by permission of the publisher and author from *Journal of Finance*, May 1972, pp. 343–54.

*This paper has been substantially improved by comments from Fischer Black, Philip Brown, Eugene Fama, and Nicholas Gonedes.

1. Ball and Brown [2].
2. Kaplan and Roll [19] provide an exception. Their research is discussed in fn. 13 below.
3. This paper emphasizes methodological issues. More detailed results are described elsewhere [1].

II. Equilibrium in the Central Market

If the capital market is in equilibrium at the end of any period $(t - 1)$ then, given the available information at that point, all assets are "correctly" priced. That is, each asset is priced such that its probability distribution of yield over any immediately ensuing period t is exactly the distribution required for that asset. In a two-parameter model one need only refer to the expected values and risks of the distributions. Thus, for each asset:

$$E(\widetilde{R}_{jt}|\phi_{t-1}) = E(\widetilde{R}_{jt}|\lambda_{jt}),\qquad (1)$$

where:

$\widetilde{R}_{jt}$ = rate of return on asset j over the period t, a random variable (denoted by the tilde);

ϕ_{t-1} = the set of all data available at the end of $(t - 1)$ concerning the probability distribution of returns from all assets during t;

λ_{jt} = risk (however defined) of asset j in period t, a characteristic of the uncertainty of rates of return and a subset of ϕ_{t-1}; and

E = the expectation operator, taken immediately prior to t.

The two-parameter models of Sharpe [25] and Black [4] provide identical definitions of risk and similar relationships between risk and expected value of rate of return. In the Black formulation:

$$E(\widetilde{R}_{jt}|\lambda_{jt}) = E(\widetilde{R}_{zt}) + [E(\widetilde{R}_{mt}) - E(\widetilde{R}_{zt})]\beta_{jt},\qquad (2)$$

where:

$\widetilde{R}_{mt}$ = rate of return on wealth during period t, commonly known as the "market index,"

$$= \sum_{j=1}^{M} x_i E(\widetilde{R}_{jt}), \text{ where } x_i \text{ is the proportion of the value of asset } i \text{ to}$$

the value of all M assets in the economy, measured at the beginning of t, with

$$\sum_{i=1}^{M} x_i = 1;$$

$\widetilde{R}_{zt}$ = rate of return on the "efficient" portfolio[4] with $\text{cov}(\widetilde{R}_{zt}, \widetilde{R}_{mt}) = 0$;

β_{jt} = the ratio of $\text{cov}(\widetilde{R}_{jt}, \widetilde{R}_{mt})$ to $\text{var}(\widetilde{R}_{mt})$.

In the Sharpe formulation, $\widetilde{R}_{zt}$ is assumed to have no variance,[5] and can be replaced by a known rate, R_{ft}.

III. Disequilibrium in the Capital Market

Receipt of new data over the period t could cause R_{jt} to differ from its expectation:

$$\widetilde{\xi}_{jt}(\phi_t) = \widetilde{R}_{jt}(\phi_t) - E(\widetilde{R}_{jt}|\phi_{t-1}). \tag{3}$$

If equilibrium existed before the new data in ϕ_t became available, then $\widetilde{\xi}_{jt}$ measures the market adjustment to the new data. Thus, we may use (1) to substitute for $E(\widetilde{R}_{jt}|\lambda_{jt})$ in (2) and may rewrite (3) as:

$$\widetilde{\xi}_{jt}(\phi_t) = \widetilde{R}_{jt}(\phi_t) - E(\widetilde{R}_{zt}) - [E(\widetilde{R}_{mt}) - E(\widetilde{R}_{zt})]\beta_{jt}$$

$$= \widetilde{R}_{jt}(\phi_t) - [1 - \beta_{jt}]E(\widetilde{R}_{zt}) - \beta_{jt}E(\widetilde{R}_{mt}). \tag{4}$$

In a "perfect" market, $E(\widetilde{\xi}_{jt}) = 0$. In an "efficient" market, $E(\widetilde{\xi}_{jt}) \doteq 0$: that is, in an "efficient" market, disequilibria are "rapidly" removed.[6]

Sources of Disequilibrium

The two-parameter models imply many sources of disequilibrium, including:

1. Information concerning the expected value of the uncertain *dollar* return to be generated by an individual investment. A firm's income report appears to contain information of this nature [2] .

---

4. A portfolio (which may consist of only one asset) is "efficient" if no other portfolio dominates it. The Markowitz definition of domination is the existence of another portfolio with either (a) higher expected return, given variance, or (b) lower variance, given expected return. The definition is generalized to cover symmetric stable distributions of return in [14, Chapters 6 and 7].

5. If such an asset existed, it obviously would be Black's efficient (minimum-variance), zero-covariance asset.

6. The efficient market hypothesis is limited in operational content until the speed of adjustment is specified precisely.

2.   Information concerning the risk of the uncertain *dollar* return from an individual investment. A change in relative risk $[\beta_{jt}]$ would change the expected *rate* of return $[E(\widetilde{R}_{jt})]$.

3.   Information concerning the expected value of the uncertain *dollar* returns to be generated by assets, in general. A report on housing starts might contain such information.

4.   At the aggregate market level, factors which change the relationship between relative risk and expected *rate* of return. An increase in aggregate risk $[\text{var}(\widetilde{R}_{mt})]$ would perhaps increase the premium for a unit of relative risk, $[E(\widetilde{R}_{mt}) - E(\widetilde{R}_{zt})]$. The expected return on the riskless asset $[E(\widetilde{R}_{zt})]$ can also change over time.

Each of these could cause $\widetilde{R}_{jt}(\phi_t)$ to differ from its expectation, with the second and fourth (involving *rates* of return) being more than temporary disturbances.

Two problems arise. First, the efficient market hypothesis implies that each source should be digested very rapidly by the market. Yet the evidence, almost without exception, relates to the first of these sources. In this sense, it is far from complete. Second, the various disequilibria can occur simultaneously, which presents numerous specification problems. Most studies ignore disequilibrium from all but the first source, but we shall see in this study that the models which ignore other sources of disequilibrium are not always satisfactory.

The Market Model

There are many possible methods (models) of measuring $\widetilde{\xi}_{jt}$. If one assumes that probability distributions of return are constant, then a perfect market will generate rates of return which are serially independent.[7] Since $E(\widetilde{R}_{jt})$ is then constant, the serial covariances of $\widetilde{R}_{jt}$ and $\widetilde{\xi}_{jt}$ are identical. Fama finds the sample serial covariances of $\widetilde{R}_{jt}$ to be reasonably close to zero [11], which implies (under the constant-distribution assumption) that the $\widetilde{\xi}_{jt}$ do not persist and that the market reacts quickly to information in general.

Fama *et al.* [13] wish to investigate a specific datum: the stock split. They are not satisfied with inspecting deviations from the sample mean, and propose the market model, with less restrictive assumptions about the distribution of returns, namely:

1. β_j and $E(\widetilde{R}_z)$ are constant (and therefore independent of *t*);

2. $\widetilde{R}_{mt} = E(\widetilde{R}_{mt}) + \epsilon_t$, where ϵ_t has zero expectation and is serially independent; and

---

7. This has come to be known as the "random walk hypothesis"[12].

3. $\tilde{R}_{mt}$ is measured without error.[8]

Then, substituting and rearranging in (4), we have:

$$R_{jt}(\phi_t) = [1 - \beta_j]E(\tilde{R}_z) + \beta_j\tilde{R}_{mt} + \tilde{\xi}_{jt}(\phi_t) - \beta_j\tilde{\epsilon}_t. \tag{5}$$

The residual (or error) $\hat{V}_{jt}$ from the Ordinary Least Squares (OLS) regression:

$$R_{jt} = \hat{b}_{1j} + \hat{b}_{2j}R_{mt} + \hat{V}_{jt} \tag{6}$$

provides an estimate of $\tilde{\xi}_{jt}(\phi_t) - \beta_j\tilde{\epsilon}_t$, where:

$\hat{bf}$ = constants for firm j, estimated by OLS; and

$\hat{V}_{jt}$ = estimated residual for firm j and period t.

Residuals are averaged across sample members to remove price movements which are unrelated to the data source under consideration.[9] Averaging is conducted across members at a point in time, with time measured relative to the dates at which the data were released. If 0 is the date of the data release (which differs among firms), then the average residual for a sample of N, cumulated from n observations before that date, is CAR_T, for each period (say, month) τ:

$$CAR = \frac{1}{N}\sum_{j=1}^{N}\sum_{t=-n}^{\tau}\hat{V}_{jt}.$$

The cumulative average residual is then inspected for systematic differences from zero. If N is "large," and if the various stocks' $\hat{V}_{jt}$ are independent, then the standard error of the CAR is "small," relative to the standard error of the V_{jt}, and the differences from zero are presumed to be significant.[10]

The market and serial-correlation models would provide alternative measurements of $\tilde{\xi}_{jt}$. Viewed in the context of the equilibrium models of Black and Sharpe, the major innovation of the market model is to allow $E(\tilde{R}_j)$ to be conditional on $E(\tilde{R}_m)$: that is, to allow the premium of a risky asset to vary.

---

8. Which is unlikely to be met by available "market" indexes of wealth. See [5, 21].

9. That is, to reduce the standard error of the average.

10. Officer [23] establishes that the standard error is well-behaved for stock price rates of return. Ball [1] and Kaplan and Roll [19] attempt to assess the significance of the differences explicitly, by estimating a stable density function for the market model residuals of each firm.

In other respects the serial-correlation and market models have identical implications for the measurement of $\widetilde{\xi}_{jt}$.[11]

Fama *et al.* find the market model "a satisfactory method for abstracting from the effects of general market conditions" [13, p. 7] . The model is used by Ball and Brown [2] , Beaver [3] , Brown [8] , Brown and Kennelly [10] , Kaplan and Roll [19] , Scholes [24] and Waud [26] to assess the impact of various data sources.

Potential Limitations of the Market Model

As a model of disequilibrium, the market model possesses several weaknesses. Many of these appear when the model is applied to a sample of 430 changes in accounting techniques over the 15 years 1947-61.[12]

1. *Aggregate disequilibrium.* —Since $\hat{V}_{jt}$ is an estimate of $(\widetilde{\xi}_{jt} - \beta_j \widetilde{\epsilon}_t)$, errors in anticipation of the market index $(\hat{\epsilon}_t)$ are impounded in the model's measurements of disequilibria. If the $\hat{V}_{jt}$ are averaged across firms at similar points in *chronological* time, then the standard deviation of the average is not relatively "small," regardless of any industry domination of one's sample, because individual-firm residuals then impound the market communality. This should not be important in this study, however, since the accounting changes are spread rather uniformly over the 15 years.[13]

2. *Mean disequilibrium for a firm.* —The *OLS* regression (6) constrains the mean $\hat{V}_{jt}$ to zero. Hence, the average amount of disequilibrium for an individual firm[14] is impounded in the intercept, $\hat{b}_{1j}$, and $\hat{V}_{jt}$ is an estimate of $(\widetilde{\xi}_{jt} - \overline{\xi}_j)$

---

11. This is a substantial improvement. One should not be confused by the historical fact that the models have been used to test market efficiency with respect to different ϕ's [12] . One could, for example, test for serial correlation in residuals from the market models, as in Ball and Brown [2, p. 167] . One could also investigate the market adjustment to an income report by plotting a cumulative average deviation of $\widetilde{R}_j$ from its sample mean, or (introducing a different model) by comparing the probabilities of (or runs in) signs of rate-of-return changes before and after the report.

12. The sample is described in [1] .

13. Note that any errors in measuring the market index and any industry communalities are also impounded in the model's estimated disequilibria.

This analysis might help to explain the results of Kaplan and Roll [19] , who use the market model for two samples of firms changing accounting techniques. The first sample is small and, furthermore, 38 of its 71 changes appear to be dominated by two industries: paper in 1965 and steel in 1968. The second sample is larger, but the accounting changes cluster in a very short period, probably in January to March, 1965 (the sample arises from the first use of the Accounting Principles Board Opinion No. 4 on accounting for the investment credit). The Kaplan and Roll results could thus reflect communalities in both samples: industry effects in one, and market-error communalities in the other. Their results for a control group [19, Figure 1, Panel B] indicate that the market model's performance as a model of disequilibrium is at least suspicious, regardless of whether the results are generated by communalities.

14. Which, under the efficient market hypothesis, can be nonzero (in retrospect) by chance.

$-\beta_j \tilde{\epsilon}_t$. This problem can be overcome by excluding from the regression those periods in which $\tilde{\xi}$ is suspected to differ from zero.

This course is followed by Fama *et al.*, who report [13, n. 9] that excluding observations makes little difference. However, they provide indirect evidence to the contrary: including all observations, no month earlier than – 15 has the number of positive residuals differing "substantially" from the number of negatives [13, p. 5]; yet, excluding such months with "substantial" differences, the average residual becomes consistently positive at month –29 [13, p. 13]. Further exclusion of months –29 to –15 from the regressions would remove more of the negative bias to their $\hat{V}_{jt}$'s and their inferences concerning pre-split information and market efficiency are therefore biased. That is, excluding those months would increase both the pre- *and* post-split residuals.

Any violation of the *OLS* assumption that $E(\hat{V}_{jt}) = 0$ leads to an under-assessment of the *CAR*'s pre-month-zero movements and a post-announcement-date bias toward zero.[15] Unless one's prior estimate of the period to exclude from the regressions includes all the abnormal residual behavior, a recursive extension of the Fama *et al.* exclusion procedure must be adopted. The regressions must be run, the residuals (or errors) inspected for abnormal behavior and the regressions re-run until the market disequilibrium appears to be entirely contained in the errors from the excluded period.

This is a clumsy and dangerous procedure. It is clumsy because: (a) *OLS* is used to identify periods of nonzero residuals to exclude, whereas (b) they are biased toward zero and thus difficult to identify. It is dangerous because the data are over-worked.[16]

Results from this procedure are presented in Table 21-1. The initial run reveals unfavorable pre-announcement performance and the hypothesized post-announcement bias. The former is accentuated and the latter is reduced in successive iterations, excluding more and more observations. The cumulative average residual at the month of change is finally estimated at – .32 or 32 per cent, over a total of 13 years and 3 months. The post-change residuals (errors) are no longer of predominantly opposite sign to their pre-change counterparts.

3. *Disequilibrium in R_z.*—The "riskless" rate is endogenous in the market model.[17] The intercept $\hat{b}_{1j}$ is an estimate of $(1 - \beta_j)\bar{R}_z$ is the implicit sample mean R_z. The $\hat{V}_{jt}$ impound $(1 - \beta_j) [E(\tilde{R}_{zt}) - \bar{R}_z]$, which can be nonzero due to both sampling fluctuations and changes in $E(\tilde{R}_{zt})$.[18]

Black, Jensen and Scholes [6, Table 5] give evidence that R_z increased steadily through 1931-65. This could be a problem because the market model regressions are conducted over predominantly post-change data, whereas the regression estimates are also used in predictions for *earlier* months, in which R_z

---

15. When *no* observations are excluded the *CAR* returns to zero. A similar, though lesser, bias occurs in the case of partial exclusion.

16. A cross-validation would remove this objection.

17. One version of the model [(2, n.16), 19] uses a government bond series as a surrogate for the riskless rate. In [2] this offers no discernible improvement.

18. Sampling fluctuations do not exist in the Sharpe version.

320 THE TWO-PARAMETER PRICING MODEL

Table 21-1
Cumulative Average Residuals—Market Model[a]

Regression Run	Number of Changes[b]	Months for Regressions			CAR		
		Total	Excluded	Included[c]	Month 0	Month + 99	Difference
1	430	− 99 to +99	none	− 99 to + 99	−.10	−.01	+.09
2	291	− 99 to +99	− 79 to +19	− 99 to − 80 +20 to + 99	−.16	−.13	+.03
3	276	−139 to +99	−119 to +19	−139 to −120 + 20 to + 99	−.24	−.22	+.02
4	267	−159 to +99	−139 to +19	−159 to −140 + 20 to + 99	−.32	−.36	−.04

[a]Errors (not residuals) in excluded period.

[b]Sample size decreases as more price data are required for regressions.

[c]Regressions are run on predominantly post-change months to avoid losing many more sample members. The length of the period investigated is due to the prior belief that accounting changes are "important" events and thus are possibly associated with "long term" market responses.

presumably is lower. If the average sample value of $(1 - \beta_j)$ is nonzero, then rates of return are systematically over- or under-predicted in pre-change months, giving a false appearance of disequilibrium.

An alternative to the market model is suggested by Fama. This "cross-sectional" model is adapted from the grouping technique of Fama and Officer [15], which follows the work of Black *et al.* [6] and Miller and Scholes [22]. It provides estimates of the intercept which can vary over time and which are essentially independent of the mean information for an individual firm. It thus attempts to overcome two of the major weaknesses of the market model.

The Cross-Sectional Model

Disequilibria in the cross-sectional model are estimated by a multi-stage procedure. One such procedure is outlined below.

Stage 1.—The *OLS* regression (6) is used to estimate the relative risks (β_j) of each of the stocks on the CRSP file of NYSE common stocks, using all available *even* months of data.[19] Stocks are ranked by their estimated risks. Ten portfolios of relatively homogeneous risk are formed by grouping together the stocks which fall between the deciles of the distribution of risks (thus, the highest 10 per cent are grouped together and so on down to the portfolio of the 10 per cent lowest estimated risks).

Stage 2.—The relative risks (β_p) of the 10 portfolios are estimated, again using (6), but this time using only the *odd* months. Separate data are used in the first two stages to ensure that the β_p are estimated from data which are independent of those used to form portfolios.[20]

Stage 3.—A separate risk-return relationship is estimated across portfolios in each period:

$$R_{pt} = c_{1t} + c_{2t}\beta_p + U_{pt}, \text{ in each } t, \tag{7}$$

where: bf_t = constants for each t. Aggregating into portfolios is designed to reduce measurement error in the independent variable of (7), which arises because the $\hat{\beta}_p$ are regression estimates subject to sampling error.[21]

---

19. For example, over CRSP months 248, 250, . . . , 354 for a firm with price data from month 248 to 355.

20. The portfolio rate of return is calculated as a simple average of its members' rates of return.

21. Forming portfolios on *ranked* individual risks maximizes the dispersion of the independent variable in (7). The choice of 10 portfolios is an arbitrary trade-off between reducing the standard error of estimate of a portfolio's risk, as its size increases, and reducing the number of observations for (7). Note that many different ways of estimating a cross-sectional relationship are possible. See [15].

Disequilibria for a firm are then measured as errors from a monthly prediction:

$$\hat{U}_{jt} = R_{jt} - \hat{C}_{1t} - \hat{C}_{2t}\hat{\beta}_{jt}. \tag{8}$$

The cross-sectional intercept $\hat{C}_{2t}$ is an estimate of the realized "riskless" rate, R_{zt}, and the cross-sectional slope $\hat{C}_{2t}$ is an estimate of the realized risk premium, $(R_{mt} - R_{zt})$. Since (7) is estimated each period, both the intercept and the slope can vary over time. Furthermore, $\hat{C}_{1t}$ depends only marginally upon individual-firm disequilibrium, since all firms are represented in the cross-sectional regressions.

Risk Changes

Four broad categories of disequilibrium were initially distinguished. The market model, when compared with a "serial correlation" model, was seen to isolate the third category, the effect of the "market." One advantage of the cross-sectional model was seen to be its control for the fourth category, changes in risk premiums.[22] So far, no attempt has been made to distinguish the first and second categories. That is, risk changes are problematic.

Prior evidence indicates that accounting techniques are grouped by industries.[23] It is also known that industries differ in average risks [9, 20]. Thus, changes in accounting techniques could be associated with changes in industry emphasis and changes in the β_j. The two-parameter models (2) would then predict different rates of return over the periods with different risks. The different rates of return could easily be confused by both the cross-sectional and market models with the existence of persistent disequilibrium. Thus, it is important to investigate the possibility of risk changes.

A moving series of 101 months' observations is used to estimate the β_j, employing *OLS*. For example, the observations used to estimate the β_j for month -109 are the rates of return for month -159 through month -49. The β_j for month -108 are estimated from -158 through -48, and so on. Results for the 267 accounting changes reported in Table 21-1 are surprising: the average β shifts distinctly upward, from .909 at month -109 to .995 at month 0 and

---

22. Once one controls for R_m, controlling for R_z involves controlling for $(R_m - R_z)$, the standardized risk premium.

23. It is well-known that audit firms both specialize by industries and have preferred accounting techniques. Further, Gonedes provides evidence [17, Table 4] that there is a very low probability that accounting techniques are independent of industry classes, his interpretation notwithstanding.

1.028 at month +49.[24] The constant-risk assumption possibly has led to an over-estimation of risk in the early months and thus to an over-prediction of expected returns. An over-prediction of returns would induce the negative errors which are observed in Table 21-1.

Cross-Sectional Model with Risk Changes

Changes in risk present a formidable estimation problem because few observations are available when the parameters can be assumed constant. The procedure adopted is arbitrary but, in the absence of independent evidence on the timing of risk shifts, it will have to do.

The procedure is an *OLS* estimate from a moving series of 100 observations. Thus, the β_{jt} for (8) are estimated from data for $(t - 50)$ through $(t + 50)$, excluding month t.

Results

Results fall into three categories.

1. The cumulative error, cumulated from month -109, is now $-.05$ at the month of the accounting change. This represents an average *monthly* rate of approximately $-.05$ of 1 per cent, which does not differ significantly from zero. Thus, most of the disequilibrium apparent in Table 21-1 has been explained. The remaining $-.05$ is quite possibly due to errors in measuring risk in individual periods.

2. The market appears to adjust to the disequilibrium caused by risk changes. The sample average rate of return increases concurrently with the increase in risk, a result which is consistent with the asset pricing models and therefore with market efficiency.

3. Averages conceal differences between individual firms and different accounting changes. One analysis of individual firms is to separate those changes which increased income from those which decreased income. On the basis of χ^2 tests one can conclude that there is no association between the signs of the $\hat{U}_{jt}$ and the sign of the effect on income of the accounting change. This even holds in the 12 months before the annual report is released. Interim income reports and income forecasts can reflect changes in accounting techniques which are not necessarily disclosed until the annual report, yet the market does not appear to react to the accounting change in the pre-disclosure months. These

---

24. There is no reason to suspect that firms in general which change accounting techniques should increase in risk. However, one might argue that any changes which do occur would, on average, be toward unity. Note that the observations for O and +49 are not independent. For work on risk changes, see [7, 16, 18].

results contrast with those of Ball and Brown [2] for typical income changes. Thus, the market appears to react "efficiently" to an income report which reflects a change in accounting technique. It is able to ignore the change in accounting method.

IV. Conclusions

Measuring disequilibrium is complicated by the simultaneity of the various sources of disequilibrium. To isolate particular sources, such as those which are unique to the individual firm, one must take a model of equilibrium and identify its major violations. The "cross-sectional" model appears to be an improvement in this regard.

After isolating various sources of disequilibrium, it appears that the average risk of the sample of firms changing accounting techniques has increased. This is unlikely to hold for all firms which change accounting techniques. It is difficult to handle risk changes in the disequilibrium models. Using a moving-average procedure for measuring risk, it appears that changes in accounting techniques are not associated with other market disequilibria and that the efficient market hypothesis is not contradicted. Further results are presented in [1].

References

1. Ray Ball. "Changes in Accounting Techniques and Stock Prices," *Empirical Research in Accounting: Selected Studies, 1972.* Supplement to the *Journal of Accounting Research.*
2. —— and Philip Brown. "An Empirical Evaluation of Accounting Income Numbers," *Journal of Accounting Research* VI (Autumn, 1968), 159–178.
3. William H. Beaver. "The Information Content of Annual Earnings Announcements," *Empirical Research in Accounting: Selected Studies, 1968.* Supplement to the *Journal of Accounting Research* VI, 67–92.
4. Fischer Black. "Capital Market Equilibrium with Restricted Borrowing," Unpublished manuscript (April, 1971). Forthcoming in *Journal of Business.*
5. —— and M. Jensen. "Incomplete Measurement of Market Returns and Its Implications for Tests of the Asset Pricing Model," Unpublished manuscript, November, 1970.
6. ——, —— and M. Scholes. "The Capital Asset Pricing Model: Some Empirical Results," *Studies in the Theory of Capital Markets.* M. Jensen (ed.). New York: Praeger, 1972.
7. Marshall E. Blume. "Portfolio Theory: A Step Toward its Practical Application," *Journal of Business* XLIII (1970), 152–173.

8. Philip Brown. "The Impact of the Annual Net Profit Report on the Stock Market," *The Australian Accountant* XL (July, 1970), 277–283.
9. —— and Ray Ball. "Some Preliminary Findings on the Association Between the Earnings of a Firm, Its Industry, and the Economy," *Empirical Research in Accounting: Selected Studies, 1967.* Supplement to the *Journal of Accounting Research* V, 55–85.
10. —— and John W. Kennelly. "The Information Content of Quarterly Earnings: A Clarification and an Extension," Forthcoming in *Journal of Business.*
11. Eugene F. Fama. "The Behavior of Stock Market Prices," *Journal of Business* XXXVIII (January, 1965), 34–105.
12. ——. "Efficient Capital Markets: A Review of Theory and Empirical Work," *Journal of Finance* XXV (May, 1970), 383–417.
13. ——, Lawrence Fisher, Michael C. Jensen and Richard Roll. "The Adjustment of Stock Prices to New Information," *International Economic Review* X (February, 1969), 1–21.
14. —— and Merton Miller. *The Theory of Finance.* New York: Holt, Rinehart and Winston, Inc., 1972.
15. —— and R.R. Officer. "Risk, Return and Equilibrium: Empirical Tests." Unpublished manuscript, University of Chicago, July, 1971.
16. Lawrence Fisher. "The Estimation of Systematic Risk: Some New Findings." (In preparation.) Preliminary results discussed at the Seminar on the Analysis of Security Prices, University of Chicago, May, 1970.
17. Nicholas J. Gonedes. "The Significance of Selected Accounting Procedures: A Statistical Test," *Empirical Research in Accounting: Selected Studies, 1969.* Supplement to the *Journal of Accounting Research* VII, 90–113.
18. ——. "Evidence on the Information Content of Accounting Numbers," Paper presented at the Workshop in Accounting Research, Graduate School of Business, University of Chicago, January 12, 1971.
19. Robert Kaplan and Richard Roll. "Investor Evaluation of Accounting Information: Some Empirical Evidence," Unpublished manuscript, Carnegie-Mellon University, October, 1970. (Forthcoming in *Journal of Business.*)
20. Benjamin F. King. "Market and Industry Factors in Stock Price Behavior," *Journal of Business* XXXIX (Supplement, 1966), 139–190.
21. David Mayers. "Non-Marketable Assets and Capital Market Equilibrium under Uncertainty," *Studies in the Theory of Capital Markets.* M. Jensen (ed.). New York: Praeger, 1972.
22. Merton H. Miller and Myron Scholes. "Rates of Return in Relation to Risk: A Re-examination of Some Recent Findings," *Studies in the Theory of Capital Markets.* M. Jensen (ed.). New York: Praeger, 1972.
23. Robert R. Officer. "Time Series Examination of the Risks Implied by the Market Model." Unpublished manuscript, University of Chicago, August, 1970.
24. Myron Scholes. "A Test of the Competitive Market Hypothesis: An Examination of the Market for New Issues and Secondary Offerings."

Doctoral dissertation, Graduate School of Business, University of Chicago, 1970.

25. William F. Sharpe. "Capital Asset Prices: A Theory of Market Equilibrium Under Conditions of Risk," *Journal of Finance* XIX (September, 1964), 425–442.

26. Roger N. Waud. "Public Interpretation of Discount Rate Changes: Evidence on the 'Announcement Effect.' " Forthcoming in *Econometrica*.

Part VIII
Ex Post Portfolio Performance

22 Risk-Return Measures of Ex Post Portfolio Performance*

Keith V. Smith
University of California, Los Angeles

Dennis A. Tito
University of California, Los Angeles

Risk continues to be a widely discussed topic within the field of finance. Academicians add risk variables to their quantitative models, while financial practitioners include risk considerations in their qualitative deliberations. In both contexts, risk—together with some measure of profit or return—generally comprise a dual or composite criteria for investment decision-making purposes. Whereas the decision-making situation can be described as *ex ante*, this article deals with risk in an *ex post* context. In particular, it reports an investigation of alternative risk-return measures which are designed to rank and evaluate the *ex post* performance of investment portfolios. Section I reviews three composite measures of performance and examines their interrelationships. A fourth alternative measure is also suggested. In Section II, the measures are used to rank the portfolio performance of a sample of mutual funds. Some difficulties in making performance comparisons of these funds against the market are discussed in Section III. The final section briefly explores the implications of the study and suggests areas for subsequent research.

I. Three Alternative Ranking Methods

Recent developments in the theory of portfolio management have led to an improved understanding of the criteria necessary for evaluation of investment performance. A large part of this effort has been directed toward the assessment of mutual fund performance. Comparisons have been made between funds and with randomly selected portfolios. The consensus now prevailing in the literature is that mutual funds, on the average, have not been able to

Reprinted by permission of the publisher and author from *Journal of Financial and Quantitative Analysis*, December 1969, pp. 449–470.

*The authors acknowledge the helpful comments of Professors J. Fred Weston and John P. Shelton and the useful suggestions of the referee. The research study was supported, in part, through a grant from Shareholders Management Company to the U.C.L.A. Division of Research.

329

outperform the market and that there is little reason to believe that individual funds can do any better than can be expected to occur as a result of chance.[1] Comparisons of investment performance traditionally have been based on measures of the return achieved by certain portfolios as well as by the overall market as represented by certain indices or averages. Only recently has the concept of risk been explicitly considered in such performance comparisons. Since risk is not, by itself, a particularly useful quantity, composite measure of risk and return become appropriate. Recent studies by Treynor, Sharpe, and Jensen include alternative composite measures for ranking *ex post* investment performance.

Nevertheless, it is well to build the discussion of *ex post* composite measurements upon a theoretical concept that was developed for the *ex ante* case. Both Lintner [4] and Sharpe [5, 6] have demonstrated that the important dimensions of risk and return can be combined in the expression,

$$\theta = \frac{E - r^*}{\sqrt{V}},\tag{1}$$

where E represents expected portfolio return, V is the variance of portfolio return, and r^* is the certain return from a risk-free investment. In addition to portfolio selection, Lintner [4] also suggests a version of θ for selecting one stock among many, or one mutual fund among many, to hold along with a risk-free asset.

The composite measure θ may be interpreted as the excess portfolio return per unit of portfolio risk—but where measurement is based on expectations rather than observation. Lintner demonstrated that that portfolio of risky investments which maximizes θ should be viewed as the optimal (and unique) solution to the problem of portfolio selection, and thus the θ criterion effectively combines *ex ante* return and risk. The three *ex post* measures of investment performance are closely related to this theoretical concept. The three measures will be referred to as Sharpe variability, Treynor Volatility, and Jensen Predictability.

Sharpe Variability

In a recent paper on mutual fund performance, Sharpe [5] presented a composite measure, Φ, which exhibits a similar form to θ, as follows

$$\Phi = \frac{\bar{Y} - r^*}{S},\tag{2}$$

---

1. For example, see [9].

where $\bar{Y}$ is the average yield over N prior periods and S is the standard deviation of those N historical observations. In other words, Φ is interpreted as the excess portfolio yield per unit of *ex post* risk.[2] The reward-to-variability measure Φ, if calculated for each member of a sample of funds or portfolios, can be used as a composite measure for ranking and comparing *ex post* performance.

As will be shown presently, variance S^2, which is taken as a measure of portfolio risk, can be decomposed into two important components. The first component is referred to as systematic risk and has to do with the riskiness of the portfolio that is inherent in the market itself. The second component— residual risk—is not attributed to general market movements but is unique to the particular security or portfolio under consideration.[3]

Treynor Volatility

To be more explicit about systematic and residual risk, it is convenient to turn to another composite measure which was suggested in a well-publicized paper by Treynor [7]. His procedure was to plot for each of N prior years, the annual values of *ex post* yield Y_t by a given portfolio versus the corresponding yields I_t which were achieved by the market as a whole. Figure 1 illustrates a plot of ten sets of values (Y_t, I_t) for a hypothetical portfolio. Treynor referred to the straight line, fitted by the method of least squares, through these points as the Characteristic Line of the fund or portfolio. As indicated in Figure 1, A and B refer respectively to the intercept and slope of the characteristic line. The underlying model is:

$$Y_t = A + BI_t + u_t, \tag{3}$$

where U_t is an error term with expected value of zero, but with a finite variance. The Characteristic Line portrays the responsiveness of portfolio yields to changes in yields obtainable from the market.

The component of total variation in Y_t, which is explained by the characteristic line, is simply a measure of the systematic risk as described above, while the unexplained variation corresponds to residual risk. Presumably, an individual portfolio manager has little if any effect on the systematic risk of the market. Since investors are thought to be adverse to risk as measured by the variation in Y_t, then any attempts of the portfolio manager to reduce risk via diversification must be manifested in the residual risk component. Therefore, if all points fall

---

2. Use of these particular measures of return and risk will not be defended at this point. For an excellent discussion of measures of return, see Levy [3]. Conversely, measures of *ex post* risk have been discussed by Friend and Vickers [1]. Among their measures, intertemporal.variability is usually preferred.

3. For further discussion of these risk components, see Lintner [4] and Sharpe [5].

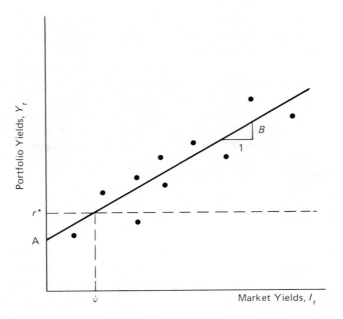

Figure 1. Characteristic Line, Volatility, and Composite Performance Measure for a Representative Portfolio

on the Characteristic Line the portfolio exhibits only systematic risk. Since mutual funds generally exhibit widespread diversification, Treynor suggested that the slope of the Characteristic Line, B, be taken as a measure of *ex post* risk. It is often referred to as portfolio or fund volatility in contrast with portfolio variability which includes both components of risk.

In formulating his performance measure, Treynor substituted portfolio volatility for variability in Sharpe's performance measure as follows

$$\psi' = \frac{\bar{Y} - r^*}{B}. \tag{4}$$

Treynor then demonstrated that rankings consistent with this measure of fund performance could be obtained directly from the coefficients of (3). Moreover, the measure as denoted by ψ in Figure 1, is defined by the intersection of the Characteristic Line and a horizontal line through the risk-free rate, r^*, which is measured on the vertical axis. In terms of the parameters which have been identified,

$$\psi = \frac{r^* - A}{B}.$$

(5)

This measure may be interpreted as the particular level of the market for which the portfolio manager has been able, over a past period of time, to produce a portfolio yield equal to the risk-free yield attainable, for example, from a savings-and-loan account. The smaller the value of ψ, the better the *ex post* performance of the fund. If two characteristic lines were exactly parallel, then the one higher in the space would exhibit a lower ψ and thus would exhibit the preferred performance.

It can be shown that ψ is consistent with Φ if a fund is assumed to be perfectly diversified. To do so, let yield, as given by (3), be viewed as a random variable having as parameters, mean

$$\bar{Y} = A + B\bar{I}$$

(6)

and variance

$$S^2 = V(Y_t) = B^2 V(I_t) + V(U_t),$$

(7)

where $\bar{I}$ and $V(I_t)$ are the mean and variance of market yield which is the independent variable. On the right side of (7), the first term represents systematic risk while the second is residual risk. If the latter is assumed to be zero, then $S^2 = B^2 V(I_t)$ and upon taking the square root of both sides

$$S = B\sigma_I,$$

(8)

where σ_I is the standard deviation of market yield. Substituting (6) and (8) into (2) gives

$$\Phi = \frac{A + B\bar{I} - r^*}{B\sigma_I},$$

(9)

which, upon re-arrangement, gives

$$\Phi = \frac{\bar{I}}{\sigma_I} - \frac{1}{\sigma_I}\left[\frac{r^* - A}{B}\right],$$

(10)

where the bracketed quantity is recognized as ψ. Because $\bar{I}$ and σ_I pertain to the market, the inverse relationship between Φ and ψ is noted. That is, as ψ gets smaller (preferred performance according to Treynor), Φ gets larger (preferred performance according to Sharpe). Hence, Treynor Volatility and Sharpe Variability are equivalent measures for portfolios with no residual risk.

Jensen Predictability

A somewhat different approach was taken by Jensen [2]. In contrast to the (Y_t, I_t) space of Figure 1, Jensen worked with the excess yields $Y_t - r^*$ and $I_t - r^*$ as indicated in Figure 2. Based on an underlying capital asset model, Jensen developed the following

$$Y_t - r^* = \alpha + \beta[I_t - r^*] + e_t, \tag{11}$$

where α and β are the intercept and slope terms, respectively, of a least squares

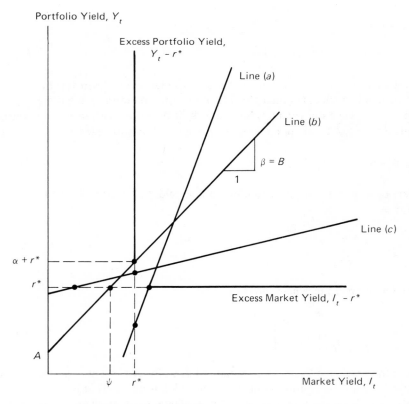

Figure 2. Geometric Comparison of Treynor Volatility and Jensen Predictability

line, and e_t is a random term with zero mean. The logic behind this model suggests that if the portfolio manager is a superior predictor of security prices, then the intercept term will turn out to be positive. Moreover, if the least squares line is based on past performance, α becomes another candidate scheme for ranking and comparing *ex post* performance. Once again, it is a composite measure with the property that, for a given fund or portfolio, the higher α is, the better the performance. Not unlike Treynor's ψ measure, Jensen's method assumes that portfolios are well diversified such that residual risk is not considered.

In subsequent discussion, Treynor [8] points out that while Jensen's α measure is appropriate for determining whether a fund "outperformed" a "buy-the-market and hold" strategy, it is not suitable for ranking portfolios relative to one another. The relationship between the A and B of Treynor and the α and β of Jensen is illustrated in Figure 2. Rewriting expression (3) and excluding the error term, one obtains

$$Y_t = [A - (1 - B)r^*] + B(I_t - r^*) \tag{12}$$

which, when compared with (11), indicates the identities $\beta = B$ and $\alpha = A - (1 - B)r^*$.

It is not clear, however, that ranking by Jensen's predictability measure, α, is consistent with a ranking by Treynor's volatility measure, ψ. For example, Characteristic Line (c) in Figure 2 simultaneously has a smaller ψ (superior performance) and a smaller α (inferior performance) than Characteristic Line (b). This is an inconsistency. If only parallel Characteristic Lines were involed this phenomenon would never occur. It serves to indicate the importance of fund volatility, β, in ranking portfolio performance.

This may be made explicit by substituting the above identities into (5) as follows

$$\psi = \frac{r^* - [\alpha + (1 - B)r^*]}{\beta}. \tag{13}$$

This simplifies to

$$\psi = r^* - \frac{\alpha}{\beta} \tag{14}$$

which was used by Treynor [8] to show how his ψ measure is related to Jensen's α index.

During the development of the composite measures for *ex post* portfolio performance, the risk-free rate r^* has been assumed to be constant. Although this is reasonable within a given period, it may not be so over a longer horizon. The next section will include the risk-free rate as a variable. Because r^* is treated as a constant in (14), however, an alternative version of the Treynor measure would be to ignore r^* and concentrate on the ratio α/β. By using this version, the measures of Treynor and Jensen would rank portfolio performance in the same direction; that is, the higher the value the better the management. It also focuses on their basic difference—namely, the slope parameter β. The ratio α/β will be included, along with the other three composite measures, in the empirical analysis which follows. It will be referred to as the "modified Jensen" measure since its calculation and use depends on the statistical model proposed by Jensen.

II. Empirical Comparisons Among Portfolios

The remainder of the paper is concerned with the application of composite measures to *ex post* portfolio performance. In this section, a comparison is made of the composite measures when they are used to rank performance among a group of mutual funds.[4] The next section deals with comparisons of fund performance against the overall market.

The mutual fund performance data used in this study consisted of quarterly observations of prices, dividends, and capital gains distributions for each fund. The investigation covered the 40-quarter period, 1958–1967. The continuously compounded quarterly return Y_t for each fund during period t was computed from

$$Y_t = \log_e \left[\frac{P_t + D_t + C_t}{P_{t-1}} \right],$$ \hfill (15)

where P_t is the share price of each fund at the end of period t, D_t is the per-share cash dividend paid during period t, and C_t is the capital gains distributed during period t. In calculating these returns for all funds and periods, it was assumed that dividends and capital gain distributions were taken in cash and held to the end of the period at which time they were re-invested in the fund.

The sample consisted of 38 mutual funds. It was randomly selected from a larger population of 77 funds for which data were readily available.[5] The

---

4. Although mutual funds are but one of several distinct examples of professional investment management, they are typically the subject of empirical analyses because of data availability. The theoretical concepts should apply, of course, to all institutional portfolios.

5. Source of the data was selected issues of *Barrons*. Because quarterly data in that source does not provide proper adjustment of dividend and capital gains distribution data during stock splits, the larger population was limited to those funds not making stock splits during the observation period.

Table 22-1
Identification of Mutual Funds in the Sample

Fund Member	Mutual Fund	Classification*
1	American Mututal Fund	Growth with Income
2	Concord Fund	Growth
3	Crown West Dallas Fund	Growth
4	General Investors Trust	Growth, Income, and Stability
5	Growth Industry Shares	Growth
6	Income Fund of Boston	Income
7	Keystone S-1	Growth with Income
8	Massachusetts Investors Trust	Growth with Income
9	National Securities–Balanced	Growth, Income, and Stability
10	National Securities–Stock	Income with Growth
11	Puritan Fund	Income
12	Shareholders Trust of Boston	Growth, Income, and Stability
13	Sovereign Investors Fund	Income with Growth
14	United Accumulative Fund	Growth with Income
15	Wisconsin Fund	Growth with Income
16	Affiliated Fund	Growth with Income
17	L.B. Allen Fund	Growth
18	American Business Shares	Growth, Income, and Stability
19	Axe-Houghton A	Growth, Income, and Stability
20	Colonial Fund	Income with Growth
21	Counselors Investors Fund	Growth, Income, and Stability
22	deVegh Mutual Fund	Growth
23	Equity Fund	Growth with Income
24	Fidelity Fund	Growth with Income
25	Financial Indicators Fund	Growth with Income
26	Group Securities–Aerospace	Growth
27	Guardian Mutual Fund	Growth with Income
28	Investors Stock Fund	Growth with Income
29	Keystone K-1	Income
30	Keystone S-2	Income with Growth
31	Rexington Trust Fund	Growth, Income, and Stability
32	Mutual Trust	Income with Growth
33	National Securities–Dividend	Income with Growth
34	State Street Investors	Growth with Income
35	Sterling Investors Fund	Growth, Income, and Stability
36	Texas Fund	Growth
37	Wall Street Investors	Income with Growth
38	Value Line–Income	Income

*As classified by *Fundscope*.

selected funds are identified and classified in Table 22-1. The sample is seen to be representative across the different fund categories.

The standard used for the computation of market returns was the Standard and Poor's Composite Stock Price Index which consists of 500 issues. The continuously compounded market returns I_t for a given quarter t were obtained from

Table 22-2
Selected Regression Statistics for Mutual Fund Sample, 1958-1967

Fund Member	MODEL: $Y_t = A + BI_t + u_t$			MODEL: $Y_t - r_t^* = \alpha + \beta(I_t - r_t^*) + e_t$		
	$\hat{A}$	$\hat{B}$	Regression Coefficient	$\hat{\alpha}$	$\hat{\beta}$	Regression Coefficient
1	.004255	.8868	.9747	.003308	.8865	.9753
2	-.007975	1.0863	.8493	-.007061	1.0776	.8492
3	-.005274	1.2442	.8938	-.002981	1.2333	.8929
4	.004173	.6144	.9031	.000824	.6190	.9051
5	.004173	1.1667	.9586	-.002622	1.1598	.9583
6	.009304	.5604	.8913	.005408	.5693	.8912
7	-.001575	.9639	.9756	-.001867	.9633	.9760
8	-.002172	.9948	.9889	-.002220	.9950	.9891
9	.004104	.5361	.8925	.000057	.5425	.8939
10	.002050	.8896	.9469	.001071	.8919	.9479
11	.012264	.7915	.8936	.010454	.7940	.8956
12	.006332	.7324	.8800	.004131	.7299	.8829
13	-.001983	.9615	.9675	-.002332	.9627	.9681
14	.000000	.9497	.9710	-.000438	.9505	.9716
15	.004270	.8900	.9533	.003353	.8896	.9542
16	.005406	.8843	.9747	.004414	.8850	.9754
17	.012551	.7385	.8071	.010360	.7379	.8102
18	.007608	.4993	.8963	.003286	.5041	.8994
19	.010854	.7898	.7747	.009252	.7818	.7760
20	.005703	.8396	.9544	.004342	.8400	.9554
21	.001336	.6655	.8851	-.001543	.6683	.8878
22	.001580	1.0285	.9031	.001971	1.0214	.9034
23	.002129	.9231	.9722	.001487	.9229	.9728
24	.003006	1.0050	.9652	.003089	1.0031	.9656
25	-.003657	1.1225	.9423	-.002491	1.1162	.9423
26	-.012601	1.2170	.8183	-.010377	1.1985	.8153
27	-.007499	.8827	.9542	.006547	.8810	.9552
28	-.005024	1.0509	.9821	-.004583	1.0503	.9824
29	.008571	.5375	.8822	.004567	.5425	.8850
30	.000171	.9683	.9616	-.000139	.9704	.9624
31	.003446	.5994	.8507	-.000046	.6049	.8537
32	-.006134	.8727	.9468	-.007197	.8723	.9479
33	.008036	.8005	.8315	.006276	.8042	.8347
34	.005030	.9234	.9314	.004456	.9201	.9324
35	.004505	.6315	.9099	.001299	.6362	.9116
36	.003730	.8582	.9479	.002483	.8606	.9489
37	.001549	.8177	.9611	.000021	.8173	.9622
38	.010302	.7025	.8371	.007734	.7054	.8404

$$I_t = \log_e \left[\frac{H_t + Q_t}{H_{t-1}} \right], \tag{16}$$

where H_t is the level of the index at the end of period t and Q_t is the dividend paid during that period.

Estimates of the risk-free interest rate were computed from the 91-day Treasury Bill discount rates existing at the beginning of each quarter during the horizon. The continuously compounded rates r_t^* were calculated by

$$r_t^* = \log_e \left[1 + \frac{d_{t-1}}{4(1 - d_{t-1})} \right], \tag{17}$$

where d_{t-1} is the 91-day maturity discount rate expressed as an annual rate and measured at the beginning of period t.

Using the quarterly values of Y_t, I_t, and r_t^* so calculated, two least-squares regressions were performed for each fund. The first regression was based on the statistical model given in (3), while the second regression made use of (11). Estimates of the intercept and slope coefficients, together with values of the regression coefficient, for each fund are presented as Table 22-2.

The statistical estimators from the regression analyses were then used to compute the composite measures for each mutual fund in the sample. Comparison were then made of the *ex post* performance rankings according to Sharpe Φ, Treynor ψ, Jensen α, and the modified Jensen α/β. Selected paired rankings appear as Figure 3. The comparisons reveal that the four composite measures are highly correlated. Not surprisingly, the Treynor ψ and the modified Jensen α/β measures exhibited the highest (.999) correlation. Also to be noted is the higher (.986) correlation between the Jensen α and Treynor ψ measures than between the Sharpe Φ and Treynor ψ measures (.968). This is also not unexpected since the Sharpe measure includes residual risk while the Jensen and Treynor methods include only the systematic component of risk. The rank correlation across all four composite measures was .983. From these results, one concludes that the risk-return measures do a comparable job of ranking and evaluating *ex post* performance among a group of funds or portfolios.

III. Empirical Comparisons With the Market

Having considered inter-fund performance comparisons, attention is now turned to comparisons of fund performance with a market standard. In a recent paper, Sharpe [6] computed his reward-to-variability measure, Φ, for 14 funds based on their annual performance during the period 1954–1963. A constant risk-free interest rate was assumed. A comparison of fund performance with that of a portfolio consisting of the thirty common stocks comprising the Dow Jones Industrial Average revealed that eleven funds did better than the Dow-Jones portfolio, while 23 did worse. The average Φ value for the funds in the sample was 0.633, as compared to 0.667 for the popular market average. An additional comparison using gross performance data revealed that 19 funds did better than the market and 15 funds did worse.

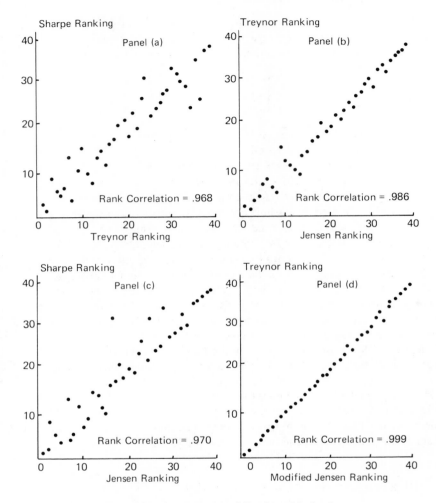

Figure 3. Comparison of Ranking Methods

    In the empirical study of mutual fund performance by Jensen [2], an
analysis was made of the returns on the portfolios of 115 open-end mutual funds
during the period 1945-1964. As a market standard, Jensen used the Standard
and Poor's Composite (500 stocks) Index. Using his α index as a measure of
performance, Jensen found that the average fund earned about 1.1 percent less
per year than it should have earned given its level of systematic risk. He also
found that a frequency distribution of the estimated α̂ measures was skewed
toward the low side with 76 funds having α̂ < 0 (performance inferior to
the Standard and Poor's market standard), and only 39 funds with α̂ > 0.

Estimates based on gross returns provided an average $\hat{\alpha}$ of $-.4$ percent per year, with 67 funds having $\hat{\alpha} < 0$ and 48 for which $\hat{\alpha} > 0$. Then, in an effort to determine if any individual fund possessed a superior forecasting ability, a study was made of the frequency distributions of "t" values of the $\hat{\alpha}$ performance estimates. The distributions revealed a definite skewness toward negative values and no evidence of an ability to forecast security prices. This conclusion held even when gross returns were used to compute such a statistic.

The problem with both of these studies is that their conclusions, as to whether mutual fund managers do better or worse than unmanaged market portfolios, depend critically on certain assumptions and the particular method which was used.[6] The rest of this section is devoted to a closer analysis of assumptions, empirical data, and procedures for statistical estimation.

First, in continuing the empirical analyses of the Sharpe and Jensen studies, it was necessary to determine the extent to which the exclusion of residual risk in the Jensen study biases its results in favor of the funds. The influence of residual risk may be determined from Figure 4, which presents summary frequency distributions of the performance estimates for the 38 funds of this study, but using the measurement technique of Sharpe and Treynor, respectively.[7]

A comparison of the two measures reveals that the Treynor Volatility measure provides a much more favorable view of fund performance than does the Sharpe Variability index. The vertical line at .0214 in Figure 4 represents the performance of the Standard and Poor's Composite Index. The average Treynor Volatility index value of .0237 for the sample of 38 funds indicates that the performance of these funds was considerably better than the market standard. The average performance as measured by the Sharpe Variability index (.0216), however, was only slightly larger than the market standard. Further, it was found that 18 of the 38 funds out-performed the market according to the Sharpe Variability index, while 25 of the 38 provided superior performance according to the Treynor Volatility index. From the rather significant differences in mutual fund performance, as measured by Sharpe and Treynor measures, it does appear that residual risk is an important factor in determining whether funds outperform market portfolios.

The second factor to be considered was the effect of including the risk-free interest rate, r_t^*, as part of both the dependent and independent variables in Jensen's estimating-equation (11). Since r_t^* is subject to measurement error as well as random disturbances, spurious correlations may be introduced together

---

6. It can be argued that an unmanaged market portfolio, such as given by one of the popular stock price indices, is not an appropriate standard for comparison with a managed fund. This interesting question is not pursued here, however.

7. The Sharpe Variability measure used in this comparison was modified slightly by multiplying Φ by σ_I. The reason for this was to standardize Sharpe's performance measure into the same units as Treynor's ψ' measure.

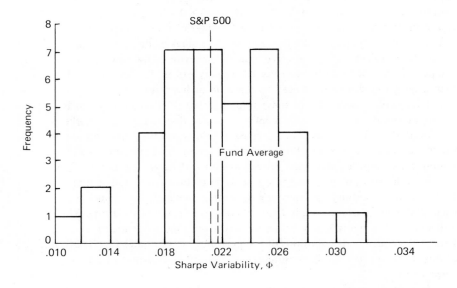

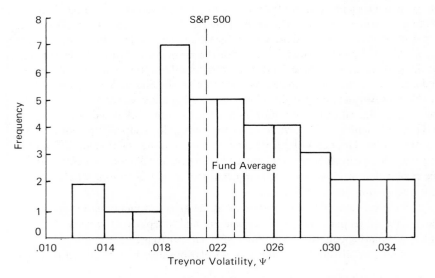

Figure 4. Frequency Distribution of 38 Fund Rankings by Sharpe Variability and Treynor Volatility

with biases in the slope coefficient. Since the regression line must continue to pass through the point of sample means, this would change the intercept term which is used as a performance measure.

Table 22-2 contains the regression statistics for (3) and (11), including the estimates, $\hat{B}$ and $\hat{\beta}$, respectively. They reveal that Jensen's estimating equation does not introduce biases that result in noticeably different volatility coefficients. The small differences in the coefficients that do exist are most likely attributable to the differences in the models used for estimating fund parameters. A comparison of the correlation coefficients given in Table 22-2 reveals that the Jensen estimating equation provides a better statistical fit in 33 out of 38 of the regressions.[8]

A third factor related to the Jensen study was the bias caused by not including the volatility coefficient β in his performance measure. A scatter diagram of the Treynor Volatility measure, ψ, versus slope coefficient, β, for the 38 mutual funds indicates that fund performance is inversely related to fund volatility. The implication of this relationship is shown in Figure 2. Characteristic Lines (a), (b), and (c) intersect the horizontal axis at equal-distance points—thus exhibiting a uniform distribution of Treynor performance estimates for three hypothetical funds. The slopes, however, are shown increasing from left to right as one proceeds from higher to lower values of Treynor Volatility. The distortion effect on the Jensen index is evident from the skewed α values defined by the intersection of these lines with the vertical axis. Although such a distortion would not influence the number of funds doing either better or worse than the market, it would influence the average value of the index computed for the entire sample of funds.

The existence of such a distortion effect is illustrated in the frequency distributions given in Figure 5. One immediately notes that the skewness toward higher values that is evident in the modified Jensen distribution is not found in the Jensen distribution. The bias is evidenced by noting the difference in average fund performance (.00142) obtained from the α measure and the estimate found by using the α/β measure (.00230).[9]

A fourth consideration concerning the Jensen study is the influence of introducing the modified-Jensen measure and its sampling distribution into Jensen's significance test for funds with superior forecasting ability. Although it is not possible to obtain direct estimates of the sampling distribution of the α/β index, it is possible to obtain estimates by expressing the variance of α/β as

---

8. These results suggest that the modified Jensen measure α/β may be superior to the Treynor ψ measure of fund performance since the estimates of α and β are obtained from Jensen's estimating equation.

9. A small part of this increase is attributable to the average volatility of the sample being less than the market. Without the bias being introduced by the distortion effect, one would expect an average α/β of .00165 (obtained by dividing .00142 by .859 which is the average volatility for the sample of funds).

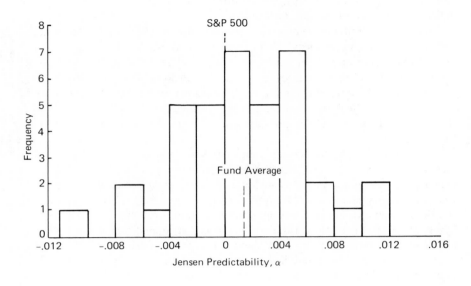

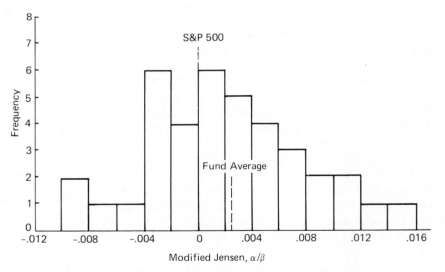

Figure 5. Frequency Distribution of 38 Fund Rankings by Jensen Predictability and Modified Jensen

$$\sigma^2_{\alpha/\beta} = \xi[\alpha/\beta - \hat{\alpha}/\hat{\beta}]^2,$$ (18)

where $\hat{\alpha}$ and $\hat{\beta}$ are the expected values of α and β, respectively, which can be estimated from (11). The first term within the brackets can be replaced by a Taylor Series of α/β about $\hat{\alpha}/\hat{\beta}$. By assuming that $(B - \hat{\beta})/\hat{\beta} \ll 1$ and $\sigma_{\beta/\hat{\beta}} \ll 1$, one may ignore higher-order terms in the series expansion. Assume further that α and β are normally distributed, independent random variables with variances σ^2_α and σ^2_β, respectively, this leads finally to

$$\sigma^2_{\alpha/\beta} = \frac{1}{\hat{\beta}^2} \sigma^2_\alpha + \frac{\hat{\alpha}^2 + \sigma^2_\alpha}{\hat{\beta}^4} \sigma^2_\beta$$ (19)

Under these assumptions, expression (19) gives the variance of the modified Jensen measure.

An examination of performance estimates, standard errors, and "t" values for both the Jensen and modified Jensen indices indicates that the Jensen performance estimates have greater statistical significance than the modified Jensen measure. This results from the added variance given by the second component in expression (19). A frequency distribution summary of "t" values presented in Figure 6, however, reveals no major differences between the two performance measures. It may be noted that these results parallel those of Jensen, and one concludes that there is very little evidence that any individual fund could do better than what was expected from mere random chance.

In addition to the considerations cited above, there are other factors that may have an important bearing on mutual fund performance. These include (1) the use of quarterly versus annual data, (2) the particular value of the risk-free rate used in computing the Φ measure of Sharpe, and (3) the time horizon used in comparing fund performance with the market. Concerning the use of quarterly data, it is suspected that this may have increased fund performance because of the increased return obtained by compounding dividends and capital gains distributions.[10] The use of a constant 3 percent risk-free interest rate by Sharpe also appears to have resulted in a bias against the funds. An analysis of the average return in Sharpe's study revealed that a reduction in the risk-free interest rate would introduce a slight increase in the number of funds outperforming the Dow-Jones market portfolio. As to time period, one can speculate that fund performance has improved slightly in recent years as a result of greater emphasis on short-range performance, as well as more systematic usage of available information.

---

10. In part, this explains why only 14 (37 percent) of the 38 funds in Table 22–2 had a negative value of α, while in the Jensen study, 76 (66 percent) of the 115 funds exhibited negative predictability measures.

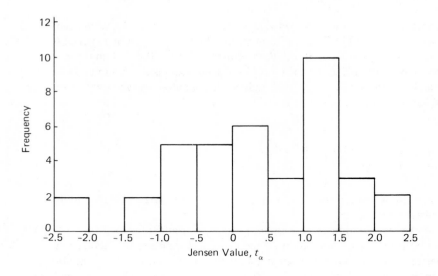

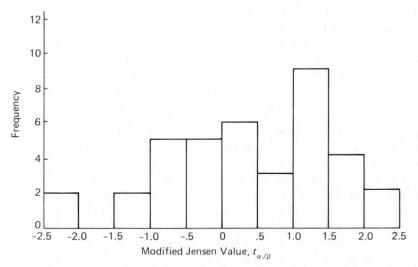

Figure 6. Frequency Distribution of "t" values for Jensen Predictability and Modified Jensen

IV. Conclusion

This study has dealt with composite measures of *ex post* portfolio performance. The alternative measures have been compared conceptually and empirically, and important differences have been indicated. When used to rank a series of funds on the basis of *ex post* performance, it was seen that there is little difference between the alternative measures. In contrast, when performance comparisons are made with the market, conclusions are not as obvious as some prior studies would suggest. In addition to statistical problems, assumptions as to residual risk, data selection, and handling of the risk-free rate are all critical inputs into market comparisons. The modified Jensen measure is recommended because it is based on a preferable estimating equation and because it does not exclude the important slope coefficient. Finally, much attention has been given to the problem of whether or not portfolio managers have performed well enough to justify their management fees. Although that problem has not been addressed here, its eventual solution must certainly rely heavily on risk-return measures of investment performance.

References

1. Friend, I., and D. Vickers, "Portfolio Selection and Investment Performance," *Journal of Finance*, 20 (September 1965), pp. 391–415.
2. Jensen, M.C., "The Performance of Mutual Funds in the Period 1945–1964," *Journal of Finance*, 23 (May 1968), pp. 389–419.
3. Levy, R.A., "Measurement of Investment Performance," *Journal of Financial and Quantitative Analysis*, 3 (March 1968), pp. 35–58.
4. Lintner, J., "Security Prices, Risk and Maximal Gains from Diversification," *Journal of Finance*, 20 (December 1965), pp. 587–615.
5. Sharpe, W.F., "Capital Asset Prices: A Theory of Market Equilibrium Under Conditions of Risk," *Journal of Finance*, 19 (September 1964), pp. 425–444.
6. ———, "Mutual Fund Performance," *Journal of Business*, 39, Part 2 (January 1966), pp. 119–138.
7. Treynor, J.L., "How to Rate Management of Investment Funds," *Harvard Business Review*, 43 (January–February 1965), pp. 63–75.
8. ———, "Discussion: The Performance of Mutual Funds in the Period 1945–1964," *Journal of Finance*, 23 (May 1968), pp. 418–419.
9. United States Congress, House of Representatives, Committee on Interstate and Foreign Commerce, *A Study of Mutual Funds*, Report No. 2274, 87th Congress, 2nd Session, August 1962.

23

Components of Investment Performance*

Eugene F. Fama
University of Chicago

I. Introduction

This paper suggests methods for evaluating investment performance. The topic is not new. Important work has been done by Sharpe [21, 22], Treynor [23], and Jensen [13, 14]. This past work has been concerned with measuring performance in two dimensions, return and risk. That is, how do the returns on the portfolios examined compare with the returns on other "naively selected" portfolios with similar levels of risk?

This paper suggests somewhat finer breakdowns of performance. For example, methods are presented for distinguishing the part of an observed return that is due to ability to pick the best securities of a given level of risk ("selectivity") from the part that is due to predictions of general market price movements ("timing"). The paper also suggests methods for measuring the effects of foregone diversification when an investment manager decides to concentrate his holdings in what he thinks are a few "winners."

Finally, most of the available work concentrates on single period evaluation schemes. Since almost all of the relevant theoretical material can be presented in this context, much of the analysis here is likewise concerned with the one-period case. Eventually, however, a multiperiod model that allows evaluations both on a period-by-period and on a cumulative basis is presented.

II. Foundations

The basic notion underlying the methods of performance evaluation to be presented here is that the returns on managed portfolios can be judged relative to those of "naively selected" portfolios with similar levels of risk. For purposes of exposition, the definitions of a "naively selected" portfolio and of "risk" are obtained from the two-parameter market equilibrium model

Reprinted by permission of the publisher and author from *Journal of Finance*, June 1972, pp. 551–67.
*Research on this paper was supported by a grant from the National Science Foundation.

of Sharpe [20], Lintner [15, 16], Mossin [18] and Fama [10, 11]. But it is well to note that the two-parameter model just provides a convenient and somewhat familiar set of naively selected or "benchmark" portfolios against which the investment performance of managed portfolios can be evaluated. As indicated later, other risk-return models could be used to obtain benchmark portfolios consistent with the same general methods of performance evaluation.

In the simplest one-period version of the two-parameter model, the capital market is assumed to be perfect—that is, there are no transactions costs or taxes, and all available information is freely available to everybody—and investors are assumed to be risk averse expected utility maximizers who believe that return distributions for all portfolios are normal. Risk aversion and normally distributed portfolio returns imply that the expected utility maximizing portfolio for any given investor is mean-standard deviation efficient.[1] In addition, investors are assumed to have the same views about distributions of one-period returns on all portfolios (an assumption usually called "homogeneous expectations"), and there is assumed to be a riskless asset f, with both borrowing and lending available to all investors at a riskless rate of interest R_f.

It is then possible to show that in a market equilibrium all efficient portfolios are just combinations of the riskless asset f and one portfolio of risky assets m, where m, called the "market portfolio," contains every asset in the market, each weighted by the ratio of its total market value to the total market value of all assets. That is, if $\widetilde{R}_m$, $E(\widetilde{R}_m)$ and $\sigma(\widetilde{R}_m)$ are the one-period return, expected return, and standard deviation of return for the market portfolio m, and if x is the proportion of investment funds put into the riskless asset f, then all efficient portfolios are formed according to[2]

$$\widetilde{R}_x = xR_f + (1-x)\widetilde{R}_m \qquad x \leqslant 1, \tag{1}$$

so that

$$E(\widetilde{R}_x) = xR_f + (1-x)E(\widetilde{R}_m) \tag{2}$$

$$\sigma(\widetilde{R}_x) = (1-x)\sigma(\widetilde{R}_m). \tag{3}$$

Geometrically, the situation is somewhat as shown in Figure 1. The curve $b\,m\,d$ represents the boundary of the set of portfolios that only include risky assets. But efficient portfolios are along the line from R_f through m. Points

---

1. By definition, a mean-standard deviation efficient portfolio must have the following property: No portfolio with the same or higher expected one-period return has lower standard deviation of return.

2. Tildes (~) are used throughout to denote random variables. When we refer to realized values of these variables, the tildes are dropped.

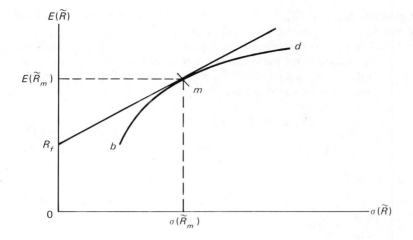

Figure 1. The Efficient Set with Riskless Borrowing and Lending

below m (that is, $x \geqslant 0$) involve lending some funds at the riskless rate R_f and putting the remainder in m, while points above m (that is, $x < 0$) involve borrowing at the riskless rate with both the borrowed funds and the initial investment funds put into m.

In this model the equilibrium relationship between expected return and risk for any security j is

$$E(\widetilde{R}_j) = R_f + \left[\frac{E(\widetilde{R}_m) - R_f}{\sigma(\widetilde{R}_m)} \right] \frac{\text{cov}(\widetilde{R}_j, \widetilde{R}_m)}{\sigma(\widetilde{R}_m)} \quad \textit{(Ex ante market line)}. \quad (4)$$

Here $\text{cov}(\widetilde{R}_j, \widetilde{R}_m)$ is the covariance between the return on asset j and the return on the market portfolio m. In the two-parameter model $\sigma(\widetilde{R}_m)$ is a measure of the total risk in the return on the market portfolio m. Since the only risky assets held by an investor are "shares" of m, it would seem that, from a portfolio viewpoint, the risk of an asset should be measured by its contribution to $\sigma(\widetilde{R}_m)$. In fact this contribution is just $\text{cov}(\widetilde{R}_j, \widetilde{R}_m)/\sigma(\widetilde{R}_m)$. Specifically, if x_{jm} is the proportion of asset $j, j = 1, \ldots, N$, in the market portfolio m

$$\sigma(\widetilde{R}_m) = \sum_{j=1}^{N} x_{jm} \frac{\text{cov}(\widetilde{R}_j, \widetilde{R}_m)}{\sigma(\widetilde{R}_m)}. \quad (5)$$

In this light (4) is a relationship between expected return and risk which says that the expected return on asset j is the riskless rate of interest R_f plus a risk premium that is $[E(\widetilde{R}_m) - R_f]/\sigma(\widetilde{R}_m)$, called the market price per unit of risk, times the risk of asset j, $\text{cov}(\widetilde{R}_j, \widetilde{R}_m)/\sigma(\widetilde{R}_m)$.

Equation (4) provides the relationship between expected return and risk for portfolios as well as for individual assets. That is, if x_{jp} is the proportion of asset j in the portfolio p (so that $\Sigma_{j=1}^{N} x_{jp} = 1$), then multiplying both sides of (4) by x_{jp} and summing over j, we get

$$E(\widetilde{R}_p) = R_f + \left[\frac{E(\widetilde{R}_m) - R_f}{\sigma(\widetilde{R}_m)}\right] \frac{\text{cov}(\widetilde{R}_p, \widetilde{R}_m)}{\sigma(\widetilde{R}_m)} \qquad (6)$$

where, of course,

$$\widetilde{R}_p = \sum_{j=1}^{N} x_{jp} \widetilde{R}_j.$$

But (4) and (6) are expected return-risk relations derived under the assumption that investors all have free access to available information and all have the same views of distributions of returns on all portfolios. In short, the market setting envisaged is a rather extreme version of the "efficient markets" model in which prices at any time "fully reflect" available information. (See, for example [7].) But in the real world a portfolio manager may feel that he has access to special information or he may disagree with the evaluations of available information that are implicit in market prices. In this case the "homogeneous expectations" model underlying (4) provides "benchmarks" for judging the manager's ability to make better evaluations than the market.

The benchmark or naively selected portfolios are just the combinations of the riskless asset f and the market portfolio m obtained with different values of x in (1). Given the *ex post* or realized return R_m for the market portfolio, for the naively selected portfolios, *ex post* return is just

$$\widetilde{R}_x = xR_f + (1 - x)\widetilde{R}_m, \qquad (7)$$

that is, (1) without the tildes. Moreover,[3]

$$\beta_x = \frac{\text{cov}(\widetilde{R}_x, \widetilde{R}_m)}{\sigma(\widetilde{R}_m)} = \frac{\text{cov}([1 - x]\widetilde{R}_m, \widetilde{R}_m)}{\sigma(\widetilde{R}_m)} = (1 - x)\sigma(\widetilde{R}_m)$$

$$= \sigma(\widetilde{R}_x). \qquad (8)$$

---

3. Henceforth the risk $\text{cov}(\widetilde{R}_j, \widetilde{R}_m)/\sigma(R_m)$ of an asset or portfolio j will be denoted as β_j.

That is, for the benchmark portfolios risk and standard deviation of return are equal. And the result is quite intuitive: In the homogeneous expectations model these portfolios comprise the efficient set, and for efficient portfolios risk and return dispersion are equivalent.

For the naively selected portfolios, (7) and (8) imply the following relationship between risk β_x and *ex post* return R_x:

$$R_x = R_f + \left(\frac{R_m - R_f}{\sigma(\widetilde{R}_m)} \right) \beta_x \qquad (\textit{ex post} \text{ market line}). \qquad (9)$$

That is, for the naively selected portfolios there is a linear relationship between risk and return that is of precisely the same form as (4) except that the expected returns that appear in (4) are replaced by realized returns in (9).

In the performance evaluation models to be presented, (9) provides the benchmarks against which the returns on "managed" portfolios are judged. These "benchmarks" are used in a sequence of successively more complex suggested performance evaluation settings. First we are concerned with one-period models in which a portfolio is chosen by an investor at the beginning of the period, its performance is evaluated at the end of the period, and there are no intermediate cash flows or portfolio decisions. Then we consider multiperiod evaluation models that also allow for fund flows and portfolio decisions between evaluation dates. We find, though, that almost all of the important theoretical concepts in performance evaluation can be treated in a one-period context.

III. The Benchmark Portfolios: Some Empirical Issues

Before introducing the evaluation models, however, it is well to discuss some of the empirical issues concerning the so-called "market lines" (4) and (9). Since this paper is primarily theoretical, and since empirical problems are best solved in the context of actual applications, the discussion of empirical issues will be brief.

First of all, to use (9) as a benchmark for evaluating *ex post* portfolio returns requires estimates of the risk, β_p, and dispersion, $\sigma(\widetilde{R}_p)$, of the managed portfolios as well as an estimate of $\sigma(\widetilde{R}_m)$ the dispersion of the return on the market portfolio. If performance evaluation is to be objective, it must be possible to obtain reliable estimates of these parameters from historical data. Fortunately, Blume's evidence [3, 4, 5] suggests that at least for portfolios of ten or more securities, β_p and $\sigma(\widetilde{R}_p)$ seem to be fairly stationary over long periods of time (e.g., ten years), and likewise for $\sigma(\widetilde{R}_m)$.

But other empirical evidence is less supportive. Thus throughout the analysis here normal return distributions are assumed, though the data of

Fama [6], Blume [3], Roll [19] and others suggest that actual return distributions conform more closely to non-normal two-parameter stable distributions. It would conceptually be a simple matter to allow for such distributions in the evaluation models (cf. Fama [11]). But since the goal here is just to suggest some new approaches to performance evaluation, for simplicity attention will be restricted to the normal model.

Finally, the available empirical evidence (e.g., Friend and Blume [12], Miller and Scholes [17], and Black, Jensen and Scholes [2]) indicates that the average returns over time on securities and portfolios deviate systematically from the predictions of (4). Though the observed average return-risk relationships seem to be linear, the tradeoff of risk for return (the price of risk) is in general less than would be predicted from (4) or (9). In short, the evidence suggests that (4) and (9) do not provide the best benchmarks for the average return-risk tradeoffs available in the market from naively selected portfolios.

Even these results do little damage to the performance evaluation models. They indicate that other benchmark portfolios than those that lead to (9) might be more appropriate, but given such alternative "naively selected" portfolios, the analysis could proceed in exactly the manner to be suggested. For example, Black, Jensen and Scholes [2] compute the risks (β's) for each security on the New York Stock Exchange, rank these, and then form ten portfolios, the first comprising the $.1N$ securities with the highest risks and the last comprising the $.1N$ securities with the lowest risks, where N is the total number of securities. They find that over various subperiods from 1931–65 the average monthly returns among these portfolios are highly correlated, and when plotted against risk the average returns on these portfolios lie along a straight line with slope somewhat less than would be implied by the "price of risk" in (4) or (9). As benchmarks for performance evaluation models, their empirical risk-return lines seem to be natural alternatives to (9). And with these alternative benchmarks, performance evaluation could proceed precisely as suggested here. But again, for simplicity, we continue on with the more familiar benchmarks given by (9).

It would be misleading, however, to leave the impression that all important empirical problems relevant in the application of performance evaluation models have been solved. To a large extent the practical value of such models depends on the empirical validity of the model of market equilibrium—that is, the expected return-risk relationship—from which the benchmark or "naively selected" portfolios are derived. And though much interesting work is in progress, it would be rash to claim that all empirical issues concerning models of market equilibrium have been settled.

For example, an important (and unsolved) empirical issue in models of market equilibrium is the time interval or "market horizon period" over which the hypothetical expected return-risk relationship is presumed to hold. Does the model hold continuously (instant by instant), or is the market horizon period some discrete time interval? This is an important issue from the viewpoint of performance evaluation since if the market horizon period is discrete, evaluation periods should be chosen to coincide with horizon periods.

The evidence of Friend and Blume [12] and that of Black, Jensen, and Scholes [2] suggests that meaningful relationships between average returns and risk can be obtained from monthly data, while the evidence of Miller and Scholes [17] indicates that this is not true for annual periods. Within these broad bounds, however, the sensitivity of risk-return relations to the time interval chosen remains an open issue.

But unsolved empirical questions are hardly a cause for disheartenment. It is reasonable to expect that some of the empirical issues will be solved in the process of applying the theory. And in any case, application of a theory invariably involves some empirical approximations. The available evidence on performance evaluation, especially Jensen's [13, 14], suggests that the required approximations need not prevent even more complicated evaluation models from yielding useful results.

IV. Performance Evaluation in a One-Period Model When There Are No Intraperiod Fund Flows

Let $V_{a,t}$ and $V_{a,t+1}$ be the total market values at t and $t + 1$ of the actual (a = actual) portfolio chosen by an investment manager at t. With all portfolio activity occurring at t and $t + 1$, that is, assuming that there are no intraperiod fund flows, the one-period percentage return on the portfolio is

$$R_a = \frac{V_{a,t+1} - V_{a,t}}{V_{a,t}}.$$

One benchmark against which the return R_a on the chosen portfolio can be compared is provided by $R_x(\beta_a)$, which by definition is the return on the combination of the riskless asset f and the market portfolio m that has risk β_x equal to β_a, the risk of the chosen portfolio a. One measure of the performance of the chosen portfolio a is then

$$\text{Selectivity} = R_a - R_x(\beta_a). \tag{10}$$

That is, *Selectivity* measures how well the chosen portfolio did relative to a naively selected portfolio with the same level of risk.

Selectivity, or some slight variant thereof, is the sole measure of performance in the work of Sharpe [21, 22], Treynor [23] and Jensen [13, 14]. But more detailed breakdowns of performance are possible. Thus consider

$$\overbrace{[R_a - R_f]}^{\text{Overall Performance}} = \overbrace{[R_a - R_x(\beta_a)]}^{\text{Selectivity}} + \overbrace{[R_x(\beta_a) - R_f]}^{\text{Risk}}. \tag{11}$$

That is, the *Overall Performance* of the portfolio decision is the difference between the return on the chosen portfolio and the return on the riskless asset. The Overall Performance is in turn split into two parts, *Selectivity* (as above) and *Risk*. The latter measures the return from the decision to take on positive amounts of risk.[4] It will be determined by the level of risk chosen (the value of β_a) and, from (9), by the difference between the return on the market portfolio, R_m, and the return on the riskless asset, R_f.

These performance measures are illustrated in Figure 2. The curly bracket along the vertical axis shows *Overall Performance* which in this case is positive. The breakdown of performance given by (11) can be found along the vertical line from β_a. In this example, *Selectivity* is positive: A portfolio was chosen that produced a higher return than the corresponding "naively selected" portfolio along the market line with the same level of risk. *Risk* is also positive, as it is whenever a positive amount of risk is taken and the return on the market portfolio turns out to be higher than the riskless rate.

A. Selectivity: A Closer Look

If the portfolio chosen represents the investor's total assets, in the mean-variance model the risk of the portfolio to him is measured by $\sigma(\widetilde{R}_a)$, the standard deviation of its return. And the risk of the portfolio to the investor, $\sigma(\widetilde{R}_a)$, will be greater than what might now be called its "market risk," β_a, as long as the portfolio's return is less than perfectly correlated with the return on the market portfolio. To see this, note that the correlation coefficient k_{am} between R_a and R_m is

$$k_{am} = \frac{\text{cov}(\widetilde{R}_a, \widetilde{R}_m)}{\sigma(\widetilde{R}_a)\sigma(\widetilde{R}_m)}.$$

It follows that

---

4. For greater descriptive accuracy, we should, of course, say "return from risk" or even "return from bearing risk," rather than just *Risk*. Likewise, "return from selectivity," would be more descriptive than *Selectivity*. But (hopefully) the shorter names save space without much loss of clarity.

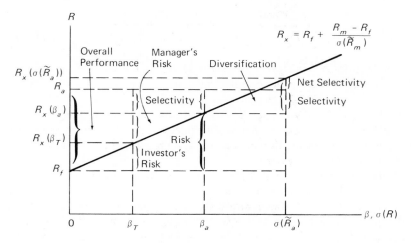

Figure 2. An Illustration of the Performance Measures of Equations (11), (12), and (13).

$$\beta_a = \frac{\text{cov}(\widetilde{R}_a, \widetilde{R}_m)}{\sigma(\widetilde{R}_m)} = k_{am}\,\sigma(\widetilde{R}_a)$$

so that $\beta_a \leqslant \sigma(\widetilde{R}_a)$ depending on whether $k_{am} \leqslant 1$.[5]

Intuitively, to some extent the portfolio decision may have involved putting more eggs into one or a few baskets than would be desirable to attain portfolio efficiency—that is, the manager places his bets on a few securities that he thinks are winners. In other words, to the extent that $\sigma(\widetilde{R}_a) > \beta_a$, the portfolio manager decided to take on some portfolio dispersion that could have been diversified away because he thought he had some securities in which it would pay to concentrate resources. The results of such a decision can be evaluated in terms of the following breakdown of *Selectivity*:

$$\overbrace{[R_a - R_x(\beta_a)]}^{\text{Selectivity}} = \text{Net Selectivity} + \overbrace{|R_x(\sigma(\widetilde{R}_a)) - R_x(\beta_a)|}^{\text{Diversification}};$$ (12a)

or

---

5. In fact the naively selected portfolios are the only ones whose returns are literally perfectly correlated with those of the market portfolio (cf. equation (8). But the theoretical work of Fama [9] and the empirical work of Black, Jensen and Scholes [2] suggests that the return on any well-diversified portfolio will be very highly correlated with R_m.

$$\text{Net Selectivity} = \overbrace{[R_a - R_x(\beta_a)]}^{\text{Selectivity}} - \overbrace{|R_x(\sigma(\widetilde{R}_a)) - R_x(\beta_a)|}^{\text{Diversification}}. \qquad (12b)$$

By defintion, $R_x(\sigma(\widetilde{R}_a))$ is the return on the combination of the riskless asset f and the market portfolio m that has return dispersion equivalent to that of the actual portfolio chosen. Thus *Diversification* measures the extra portfolio return that the manager's winners have to produce in order to make concentration of resources in them worthwhile. If *Net Selectivity* is not positive, the manager has taken on diversifiable risk that his winners have not compensated for in terms of extra return.

Note that, as defined in (12), *Diversification* is always non-negative, so that *Net Selectivity* is equal to or less than *Selectivity*. When $R_m > R_f$, *Diversi fication* measures the additional return that would just compensate the investor for the diversifiable dispersion (that is, $\sigma(\widetilde{R}_a) - \beta_a$) taken on by the manager. When $R_m < R_f$ (so that the market line is downward sloping), *Diversification* measures the lost return from taking on diversifiable dispersion rather than choosing the naively selected portfolio with market risk *and* standard deviation both equal to β_a, the market risk of the portfolio actually chosen.

The performance measures of (12) are illustrated in Figure 2 along the dashed vertical line from $\sigma(\widetilde{R}_a)$. In the example shown, *Selectivity* is positive but *Net Selectivity* is negative. Though the manager chose a portfolio that outperformed the naively selected portfolio with the same level of market risk, his *Selectivity* was not sufficient to make up for the avoidable risk taken, so that *Net Selectivity* was negative.

The breakdown of *Selectivity* given by (12) is the only one that is considered here. The rest of Section IV is concerned with successively closer examinations of the other ingredient of *Overall Performance, Risk*. Before moving on, though, we should note that (12) itself is *only* relevant when diversification is a goal of the investor. And this is the case only when the portfolio being evaluated constitutes the investor's entire holdings, and the investor is risk averse. For example, an investor might allocate his funds to many managers, encouraging each only to try to pick winners, with the investor himself carrying out whatever diversification he desires on personal account. In this case *Selectivity* is the relevant measure of the managers' performance, and the breakdown of *Selectivity* of (12) is of no concern.

B. Risk: A Closer Look

If the investor has a target risk level β_T for his portfolio, the part of *Overall Performance* due to *Risk* can be allocated to the investor and to the portfolio manager as follows:

$$\overbrace{[R_x(\beta_a) - R_f]}^{\text{Risk}} = \overbrace{[R_x(\beta_a) - R_x(\beta_T)]}^{\text{Manager's Risk}} + \overbrace{[R_x(\beta_T) - R_f]}^{\text{Investor's Risk}} \qquad (13)$$

$R_x(\beta_T)$ is the return on the naively selected portfolio with the target level of market risk. Thus *Manager's Risk* is that part of *Overall Performance* and of *Risk* that is due to the manager's decision to take on a level of risk β_a different from the investor's target level β_T, while *Investor's Risk* is that part of *Overall Performance* that results from the fact that the investor's target level of risk is positive. These performance measures are illustrated in Figure 2 along the dashed vertical line from β_T.

Manager's Risk might in part result from a timing decision. That is, in part at least the manager might have chosen a portfolio with a level of risk higher or lower than the target level because he felt risky portfolios in general would do abnormally well or abnormally poorly during the period under consideration. But if an estimate of $E(\widetilde{R}_m)$ is available, a more precise measure of the results of such a timing decision can be obtained.[6] Specifically, making use of the *ex ante* market line of (4)[7] we can subdivide *Risk* as follows:

$$\overbrace{[R_x(\beta_a)' - R_f]}^{\text{Risk}} = \overbrace{\Big\{ \underbrace{[R_x(\beta_a) - E(\widetilde{R}_x(\beta_a))]}_{\text{Total Timing}} - \underbrace{[R_x(\beta_T) - E(\widetilde{R}_x(\beta_T))]}_{\text{Market Conditions}} \Big\}}^{\text{Manager's Timing}}$$

$$+ \underbrace{[E(\widetilde{R}_x(\beta_a)) - E(\widetilde{R}_x(\beta_T))]}_{\text{Manager's Exp. Risk}} + \underbrace{[R_x(\beta_T) - R_f]}_{\text{Investor's Risk}}. \qquad (14)$$

---

6. $E(\widetilde{R}_m)$ might be estimated from past average returns on the market portfolio m. Alternatively, past data might be used to estimate the average difference between R_m and R_f. In any case, it should become clear that the expected values used must be naive or mechanical estimates (or at least somehow external to those being evaluated), otherwise the value of the timing measures is destroyed.

Admittedly, given the current status of empirical work on the behavior through time of average returns on risky assets, we can at most speculate about the best way to estimate $E(\widetilde{R}_m)$. Hopefully empirical work now in progress will give more meaningful guidelines. And perhaps the development of theoretical methods of performance evaluation will itself stimulate better empirical work on estimation procedures. In any case, the discussion in the text should help to emphasize that one cannot obtain precise measures of returns from timing decisions without mechanical or naive estimates of equilibrium expected returns.

7. That is,

$$E(\widetilde{R}_x(\beta_a)) = R_f + \left[\frac{E(\widetilde{R}_m) - R_f}{\sigma(\widetilde{R}_m)} \right] \beta_a$$

and similarly for $E(\widetilde{R}_x(\beta_T))$.

The first three terms here sum to the *Manager's Risk* of (13). *Manager's Expected Risk* is the incremental expected return from the manager's decision to take on nontarget level of risk. *Market Conditions* is the difference between the return on the naively selected portfolio with the target level of risk and the expected return of this portfolio. It answers the question: By how much did the market deviate from expectations at the target level of risk? *Total Timing* is the difference between the *ex post* return on the naively selected portfolio with risk β_a and the *ex ante* expected return. It is positive when $R_m > E(\widetilde{R}_m)$ (and then more positive the larger the value of β_a), and it is negative when $R_m < E(\widetilde{R}_m)$ (and then more negative the larger the value of β_a). The difference between *Total Timing* and *Market Conditions* is *Manager's Timing*: it measures the excess of *Total Timing* over timing performance that could have been generated by choosing the naively selected portfolio with the target level of risk. *Manager's Timing* is only positive when the sign of the difference between β_a and β_T is the same as the sign of the difference between R_m and $E(\widetilde{R}_m)$, that is, when the chosen level of market risk is above (below) the target level and R_m is above (below) $E(\widetilde{R}_m)$. It is thus somewhat more sensitive than *Total Timing* as a measure of the results of a timing decision.

A target level of risk will not always be relevant in evaluating a manager's performance. For example, an investor may allocate his funds to many managers, with the intention that each concentrates on selectivity and/or timing, with the investor using borrowing or lending on personal account to attain his desired level of market risk.

If a target level of risk is not relevant but the expected value or *ex ante* market line is still available, a breakdown of *Risk* similar to (14) can be obtained by treating the market portfolio (or the approximate proxy)[8] as the target portfolio. That is,

$$
\underbrace{[R_x(\beta_a) - R_f]}_{\text{Risk}} = \underbrace{\{\underbrace{[R_x(\beta_a) - E(\widetilde{R}_x(\beta_a))]}_{\text{Total Timing}} - \underbrace{[R_m - E(\widetilde{R}_m)]\}}_{\text{Market Conditions}}}_{\text{Manager's Timing}}
$$

$$
+ \underbrace{[E(\widetilde{R}_x(\beta_a)) - E(\widetilde{R}_m)]}_{\substack{\text{Expected Deviation} \\ \text{from Market}}} + \underbrace{[R_m - R_f]}_{\text{Market Risk}}. \tag{15}
$$

The idea here is that even in the absence of a target level of risk, the measure of *Manager's Timing* must be standardized for the deviation of the market return

---

8. For example, if one were faced with portfolio evaluation in a multiperiod context, one might use the average of past levels of market risk chosen by the manager as a proxy for the target risk level when the latter is not explicitly available.

from the expected market return, that is, for the "average" spread between the *ex post* and *ex ante* market lines.

Finally, the goal of this paper is mainly to suggest some ways in which available theoretical and empirical results on portfolio and asset pricing models can provide the basis of useful procedures for performance evaluation. But the various breakdowns of performance suggested above are hardly unique. Indeed any breakdown chosen should be tailored to the situation at hand. For example, if a target level of risk is relevant but the subdivision of Risk given by (14) is regarded as too complicated, then the approximate effects of the timing decision might still be separated out as follows:

$$\overbrace{[R_x(\beta_a) - R_f]}^{\text{Risk}} = \overbrace{[R_x(\beta_a) - E(\widetilde{R}_x(\beta_a))]}^{\text{Total Timing}}$$

$$+ \overbrace{[E(\widetilde{R}_x(\beta_a)) - E(\widetilde{R}_x(\beta_T))]}^{\text{Manager's Expected Risk}} + \overbrace{[E(\widetilde{R}_x(\beta_T)) - R_f]}^{\text{Investor's Expected Risk}}. \quad (16)$$

The one new term here is *Investor's Expected Risk*, which measures the expected contribution to *Overall Performance* of the investor's decision to have a positive target level of risk. Alternatively if a target level of risk is not relevant for the situation at hand, but an expected value line is available, *Risk* can nevertheless be subdivided as follows,

$$\overbrace{[R_x(\beta_a) - R_f]}^{\text{Risk}} = \overbrace{[R_x(\beta_a) - E(\widetilde{R}_x(\beta_a))]}^{\text{Total Timing}} + \overbrace{[E(\widetilde{R}_x(\beta_a)) - R_f]}^{\text{Total Expected Risk}}. \quad (17)$$

And these few suggestions hardly exhaust the possibilities.

V. Components of Performance:
Multiperiod Models with Intraperiod
Fund Flows

In the one-period evaluation model presented above, (i) the time at which performance is evaluated is assumed to correspond to the portfolio horizon date, that is, the time when portfolio funds are withdrawn for consumption; and (ii) there are assumed to be no portfolio transactions or inflows and out-flows of funds between the initial investment and withdrawal dates, so that there is no reinvestment problem. If in a multiperiod context we are likewise willing to assume that: (i) though there are many of them, evaluation dates nevertheless correspond to the dates when some funds are withdrawn for

consumption, and (ii) all reinvestment decisions and other portfolio transactions are also made at these same points in time, then generalization of the
one-period model to the multiperiod case is straightforward.[9] Indeed the
basic procedure could be period-by-period application of the performance
measures presented in the one-period model. The major embellishments would
not be in the nature of new theory, but rather would arise from the fact that
multiperiod performance histories allow statistically more reliable estimates
of the various one-period performance measures.

But this pure case is unlikely to be met in any real world application.
Often performance evaluation would be carried out by someone with little or
no knowledge of the dates when funds are needed for consumption by the
owner of the portfolio, and often (e.g., in the case of a mutual fund or a pension
fund) the portfolio is owned by many different investors with different consumption dates. As a result evaluation dates, withdrawal dates, and reinvestment
dates do not usually coincide.

The rest of this paper is concerned with how the concepts of the one-period
model must be adjusted to deal with such intraevaluation period (or more
simply, intraperiod) fund flows. The procedure is to first present detailed
definitions of variables of interest in models involving intraperiod fund flows,
and then to talk about actual measures of performance. And it is well to keep
in mind that though the analysis is carried out in a multiperiod context, the
problems to be dealt with arise from intraperiod fund flows. With such fund
flows, the same problems would arise in a one-period evaluation model.

A. Definitions

Suppose the investment performance of a portfolio is to be evaluated at
discrete points in time, but that there can be cash flows between evaluation
dates. That is, there can be intraperiod inflows in the form of either cash
receipts (dividends, interest) on existing portfolio holdings or net new contributions of capital by new or existing owners. And there can be intraperiod outflows
in the form of dividend payments to the portfolio's owner(s) (e.g., a mutual
fund declares dividends) or withdrawals of capital (e.g., by a mutual fund's
shareholders).

In simplest terms, the major problem with intraperiod cash flows is
obtaining a measure of the return on the beginning of period market value of a
portfolio that abstracts from the effects of intraperiod new contributions and
withdrawals on the end of period value of the portfolio. One approach is what
might be called the mututal fund method. Specifically, when performance
evaluation is first contemplated, the market value of the portfolio is subdivided

---

9. For the development of the underlying models of consumer and market equilibrium
for this case see [8].

into "shares." Subsequently, whenever there are contributions of new capital or withdrawals of capital from the portfolio, the current market value of a share is computed and the number of shares outstanding is adjusted to reflect the effects of the cash flow.[10]

Thus let evaluation dates correspond to integer values of t and define

$V'_{a,t}$ = actual market value of the portfolio at time t. It thus includes the effects of investment of new capital or reinvestment of any cash income received on securities held in the portfolio, and it is net of any dividends paid out to owners or other withdrawals of funds prior to t.

$V_{a,t}$ = market value the portfolio would have had at t if no dividends were paid out to owners since the previous evaluation date. In computing $V_{a,t}$ it is simply assumed that dividends paid to the portfolio's owners were instead reinvested in the entire portfolio. At the beginning of each evaluation period, however, $V_{a,t}$ is set equal to $V'_{a,t}$.

n_t = number of shares outstanding in the portfolio at t. As indicated above, this is adjusted when new capital comes into the portfolio and when capital is withdrawn, but it is unaffected by reinvestment of cash income received on securities held or by dividends paid to the portfolio's owners.

$p'_{a,t}$ = $V'_{a,t}/n_t$ = actual market value at t of a share in the portfolio.

$p_{a,t}$ = $V_{a,t}/n_t$ = value of a share at t under the assumption that dividends paid to owners of the portfolio were instead reinvested in the entire portfolio.

$R_{a,t}$ = $(p_{a,t} - p'_{a,t-1})/p'_{a,t-1}$. Assuming t corresponds to an evaluation date, this is the one-period return on a share with reinvestment of all dividends paid on a share since the last evaluation date.

$R_{a,t}$ is an unambiguous measure of the return from $t-1$ to t on a dollar invested in the portfolio at $t-1$. This is not to say, however, that it is unaffected by intraperiod fund flows. Such fund flows are usually associated with redistributions of portfolio holdings across securities and these affect the return on a share. Moreover, $R_{a,t}$ as defined above is not the only unambiguous measure of the return from $t-1$ to t on funds invested in the portfolio at $t-1$. For example, one could define $R_{a,t} = (p'_{a,t} + d_t - p'_{a,t-1})/p'_{a,t-1}$, where d_t is the dividend

---

10. This is in fact the method of accounting used by open end mutual funds. It is also closely related to the "time-weighted rate of return" approach developed by Professor Lawrence Fisher. On this point see [1, Appendix I and p. 218].

per share paid during the evaluation period to the portfolio's owners. The more complicated definition, that is, with dividends assumed to be reinvested, is "purer" (especially for the purpose of interportfolio comparisons of performance) in the sense that funds invested at the beginning of a period remain invested for the entire period, but it is less pure in the sense that it assumes a reinvestment policy not actually followed in the portfolio.

The next step is to define prices per share for the benchmark or naively selected portfolios that also take account of intraperiod fund flows.

$p_{xt}(\beta_T)$ = price at t per share of the naively selected portfolio with the target risk level. To avoid double-counting of past performance, at the beginning of any evaluation period (for example, just after an evaluation takes place at $t-1$) this price is set equal to the price per share of the actual portfolio. Then this amount is invested in the naively selected portfolio with the target risk level, and the behavior of the market value of this portfolio during the evaluation period determines the end-of-period price per share, $p_{xt}(\beta_T)$. Any intraperiod cash income generated by the securities of this naively selected portfolio is assumed to be reinvested in this portfolio.

These conventions for the treatment of beginning-of-period values and intraperiod cash income will be taken to apply in the definitions of all the benchmark portfolios. Thus

$p_t(R_f)$ = price at t per share of the naively selected portfolio obtained by investing all funds available at $t-1$ in the riskless asset.

The benchmarks provided by $p_{xt}(\beta_T)$ and $p_t(R_f)$ are unaffected by intraperiod fund flows in the actual portfolio. This is not true of the following two benchmarks.

$p_{xt}(\beta_a)$ = price at t per share of the naively selected portfolio with market risk equal to that of the actual portfolio. At the beginning of any evaluation period and after any transaction in the actual portfolio during an evaluation period (that is, after any cash flow or exchange of shares in the actual portfolio) the market risk of the actual portfolio is measured, and the current price per share of this benchmark is shifted into the naively selected portfolio with that level of market risk. Thus the value of β_a could be shifting more or less continuously through time as a result of inflows and outflows of funds and decisions to shift the holdings in the portfolio.[11]

$p_{xt}(\sigma(\widetilde{R}_a))$ = price at t per share of the naively selected portfolio with return dispersion equal to that of the actual portfolio. The definition of $p_{xt}(\sigma(\widetilde{R}_a))$ is obtained by substituting $\sigma(\widetilde{R}_a)$ for β_a in the definition of $p_{xt}(\beta_a)$ above.

Thus $p_{xt}(\beta_a)$ and $p_{xt}(\sigma(\widetilde{R}_a))$ take account of changes in β_a and $\sigma(\widetilde{R}_a)$ that result from intraperiod fund flows and portfolio shifts. Computationally, keeping tract of β_a and $\sigma(\widetilde{R}_a)$ in the way required for these benchmarks is not a difficult problem. At any point in time the market risk β_a of the chosen portfolio is just the weighted average of the market risks of the individual assets in the portfolio, where the weights are the proportions of total portfolio market value represented by each asset. Thus if one has estimates of the market risks of the assets from which portfolios are chosen, the value of β_a is updated by combining these with current measures of the weights of individual assets in the chosen portfolio. And a similar procedure can be followed with respect to updating values of $\sigma(\widetilde{R}_a)$.[12]

B. Multiperiod Measures of Performance

Given the beginning and end-of-period prices per share for these benchmark portfolios, their one-period returns are obtained in the usual way. Then the performance history of a portfolio can be built up (for example) through period-by-period application of the breakdowns given by (11)–(13). Alternatively, one can define performance measures in terms of profit per share rather than return. Thus, in line with (13) and using end of evaluation period prices, define

$$\overbrace{[p_{a,t} - p_t(R_f)]}^{\substack{\text{Overall} \\ \text{Performance}}} = \overbrace{[p_{a,t} - p_{xt}(\beta_a)]}^{\text{Selectivity}}$$

$$+ \overbrace{[p_{xt}(\beta_a) - p_{xt}(\beta_T)]}^{\text{Manager's Risk}} + \overbrace{[p_{xt}(\beta_T) - p_t(R_f)]}^{\text{Investor's Risk}}. \qquad (18)$$

---

11. Indeed even if there are no transactions taking place, the value of β_a shifts continuously through time as a result of shifts in the relative market values of individual securities in the portfolio. Aside from adjusting the value of β_a at the beginning of each evaluation period, we have chosen to ignore the effects of such "non-discretionary" shifts here.

12. Keeping track of $\sigma(\widetilde{R}_a)$ is especially simple if one assumes that returns are generated by the so-called "market model." On this, and for additional computational suggestions, see Blume [3, 4, 5].

This type of breakdown can of course be computed both period-by-period and cumulatively. And from such multiperiod histories one can get more reliable measures of a portfolio manager's true abilities than can be obtained from a one-period analysis. For example, one can determine whether his *Selectivity* is systematically positive or simply randomly positive in some periods.

For some purposes one may wish to compare the multiperiod performance histories of different portfolios. For example, an investment company may be interested in the relative abilities of its different security analysts and portfolio managers. Or an investor who has allocated his funds to more than one manager may be interested in comparing their performances. On a period-by-period basis such performance comparisons can be carried out in terms of percentage returns. Alternatively, if the prices of shares in different portfolios are set equal at the beginning of comparison periods, profit-based performance measures such as (18) could be computed both on a period-by-period basis and cumulatively.

One must not get the impression, however, that all the problems caused by intraperiod fund flows have been solved. Though the performance of a "share" during any given evaluation period (or across many periods) gives an unambiguous picture of the investment history of funds invested in a given portfolio at a given point in time, comparisons of the performances of shares in different portfolios are not completely unambiguous. This is due to the fact that even when things are done on a per share basis, intraperiod fund flows necessitate portfolio decisions that usually have some effect on the performance of a share. And when such fund flows occur at different times (and thus during different market conditions) in different portfolios, the observed performances of shares in the portfolios may differ, even if the portfolios are managed by the same person trying to follow the same policies in all of his portfolio decisions. But though such ambiguities seem unavoidable and to some extent unsolvable, their effects on performance comparisons should be minor except in cases where portfolios experience large cash flows (relative to their total market values) in short periods of time and/or when evaluation periods are long.

Finally, if an *ex ante* market line is available to compute expected values through time for the three benchmarks, $p_{xt}(\beta_T)$, $p_{xt}(\beta_a)$ and $p_{xt}(\sigma(\widetilde{R}_a))$, then the one-period performance breakdowns of (14)–(17) can be carried out either in terms of returns or market values, and these can be used as the basis of even more detailed multiperiod performance histories.

But we terminate the discussion at this point. We do this not because of a lack of additional interesting problems, but because in the absence of actual applications, suggested solutions become increasingly speculative and thus of less likely usefulness.

VI. Summary

Some rather detailed methods for evaluating portfolio performance have been suggested, and some of the more important problems that would arise in implementing these methods have also been discussed. In general terms, we have suggested that the return on a portfolio can be subdivided into two parts: the return from security selection (*Selectivity*) and the return from bearing risk (*Risk*). Various finer subdivisions of both *Selectivity* and *Risk* have also been presented.

To a large extent the suggested models can be viewed as attempts to combine concepts from modern theories of portfolio selection and capital market equilibrium with more traditional concepts of what constitutes good portfolio management.

For example, the return from *Selectivity* is defined as the difference between the return on the managed portfolio and the return on a naively selected portfolio with the same level of market risk. Both the measure of risk and the definition of a naively selected portfolio are obtained from modern capital market theory, but the goal of the performance measure itself is just to test how good the portfolio manager is at security analysis. That is, does he show any ability to uncover information about individual securities that is not already implicit in their prices?

Likewise, traditional discussions of portfolio management distinguish between security analysis and market analysis, the latter being prediction of general market price movements rather than just prediction of the special factors in the returns on individual securities. The various timing measures suggested in this paper provide estimates of the returns obtained from such attempts to predict the market. And modern capital market theory again plays a critical role in defining these estimates.

References

1. Bank Administration Institute. *Measuring the Investment Performance of Pension Funds*. Park Ridge, Illinois: B.A.I., 1968.
2. Fisher Black, Michael Jensen, and Myron Scholes. "The Capital Asset Pricing Model: Some Empirical Tests." To appear in *Studies in the Theory of Capital Markets*, edited by Michael Jensen and published by Praeger.
3. Marshall Blume. "The Assessment of Portfolio Performance," unpublished Ph.D. dissertation, University of Chicago, 1968.
4. ———. "Portfolio Theory: A Step Toward Its Practical Application." *Journal of Business* XLIII (April, 1970), 152–173.

5. ——. "On the Assessment of Risk," *Journal of Finance* XXVI (March, 1971), 1–10.
6. Eugene F. Fama. "The Behavior of Stock Market Prices," *Journal of Business* XXXVIII (January, 1965), 34–105.
7. ——. "Efficient Capital Markets: A Review of Theory and Empirical Work," *Journal of Finance* XXV (May, 1970), 383–417.
8. ——. "Multiperiod Consumption-Investment Decisions," *American Economic Review* XL (March, 1970), 163–174.
9. ——. "Portfolio Analysis in a Stable Paretian Market," *Management Science* XII (January, 1965), 404–419.
10. ——. "Risk, Return and Equilibrium: Some Clarifying Comments," *Journal of Finance* XXIII (March, 1968), 29–40.
11. ——. "Risk, Return, and Equilibrium," *Journal of Political Economy* LXXIX (January–February, 1971), 30–55.
12. Irwin Friend, and Marshall Blume. "Measurement of Portfolio Performance under Uncertainty," *American Economic Review* XL (September, 1970), 561–575.
13. Michael Jensen. "The Performance of Mutual Funds in the Period 1945–64," *Journal of Finance* XXIII (May, 1968), 389–416.
14. ——. "Risk, the Pricing of Capital Assets, and the Evaluation of Investment Portfolios," *Journal of Business* XLII (April, 1969), 167–247.
15. John Lintner. "Security Prices, Risk, and Maximal Gains from Diversification," *Journal of Finance* XX (December, 1965); 587–615.
16. ——. "The Valuation of Risk Assets and the Selection of Risky Investments in Stock Portfolios and Capital Budgets," *Review of Economics and Statistics* XLVII (February, 1965), 13–37.
17. Merton Miller, and Myron Scholes. "Rates of Return in Relation to Risk: A Reexamination of Some Recent Findings." To appear in *Studies in the Theory of Capital Markets*, edited by Michael Jensen, and published by Praeger.
18. Jan Mossin. "Equilibrium in a Capital Asset Market," *Econometrica* XXXIV (October, 1966), 768–783.
19. Richard Roll. *The Behavior of Interest Rates: Application of the Efficient Market Model to U.S. Treasury Bills*. New York: Basic Books, Inc., 1970.
20. William F. Sharpe. "Capital Assets Prices: A Theory of Market Equilibrium under Conditions of Risks," *Journal of Finance* XIX (September, 1964), 425–442.
21. ——. "Mutual Fund Performance," *Journal of Business* XXXIX (Special Supplement, January, 1966), 119–138.
22. ——. "Risk Aversion in the Stock Market," *Journal of Finance* XX (September, 1965), 416–422.
23. Jack L. Treynor. "How to Rate Management of Investment Funds," *Harvard Business Review* XLIII (January–February, 1965), 63 75.

About the Editors

James L. Bicksler received the B.A. from Beloit College (1959), the M.B.A. and the Ph.D. from New York University in 1960 and 1967. He is associate professor at Rutgers University, Graduate School of Business, where his current research is in micro capital theory.

Paul A. Samuelson received the B.A. from the University of Chicago in 1935 and the M.A. and the Ph.D. from Harvard University in 1936 and 1941. He is Institute Professor at the Massachusetts Institute of Technology, where his research embraces analytic micro and macro economics.